THE ART
AND ARCHITECTURE
OF FREEMASONRY

THE ART
AND ARCHITECTURE
OF FREEMASONRY

An Introductory Study

JAMES STEVENS CURL

B.T. Batsford Ltd · London

By the same author

European Cities and Society. The Influence of Political Climate on Town Design (Leonard Hill, London, 1970 and 1972)

The Victorian Celebration of Death (David & Charles, Newton Abbot, 1972)

City of London Pubs (Co-author Timothy M. O. Richards) (David & Charles, Newton Abbot, 1973)

Victorian Architecture: its Practical Aspects (David & Charles, Newton Abbot, 1973)

The Erosion of Oxford (Oxford Illustrated Press, Oxford, 1977)

English Architecture: an Illustrated Glossary (David & Charles, Newton Abbot, 1977 and 1987)

Mausolea in Ulster (Ulster Architectural Heritage Society, Belfast, 1978)

Moneymore and Draperstown. The Architecture and Planning of the Estates of The Drapers' Company in Ulster (Ulster Architectural Heritage Society, Belfast, 1979)

A Celebration of Death. An introduction to some of the buildings, monuments and settings of funerary architecture in the Western European tradition (Constable, London, and Scribners, New York, 1980)

Classical Churches in Ulster (Ulster Architectural Heritage Society, Belfast, 1980)

The History, Architecture, and Planning of the Estates of The Fishmongers' Company in Ulster (Ulster Architectural Heritage Society, Belfast, 1981)

The Egyptian Revival. An Introductory Study of a Recurring Theme in the History of Taste (George Allen & Unwin, London, 1982)

The Life and Work of Henry Roberts (1803–76), Architect (Phillimore, Chichester, 1983)

The Londonderry Plantation 1609–1914. The History, Architecture, and Planning of the Estates of the City of London and its Livery Companies in Ulster (Phillimore, Chichester, 1986)

Victorian Architecture (David & Charles, Newton Abbot, 1990)

© James Stevens Curl 1991
First published 1991

ISBN 0 7134 5827 5

Typeset by Keyspools Ltd, Golborne, Warrington
and printed in Great Britain by
Courier International

for the Publisher
B. T. Batsford Ltd
4 Fitzhardinge Street
London W1H 0AH

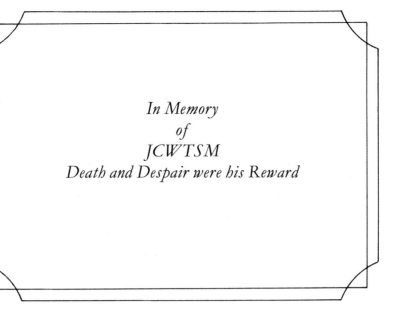

In Memory
of
JCWTSM
Death and Despair were his Reward

The most satisfactory definition of freemasonry from the masonic
historian's point of view would appear to be the organisation and practices
which have from time to time prevailed among medieval
working masons and their 'operative' and 'speculative' successors, from the
earliest date from which such organisation is traceable
down to the present time.

Douglas Knoop and G. P. Jones
The Genesis of Freemasonry
Manchester, 1949, p11

By 'speculative masonry', or what Murray Lyon calls 'symbolic masonry',
we understand a peculiar system of morality, veiled in allegory and
illustrated by symbols. In other words, we regard it as synonymous
with 'freemasonry' in its modern sense.

Ibid., p129

A definition of freemasonry should only include the operative
craft of masonry once its members developed beliefs and practices which
rendered it qualitatively different from other crafts. There is
no evidence of this in the Middle Ages, though the elaborate traditional
history of the mason craft and the mobility of its members
made it a relatively unusual one.

David Stevenson
The Origins of Freemasonry:
Scotland's Century, 1590–1710
Cambridge, 1988, p11

ACKNOWLEDGEMENTS

The allegories that veil freemasonry, as also
the symbols that illustrate it, are . . . drawn
from the lore of architecture and building.

Bernard E. Jones
Freemasons' Guide and Compendium
London, 1959, p19

This study acknowledges its intellectual debt to the great pioneering works of the German Masonic historians Georg Kloss (1787–1854), J. G. Findel (1828–1905), and Georg E. Wilhelm Begemann (whose best work saw the light of day in the period just before the catastrophe of 1914). In England the chief foundation works have been by A. F. A. Woodford (1821–87), R. F. Gould (1836–1915), and W. J. Hughan (1841–1911). Douglas Knoop, G. P. Jones, and Douglas Hamer have contributed an enormous range of scholarship since the 1930s, and their endeavours are especially useful in considerations of medieval Freemasonry. The works of Knoop and Jones are essential as scholarly bases of Masonic history, and are mercifully free from any taint of the sensational or the half-baked. Other studies relevant to an understanding of Freemasonry have been undertaken by Frances A. Yates (whose delvings into previously obscure byways of Renaissance culture have served to illumine some of the stranger ideas prevalent in the sixteenth and seventeenth centuries), and by Margaret C. Jacob (whose *The Radical Enlightenment: Pantheists, Freemasons, and Republicans*, published in London in 1981, is a useful text).

Knoop and Jones recognized the importance of Scotland in the history of Freemasonry since the six-teenth century, while Murray Lyon and Begemann had earlier produced substantial studies that acknowledged the significance of Scottish Masonic beginnings. More recently, David Stevenson has demonstrated that Scotland's contribution was indeed immense, and has attempted to correct what he claims is an 'Anglocentric' tendency present in many standard works. His *The Origins of Freemasonry: Scotland's Century 1590–1710* (Cambridge, 1988) was published after I had completed my first drafts. I refer to some of his findings in my own text, acknowledge my debt to his scholarly exposition of much interesting material, and am grateful to Doctor Stevenson for permission to quote from his book.

Bernard E. Jones's *Freemasons' Guide and Compendium* is of considerable value in explaining much of the basic stuff of Freemasonry (although even that volume is unnecessarily coy on occasion), while Albert G. Mackey's *A Lexicon of Freemasonry* and Gould's great *History* offer much food for thought, although the latter book must be treated with great caution. Also of considerable value is C. Lenning's *Allgemeines Handbuch der Freimaurerei*, while other German sources quoted in the Bibliography are very rewarding.

Professor Anthony Vidler, in *Oppositions, AA Files, Lotus International*, and in his more recent *The Writing of the Walls: Architectural Theory in the Late Enlightenment* (Princeton, 1987), has considered various aspects of eighteenth-century French Architecture and discussed building types, including Masonic Lodges. I had the pleasure of reviewing the latter book, and I paid tribute to the definitive flavour of the wide range of architectural preoccupations during a period when Europe erupted with change which Vidler evoked. He and I have inevitably been over similar ground in our consideration of the extraordinary vein of Masonic material and its manifestations in France during the *Ancien Régime* and the Revolutionary and Napoleonic periods. In some cases I have incorporated points made by Vidler: I thank him most warmly for permission to quote from his work.

In any study such as this it is inevitable that many ideas and much material are drawn from a huge range of sources, for the sheer mass of works consulted was enormous (some more profitable than others) and distillation was a grave problem. The Select Bibliography and Notes give an indication of what is only the tip of an enormous iceberg of Masonic and related publications, and there must be many ideas and images I have absorbed over some thirty years of considering the subject which have simply become part of my understanding, and which I can no longer recall as being anything other than part of the total picture I have formed. Once a subject begins to bite, and interest is aroused, the mind and eye are open to all sorts of stimuli and connections that help to build up an overall impression: inevitably that conspectus contains elements from countless sources, and I acknowledge their contribution to the sum of ideas, facts, and hypotheses that help to form the kernel of a work such as this. Some specific acknowledgements other than those outlined above are necessary, and it is my pleasure to thank the many people who have helped me to assemble my material.

First of all, I am grateful to Mr John Hamill, Librarian and Curator of the Library and Museum of the United Grand Lodge of England, and to his predecessor, Mr T. O. Haunch, without whose help in finding some marvellous material the preparation of the book would have been impossible. Mr Hamill, Mr Haunch, Mr Page, and Mr Meacham of the United Grand Lodge dealt with my endless queries and requests with unfailing courtesy. I am also grateful to the Rev. Neville Barker Cryer (Secretary of the Quatuor Coronati Lodge No. 2076), to Mr Arthur O. Hazel, O St J (of the Grand Lodge of Scotland), and to Mr R. J. C. Jamieson for encouragement. Doctor Brent Elliott made some useful suggestions for reading: I am grateful to him for his advice.

I have enjoyed the help of Mr Ralph Hyde, Keeper of Prints and Maps, and the staff of the Guildhall Library, City of London, who have all been more than kind. I have also received assistance from the staffs of the following: the RIBA British Architectural Library; the RIBA Library Drawings Collection; Sir John Soane's Museum (especially Mr Peter Thornton and Mrs Margaret Richardson); the Statens Konstmuseer Stockholm; the Staatliche Museen Preussischer Kulturbesitz; the Deutsches Theatermuseum, Munich; the Theatermuseum, Cologne; the Matica Slovenská; the Cooper-Hewitt Museum; the Smithsonian Institute's National Museum of Design; the Rare Book and Manuscript Library of Columbia University in the City of New York; the Royal Commission on the Historical Monuments of England (especially Mr Ian Leith and Mr Robert Blow); the Royal Commission on the Ancient & Historical Monuments of Scotland; the Staatliche Schlösser and Gärten Wörlitz, Oranienbaum, Luisium in the DDR (especially Dr Hartmut Ross and Dr Reinhard Alex for illustrations of Wörlitz); the Germanisches Nationalmuseum Nürnberg; the Musée Carnavalet, Paris; the Center for Studies in Landscape Architecture, Dumbarton Oaks, Washington DC; the Society of Antiquaries of London; the Bodleian Library, University of Oxford; the British Library (especially Miss Pam Taylor); the Bibliothèque Nationale, Paris; the Bischöfliches Ordinariat Würzburg; the Museen der Stadt Wien; the Bibliothèque Royale Albert 1er, Brussels, and many other museums and collections too numerous to name individually, for the many answers to enquiries I have made. I am grateful to them all.

I also thank Mr Geremy Butler, Miss Iona Cruickshank, and Mr Rodney C. Roach for help with photography. Mr John Gamble, Mr Michael Goldmark, Mr Jeremy Ridge, and Mr Meaburn Staniland all helped to locate documents and books, for which I am most grateful. My much-altered manuscripts were translated into typescript by Mrs Pamela D. Walker, who has my gratitude. I also thank my many scholarly friends in the German Democratic Republic who have shown me the buildings, gardens, and cemeteries of what used to be Prussia and Saxony. If I have omitted anyone by name from these acknowledgements it is not for lack of appreciation: there have been so many that it would be an immense task to thank them all. I hope that this sincere expression of my indebtedness will suffice, for without the generous assistance of friends, colleagues past and present, and very many other people, the task of writing this book would have been very much more difficult than it actually was.

James Stevens Curl
1986–90

PREFACE

As close as oak, an absolute freemason for secrecy

George Colman the Elder
The Deuce is in Him. Act II

This book is intended as an introduction to a subject that perhaps has generated more heat than light, yet the importance of that subject is obvious to anyone with any interest in European civilization, especially during the eighteenth and early nineteenth centuries.

I first realized there was a book to be written on the topic when carrying out research for my *The Egyptian Revival. An Introductory Study of a Recurring Theme in the History of Taste*, which came out in 1982, although it had dawned on me very much earlier that *that* was a book which needed to be written when viewing the marvellous Schinkel stage-sets for *Die Zauberflöte* in a special 1960 Festival Exhibition in Mozart's birthplace in Salzburg. Although twenty-two years elapsed after that exhibition before *The Egyptian Revival* appeared, the enormous trawl of material I acquired pointed to something I had only half-suspected when I first explored seventeenth- and eighteenth-century Egyptianisms: the significance of Freemasonry in design.

There is an obvious danger in seeing allusions everywhere, and of ascribing to buildings connotations that are, at best, tentative. That danger I have tried to avoid, proposing Masonic influences only where there are clear indications that they are real. Some Masonic emblems and motifs are shared by other societies and bodies, and some are simply part of an enormous range of images and elements that can be found within the rich language of European Classical and pre-Classical design. Two columns or a triangle, for example, are not necessarily indicative of Masonic allusions, but on the other hand they might be: I have tried to differentiate where possible. Broken columns do indeed signify a life cut off, but they are not necessarily Masonic, yet they can be. All this sounds vague and difficult, and so it is, but there is no doubt in my mind that a careful study, as far as it is possible, reveals many interesting and relevant byways in the history of Architecture and design that are closely connected with upheavals of organization at the time of the Reformation, and that have links with certain esoteric themes linking Renaissance studies with the worlds of the Magus and of the mysteries of Antiquity in the Graeco-Roman world.

Many personalities of the European Enlightenment were Freemasons, and some of the most familiar and celebrated of works created in the eighteenth century were steeped in Masonic allusion including, of course, *Die Zauberflöte*, Mozart and Schikaneder's masterpiece that has infuriated, baffled, and delighted many commentators for almost two centuries, although its meaning was probably clearer to minds steeped in the Enlightenment than those filled with other notions and layers of understanding (or lack of it) today. One must take seriously the fact that no less a person than Goethe (himself a Freemason) held *Die Zauberflöte* in the highest regard, and himself prepared a sketch for a sequel.

Musicians, Architects, writers, theorists, philosophers, and even Churchmen (of many persuasions) of the time joined Masonic Lodges in numbers, and there can be no doubt that Freemasonry not only offered many of the finest minds of the Enlightenment something not available in other organizations (including the Church), but attracted the loyalty and interest of an astonishing number of significant historical figures, and unquestionably influenced aspects of endeavour in an age of fecund creativity.

It is regrettable that Masonic studies have been bedevilled by certain writings of a journalistic and sensational type. The secret nature of much of Masonic ritual has, of course, encouraged speculation and a certain wild denunciation verging on the hysterical: it is not to the credit of many in public life today that exaggeration and condemnation have come so easily to them. This is all the more peculiar since so much about Freemasonry is readily available in standard reference works (although certain Masonic writers have not helped their cause by coyness and deliberate obfuscation). The conclusion is melancholy: it can only be assumed that the over-simplified messages emanating from the media, from politicians, and from those in public life (who ought to know better) reflect a growing reluctance to read, to delve, to ascertain. The sensational, the 'controversial', the inaccurate, the disastrous, the sordid, and the 'newsworthy' are regarded as more important than the truth, because the effort of finding out seems to be beyond those who live by the vulgarities of populist 'culture'.

The Masonic allusions in *Die Zauberflöte* are clear to those who bother to read the libretto and listen to the music; the literary origins of *Die Zauberflöte* can also be found among certain texts popular in the eighteenth century, while the musical aspects of Masonic allusions are not obscure, difficult, or unworthy of attention—in fact, *Die Zauberflöte* is meaningless if the Masonic, clerical, political, and cultural concerns of the Central-European intellectual climate of 1791 are ignored. Similarly, the design of many late eighteenth-century buildings, gardens, and cemeteries, and the contents of some well-known Continental literary texts, can make sense only when their implicit Masonic content is understood and recognized.

So it is with Architecture. Once a few points are understood, a considerable number of buildings will be shown to have Masonic elements. This is hardly surprising, given the architectural content explicit in Freemasonry, while the Great Architect Himself is a Masonic metaphor that will need little elaboration. There are texts dealing with Masonic ceremony, initiation, and ordeal, and these have been around for quite some time; I have used them freely, and I make no apology for doing so.

In an age when death is regarded as a sensational disaster if it occurs to large numbers of people in public (as in an aircraft, train, ship, or car), used as the excuse for 'entertainment', relegated to embarrassed shuffling when it occurs normally, or treated with horror if it happens as a result of disease, it is not peculiar that reflections about death, the ending of life, the position of individual existence, and the celebration of death are not given much consideration in current times in Britain. We are too busy showing how 'caring' we are to face the realities or to challenge the supposition that death and bereavement can be treated as antiseptically as rubbish disposal (and given less significance).

Death, and facing death, however, are central to eighteenth-century Masonic texts, and involve the idea of a journey, trials, and rebirth. In Architecture and in the design of gardens, the themes of a route, a progression, of allusion, of metaphor, of mnemonics, of conjuring moods, cultures, or exotica, and of passing through to a climactic end are not unusual, and yet the Masonic content of such designs often escapes commentators. Masonic concepts of death, trial, and descent to the depths are clearly described in many books, and are explicit in the text of *Die Zauberflöte*, although obscured in the opera houses of today where productions and designs strive after 'originality' and 'contemporary meaning' only to make nonsense of the work and display an abysmal ignorance of the essence of the piece. *Die Zauberflöte* with no Masonic iconography and no Egyptian Architecture for the sets misses the point entirely and leaves the audience mystified, bored, or irritated by what appears to be a nonsensical story. Operatic embarrassment is nothing new, but to make it inevitable by crassness, by omitting chunks of dialogue that are essential to understanding, and by failure to use the potential of Masonic allusion is indicative of something rather alarming in the culture of the late 1980s. Would it be too much to hope that in 1991, the bicentenary of Mozart's death and of the first performance of *Die Zauberflöte*, we might have a production with Schinkel's Egyptian sets, with the text uncut, and where the Masonic elements are used and exploited rather than ignored?

This book draws on many sources and attempts to explain the Masonic content in Art and Architecture; it is necessarily only an introduction, for a detailed study would be very much larger than my publishers are prepared to allow me. The Select Bibliography, though fairly wide in scope, is by no means exhaustive: even the collection in Freemasons' Hall in London, if listed as a Bibliography, would fill this entire book (and more), leaving no room for text or illustrations.

It must be emphasized that the subject is vast and that there is no shortage of material, yet the odd thing is that, with several exceptions, most scholars writing in English have tended to avoid any mention of Freemasonry when discussing Architecture or the design of gardens. The French have not been so inhibited, while German scholarship also touches upon the subject, but more warily. The problem lies partly in the fact that Continental Freemasonry has tended to be associated with political and cultural ideas alien to modern British Freemasonry (but not so alien in the seventeenth and eighteenth centuries), and that the anti-clerical (even anti-religious) and anti-establishment nature of many Continental Lodges (both before and after the French Revolution) raises questions that, even today, are difficult to deal with, for much of the literature in English that has attempted to discuss the matter tends to be based upon sources biased against Illuminism and its Masonic counterparts. French, German, Dutch, and Scandinavian writers have been much more adventurous.

This study will attempt to avoid speculation as far as is possible, and will be concerned with iconography, Architecture, types, gardens, literature, music, and stage-design. It will try to avoid the sensational and will be based on sound sources, although reasoned hypotheses are offered on more than one occasion, parallels are drawn, and comparisons are made on a logical basis. To the enquiring mind all subjects offer scope for investigation: the Art and Architecture associated with Freemasonry are eminently reasonable topics with which to be concerned. Unfortunately, some writers have tended to jeopardize Masonic studies by indulging in wild claims and sensationalism: John Saltmarsh in *The Economic History Review* of 1937 described Masonic history as 'obscure and highly controversial', and 'by ill-luck the happiest of all hunting grounds for the light-headed, the fanciful ... and the lunatic fringe of the British Museum Reading Room'. Having waded through some weird stuff in the course of my research, I can confirm that, although much serious work has been done, much tedious, barmy, entirely fanciful, and usually nonsensical material has appeared since Saltmarsh's comments of over half a century ago, and only serves to obscure and cloud issues that deserve careful attention and clarity of thought. Like some recent investigations into the peculiar world of pre-Newtonian European culture, any study of Freemasonry is bedevilled by the existence of a vast 'literature' of worthless speculation and inaccurate outpourings from the loony fringe of occultism. This does not mean that an attempt to study the relatively small percentage of what may be described as sound Masonic material should be avoided, for Freemasonry does have a serious, respectable, and important history that is essential to approach and consider in any evaluation of certain aspects of architectural and cultural history—indeed it would be irresponsible to ignore it. This book therefore, is intended to offer a flavour of what might lie in wait for future historians sufficiently inquisitive to delve further.

CONTENTS

LIST OF ILLUSTRATIONS

Sources are given in brackets after each caption, with the abbreviated form of the publication or collection indicated in either the caption or the source in parentheses. Abbreviations indicate the collection from which the illustrations derive, with the reference number or shelf-mark after the abbreviation. The key to abbreviations is given as follows:

A	The Author, or from the Author's collection
AC	Lequeu, *Architecture Civile*
L'Architecture	Ledoux, C.-N., *L'Architecture considérée sous le rapport de l'Art des Moeurs et de la Législation.* Paris, 1804
Bernigeroth	Bernigeroth, J.M., *Les Coutumes des Francs-Maçons dans leurs Assemblées . . .* Leipzig, 1745
BL	The British Library, London
BN	Bibliothèque Nationale, Paris
BO	The Bodleian Library, University of Oxford
CE	Cabinet des Estampes, Bibliothèque Nationale, Paris
DT	Deutsches Theatermuseum, Munich, Früher Clara Ziegler-Stiftung
Entwurff	Fischer von Erlach, Johann Berhard, *Entwurff einer Historischen Architektur, in Abbildung unterschiedener verühmter Gebäude, des Alterthums und fremder Völker.* Leipzig, 1725
GLCL	Guildhall Library, City of London
Handzeichnungen	*Handzeichnungen Zum Theater Gebrauch von Carl Maurer, Fürstlich Esterhayzyscher Hof Theater Decorateur.* Eisenstadt, 1812
Krafft	Krafft, J.C., *Recueil d'Architecture civile.* Paris, 1812
Laborde	Laborde, Alexandre-Louis-Joseph, Comte de, *Descriptions des Nouveaux Jardins de la France et de ses anciens châteaux; mêlée d'observations sur la vie de la campagne et la composition des jardins, par Alexandre de Laborde.* Paris, 1808–15
Lamy	Lamy, Bernard, *De Tabernaculo Foederis, de Sancta Civitate Jerusalem, et de Templo EJUS.* Paris, 1720
Larudan	Larudan, Abbé, *Les Francs-Maçons écrasés. Suite du livre intitulé, L'Ordre*

Black and white

The front jacket illustration shows: *Decoration by Friedrich Jügel after a design by Karl Friedrich Schinkel for the second scene of Act I of the Opera* Olimpia *by Gasparo Luigi Pacifico Spontini (1774–1851). The original project is in watercolour, and is held in the Schinkel Museum in Berlin (TH/15): it shows Schinkel's version of the interior of the celebrated Temple of Artemis at Ephesus based on descriptions in Pliny and Pausanias, and the Ionic and Corinthian Orders are in evidence (Doric was used for the design of the exterior, so all three main Orders were incoroporated in the sets). Behind the altar is the cult statue of Artemis with her bound body, crowned disc, and rings of objects that are now thought to represent the testicles of sacrificed animals rather than 'many breasts'.*

Olimpia *has other Masonic connections besides the identification of Artemis with Isis and the Egyptian Mysteries: the libretto was by E. T. A. Hoffmann, based on the original French by Dieulafoy and Brifaut, which was in turn derived from the tragedy by that great Freemason, Voltaire. This production was given at the Court Opera in Berlin in 1821, and exhibits some of the most refined and brilliant Masonic/Neoclassical designs ever made for the stage.* From Thiele (BL).

The back jacket illustration shows: *The Building of the Tower of Babel, showing Masons preparing stone, hoisting blocks into position, and working on the flimsy cantilevered scaffolding at the top. The Angels of Heaven are distorting the speech of the men so that they start fighting, fall to their deaths, and the Tower falls with them. On the left is the Lodge in which the Masons are preparing lime-mortar which is then carried on hods on the shoulders of the hod-carriers. A fifteenth-century illumination from the Duke of Bedford's* Book of Hours *(Bl. Add. 18 850, Fol. 17V).*

CHAPTER I

AN OUTLINE OF SOME OF THE HISTORY OF THE CRAFT

Introduction; Freemasonry and Freemasons; the Lodge

The origin of Freemasonry is one of the most debated,
and debatable, subjects in the whole realm of historical enquiry. One has to distinguish
between the legendary history of Freemasonry and the problem of when it actually
began as an organized institution. According to masonic legend,
Freemasonry is as old as architecture itself. . . .

Frances A. Yates
The Rosicrucian Enlightenment
London, 1972, p209

Introduction

One of the most common features of esoteric cults and secret societies is a tendency to claim hidden knowledge not available to the outsider. Such claims are frequently enhanced by associating knowledge or wisdom with lost civilizations, and especially with the great civilizations of Antiquity (Ancient Egypt, the Hellenistic cultures, and the Graeco-Roman World of the Mediterranean lands). The longing to recover what had been lost, the attempt to find once again what was perfect, and the widespread tendency towards syncretism, or blending of legends, religions, cults, and ideas, are not recent phenomena, and have played no small part in Western European civilization. The Garden of Eden, the Temple of Solomon, the Wonders of the Ancient World, the glories of Greek and Roman Architecture, and the stories of Lost Continents and Lost Tribes are potent examples of that sense of loss, and of a desire to rediscover something infinitely precious, essential, uplifting, noble, and powerful. The realms of magic, of divine authority, of mystery, and of super-creativity are never far away.

The term 'Architecture' will be used throughout this book, as will 'Geometry', 'Masonry', and other terms, so it is as well to remind ourselves what they mean. 'Architecture' implies something much more than mere building: it signifies the art or science of constructing edifices (or making designs for such edifices) that have aesthetic pretensions, that have qualities on a higher plane than those of purely utilitarian structures, and that have complexities, aspects capable of moving the beholder, and an intellectual rigour raising them to heights considerably loftier than those of the bicycle-shed or similar mundane buildings. Early definitions of Architecture mention science, art, monumental quality, ingenuity, and composition of parts. Ruskin's suggestion that Architecture is the art which so disposes and adorns the edifices raised by man that the sight of those edifices contributes to mental health, power, and pleasure seems to indicate something different, while George Gilbert Scott's contention that Architecture is the decoration of construction is something few would entertain, least of all the Renaissance thinkers and writers on the subject. An Architect is a master-builder, a skilled professor of the art or science of building, who prepares designs and supervises the erection of his designs: he designs and frames any complex structure, arranges elementary materials on a comprehensive plan, and is a creator, even The Creator, because he creates Order out of Chaos, or superimposes order where there was none.

Geometry is an essential part of Architecture, for it is the science which investigates the properties and relationships of magnitudes in space, as lines, as surfaces, and as solids. In ancient texts Geometry was seen as a practical art for measuring and planning, and was indissolubly associated with Architecture. It was a necessary means of measuring ground, marking out plots, establishing areas, and imposing ordered subdivisions on territories, but an understanding of Geometry was a necessary skill of the stonemason, who created the most respected and highest form of Architecture, that of an Architecture of stone. In Bradshaw's *St Werburge* of 1513 we read of 'masons . . . Counnynge in geometrie', while John Dee, in 1570, states that 'Geometrie is the Arte of Measuring sensible magnitudes, their iust quantities and contents'. Architects, Masons, and Geometers, then, had a close working knowledge of the art or science of Geometry, or that branch of Mathematics which treats of the description and properties of magnitudes in general.

A Mason, of course, is a builder and worker in stone, a person who dresses and lays stone in building. To mason is to build with stone, to construct of masonry, to build up or strengthen with stone. To say that something was masoned is to mean that it was built of stone.[1]

It seems that the first 'histories' of Freemasonry date from the Middle Ages: in these curious documents Geometry is regarded as one of the Seven Liberal Arts, and Masonry, in the sense of the craft of building with stone, was seen as equivalent to Geometry in significance. Given its importance, therefore, it is not surprising to find that Euclid was held to be a figure of great wisdom, and indeed was identified syncretically with the wisest of the ancients, and was himself the keeper of mysteries and the deepest founts of knowledge.[2] The *MS Constitutions of Masonry*, known as the Old Charges (of which the well-known *Regius* and *Cooke* MSS of the late fourteenth and early fifteenth centuries respectively are the earliest versions so far identified), contain details of regulations, wages, and other matters concerning the degrees of masters, craftsmen, and apprentices.[3] Knoop, Jones, and Hamer have edited *The Two Earliest Masonic MSS*, which appeared in 1938, but the reasons for the compilation of the manuscripts remain obscure: speculation as to why exactly these strange accounts developed would be profitless, but they are important as links between 'operative' and 'speculative' Freemasonry, for they stress the venerable nature of the connections of the Craft with myth, Antiquity, and a moral system of conduct. James Anderson's *The New Book of the Constitutions of the Antient and Honourable Fraternity of Free and Accepted Masons*, published in London in 1738 (a development of the earlier *Book of Constitutions* of 1723),

collated and enlarged upon the medieval Masonic texts, introducing many claims that do not stand up to serious examination: the Emperor Augustus as Grand-Master of a Lodge in Rome, and similar promotion of King Nebuchadnezzar as a Masonic figure in Babylon, are only two examples of spurious notions that gathered further accretions in the course of time, and only served to cloak real Masonic history in fictions, fairy-stories, and obfuscatory stuff.

The really important elements of Masonic history are those concerned with the Geometry–Architecture–Masonry links, and these seem to occur first in England in the *Regius* MSS of around 1390. The Greeks gave high regard to Geometry, and it was part of the educational system of the Ancient Greeks: it was studied as a Liberal Art on a theoretical basis by both the Greeks and the Romans. These Liberal Arts were defined as seven by the fifth-century Carthaginian Martianus Capella in his *Nuptiae Philologiae et Mercurii* as Grammar, Dialectic, Rhetoric, Geometry, Arithmetic, Astronomy, and Harmony. The seventh-century Bishop of Seville, St Isidore (*c*.560–636) (whose attributes, interestingly enough, include the hive of bees, a Masonic emblem), lists Geometry, comprehending the measured and dimensions of the Earth, as the sixth Liberal Art, but, by the time of the medieval manuscripts referred to above, Geometry had become something more: it was the introductory source of all knowledge.[4] Thus, as early as the Middle Ages, Geometry had acquired an awesome status rather grander than we might suspect from the perspective of the twentieth century. Although Geometry was associated with the measurement of land, it began to be connected with the art and science of Masonry. There can be no question but that the association with exact measurements and with buildings of importance made of stone was a stimulus to accord Geometry a new grandeur connected with mysteries, with power (both secular and sacred), and with political clout. Builders of stone monuments, great churches, and the like, enjoyed a certain status, and the creators of the Houses of God on such a spectacular scale as those of the cathedrals of the Middle Ages were no ordinary artisans, and appear to have been far more mobile than members of other crafts with different skills. The idea of Geometry as holding within it the kernel of all advancement, all truth, and the ultimate mystery elevated that art to the highest pinnacle in the respect and awe of Mankind. Geometry was a kind of First Cause, a touchstone of power and knowledge, and the art by which mighty expressions of the truth could be realized: it held within it the possibility to re-create the Divine in building, the lost Temple of Solomon itself.

The manuscripts contain early Masonic legends that

relate to the *invention* of Geometry. Clearly, Geometry, Masonry, and Architecture are connected, but Geometry was considered to have been discovered before the Flood by Jabal, who was Master-Mason in charge of the building of Enoch, the first city, for Cain.[5] From the Hebrew *Apocrypha* and from Flavius Josephus's (37–c.98) *Jewish Antiquities* comes the legend that Abraham instructed the Egyptians in arithmetic and astronomy, the source for the twelfth-century claims in Honorius Augustodunensis's *De Imagine Mundi* and in Petrus Comestor's *Historia Scholastica* that Abraham taught the Egyptians Geometry.[6] Later versions of this legend grant Euclid the distinction of having founded Geometry, in the basic principles of which he had been instructed by Abraham.[7] Here then, is an example of syncretism in which Jewish legend and the civilizations of Antiquity merge: this will be a familiar process throughout this study. A tendency to telescope history and to create connections by ignoring the time-gap of millennia is not an unusual feature of the medieval world, and indeed syncretism, by which various figures merged with deities, and by which deities themselves became identified with other deities and personages, was a strong characteristic of Classical Antiquity itself.[8] Even more interesting in this respect is the legend that Geometry was invented as a corollary of Nilotic flooding: this attribution is recorded by Diodorus Siculus (who lived at the time of Julius Caesar and Augustus, and whose *Bibliotheca* included six books dealing with the history and mythology of the Ancient Egyptians), and was repeated by St Isidore of Seville, in his *Originum seu Etymologiarum Libri XX*, who specifically credits the Egyptians with the invention of Geometry because they were obliged to divide the mud-covered lands by means of measured sections.[9] The good Bishop (whose encyclopaedia was one of the most influential books of the Middle Ages) omits any mention of Abraham in this weighty matter, for the great Geometer becomes Hermes, the Messenger, no less. Nilotic flooding, and measurement by Cubits (the units by which the amount of flooding was calculated) became associated with the Masonic legend in which Hermes Trismegistus and Euclid were identified as one and the same.[10] Hermes Trismegistus, of course, is identified with Thoth and with Mercury, and instructed Isis (the Great Goddess herself, whose tears for the murdered Osiris caused the Nile to flood) in many matters, including Geometry.[11] Diodorus Siculus tells us that instruction in mathematics and Geometry was given to the sons of priests alone, and thus the idea of Geometry, the root of Masonry, as an exclusive and secret art or science, handed down to the deities, to an élite, or to a specific class, has an obvious connotation with Freemasonry in later times.[12]

Freemasonry and Freemasons

So what is Freemasonry? The precise derivation has been much disputed, and doubtless will continue to arouse passions. The notion that a Freemason was a Free-Stone Mason seems to come from a reference to a 'master mason of free stone' (*mestre mason de franche peer*) in Act 25 Edward III St II, c3, of 1350, while the phrase *sculptores lapidum liberorum*, or 'carvers of free stones', is supposed to occur in a document of 1217 in the London Assize of Wages of that year. Although 'Freemason' and 'Mason' seem to be synonymous sometimes, this is not always so. The term 'Mason', however, seems to cover all people working with stone, while a 'Freemason' was one who could be contrasted with a roughmason, hard-hewer, layer, or rowmason, the latter four terms signifying those who roughly shaped stone with an axe or a scappling hammer. Freemasons were a cut above, therefore, and the term meant 'craftsmen who would hew and set freestones'. A freestone, meaning any finely-grained limestone or sandstone that can be freely worked in any direction and sawn, has always been used for carving, undercutting, and fine work, so a Freemason, in one sense, was one who worked with freestone. In 1351 a *Magister Lathomus Liberarum Petrarum* is mentioned in connection with the building works at Oxford. This interpretation was held by Wyatt Papworth, Joseph Gwilt,[13] Dr Wilhelm Begemann,[14] and many others.[15]

Interestingly enough, in Scotland there is not much freestone: the sandstones tend to be very hard, and the term 'Freemason', meaning someone involved in building, was not common, if it was used at all,[16] although there are instances of its occurrence in seventeenth-century Scottish Lodge minutes.[17] In Scotland and in the north we find reference to Cowans, who appear to have been workmen who were semi-skilled in working with stone, and who were equivalent to the roughmasons of England. A Cowan was forbidden to work with lime-mortar, as was a dry-stone waller or diker: the term was applied derogatorily to a labourer who worked with stone, but who had not been regularly apprenticed, so it was given to anyone who was uninitiated into the secrets of Freemasonry. The Mother Kilwinning Lodge of Ayrshire describes a Cowan as a Mason without the Word, and Freemasons were to guard the Lodge with a drawn sword to protect if from all 'Cowens and Eves-Droppers'. Freemasons had regulated wages, and were superior to Cowans, who were regarded with suspicion and hostility for trying to find the secrets of Freemasonry which would enhance their position. Cowans, therefore, became defined as sneaks or prying persons, the uninitiated, the outsiders, the profane. So it is quite clear that Freemasons had an interest in maintaining their position as craftsmen of a superior nature, and that their secret signs were a means of ensuring status, wealth, and keeping the untrained at bay. Thus a Freemason, in the Craft sense, would have been familiar with the trowel, but a Cowan would have no use for such a tool, as he was forbidden to use lime at all. Lime is therefore of singular importance in many senses in the history of operative and speculative Masonry.

The terms *Cementarius, Lathomus, Lapicida, Masonn, Masoun, Mazon* are all found in documents, so the Latin and Norman-French words were in common use.[18] It appears that 'Freemason' first occurs in English in the City of London *Letter-Book H* of 9 August 1376.[19] This was the date when the Common Council of the City of London was elected from the Mysteries, or Guilds, or Livery Companies. Mysteries, of course, is a corruption of the Latin *mysterium*, confused with *ministerium*, which in due course became associated with the old French word *mistere*, meaning trade, occupation, service, or craft, derived from the old French *mestier* (modern equivalent *métier*, meaning trade). An example of the use of the term can be found in the grandiose titles of some of the Livery Companies of the City of London, as in 'The Master and Wardens and Brethren and Sisters of the Guild or Fraternity of the Blessed Mary the Virgin of the Mystery of Drapers of the City of London'. W. J. Williams, in his useful article on the 'Use of the word "Freemason" before 1717',[20] points out that 'Freemason' recurs in documents, though 'Mason' is more usual. The City of London *Letter-Book H* of 1376 describes two individuals as 'Freemasons', but this entry is deleted and replaced by an entry of the two names and two others, the four being described as 'Masons'. Did this mean that the men were roughmasons, or was 'Mason' substituted as a loose term to include 'Freemasons'? Whatever the case, it is clear that the four were elected to represent the Mystery of Masons, which seems to have been of fourteenth-century date, probably established between 1356 and 1376. Knoop and Jones,[21] however, mention twelve freemen of Norwich admitted as 'Freemasons', eleven as 'Roughmasons', and 135 as 'Masons' in the fifteenth and sixteenth centuries, which indicates some differentiation. According to Knoop and Jones the terms 'Mason' and 'Freemason' became interchangeable, although it does seem that there was a definite distinction at one time denoting the actual skills of the persons concerned, but that the distinction became blurred quite early. Even the London muniments concerned with the organization of the trade of Masonry refer to a Company of Masons and of Freemasons.[22]

Another view of the origin of the term 'Freemasonry' concerns that of Free Masons, that is persons who were 'Free' of the Masons' Guilds. 'Free' in this usage indicates status, as in a municipal organization or in a Company or Guild (e.g. Freeman of the City of London or Freeman of a London Livery Company), or as an indication of freedom from some kind of obligation or serfdom. As Knoop and Jones[23] have pointed out, though, most Masons would not have been 'free' of a Company or Guild. It seems fairly clear that apprentices, in the fourteenth-century manuscripts, were not to be of servile status or birth, and that the peripatetic nature of domicile connected with the Mason's trade made any binding to a Manor impossible; yet the apprentice was not exactly free, and his status was rather like that of a servant.[24] G. W. Speth has claimed[25] that itinerant Masons were called 'Free' precisely because they were *not* under the control of local Guilds of the towns and cities in which they settled on a temporary basis.

It has also been suggested that the term refers to the practice of emancipating skilled workmen so that they could travel and give their services to any great building project.[26] A Freemason was a member of a class of skilled workers engaged in hewing and/or setting freestone, and in the fourteenth and following centuries was sometimes mentioned in contradistinction to roughmasons or *ligiers*. Freemasons travelled to find work where important buildings were to be erected, and seem to have used a system of secret signs and passwords to identify the level of skill attained, although these systems of words and signs were probably as much to secure status and pay as to indicate skills. From the sixteenth century the term seems to have implied that the craftsman belonged to a higher grade than that of an ordinary Mason. In 1444[27] a *frank mason* is differentiated from a *rough mason*, and similar distinctions are drawn elsewhere.[28]

A new meaning of the term developed during the seventeenth century. While a Freemason in the sixteenth and seventeenth centuries was still a word denoting an 'operative' Mason who cut or set freestone (as is clear from a letter of the second Earl of Nottingham who complained of a shortage of 'freemasons to prepare stone' for his great house at Burley-on-the-Hill in Rutland), it also began to mean a member of a Fraternity called Free and Accepted Masons. Early in the seventeenth century it appears that the societies of Freemasons began to admit honorary members who were not necessarily connected with the building trades, but who might have achieved a certain eminence in architectural and/or antiquarian scholarship. These persons were called 'Accepted Masons', although the name of 'Freemasons' was often applied: they were given knowlege of the secret signs, instructed in the Legends of the Craft, and took part in convivial and social gatherings.

Some scholars, however, do not accept that 'speculative' Freemasonry developed from the 'operative'

Lodges at all, but consider that it evolved more as groups of men seeking esoteric knowledge of Antiquity and enlightenment derived from Hermetic Wisdom. As Freemasonry claimed to guard knowledge passed down from Ancient Egypt itself, men who sought the eternal truths of the lost mysteries gravitated to Freemasonry. Elias Ashmole became a Freemason in 1646, and in 1682 he attended a meeting of a Lodge at Mason's Hall in London where several people were admitted into the Fellowship of Free Masons.[29] Ample evidence suggests that various antiquarians, such as Aubrey, became Freemasons in the 'Accepted' sense during the course of the seventeenth century, and that several societies and fraternities developed. It appears that these societies evolved in the eighteenth century, and were largely convivial: one reads of 'Free Masons and other Learned Men, that used to get drunk' in the English translation of a French book in praise of drunkenness, and it appears that the Brotherhood of the Craft was often in its cups during the Georgian Age.[30] This does not mean, of course, that the Freemasons were more given to Bacchic excess than others of the period, for most convivial societies of the time seem to have drunk deep, and indeed it was a national tendency to drink so heavily that visitors from other European countries could hardly fail to notice the fact. It was not only obeisance to Bacchus that engaged the Freemasons of Georgian England, however, for lectures on Architecture and Geometry were often given in Lodges (and the importance of Geometry as a source of knowledge must be stressed). Aubrey, in 1691, wrote of a convention in St Paul's church of the fraternity of the Accepted Masons at which Sir Christopher Wren was to be 'adopted as a Brother'.[31]

Freemasonry is therefore the Craft or occupation of a Freemason; it is the principles, practices, and institutions of Freemasons; it is a secret or tacit brotherhood, which can also indicate instructive sympathy. Freemasonry is a brotherhood of men joined together through initiation rites that are supposedly secret, the members of which recognize each other by secret methods of identification (such as handgrips or signs), and which is organized in groups called Lodges. A Lodge is the group of Freemasons comprising a branch of the brotherhood, the place of meeting for members (whether it be a permanent building or suite of rooms set aside for such meetings or a temporary marked out space in a room), and the meeting itself.

Yet a connection between organizations of Freemasons in medieval times and the Lodges of later periods is often obscure, although modern scholarship has shed light in some dusty corners. It is clear there were many organizations of bodies of Masons. Various *Corps de Métiers* and *Compagnonnages* existed in France; there were the *Steinmetzen* in the German-speaking lands; Guilds in Flanders and in the Free Cities of Europe; Architect-Mason Companies in Italy; Lodges and Incorporations in Scotland and Assemblies, Craft-Guilds, and Companies in England.[32] The key to such a connection lies in the upheavals of organization and observance caused by the Reformation and in the peculiar climate in which lost knowledge was sought. We enter that strange world of Hermetic Wisdom, of the Magus, and of lost 'Egyptian' (and therefore doubly obscure) knowledge.

The Lodge

A Freemasons' Lodge was originally a Masons' workshop, such as would be necessary for the construction of a cathedral, and this term seems to have been in use as early as 1278. The word 'Lodge' was also used to denote a group of Masons working on any major project, or associated with any particular town or district. A Lodge could assign Marks, establish rules for terms and conditions of apprenticeship, settle disputes, and collect and distribute funds for the relief of distressed Masons and their families.[33]

---

1 *The construction of the Abbey-Church of Schönau, dating from the sixteenth century. At the top left-hand is the quarry where stone is being extracted, blocks are being moved by means of crowbars, and transported by means of ox-carts to the site. In the foreground lime mortar is being mixed and carried up the ladder to the area where dressed stone is being lowered into position by means of a primitive hoist. To the right is the Lodge, a lean-to structure, in which stone is being prepared by means of a pickaxe and a gavel, and within which the square and a template are prominently displayed.*

The figure in the foreground about to cross the river and carrying a rule and a square is presumably the Master-Mason; to the right one of the Brethren (who seem to be Lay-Brothers of the Abbey) is drinking from a flask, while the main supplies of drink are in large containers, one of which is cooling in the river. Two men are shifting a large undressed stone on the right by means of crowbars. Another point of interest is the flimsy cantilevered scaffold-platform just below the clerestory of the building on the right: construction work at high altitudes in the medieval period must have been extremely dangerous and terrifying.

For details see Schock-Werner, Barbara, 'Bauhütten und Baubetrieb der Spätgotik' in Die Parler und der schöne Stil 1350–1400. *Cologne, 1978, p61 (Germanisches Nationalmuseum, Nürnberg. Hz. 196).*

CONSTRVXERE DOMVM CONVERSI SCHONAVIENSEM
QVOS PIVS INDVXIT RELIGIONIS AMOR.

The subject of Masons' Marks is enormous itself, and only a few words can be expended on the topic here. Marks of operative Masons have been found on many buildings over a very long period, yet we can say for certain only that Marks were registered and properly organized in Germany and in Scotland, although it is highly unlikely that no such system existed elsewhere: the evidence is simply lacking. In England alone there are many thousands of examples of Marks cut into stone, and these were the Masons' equivalent of other Guild regulations for various trades which identified goods, makers, and quality. The Schaw Statutes in Scotland of the late sixteenth century indicate that Marks had to be recorded in Lodge minute-books, so they were, in effect, 'signatures' personal to individual Masons. Scottish operative Masons had to register their Marks on entering the Fellow Crafts, while Marks granted to or chosen by gentlemen Masons were also registered in Scottish Mark-books and minutes.

A Lodge, in the sense of a temporary structure, was erected on site to provide protection from the weather and to store tools and materials. It was usually a timber shed, either free-standing or a lean-to structure built against the new building [Colour Plates I–III; 1]. For very large and complex projects taking several years to build, Lodges comprised several rooms, and might have some architectural pretensions themselves: it appears that the Lodges erected for the construction of the cathedrals in Strasbourg and Prague were built of stone.[34] A Lodge was a *Loge* or *Chantier* in French, a *Bauhütte* in German, and other versions include *Logia, Logge, Loygge, Luge,* and *Ludge.* Lodges were workshops in which Masons cut stone, but it seems they were also establishments where the workers could eat, drink, and relax, as well as providing a place where disputes could be ironed out and meetings held. A Lodge was both the place where feasting and convivial activities took place *and* the organized body which arranged such feasts for members. In Scotland Lodges were territorial in the sense that they were associated with a town or an area.[35]

The *Steinmetzen* of the German-speaking lands had rules concerning behaviour: piety, charity, and the honour of the Craft were urged on members. Three grades, those of apprentice, journeyman, and master, were settled by custom (apprenticeship was normally five years), and there were precise rules about financial contributions and Masons' Marks. The *Steinmetzen* also had secret handshakes and forms of greeting, and were organized on a regional basis with a centre in each area. Other organizations such as local Guilds, associations on a larger territorial basis, and trade fraternities under the protection of a Saint (the Parisian Masons had St Blaise as their patron) existed on the Continent during the Middle Ages. The *Steinmetzen* appear to have had sophisticated systems of organization throughout the Holy Roman Empire, probably necessary because of the enormous geographical area and host of Principalities, Duchies, and the like that comprised the Empire. In this respect the comparative compactness of England (and that Kingdom's relative political unity) seem to have made regional centres unnecessary, even during the medieval period,[36] for the early *Regius* and *Cooke* MSS are silent on many aspects such as levies, Marks, and regional organiz-ation. This does not mean, of course, that these matters did not receive attention in England: it simply means that the fourteenth-century texts do not discuss them, yet we know that they were the concerns of Masonic organiz-ations in Scotland, as Knoop and Jones and David Stevenson have made clear.

The *Compagnonnages* of France seem to have developed from the groups of Masons working on the great French cathedrals from the twelfth century,[37] and they were probably similar to a cross between a trade union, a Livery Company (the *Compagnonnages* wore a livery), and a Guild under the patronage of a Saint.[38] As in England, French Masons travelling from place to place were given lodging by fellow-Masons, and helped with money to get them to the next Lodge. It would seem that itinerant Masons, be they French, English, or German, were able to grant and receive benefits only when passwords and signs were given (and indeed it would have been imprudent for a Mason to bestow *largesse* on *any* traveller). Because the *Compagnons* had little chance of becoming Master-Masons as the organizations became more oligarchic in character, they tended to band together against the employers and masters, so the motive for secrecy was increased. The necessity to protect the *Compagnonnages* from outside attack led the association to evolve systems of enforced discipline to punish miscreants within the group.[39] *Compagnonnages* also evolved complex rituals for admission, organized the funerals of members (as did the Guilds), and developed ceremonial for their feasts. Of prime impor-tance was the fact that they also built up Legends of the Craft to account for their beginnings.[40]

These Legends included a claim that the *Compagnon-nages* had been founded by Hiram (Master-Mason to Solomon) who had been killed by three apprentices; that they were commenced by Maître Jacques, who had made two columns embellished with pictures, and that they had been created by Father Soubise (Master-Mason to Solomon), who fell out with Maître Jacques after they had arrived in France.[41] Here there may be some esoteric connection with the Knights Templar, but M. Saint-Léon supposes that the stories of Hiram, Jacques, Soubise, and the Temple are only a vague Biblicized memory of the building works carried out by the Masons at great cathedrals to build Temples of God. Saint-Léon points to the close similarity between rituals of initiation in France and England, and suggests that English Masonic catechisms and rites of initiation were the models for the French *Compagnonnages*, although the latter did not include Masters, but only journeymen.[42] It seems that operative Masonry in England, France and Scotland had common traditions (or parts of traditions), organizations, and objects. English and Scottish operative Masonry, however, appear to have lost their rituals and organizations, and these were re-invented, elaborated, and developed by the Accepted and then by the Speculative Freemasons. It is most likely that the reason for this was the break with so much tradition (including the patronage of Saints, the formation of groups for chantries and burials, and the religious and charitable aspects) caused by the Reformation. Certainly the violence of Scottish Calvinism, and the destruction of chantries and so many Guilds in England, would have stripped much from Freemasonry in its operative phase. This is borne out by the fact that the *Compagnonnages* held on to the rituals and secrecy, continuing as charitable bodies with a strong religious flavour throughout the nineteenth century; they also remained as groups of labour organizations, and kept aloof from French speculative Masonry, which became first sceptical about religion and then violently atheistical and anti-clerical.

It is important to recognize the fact that Fraternities, Guilds, and Incorporations held the religious side to be as important as the economic aspects: Feast-Days of Patron Saints, great religious festivals, and craft pageants would find groups of liveried men taking part in processions and plays. Many Guilds and Fraternities had altars and chaplains in the great churches, for although none but the richest could afford to endow a chantry, maintain an altar, or pay for a priest, as groups this could be possible, so prayers for the dead and chantries were available to the Guilds. One of the most important of the bases of Fraternities in the Middle Ages, then, was the doctrine of Purgatory which necessitated the saying of Masses to free a soul from its toils, so this, in turn, caused chantries to be endowed as a variety of insurance policy for the hereafter. Protestantism expressly abolished Purgatory as a 'vain opinion', confiscated chantries, and left a huge void, for processions, the celebrations of great festivals, and even worship by groups such as Guilds were suppressed. Altars dedicated to Patron-Saints were destroyed or removed, and a rich mix of custom, symbol, devotions, and pageant was abandoned. The Reformation, then, dealt a severe blow to participation in ceremony, and ended the connection of collective bodies of Guilds with formal religious observance. Indeed the

Guilds and Fraternities tended to remain faithful to the old religion, though in time they conformed, while often retaining in their grand titles a connection with a Catholic past. It seems that the Reformation had the effect of forcing some crafts to develop secret ceremonies and rituals of their own, for, as David Stevenson has emphasized, the Reformed Churches discouraged religious worship and ceremony by the Guilds themselves. It does seem to have been this aspect that was one of the most important elements in the creation of Speculative Freemasonry.

Masonic organization and ritual in Scotland seem to have evolved in a response to stern Reformation principle: it was an attempt to fill the void caused by the abolition of colour, ritual, and ceremony by a grimly dour and Calvinist Church.[43] The Craft of Masonry developed more elaborate rituals than other groups, but then it was already quite a distinct Craft before the Reformation, with its own secret recognition methods and a mythology, history, and series of legends of rich complexity. The evolution of the Craft when esoteric knowledge and the search for it were producing a ferment of ideas in the Renaissance period (including a harking back to Vitruvian and earlier principles of Antiquity) attracted many non-Masons to the Lodges, perhaps in order to satisfy a need for ritual that the new Church ignored.[44] David Stevenson suggests that in the relationship of Scottish Lodges with the Reformed Church may lie the beginnings of distinctive features of later Freemasonry: 'the exclusion of overt religious elements from Lodge activities while at the same time clearly accepting the existence of God and the truth of Christianity'.[45] He goes on to point out that

> the emergence of Freemasonry in seventeenth-century Scotland as a system of morality illustrated by symbols, allegories and rituals . . . [indicates] . . . that the lodge was not a valid place for masons to indulge their [orthodox] religious inclinations in. But of course, in the long term, this exclusion from lodges of open commitment to any one brand of religion opened the way for the adoption of heterodox idea and the admission of members with divergent religious beliefs.[46]

The Church of Scotland, Stevenson argues, accepted the existence of Lodges, and of rituals to be held within them, on condition they were not *religious* rituals: this certainly goes a very long way to explaining the tolerance the Reformed Church showed towards the Lodges. This was in marked contrast to the suppression of all drama and play-acting, not only because of Papist and pagan associations, but also because of the fundamentalist position on representing images of other people. The Reformed Church in Scotland allowed some legitimacy to the arts, but only provided they were sundered from religious observance.[47] Masonic ritual, seen as unimportant in religious terms, and as a harmless activity, was not denounced: it was ceremonial and formula, without religious connotations. If this were not the case it would not have survived in the ultra-Protestant climate of sixteenth- and seventeenth-century Scotland, and it is important to recognize this point. Those who claim that Freemasonry is a 'religion', or is in some way suspect, ignore this significant fact.

Yet there was another aspect, and this, too, cannot be overlooked in the present context. Freemasonry had within it a potential of becoming something like a new religion, for it gave a new sense of belonging to men who were disillusioned with the Church, with notions of Providence, and with belief in the Supernatural. Freemasonry could offer a philosophy perhaps similar to a natural religion based on observations of the powers of Nature, Reason, and Wisdom. Ceremony and Ritual were present in Lodge meetings, and the Craft claimed descent from mysteries older than Christianity, linking the greatness of Ancient Egyptian civilization with the Temple of Solomon (Wisdom again), and the very beginnings of Time itself.

CHAPTER 2

THE IMPORTANT LEGENDS

The Two Columns or Pillars; The Hiramic Legend; the Mysteries

And he set up the pillars in the porch of the temple:
and he set up the right pillar, and called the name thereof Jachin: and he set up the left
pillar, and called the name thereof Boaz.

I Kings 7, 21

The Two Columns or Pillars

First, some definitions are necessary. A pillar is a vertical isolated, free-standing upright element, which need not be circular on plan, and must not be confused with a column or a pier. Generally speaking, pillars do not conform to the Orders. A column, on the other hand, is an upright member, usually circular on plan, but also polygonal or square, supporting a lintel. It consists of a base, a shaft, and capital, except in the case of the Greek Doric Order, which has no base. One of the problems in unravelling Masonic lore is that 'pillar' is used when 'column' is the word wanted, and vice versa.

The Two Columns, or Two Pillars, play a significant rôle in early Masonic Legend in the manuscripts known as the Old Charges.[1] They are *not* the same as the two columns erected in the porch of Solomon's Temple, although the latter, by the familiar processes of syncretism and association, became confused with the legendary 'pillars'. These Two Pillars of Masonic Legend are the medium by which the secret knowledge was saved from destruction by Fire and Water.[2] The story occurs in the *Apocrypha*, but appears to have had a Babylonian origin.[3] In this version a Babylonian priest had a vision of a flood, and proceeded to write a history of the

beginning, procedure, and end of all things on clay tablets which were then burned hard in a fiery furnace. These tablets were buried in the City of the Sun at Sippara, and were the basis for knowledge upon which the rebuilding of Babylon was made possible.[4] In Hebraic versions Eve instructed Seth and his siblings to record on tablets of stone and baked clay the words of Archangel Michael when he ordered them from the Garden of Eden. The tablets would survive whether flood or fire destroyed the world.[5] Later versions of this Legend grant Adam the credit for prophecy, and the tablets become 'pillars' on which are carried the discoveries made by the descendants of Adam and Eve:[6] the idea goes back to the beginning of things, and to a lost Paradise itself. Astronomical discoveries were inscribed on the 'pillars', and in later versions music only was carved by Jubal on them, one being brick and the other marble (which indicates a curious ignorance of the nature of marble, which would become quicklime if burned, and eroded if subjected to the action of water).[7] Zoroaster (Zarathustra) was said by Petrus Comestor to have inscribed all seven Liberal Arts on fourteen columns (seven on brass and seven on brick) to preserve them against destruction by a vengeful God:[8] this is yet another example of syncretism. Later medieval versions[9] claim that after the Flood both pillars were found, one by Pythagoras and one by Hermes Trismegistus (the Thrice-Wise), who passed on the secret knowledge inscribed.[10] In this version one pillar was of marble and the other of *lacerus* (a misreading of *lateres*, signifying burnt clay).[11]

Masonic myth has it that the pillars set up by Solomon were hollow, serving as repositories for Masonic archives; the other two pillars on which the Seven Liberal Arts (including Geometry or Masonry) were inscribed in order to preserve knowledge from attacks by fire and water appear to have been Babylonian in origin, as has been described. The early introduction of the threats by fire and water should be noted, for, as we will see, these play a significant part in many important eighteenth-century Masonic works, including those of Terrasson, Mozart, and Lequeu.

The Solomonic 'pillars' are described in the Bible:

And King Solomon sent and fetched Hiram out of Tyre. He *was* a widow's son of the tribe of Naphthali, and his father *was* a man of Tyre, a worker in brass: and he was filled with wisdom, and understanding, and cunning to work all works in brass. And he came to king Solomon, and wrought all his work.

For he cast two pillars of brass, of eighteen cubits[12] high apiece: and a line of twelve cubits did compass either of them about.

And he made two chapiters *of* molten brass, to set upon the tops of the pillars: the height of the one chapiter *was* five cubits, and the height of the other chapiter *was* five cubits:

And nets of checker work, and wreaths of chain work, for the chapiters which *were* upon the top of the pillars; seven for the one chapiter, and seven for the other chapiter.

And he made the pillars, and two rows round about upon the one network, to cover the chapiters that *were* upon the top, with pomegranates: and so he did for the other chapiter.

And the chapiters that *were* upon the top of the pillars *were* of lily work in the porch, four cubits.

And the chapiters upon the two pillars *had pomegranates* also above, over against the belly which *was* by the network: and the pomegranates *were* two hundred in rows round about upon the other chapiter.[13]

The chapiters (capitals), then, were very tall, if they were five and the 'pillars' eighteen Cubits high, so they must have looked top-heavy. More convincing is the account in *Chronicles*, which describes the pillars as being thirty-five Cubits high with capitals five Cubits high.[14] We also know from Biblical and other sources (Josephus) that the capitals were finished in 'lily-work', that is, architectural ornament similar to the fleur-de-lys or lotus-flower of Ancient Egypt. Josephus also mentions net-work interwoven with small palms made of brass,[15] which suggests the palmette ornament of Antiquity. It therefore seems likely that the capitals of the two pillars had architectural similarities to Ancient Egyptian capitals featuring lotus, papyrus, and palm motifs.

One pillar 'on the right hand' was called Jachin, and the other, 'on the left', was named Boaz: Jachin is a name associated with foundations or establishments, meaning 'he shall establish', while Boaz is associated with strength, the name meaning literally 'in it is strength'. The problem here, of course, is to decide which was right and which was left. The pillars were at the east entrance to the Temple (the Holy of Holies was at the west): on the *right*, as the worshipper entered, was Boaz (at the north-east of the entrance), and on the *left* was Jachin (to the south-east of the entrance). When we think of Jachin and Boaz as on the 'left' or 'right', we have to think of them heraldically, and how they would be viewed by someone *leaving* the east entrance to the Temple. It is quite wrong, therefore, to think of an elevation of the Temple with Jachin on the right and Boaz on the left: it was the other way round.[16] Most Masonic diagrams do indeed show Jachin on the left and Boaz on the right: the curious thing is that a Lodge is orientated with the Master's place and the Bible at the *east*, and the Two Pillars at the west. So if Masonic Lodges are laid out with the Temple in mind, the left–right problem becomes acute because the orientation is back-to-front, and it is arguable that with this mirror-image, as it were, Jachin ought to be on the right and Boaz on the left. The difficulty lies, of course, in the overlaying of Christian ecclesiastical orientation on that of the Temple. The simile of the Craft is that the sun rises in the east to bring the day, just as the Worshipful Master in the east opens the Lodge and instructs the Brethren on Freemasonry[2]. Syncretism brings problems as well as solutions.

The Solomonic Temple seems to have exercised the minds of many scholars in the early part of the Middle Ages, and the sense of acute loss implied by the destruction of the Temple certainly existed. Like the Garden of Eden the lost Temple was a potent idea. Two very strange medieval columns with multiple shafts and weird serpentine enrichment survive at Würzburg Cathedral:[17] these are called Jachin and Boaz, and seem to have been associated with an attempt to allude to the Temple of Solomon in the Architecture of Würzburg Dom. It is clear from the inscriptions that these strange

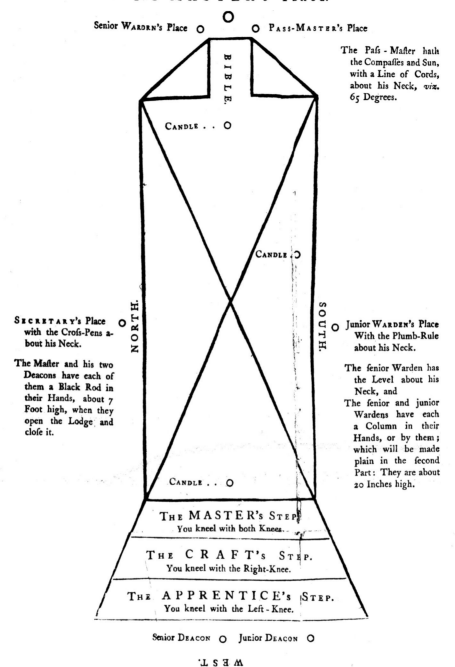

2 *Masonic Lodge layout from* The Three Distinct Knocks, Or the Door of the most Antient Free-Masonry, Opening to all Men, Neither Naked nor Cloath'd, Barefoot, nor Shod, Ec. Being an universal Description of all its Branches, from In its first Rise to this present Time, As it is deliver'd in all Lodges ... *etc. London, 1763* (UGLE).

3 *Jachin* (left) *and Boaz* (right) *in Würzburg Cathedral: two medieval columns, made by the* Steinmetzen, *probably in the thirteenth century, though they may be twelfth-century in date, and some opinion holds that they are eleventh-century carvings. The most likely date, however, is early thirteenth or late twelfth century. Stieglitz opined that they were an overt reference to the Fraternity, but other explanations include certain theological symbolism: Boaz, being tripartite, represents the Trinity, while the shafts, with their curious coiled formations, allude to the Deity without a beginning or an end, as well as to the binding of ties; Jachin represents body and soul, united by the mysterious bond, while the capital, formed of another endless band, represents the spirit and eternity. The persistence of serpentine, spiral, or twisted columns in representations of the Temple and of Lodges should be noted. Similar knotted shafts can be found at the east end of the* Broletto *in Como, where one of the* bifore *contains two such examples dating from around 1215, which ties in with the most likely Würzburg date* (Bischöfliches Ordinariat Würzburg).

columns, with their interlacing detail, show an early association in the minds of European Masons with some kind of draped column, or a column around which plants or spiral ornament were wrapped: the allusion, as will be demonstrated in this study, became more pronounced with the Renaissance and Baroque periods[3]. Serpentine ornament, therefore, especially when associated with columns, was identified very early in European iconography with the Solomonic Temple, and later with Freemasonry. It also seems to have had links with a school of Masons based on Lake Como from the time of the end of the Roman Empire (the so-called Comacine School), and indeed similar serpentine ornament to that of the columns of Würzburg occurs on the *Broletto*, completed in 1215, in the city of Como itself.

The two pillars have also been interpreted as representing the physical powers of generation or creation (i.e. a phallic symbol), the spiritual power of regeneration (i.e. salvation), and as allusions to the stone pillar of Jacob at Bethel, with names suggesting strength and firmness.

Doubtless the variations of meaning of pillars and columns can be infinite, and it is not profitable to attempt to list them here. The significant thing about Jachin and Boaz, as far as we are concerned, is their importance as celebrations of entrance, as mnemonics of the Temple and of the legends of how esoteric knowledge was preserved, and as sources for the design of columns and pillars, especially in the Renaissance and Baroque periods. The spiral form, indeed, can be found in reconstructions of the Temple by artists of the Enlightenment, in the *Baldacchino* of St Peter's in Rome, in designs for a new architectural Order suitable for the eighteenth century in France, and in the décor of Continental Lodges. The spiral, even from early medieval times, was used on columns or piers associated with an altar or an important shrine. It is also found in the chapel at Roslin in Scotland, a fifteenth-century work of remarkable richness virtually encrusted in elaborate carving. At Roslin the piers dividing the ambulatory and the east chapels are spectacular, and that to the south is called the Prentice Pillar from an apparently recent story that it was carved by a talented apprentice who was killed by a jealous Master-Mason. The parallel with Hiram is clear, but it is curious that the pier has four strips of stylized foliage draped in spirals around 180 degrees, starting from each of the cardinal points at the base, and winged serpents with entwined necks biting their tails at the foot. One of the corbelled heads in the chapel shows a wound in the forehead, purporting to be the murdered apprentice. Furthermore, it does appear that the Sinclairs, Lairds of Roslin, not only knew the Mason Word, were patrons of Architecture, and great builders for many generations, but were closely associated with Freemasonry from the seventeenth century. It is also clear that the spiral, or Solomonic, form, enjoyed a significance as something very special, even from the early Middle Ages and probably before then.

The Hiramic Legend

Various versions of this story exist, but the variant in which the Master of the Works at King Solomon's Temple was murdered by means of three blows (with a hammer, a level, and a plumb) to the head by three Apprentices, or Fellow-Crafts, who were trying to obtain the secrets of a Master-Mason, is the best known. Each blow was delivered at a different door of the Temple, and after each blow Hiram tried to escape, leaving a trail of blood around the floor until he died at the east: this trail of blood may be the origin of some of the designs around Masonic tracing-boards. Originally there had been fifteen conspirators, but twelve drew back (recanters), and these twelve were to bring Geometry and Architecture to the world[4]. The numbers as multiples of three should be noted. The three buried the body, the Fellow-Crafts sought it, and agreed that if they did not find the Word in or about Hiram then the first word associated with the finding of the body should become the Master's Word (the latter being like a 'Rabbinical tradition', in way of comment upon Jachin and Boaz, with the addition of some secret sign delivered by hand to hand, by which 'Freemasons recognize each other', as the Rev. Robert Kirk, Minister at Aberfoyle, Stirlingshire, noted in 1691)[18] The body was found under some green moss on which a sprig of acacia was placed (to deter anyone from displacing it): the finders were five of fifteen (a third), and the King ordered that the body should be re-interred. When the Masons tried to lift Hiram by pulling the forefinger, the skin came off (the Slip), so they raised him by the Five Points of Fellowship (hand to hand, foot to foot, cheek to cheek, knee to knee, and hand to back).

The body of Hiram was discovered because the seekers pulled on the sprig of acacia when climbing, but it came away in the grip, thus indicating that the sprig was newly placed, and this led to the discovery of the corpse, for acacia was planted to dissuade the curious, and marked where dead bodies lay, so travellers would pass by and not disturb the sprig. Hiram was reburied in the precincts of the Temple, suggesting possibly human sacrifice or even the sanctity conferred by interring the bodies of Saints in a church. Tombs and shrines are often one and the same, after all, and in ancient times human sacrifices were often made in order to consecrate some important building.

What seems to be a syncretic variant of this story occurs in an early eighteenth-century MS:[19] in this all things useful for the world after the Flood were placed in the Ark with Noah, so after Noah's death his three sons determined to find their father's valuable secrets in his grave, and agreed previously that if they did not find what they sought then the first thing they found was to be substituted as a secret. When they gripped Noah's finger it came off, and so with the hand and arm. The body was raised, supported by setting foot to foot, knee to knee, breast to breast, cheek to cheek, and hand to back.[20] The discovery of marrow in one of the bones by one brother, the contention that the bone was dry by the second, and the observation that the bone stank by the third led to the 'naming of the bone'.

Thus both the Noah and Hiram stories involve attempts to find secrets from dead bodies, both involve substitute 'secrets' in the absence of real ones, and both suggest necromancy or even tries at raising the dead. Elisha, it will be recalled, lay upon the Shunammite woman's dead child mouth to mouth, eyes upon eyes,

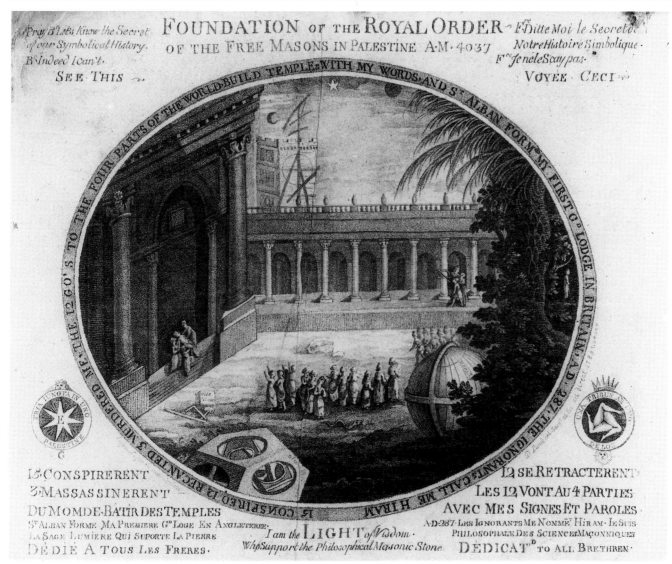

4 The Foundation of the Royal Order of the Free Masons in Palestine A.M. 4037. *Engraving by D. Lambert of 1789 showing the Murder of Hiram by the Three, and the Recanting Twelve who were to bring Geometry and Architecture into the world in four groups of three, armed with the Signs and Words. Note the two columns on either side of the arched entrance. Rods, squares, and Masonic tools are in evidence, as is the Globe. The object partially shown in the bottom left seems to be based on a polyhedral sundial, somewhat inaccurately observed, and has a vague resemblance to the Scottish sundials described elsewhere, and shown in 7–12 (GLCL).*

hands upon hands, and stretched himself upon the child, who became warm, sneezed seven times, and opened his eyes.[21] The Hiram-Noah legends are probably connected with attempts to restore the dead to life in order to find secrets which had died with them.[22] Marrow, of course, also means partner or fellow, and may have been a means of reminding Masons of the obligations of fellowship and that fellowship was an essential part of Freemasonry: it may also be a mnemonic for *matchpin* or *mahabyn*, a 'Master's Word', supposedly uttered when Hiram's skin slipped off.[23]

It is unclear whether the Master's Word was the same as the Mason Word: what is clear is that the Mason Word existed, it seems, from early times, that it has been used with the Five Points of Fellowship for ceremonies, and that it was useful out of necessity. This does not mean that the mysterious Mason Word was used to identify a skilled worker in stone from the medieval equivalent of a 'cowboy' contractor: that could have been done far more reliably by means of a practical demonstration with stone and chisel. It seems to have been an indication that a craftsman who knew it accepted certain rules and also had certain privileges because he was a member of a body: it was *not* evidence of technical ability, but of some kind of position in an association or incorporation with rules, requirements, privileges, and obligations. A Mason with the Mason Word could therefore have a better chance of finding work, and could also claim relief when he fell on evil times. Certainly in Scotland it does appear that the Mason Word was used to protect the craftsmen from persons who had not been apprenticed and who had not acquired certain skills. The very term Word, with a capital, suggests the significance of Scripture (the Word of God), as used in the Reformed Church in Scotland, and endows the Mason Word with extra properties of mystery and awe.[24] There is another point to be borne in mind: the Reformation ended the cult of Saints and the veneration of Relics. It may well be that the bone stories were connected with the importance given to Relics in earlier times, and to the need to give Freemasonry a powerful inner secret as potent as Saints' bones in former days.

There is, considering the syncretism of deities and cults of the ancient world, reason to suppose that the Hiramic Legend may also relate to consecration sacrifices common in the Middle East, and associated with the worship of Astarte-Ashtoreth-Ishtar. King Solomon himself had built shrines for the terrible Goddess,[25] and it is difficult to know where one legend begins and another ends. The murder of Osiris and the search and subsequent raising of both Osiris and Adonis have similarities to the Hiramic Legend. Yet in all initiation ceremonies there is a symbolic death and a resurrection: a young apprentice finishing his apprenticeship by some splendid work, and then 'dying', is a way of pointing to the death as an apprentice and the rebirth as a master, and recurs in many mysteries. It does, however, raise the possibility that the Hiram Legend was a remembrance of a consecration sacrifice, with the further possibility that the Temple could at one time have been dedicated to something other than tradition holds.

The problem is compounded by the fact that there were several Hirams, and that they were confused, not only with each other, but with other legends (the Noah story is one of many). There is nothing peculiar to Freemasonry about this, for throughout Antiquity and the Middle Ages legends overlapped, got mixed up, or were confused. Matters were also complicated by scribes who, when copying the work of some other crabbed hand, misread, misinterpreted, or embellished the original: multiplying those problems would create a bewildering variety of stories, while the imaginative graphics of interpreters also would create brand-new ideas, legends, and even 'histories'. It is not the purpose of this book to set out Masonic ceremonial, to speculate about Hiram or anyone else, or to offer guidance on Freemasonry: adequate books such as those by Knoop and Jones and by Bernard E. Jones should satisfy the most voracious appetite for Masonic lore. Here, we are concerned with visual aspects, and aspects of Freemasonry are discussed where they are apposite.

Finally, mention should be made of a very curious plate from Benedictus Arias Montanus's (1527–98) *Exemplar sive de sacris fabricis liber* of 1572 showing Noah's Ark as a coffin containing the body of Christ with stigmata, perhaps emphasizing the Ark as a container and means of Salvation in the real and mystical sense. This image occurs also in versions of the Holy Bible published from that date. Such ideas and images show how very complex was the world of Renaissance symbol, allegory, emblem, and idea: as in Classical Antiquity very many legends intermingled, so that in the end Hiram, Noah, Christ, and Hermetic–Egyptian ideas coalesce.[26]

The Mysteries

Mystery–religions are of great antiquity, but in the Masonic context the most interesting are those of Ancient Egypt invented by Isis herself, the Great Goddess, the Magna Mater. The Egyptian cults, Geometry, and even the Great Architect have Masonic connections that cannot be avoided. Rituals included references to secrets that are not seen or heard, but are handed down, and these secrets were presided over by the jackal-headed Anubis who, significantly, taught Isis the way when she was searching for the dismembered Osiris. Isiac mysteries were participated in by certain Roman Emperors, and involved purification, personal piety, and a variety of symbolic journeys, with a trial and degrees. Hadrian is known to have gone through two ceremonies at Eleusis that had Isiac-Egyptian connotations. Enlightenment (*photismos*), initiation as a *mysterion*, and *symbolon* (password) are words that recur in Antiquity. The term *mysterion* signifies the obtaining of esoteric wisdom after some kind of endurance test involving trials, or ordeals, has been passed. Many cults in the Graeco-Roman world required initiates to await enlightenment while being kept isolated in darkness, and there were rules concerning silence, patience, and fortitude. The concept of being reborn in the presence of the Great Goddess Isis after a symbolic death was present in the Isiac cults.[27] An initiate, once reborn, would join a sacred band of chosen ones who would be informed of the divine mysteries by being entrusted with esoteric knowledge. Mozart's

O heiliges Band der Freundschaft treuer Brüder (K148) perfectly suggests Masonic ideas of fraternity and a 'sacred band', and was written long before he became a Freemason, but such ideas were there, often just beneath the surface, and had never died, such was the strength of survival of the ancient mysteries in one form or another.

Herodotus identified Hephaestus with Ptah, the Egyptian God of Fire and Architect of the Universe, and the demi-gods, the Cabiri, as his (Hephaestus-Ptah's) sons who were born in Egypt. Late theology of Antiquity established links between the Great Goddess Isis and Memphis, where the temples of the Cabiri and of Ptah could be found. Isis, as sister-consort of Osiris, was also Mother of the God, of the Apis-Bull, and consort of Ptah. Certainly it seems that Isis was firmly ensconced, through her connections with the Cabiri, in Thessalonica as early as the third century BC.[28] Isis was therefore linked to Imhotep, known as a son of Ptah, chief Architect to King Zoser, and builder of the pyramid complex at Sakkara.[29] In due course Imhotep, who was a real figure and a real Architect, became the Divine son in the Triad of Memphis, and the subject of worship. Imhotep and Isis had a temple at Epidaurus dedicated to them, which is not surprising, as both were devoted to medicine and to the occult. Eventually Imhotep achieved precedence over Ptah, and so the Great Architect of the Universe was none other than Imhotep, Architect and sage, and builder of the Sakkara stepped pyramid: the Master-Mason, as Architect, had himself become a God. This factor seems to have escaped many Masonic commentators, but it goes a long way to explain the importance of Masonic and Egyptian attributes as mystical objects. Yet it is clear that it must be taken into account in any consideration of the history and rituals of Freemasonry, for the latter has claims to incorporate the mysteries of later Antiquity within its activities. The initiates follow the ways of the Cabiri of old, and indeed of Isis herself, who searched for Osiris. The syncretic aspects of Antiquity are clear, for Osiris, resurrected as Ptah (who began and ended the day, and who was the deity of Masons and Architects engaged on building temples and tombs), was also identified with and even superseded by Imhotep, who decreed that a building should be firmly established. In order to do this Ptah/Imhotep held a column as his attribute of stability.[30] The fact that Jachin is associated with foundations and establishment and that Boaz is identified with strength or stability indicates a syncretism so widespread as to be of considerable importance, and that Ancient Egypt is indeed of exceeding significance in the history of Freemasonry. Images of the Great Architect, of God as Divine Architect, and of Christ as Creator may be a syncretic vision based on Osiris-Ptah–Imhotep, which is not at all strange when we consider how closely Mary the Madonna, Mother of God, resembles Isis, the Great Goddess.

During the Ptolemaic period, and thereafter in the Roman Empire, Isis, her consort, and Horus/Harpocrates, had become a Trinity, associated with the rising and setting of the sun, skilled practitioners in mathematics, Geometry, and inventions, controllers of fire, bringers of heat, light, and life, dissolvers of darkness, and resurrectors of the dead (quite apart from their skills as healers and as Architects). Now it is important to realize that the veneration of Isis, Osiris, Serapis, Ptah, Imhotep, Horus, Harpocrates, and so on was not confined to Egypt, but became widespread in the Graeco-Roman world. Isiac legends (or theology) point to an interesting parallel with Freemasonry: the murder of Osiris at the hands of Seth was the great forerunner, but in the rites associated with the Cabiri one of the brothers was killed by other brothers, suggesting the death of Hiram. Apuleius tells us of degrees of trials, of oaths, of secrecy, of passwords, of hidden truths, of passages from darkness to light, and of a victory over death in the Isiac mysteries. Abstinence, fasting, patience, and endurance of long periods in the dark were part of these Isiac mysteries (the term *incubare* refers to the custom of sleeping in a sanctuary where oracular responses were sought through dreams or necromancy). The candidate was then led to a chamber and thus participated in a ritual journey, passing through all the 'elements', until at midnight the blazing sun was seen, and the Gods themselves appeared. Yet Apuleius, who speaks of journeys to the verge of death, does not tell us of any disclosures, for the rites were secret, and betrayal would bring punishment. In due course Apuleius translated his initiate to the great Isaeum in the Campus Martius in Rome (one of the greatest of all temples of Imperial Rome), where he was admitted to a new degree of Isis and Osiris, who were joined in their mother's womb as brother and sister, as husband and wife, in attributes, and in ritual. Osiris the Resurrected, the Invincible, who was also Ptah/Serapis/Ammon/Horus/Apollo/Dionysus, possessed the All-Seeing Eye.

For the third degree the candidate was guided by Osiris himself, the highest among the greatest, and the greatest among the highest, in a mystic union where two became one and the candidate was alone with the Alone in a sanctuary where serenity, stillness, and silence ruled like gods. So the journey Apuleius indicates was part of the Isiac mystery, and that which the Neoplatonist writer Plotinus (AD205–270) connects with an ecstatic elevation of the soul to the divine, could not be revealed, but involved a ritual purification by water, the ducking of the head seven times, a prayer to the Queen of Heaven, Isis, and the donning of different garments or vestments for

5 *Labyrinth in Rheims Cathedral from a sixteenth-century representation (it was destroyed in the eighteenth century). Four Master-Masons were named and shown with compasses and square, while the Archbishop was depicted in the centre (A).*

each of the regions through which the candidate would pass. During the ritual journey the candidate would undergo the *mors voluntaria*, or voluntary death, yet hoped for rescue and resurrection by Isis.[31]

The idea of a journey through various compartments, with vestments for each stage, before a goal is reached is not confined to ancient esoteric Egyptian mystery cults. Daedalus, the cunning artificer, was revered by the artists' Guilds of the ancient world, especially in Attica. An accomplished Architect, Daedalus was supposed to have invented the axe, awl, and bevel. His nephew, who invented the saw, the potter's wheel, the lathe, and other tools, attracted the jealousy of Daedalus, who slew him, and buried the body, in which act he (Daedalus) was detected. The parallels will be obvious. Daedalus fled to

Crete where he designed and built the Labyrinth at Gnosus (Knossos) for the Minotaur; he entrusted Ariadne with certain secrets (symbolized by the clue of yarn) by which she guided Theseus through the maze (note the Isiac notion of a guide through dark passages).[32] And the labyrinth, as we will see, recurs as an important element in this study.

The labyrinth as an emblem or as a form is a number of communicating passages arranged in great complexity through which it is difficult to find one's way without guidance; it is also called a maze, and is an intricate, tortuous arrangement of features designed to mystify. Labyrinthine patterns were the ancestors of the 'knots', or ornamental patterns, found in gardens in the fifteenth and sixteenth centuries. By the end of the fifteenth century a 'knot' was synonymous with a maze. Even the Greek-key pattern is derived from a labyrinthine form, and maze-like patterns recur in the ancient art of many civilizations. Apart from their complex decorative possibilities, labyrinthine designs had symbolic and even magical connotations, for they could be protective (by leading potential enemies or evil spirits literally up the garden path), and they could also suggest the journey through life itself, with its many dead ends, wrong turnings, and misleading signs, until the correct way

could be found and the prize gained. In this latter sense, the labyrinth could be a symbol of a journey through one existence, with all its trials and mistakes, until a Paradise or a rebirth could be attained.[33]

Labyrinthine designs occurred in the floors of some medieval cathedrals, and are associated with pilgrimage: the obscure maze-dance by clergy during pilgrimages to cathedrals appears to have been connected with an allegory of a journey through life to the City of God. Maze-patterns in masonry (as at Chartres Cathedral) repeat those of turf or hedge labyrinths, and of course hedge-mazes of topiary were themselves enclosed gardens, with swastika-like patterns.[34] In some of the greatest cathedrals of the medieval period large areas of nave floor were given over to labyrinthine patterns that often have even contained the names and portraits of the Architects responsible. We have pictures of the labyrinths of Amiens and Rheims [5], which portrayed the Architects and the Bishops who laid the foundation-stones. The Chartres labyrinth [6] has lost its signature-plate from the centre, but it is quite clear that the medieval Architects were not only providing a pattern which could be used for prayer, for ritual pilgrimage, for curious maze-dances, and for an allegory of life's journey with its trials and tribulations, but were showing that

6 *Labyrinth in the centre of the nave of Chartres Cathedral, which measures some 13 metres (43 feet) in diameter, and is similar to a labyrinth illustrated in Villard de Honnecourt's thirteenth-century notebooks. This labyrinth once contained a signature-plate of the Architect or Master-Builder, and the way to the central point was 230 metres (755 feet) long, representing a journey, a ritual pilgrimage, progress through life itself, with all its false turnings, and even the Holy Grail. Significantly, Parsifal, in Wagner's* Bühnenweihfestspiel, *asks 'Who is the Grail?', and Gurnemanz points out that no earthly path leads to it, and none could tread it unless guided by the Grail itself* (A).

they were the heirs of Daedalus, the builder of labyrinths and the Architect of many buildings in Egypt, Sicily, Sardinia, Greece, and Italy.[35] So Architects were identifying with Daedalus (who is shown flying from the Labyrinth in a relief by Pisano from the Cathedral of Florence): one Anselm described himself as the second Daedalus in a twelfth-century inscription in Milan.[36] Even God becomes *Architectus Mundi* in thirteenth-century representations, showing him with compasses, an image revived by Blake. This memory of Ptah-Imhotep as Sublime Architect is not an uncommon design, recurring in numerous illuminated Biblical texts of the Middle Ages. So Osiris, Ptah, Imhotep, Daedalus, God as *Architectus Mundi*, and medieval cathedral Architects have similar attributes.

In these connecting themes and motifs from Antiquity Freemasonry has certain roots: of that there can be little doubt. The actual *processes* by which certain ideas recurred remain obscure, but the rediscovery of 'Hermetic' texts, the importance of Graeco–Roman writers, the survival of elements in design, the handing down of legend by word of mouth, and the continuing mechanisms of identification, of taking over of attributes, and of syncretism no doubt played their part. Probably the most significant element of all was the development of the Cult of the Virgin Mary, the initiator, the unfading rose, the heifer who brought forth the spotless calf, the chariot of fire, the star-flaming Queen, the haven and anchorage, the Mistress of the Word, the Queen of Heaven, the Great Virgin, the Mother of the God, the Garden Enclosed, the Fountain: Isis remained what she ever was, as the source of grace and truth, the Resurrection and the Life, and the Great Goddess, who stealthily became the Virgin Mary. Isis-Sophia, the Wise, the Sister of God and His Spouse, is also Mary, the Sister and Spouse of God, the Sister of Christ, the Wearer of Diadems, the Cornucopia of all our Goods, the Fructificatio, the Lighthouse of the World, the Salvatrix, Inventrix, and Justitia. She is the moon, the cresent, the swallow, the bow, the deer, and much else. The aretalogy of Hipploytus Marraccius, *Polyanthea Mariana, in qua libris octodecim*, published in Cologne in 1710 covers this matter in exhaustive detail.

The claims of Giordano Bruno (1548–1600) that the most acceptable theologies had developed in the Egypt of Antiquity and that the cults of Isis have exerted a formative influence on Christianity itself should be clear to all but the most closed of minds: Christianity, with its Saints, emblems, veneration of the BVM, and iconography, owes more, perhaps, to lands of the Nile than to those of the Jordan, at least in the development of its Cults and its Art. The whole of Christendom is permeated with ideas born in Antiquity, with Hermetic notions, and with themes derived from the Graeco-Roman-Egyptian Cults. It is hardly surprising that Freemasonry, too, has taken on board some of those themes: a vast organization with a code of conduct, a ritual, a system of morality in which allegory and symbol play their parts, with concepts of trials, degrees, initiations, secrecies, and with the ideas of ritual, journeys, death, and rebirth after ordeals, has claims to connections with the mysteries of Graeco-Roman-Egyptian Antiquity. The All-Seeing Eye of Ptah, the Isiac mysteries, and the resurrection of Osiris are not very far from the centre of Freemasonry: Ptah's column is not unrelated to Boaz and Boaz's inner meaning, and Ptah was superseded by Imhotep, a real Architect.

CHAPTER 3

THE RENAISSANCE PERIOD AND FREEMASONRY

Introduction; the Hermetic Tradition; Mnemonic Techniques and Freemasonry; Some Visible Evidence of Freemasonry in Artefacts in Scotland; Scotland, England, Jacobites, and Hanoverians; The Effect on the Design of Early Lodges.

The great mathematical and scientific thinkers of the seventeenth century have at the back of their minds Renaissance traditions of esoteric thinking, of mystical continuity from Hebraic or 'Egyptian' wisdom, of that conflation of Moses with 'Hermes Trismegistus' which fascinated the Renaissance. These traditions survived across the period in secret societies, particularly in Freemasonry.

Frances A. Yates
The Rosicrucian Enlightenment
London, 1972, p219

Introduction

Neoplatonism (the philosophical and religious system, mainly composed of a mix of Platonic ideas and Egyptian and Asiatic mysticism, which originated in Alexandria in the third century, and is perhaps best represented in the works of Plotinus, Porphyry, and Proclus) permeated much of Renaissance thought and blurred distinctions between matter and spirit: it was, of course, fundamentally pantheistic. The whole of the cosmos was seen as an entity, and special attributes were accorded to symbols, numbers, colours, and letters: everything merged with the Divine, and the stars in the firmament were seen to be joined to Man's fortunes. Indeed, a harnessing of forces for the benefit of Mankind was the aim of the occultists, alchemists, astrologers, and magicians[1] who were associated with the remarkable rediscovery of Neoplatonic thought that had been obscured after the death of Julian 'the Apostate', who was devoted to Isis, most universal of deities.

The search for esoteric knowledge through alchemy[2] became a European obsession in the sixteenth and seventeenth centuries before the Newtonian physicists put paid to such notions. In this connection the materialistic ideas born of rationalism have been unfair to the age

of alchemists, for the seeking of the Philosopher's Stone was more a striving for some form of moral and spiritual rebirth than a cheap way of making money in the literal sense.[3] The alchemists desired to find a reality behind the physical world, and strove to understand and control forces of nature to give Mankind powers beyond his imagining.[4] The Renaissance alchemists sought a perfection of the spirit, a union with the Divine in the Universe, and a Godlike state of pure and revealed knowledge. Poetry of the period is frequently ecstatic and deeply concerned with the attainment of some unspoiled and spiritual plane of blinding clarity unknown in experience. Thomas Traherne (c.1637–74), for example, in his *Centuries of Meditation*, speaks of never enjoying the world aright

> till the sea itself floweth in your veins, till you are clothed with the heavens, and crowned with the stars: and perceive yourself to be the sole heir of the whole world, and more than so, because men are in it who are every one sole heirs as well as you.

There is an ecstatic quality in his description of the corn as 'immortal wheat, which should never be reaped, nor was ever sown', and in his thought that it had 'stood from everlasting to everlasting'. Such notions are foreign to the more prosiac world of modern physics, born of Newtonian discoveries, and to an age obsessed by measurement, ignoring the immeasurable, as though it did not exist because it cannot be measured. But they are *not* foreign to the sensibilities of the Graeco-Roman world.

Needless to say, aspects of Neoplatonic occult ideas were formulated in secrecy, not only because of possible dangers from orthodoxy or powerful individuals or groups, but because, if understanding of the hidden meanings of the universe were to be achieved, that knowledge could not be made public in order to prevent misuse, for only the pure and initiates were worthy vessels for such power. Thus secret societies existed, and were associated with the search for knowledge and the guardianship of spiritual truths too precious to be bandied about. Masonic secrecy was thus nothing unusual, for it grew from the need for the Craft to preserve the mysteries and signs of the trade, and developed at a time when exclusive and significant knowledge was treasured: sharing with all would not only devalue the knowledge, but could be dangerous if the secrets or knowledge fell into the wrong hands.

Emblems, symbols, and hieroglyphs were valued by thinkers of the Neoplatonic moulds, for they were like perceived truths of the universe: they had meanings that could be interpreted, but they also disguised those meanings in decent obscurity from the uninitiated. The sages of the time believed that the eternal truths of divine revelation had been known in Antiquity, notably by the Ancient Egyptians whose hieroglyphs offered intellects an endless source of contemplation and puzzlement (all the more so as many accessible hieroglyphs at the time were Roman or Italian works in the Egyptian Taste, and were of the bogus or decorative kind).[5] Many attempts were made to decipher hieroglyphs, of which the most interesting were those of the Jesuit priest Athanasius Kircher, whose *Lingua Aegyptiaca Restituta*,[6] *Obeliscus Aegyptiacus*,[7] *Obeliscus Pamphilius*,[8] *Oedipus Aegyptiacus*,[9] *Prodomus coptus sive Aegyptiacus*,[10] *Rituale Ecclesiae Aegyptiacae sive Cophtitarum*,[11] *Sphinx Mystagoga, sive Diatribe Hieroglyphica*, etc,[12] and *Turris Babel*,[13] are the best examples. Although all barking up wrong trees, they at least show some reasoned attempt to codify Egyptian monuments and artefacts based on those in Rome itself (the importance of Egyptian religion in the Roman Empire, the elevation of Roman Emperors as deities in conformity with Egyptian custom, and the fashion for Egyptian artefacts led to a very large collection of Egyptian and Egyptianizing objects in Rome).

Interpretation of hieroglyphs was based on the belief that sacred and eternal truths had been concealed therein, and that their meaning was inadequately expressed in mere words. This notion was derived from a consideration of obscure passages in Scripture and in other writings, for the more obscure, the more minds strove to interpret the meaning. From the awe felt for hieroglyphs grew the evolution of the emblem and symbol as means of expressing ideas, truths, and meanings which had to be concealed from the ignorant and profane, but which could be read by the pure and the initiated; it is hardly surprising that the literature on emblems of the period is enormous. Emblems consist of a picture incorporating symbols, hieroglyphs, and a composition with figures, designs, and the like, and had to have texts explaining the meaning. Emblems codified certain ideas by conventions, just as Masonic ritual used a pictorial set of emblems and a verbal catechism to suggest its truths. The invention and translation of emblems became a major part of late-Renaissance searchings for truth and revelation, and involved layers of meaning with different aspects of truth, so much so that the truth was often made even more elusive: obfuscation became an end in itself, and the unravelling of onion-like layers developed as a desirable goal. The obscure and the secret were seen as virtues, for had not the Creator concealed the secrets of the very universe? Thus much literature of the period is many-layered, as though to secrete important truths in obscurantist texts. In such a world, elements of Architecture, geometrical forms, and even the tools of the Masons' Craft were valued beyond what they were in actuality, and were given additional symbolic significances. The Mason in his Lodge considering the meaning of the square, the triangle, and the compass was imbued with the *Zeitgeist* of Neoplatonist ideas, and shared much of his outlook with the alchemist, the astrologer, and the seekers after the Philosopher's Stone.

The Hermetic Tradition

The Renaissance Hermetic tradition appears to have developed through Marsilio Ficino (1433–99) and Pico della Mirandola (1463–94), and gained a new lease of life in the seventeenth century.[14] Robert Fludd[15] was an adherent of the philosophy of the 'Egyptian' priest Hermes Trismegistus (identified with Euclid, Thoth, and others), as is apparent in his *Tractatus Apologeticus Integritatem Societatis de Rosea Cruce defendens* and *Apologia Compendiaria Fraternitatem de Rosea Cruce suspicionis & infamia aspersam, veritatis quasi fluctibus abluens & abstergens*. Fludd's works[16] set out the basic scheme developed by Pico della Mirandola when he added the Cabbala to the revival of Hermetic philosophy, encouraged by Ficino's interpretation of the recovered Hermetic texts.

Giordano Bruno and Michael Maier also figure prominently in what Dr Yates has called the 'Rosicrucian

Enlightenment'.[17] Maier was the author of *Arcana Arcanissima, Hoc est Hieroglyphica Aegyptio-Graeca*, and was himself close to the Court of the Emperor Rudolf II, who appears to have been devoted to alchemy and magic.[18] The title-page of *Arcana Arcanissima* featured two obelisks, each set on four balls on pedestals, with figures of Osiris, Isis, and Typhon, Ibis, the Apis Bull, and a cynocephalus. Maier's *Symbola Aureae Mensae duodecim Nationum* is a volume not entirely innocent of Egyptian or Egyptianizing ideas, and it contains material on *Hermetis Aegyptiorum Regis et Antesignani Symbolum*.[19] Both Maier and Fludd were published at Oppenheim, and both had connections with England, the Netherlands, the Court of the Elector Palatine, and the Court of the Emperor himself. Maier, like Fludd and Dee, did much to promote 'Egyptian Hermetic' truth. His *Symbola* enthuses over the Wisdom of Hermes, and celebrates the sacredness of the Virgin Queen Chemia, who is obviously Isis, the fount of wisdom. The Virgin Queen is also found in Elizabethan times, even to the extent of having an approved icon, and is yet another instance of a universally loved medieval Catholic image leaving a void that had to be filled by beleagured Protestantism: Isis returned in another guise.

Throughout this study reference will be made to the significance of Protestantism, Hermeticism, symbolism, and syncretism with reference to Freemasonry. There is at least one extraordinary artefact that links Scotland, emblems, labyrinths, Masonic symbolism, the Reformation, and an ill-fated bid to establish a Protestant Kingdom in Bohemia, in the heart of the Holy Roman Empire itself. The 'Winter King and Queen' established a garden at Heidelberg that, to Protestant-Renaissance minds, was the Eighth Wonder of the World. Salomon de Caus, Architect, laid out one of the most interesting and well documented of all Renaissance gardens for Frederick v, Elector Palatinate and son-in-law of King James I and VI, at Heidelberg. De Caus's designs were published in *Hortus Palatinus* by J. T. De Bry in Frankfurt in 1620, which included a panorama by Merian showing English knot-gardens, *Broderies* (or 'embroidered' gardens), fountains, grottoes, and a labyrinth of clipped hedges.

The complex iconography, the programme involving a belief in a universal harmony, and the Euclidian, Platonic, and Pythagorean systems of numbers have been adequately discussed elsewhere.[20] According to this interpretation the soul moves through various states represented by parts of the garden, through the maze (representing the confusion of life's journey), to the new harmony of the Orange Parterre where even nature is changed and understood by the intellect, and on to a new plane of revelation through astrology and the mysteries of Divine Love. Such a programme, of course, suggests the Reformation and a proto-Enlightenment based on Hermetic philosophies that had been embraced by Giordano Bruno and Pico della Mirandola, who recognized that Christianity was anything but unique, and that there was much in Roman Catholicism that owed more of a debt to Classical Antiquity than die-hard reactionaries would care to admit.

The gardens at Heidelberg evoked marvels by such means as mechanical fountains which emitted musical sounds, and were suggested by the rediscovery of ancient texts, some of which had come from Alexandria. Salomon de Caus employed systems of design in which Architecture, hydraulic engineering, perspective, Geometry, ideals of proportion based on the meaning of numbers, and mathematical science were used. There were grottoes, fountains, statues and many other devices that would have conjured up the ancient world, but, most importantly, the use of a numerical study in order to create mechanical musical instruments heralds the obsessions of the Enlightenment with gadgets, as well as evoking Antique ideas and pointing the way to industrial power in the centuries ahead. De Caus seems to have employed steam power for some of his machines, which he based on Vitruvian and Pythagorean precedents, and which looked forward to the mammoth organs and water-displays of nineteenth-century Europe and America. The Hortus Palatinus was a symbol of a proto-Enlightenment that embraced universal systems of harmony and proportion: it was a series of experiences through which one could pass and reflect, and had its parallels—though not its exact antecedents or derivatives—in ancient and later gardens. It was to be destroyed by the same forces of reaction that condemned Bruno to the stake and that stemmed the tide of inquiry in Protestant Europe.[21]

If the design of the garden is startling in the context of this study, the title-page of *Hortus Palatinus* was even odder. A massive, blocky, primitivist, almost Neoclassical architrave with bold crossettes and plain oversailing cornice framed the lettering. On the cornice a *putto* dangled a square, set-square, compasses, and other implements of Architecture and building, while holding in his left hand a lighted torch, for illumination, exposition, and truth. Two *putti* in the centre carried a polyhedral form composed of five-pointed stars, and another *putto* on the right dangled a mirror and other attributes. At the base Minerva faced Hermes with *caduceus* and dividers, while between the two seated figures were a pyramid, a cube, and various polyhedral forms.[22] It might well have been a Masonic frontispiece.

Giordano Bruno made use of Hermetic themes: he preached a reformation of the world based on a return to

'Egyptian' wisdom and religion as revealed in Hermetic treatises. Religious differences were to be overcome through love and magic, and Bruno's ideas were carried throughout northern Europe to become enshrined in the Rosicrucian movement. Bruno was to die at the stake for his conviction that the wisdom of Ancient Egypt was greater than that displayed by a repressive orthodoxy that burned dissidents. His denial of the unique nature of Christianity included the observation that even the Cross with halo was a symbol invented by the Egyptians (the *Ankh*), and he saw clearly the debt that Christian belief and practice owed to the ancient cults of Isis and Osiris, including the Virgin Birth, the ability to resurrect the dead, to heal the sick, and to restore sight. Even the attributes of the Blessed Virgin Mary were the same as those of Isis: Stella Maris, Protectress in Death, and Queen of Heaven are but three examples. Bruno must have smiled a wryly cynical smile when considering that the Inquisition demanding his life ignored the fact that the Vicar of Christ had claimed descent from Osiris through the dubious researches of Annius of Viterbo, and that the Apis Bull and other Egyptian deities and figures decorated not only the Missal of Cardinal Pompeo Colonna,[23] but the Borgia apartments themselves in the Vatican.[24]

The religion of the Egyptians was held to contain prophecies of Christianity, and seen as the 'imperfect harbinger', though modern scholarship tends to vindicate Bruno and others. The 'Hermetic' writings were, in fact, later than Christ (although this was not known in late-medieval or Renaissance times), but the ideas in Hermeticism concerned with the spiritual journey and the search of the individual found favour in Protestant circles. Renaissance minds looked back to Antiquity with admiration, and the search for ancient wisdom was paralleled by the search for the Art and Architecture of the ancients. The 'purified' religion of the Reformation sought inspiration from the examples of the Early Christians and from the texts of Antiquity in which wisdom of a spiritual nature was enshrined.

Religious strife, persecution, bloody war between Protestant and Counter-Reformation forces, and fragmentation among the Protestant ranks led to a growing tendency towards private contemplation and secret observance. It seems that apparent conformity with whatever was regarded as orthodox often disguised devotion to Hermetic ideas that were felt to be older, nobler, purer, and truer than the warring factions of Christianity. Bruno did not keep his Hermeticism secret, but argued for a sort of Egyptian Reformation mixed with ideas of Good Works and Utilitarianism for the benefit of Mankind:[25] he also deplored the passing of many of the best features of medieval organization, including the charitable and social cohesion given by the old Guilds.

Doctor Yates, in her *Giordano Bruno*,[26] wondered where there was a 'combination . . . of religious toleration, emotional linkage with the past, emphasis on good works for others, and imaginative attachment to the religion and the symbolism of the Egyptians'. The answer she came up with was Freemasonry, for Hermetic ideas and Freemasonry have points of closeness that cannot be dismissed. Freemasonry emerged with Lodges, minute-books, records, some sort of national organization, non-operative members, the development of ethical ideas and symbols, references to the Mason Word, catechisms and ceremonies, degrees or grades (Entered Apprentice, Fellow Craft, and Master) in Scotland by 1600, as David Stevenson has shown,[27] and it would be very curious if Hermetic influence so widespread throughout Europe were not injected into Freemasonry. As Doctor Stevenson has pointed out, the period

> saw the peak of the Hermetic striving for enlightenment and the spiritual rebirth of mankind, based on secret knowledge and secret societies or cults. When a system of lodges emerges in Scotland with secret rituals and identification signs, just as the great esoteric Hermetic movement was sweeping across Europe, there surely must be a link between them.[28]

Quite so: there must indeed be a link, and the strong Egyptian flavour in much Masonic design must stem from this and from the idea that obscure hieroglyphical inscriptions held sacred truths. Yet we have seen that much Isiac allusion was actually preserved in the Church as part of the Marian *cultus*, and that other ideas, such as the connections with Daedalus and the Labyrinth, were openly displayed by medieval Masons in cathedral floors such as those of Chartres and Rheims [see 5,6]. Is there therefore some possibility of truth in the Masonic claim that much ancient lore was actually passed over through the Lodges themselves from Antiquity? This idea may not be as far-fetched as has been suggested by some hitherto, although there must have been a new injection of Hermeticism during the Renaissance period which gave new life to old customs. My own view is that something *did* survive, and that it was re-interpreted and *revived* from the sixteenth century, but that the *survivals* were overlaid, obscured, and corrupted. Yet the Daedalus–Labyrinth connection with Antiquity is irrefutable, as is God as Architect (Imhotep-Ptah), and Isis transformed as Mary, so the Egyptian theme was there all the time.

Masonic legends, as encapsulated within the Old

Charges, include allusions to Hermes, the Preserver of Knowledge, who not only treasured the wisdom and methods of the Craft, but in due course passed that heritage on to Mankind after the Deluge. Here again syncretism plays its familiar rôle, for Euclid is supposed to have instructed the male offspring of the Egyptian aristocracy in the mysteries of the Craft, and there is much else that points to an Egyptian, or Graeco-Egyptian set of legends, many of which overlap, interlock, and merge with each other.

In 1600, therefore, Freemasonry would have been accepted as part of a great Hermetic movement in a time of striving, change, and intellectual ferment. It is not fanciful to identify Hermes-Trismegistus as a kind of patron of Freemasonry, for, by that curious process of syncretism and overlaying, Hermes, messenger of the deities, could also be associated with Christian Saints: and who could be regarded as more perfect for such a rôle than St John the Baptist, as the great messenger of Christ Himself?[29] Matters do not rest even there. It is recognized that many Christian Saints took over attributes from pagan deities: the myriad Madonnas of Southern Europe have their forerunners in the protean Isis, the Greatest of All Goddesses, with her crescent moon, her horns, her stars, her fountains, her roses, and her connection with the sacred unit of measurement, the Cubit. It must be of great significance that both St John the Baptist and St John the Evangelist were venerated as Patron Saints of the Mason Craft: indeed, the Companions of the Royal Arch, in what is known as 'Browne's Ritual', toast the 'pious memory of the two Saint Johns, those two great *parallels*[30] in Masonry; we follow their precepts and profit by their example'.[31] So Hermes-Trismegistus, Mercury, and SS John (Baptist and Evangelist, but probably also St John of Jerusalem, who is also known as St John the Almoner in that, by now, familiar syncretic process) mixed.

The attributes of St John the Baptist and St John the Evangelist include the camel-hair coat, rough cross, lamb, open book, dragon or serpent emerging from a chalice, and a young man with an eagle, and occur in some Masonic designs.[32] Veneration of one St John or another was not confined to the Mason Craft alone: many Guilds or Mysteries favoured the SS John, and in Wagner's *Die Meistersinger von Nürnberg*, Veit Pogner sings of *das schöne Fest, Johannistag*, indicating that St John the Baptist was significant to the medieval Guilds of Nürnberg as well, and this seems to have been true of many fraternities of the Middle Ages. The *Johannistag* was at mid-summer, so it is the Baptist's Nativity which was celebrated, and Hermes was the proto-John.

Mnemonic Techniques and Freemasonry

Central to any basic understanding of Freemasonry is the rôle of memory, for the Lodge itself was a mnemonic of the Temple, of a lost ideal, and much else. Esoteric knowledge, too, was not safe in the hands of the ignorant or the profane, so it was safer for initiates to remember such material, possibly using emblems as aids, rather than to commit secrets to the page.

Among the many facets of ancient knowledge to be rediscovered and re-interpreted during the Renaissance period was the method used in Classical Antiquity for improving memory. This interesting mnemonic technique was closely associated with Hermeticism, and was not only extremely useful, but had overtones of the divine, of cosmic relevance, and of striving for perfection. In Scotland Fellow Crafts were not admitted to the Freemasons' Lodge without 'pruife of memorie and art of craft'.[33] Thus proficiency in mnemonic technique was regarded as an essential part of the Freemason's skills.

Obviously those persons obliged habitually to speak in public—those involved in the theatre, politicians, and public performers of all sorts (including musicians)—must have a need to develop methods of memorizing a vast range of material. It will startle some to learn that Graeco-Roman mnemonic technique used Architecture as bases for their arrangement).[34] Doctor Frances Yates opposed to mere buildings, were organized, ordered, and sufficiently complex (using Geometry and mathematics as bases for their arrangement)[34] Doctor Frances Yates devoted a whole book to The Art of Memory, as it is called, so only the barest outline is possible here, and readers are referred to Doctor Yates's work for a clear and comprehensive exposition. The method used involved the detailed and careful study of a large building with architectural pretensions: the student would note the plan, the disposition of rooms, features, sculptures, finishes, and detail, and would commit these to memory, perhaps only after several visits. Naturally, this process involved a journey through the building, so the rooms, spaces, compartments, and so on were visited and viewed in a definite and logical order, involving a progression or route, a profoundly Masonic idea, as we will see. When memorizing a text, a play, a speech, or a sequence of facts or arguments, the student had to remember the *route* through the building, so that the rooms, with their features, became associated with key elements in the text, with concepts, with faces, or even with specific words or phrases. The order of the images retained in the memory, obviously, had to correspond with the order of the contents of the speech, and the remembered images then had a triggering mechanism to release associations with thoughts, ideas, words, and abstractions.

Such a technique allowed great scope for detailed personal observation, permitting tailor-made memory-routes tuned to personal taste or convenience. Relationships between images (and, of course, type of image), places, and content might be extremely obscure to all except the person involved in the exercise.[35] During the 'play-back' the student proceeded in his mind through the building complex, permitting each room, corridor, space, architectural detail, material, or colour to prompt an association whereby the desired phrase could be 'triggered'. Skilled perambulators through building groups as organized and as vast as Roman Thermae apparently could associate almost every word of a speech with the images of the sequences of the route, and prodigious examples of the success of the method were claimed.[36] Clearly such a mnemonic technique could encourage associations, abstractions, and identification by symbol and attribute in a built environment lavishly decorated and embellished with architectural ornament and statuary that themselves were derived from a sophisticated *vocabulary* and fully developed *language* of *literate* design. The point is that the technique would work with Classical Architecture, or perhaps with Gothic, but it would stand little chance of success with some of the more feeble products of the last forty years or so, most of which hardly rate as Architecture at all.

The Art of Memory could also involve elaborate symbols or emblems, which were familiar throughout the ancient world, notably in the Roman Empire. Just as the deities of Antiquity had attributes which helped to identify them and jog the memory concerning their activities and powers, or 'specializations', so Christian iconography absorbed much that already existed: Norman Douglas's crack that Christianity was partly a 'quaint Alexandrian *tutti-frutti*' is not too far off the mark in this respect. Christian Saints were depicted with virtues, instruments of martyrdom, and so on in order that they could be identified, and contemplation, based on memory of their deeds, encouraged.[37] St Catherine with her Wheel, St Laurence with his Grid-Iron, and St Andrew with his Saltire Cross are but three obvious examples. It is perhaps worth noting, *en passant*, that most Saints' Days record the day of martyrdom, of physical death: in Christian belief, though, this death is a true birth, for Saints are 're-born' by martyrdom and enter Eternal Life among the Blessed. The Masonic idea of a death and new life on initiation is a parallel, and both ideas go back to the beginning of time, but owe much to the developed ideas of death and re-birth in Antiquity. A medieval cathedral, with its labyrinths, many statues, thousands of carvings, and iconography, served also as a Temple of Memory, reminding the pilgrim of the

Temple of Solomon, Biblical stories, of the deeds of Saints, and of formulae for prayer and devotion, a point that goes a long way to explaining the extraordinary complexity of such buildings, with their labyrinths, colour-schemes, and elaborate imagery.

Mnemonic method involving perambulation through a sequence of spaces in which architectural features would be memorized was developed further by placing imaginary images or details on parts of the rooms as an aid to memory;[38] there were many variations using similar techniques that could be used to suit individual tastes and requirements. This 'Art of Memory' was revived during the Renaissance period, and, called Artificial Memory, Science or Art of Mnemonics, or System of Mnemonic Devices, was discussed in a number of Renaissance texts, including Petrus Ravennas's *Foenix; seu artificiosa memoria* of 1491, R. Copland's *The Art of Memory, that otherwyse is called the Phenix* of c.1540, and W. Fulwood's *Gratarolus's Castel of Memorie* of 1573 (which defines 'Artificiall Memorie' as a 'disposying or placing of sensible thinges in the mynde by imagination, whereunto the naturall Memorie hauing respect, is by them admonished'). Cowley, in 1647, on his Mistress, spoke of her 'Parts becoming to him "a kind of Art of Memory"', which might be a more agreeable methodology to adopt by those of less architectural turns of mind, while Hoyle, in 1747, in his *Short Treatise on the Game of Whist*, advised mnemonic methods to assist in the game in the added part entitled *An Artificial Memory: Or, An easy Method of Assisting the Memory of those that play at the Game*. So the Art of Memory was a well-known and ancient technique that was revived during the Renaissance period as part of a general rediscovery of Antiquity, and was embraced by many groups in search of esoteric knowledge, using elaborate emblems, charts, frontispieces, and the like. The phoenix, as a symbol of the Art of Memory, is a not unfamiliar motif, and was used by the Templars to denote resurrection or continuity.[39]

Considerations of Architecture were essential elements of the Neoplatonic themes of the Renaissance period, notably aspects of Hermeticism and the rediscovery of Classical memory techniques. The Art of Memory, as a so-called 'occult' art, became an important element in European intellectual life. One Giulio Camillo is credited with the invention of a memory theatre based on Vitruvian principles with Biblical (especially Solomonic) additions: he made objects designed to jog the memory which he set in 'memory-places'. Not only could memory techniques be improved, Camillo claimed, but his system was supposed to be able to control the forces within the firmament itself by using the pattern of the stars and the signs of the Zodiac as a wider, universal theatre of memory. Bruno also worked on methods of memory, and argued that his techniques could help to reveal Ancient Egyptian knowledge, enabling Man to achieve union with the Divine.[40] Alexander Dickson, a Scot and follower of Bruno, published in 1584 a work based on Bruno's ideas in which Antique techniques of memory were given overt Egypto-Hermetic settings; Dickson later used places and images in buildings in groups of ten, joined by visual associations to enable them to be memorized in the correct sequence.[41] If all this business about mystic numbers, signs of the Zodiac, and revelations of ancient knowledge sounds fishy to us, we must remember that there are plenty of people around today who consult astrologers, look for signs, and put faith in numbers some three centuries *after* Newtonian enlightenment! The Age of the Alchemical Magus, of the Faustian Seeker, of the Wanderer, did not have the benefit or otherwise of Newtonian physics and all that came after it, but it did have something else that perhaps recognized the importance of spiritual, unmeasurable, ecstatic values.

It is suggested by Doctor David Stevenson[42] that Bruno's influence may have introduced Hermetic ideas of memory into the Mason Craft in Scotland by 1599 through Bruno's disciple Alexander Dickson, and William Schaw, Master of the Works to the Scottish Crown. Schaw it was who insisted that Masons should be thoroughly tested in the Art of Memory, for the latter was of particular interest to Freemasons: it was, after all, based on the idea of studying a large and complex building, and it was recognized as giving new powers by developing mnemonic skills for acquiring knowledge and storing facts by allusions. Doctor Yates saw the connection between the Art of Memory (using Architecture in the search for Wisdom) and Freemasonry.[43] She went so far as to suggest that the Renaissance occult Art of Memory was the source of a Hermetic and mystical movement which used the imaginary, legendary, or speculative elements of the Architecture of Memory as vehicles for teaching moral and mystical ideas directed towards and from the Great Architect of the Universe.[44] Doctor Stevenson has shown[45] that the Warden of the Lodge of Kilwinning in 1599 was ordered to test every Entered Apprentice and Fellow Craft in the Art and Science of Memory, and that punishments were to be instituted for those who lost points. Masters most perfect in the Art of Memory were to test other Masons in aspects of the Art, Craft, Science, and Ancient Memory.[46] Thus it is clear from what are known as the Second Schaw Statutes that Hermetic Renaissance ideas were introduced to the Craft, indeed almost imposed by the Master of the Works himself, and that there are links between Schaw, Dickson, and Bruno, as Doctor Steven-

son has demonstrated. It is also clear that ideas concerning mystical enlightenment through an ancient technique not only developed aspects of Masonic custom, but influenced the iconography of the Craft.

These points comprise significant parts of the history of Freemasonry, linking Hermetic strands of 'Ancient Egyptian Wisdom' with the Mason Craft. The Enlightenment enthusiasm for Egyptian Architecture and mysteries *before* the scientific surveys of Egyptian buildings thus makes much more sense: the Hermetic ideas permeated Scotland, and Scotland was the *source* of much later Masonic ceremonial. It is in Scotland, too, that we find tangible and visible evidence of how deeply Renaissance themes had penetrated in that country: that evidence is so startling and so strange that it cannot be dismissed as artistic licence or as mere chance.

Visible Evidence of Freemasonry in Artefacts in Scotland

The Knights Templars, or Order of the Poor Knights of Christ and the Temple of Solomon comprised a military and religious Order, consisting of Knights, Chaplains, and men-at-arms, founded around 1118, chiefly for the protection of the Holy Sepulchre and to escort Christian pilgrims visiting the Holy Land. The Order was called thus because it occupied a building on the site of the Temple of Solomon in Jerusalem. It became immensely wealthy, with vast estates and properties throughout Western Europe, and was suppressed in 1312, having been accused of all manner of blasphemies, heresies, and wicked practices. The suppression was carried out at the instigation of King Philippe IV of France, who leaned on the Pope, Philippe's puppet Clement V, to dissolve the Order.

The Templars suffered many losses, but numerous Knights and others seem to have got away, either melting into the populace at large, or joining other Orders. Yet others may have escaped to Scotland and to the Western Isles and Ulster, where the Papal writ was not powerful, and where the political and legal frameworks at the time of Robert the Bruce were sufficiently confused to permit members of the Order to survive. There were 'Temples' in Scotland and Ulster, and there are surviving funerary monuments featuring Masonic Squares, Masonic tools, and Templar swords and crosses

7 *Obelisk-sundial from Mount Stuart, Bute, from M & R, p416* (A).

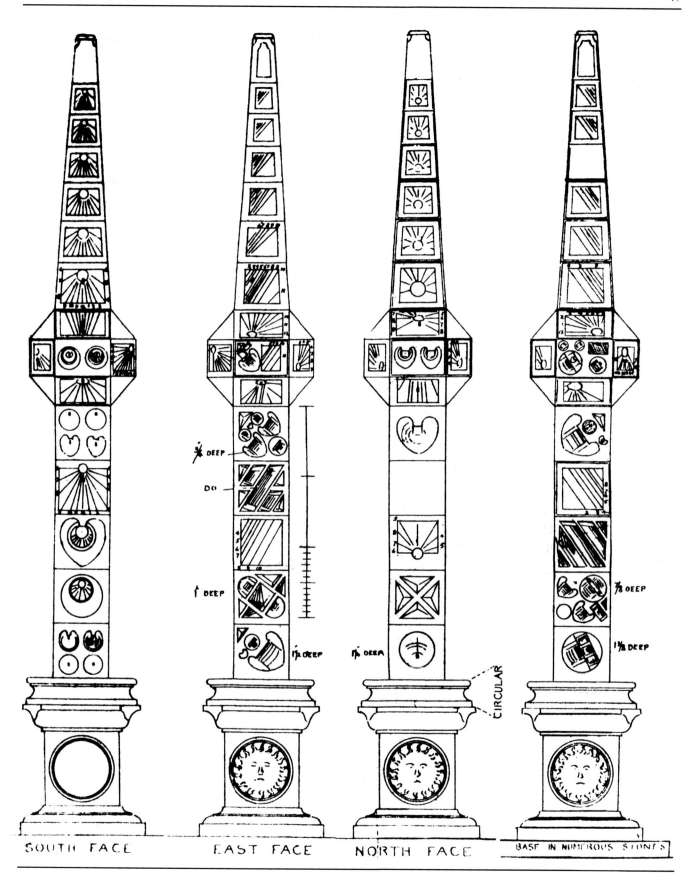

SOUTH FACE   EAST FACE   NORTH FACE   BASE IN NUMEROUS STONES

at Kilmory, Garway, Kilmartin, and other sites that have affinities with Templar memorials in the Holy Land. The fact that the Bruce was very much a law unto himself, and wished to restore an independent Celtic Kingdom of Scotland, meant that the secular agents of the Papacy could not enforce Papal policy, and so the surviving Templars went to ground in Scotland.[47]

It seems highly unlikely that the Order simply died out, but was subsumed in some way into Scottish society. Quite possibly some Masonic legends and concerns, such as ritual, the iconography of the Temple, and certain signs and symbols, derive from Templar practices, for there are rather too many signs in common for this to be entirely accidental. Obviously documentary evidence is somewhat lacking, but the visual evidence on tombstones and in sculpture does suggest that aspects of speculative Freemasonry may owe something to the Templars. The idea of loss, for example, is particularly apposite in the type of the Temple itself: the lost headquarters, the lost arts, the lost Architecture, and the lost power are all encapsulated in the Temple and its iconography. The Templar connection, and the importance of Scotland in the history of Freemasonry, mnemonics, Renaissance-Hermetic ideas, and the Reformation cannot be overlooked. A singular significance of Scotland is reflected in the proliferation of architectonic and sculptural curiosities that cannot be explained in terms of function or climate.

Two remarkably common sculpted types of artefacts survive in Scotland which indubitably display Masonic allusions. Examples of tombstones and memorials with Masonic emblems on them abound in the churchyards and cemeteries of Scotland. But the most elaborate surviving artefacts with Masonic connotations are sundials, which is an odd aspect of a rainy, frequently overcast land, not be be explained in so-called 'functional' terms.

Two very unusual sundial types deserve comment here, although sundials can be found in an incredible number of positions on buildings or as detached objects; the two are obelisk- and lectern-shaped sundials. Obelisk-sundials have overt Egyptian allusions, but Egyptian obelisks themselves were believed by some to have been gnomons, that is the 'pin' of a dial the shadow of which points the hour. These strange objects have square shafts rising from a stepped or plain base, the shaft being divided on each side into five panels, thus presenting twenty compartments to the viewer as he walks around it. These compartments are ornamented with cup-shaped, heart-shaped, triangular, and other incisions, which are usually lined to mark the hours: the sharp edges of the figures cast the shadows, while stone gnomons or metal stiles are also fixed in the hollows.

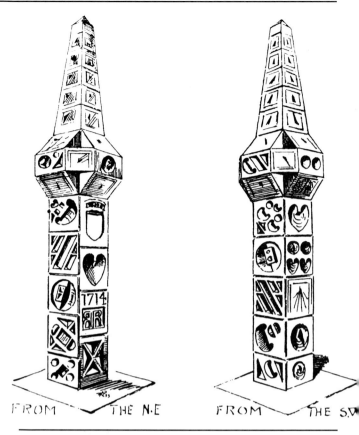

8 *Obelisk-sundial at Tongue, Sutherland, probably of 1714, from M & R, p415 (A).*

9 *Lectern-shaped sundial from Woodhouselee. Such sundials have strong Masonic allusions, and are based on the* Torquetum, *an instrument invented in the sixteenth century by Peter Apian of Ingolstadt for calculating the position of the sun, moon, and stars. The* Torquetum *is the model for many lectern-shaped sundials found especially in Scotland. The idea of a petrified astronomical instrument is somewhat bizarre, but the sun-moon-stars imagery is strong in Freemasonry. Note also the spiral form of the pedestal: the spiral alludes to the Solomonic Temple. See Gatty, H. K. F. and Lloyd, Eleanor,* The Book of Sundials, *London, 1900. From M & R, p423 (A).*

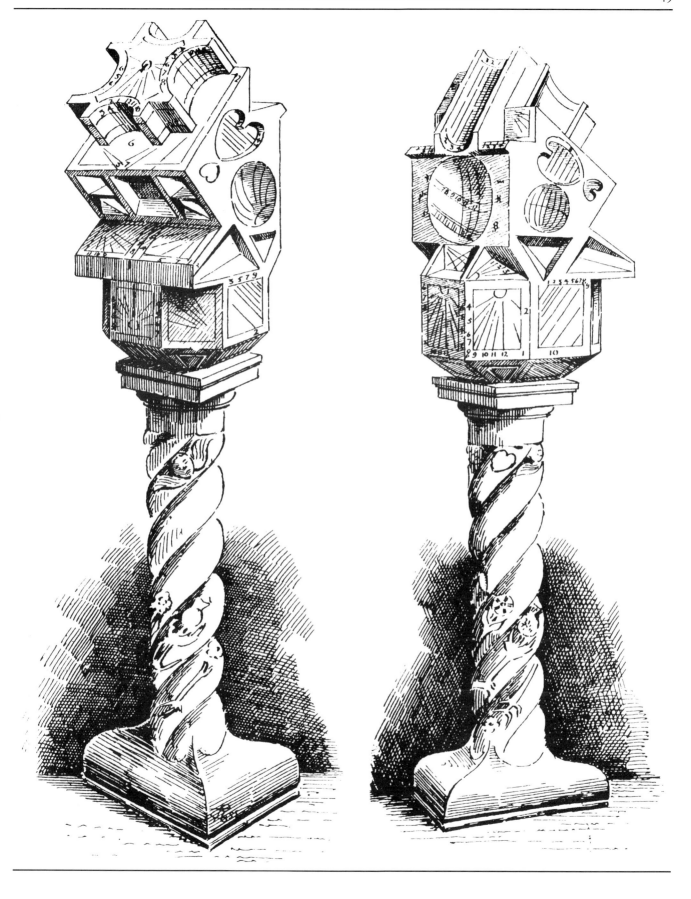

At the top of the compartmented shaft is a block which bulges out on corbelled forms to create an octagon on plan, while above and below each facet over the four sides of the shaft are sloping faces, which also have dials. The triangular pieces formed by the meeting of the square and the octagon are cut out, forming dark shadows. Above the octagon, which returns to the square plan, is an obelisk or a finial, again subdivided vertically into panels (although there does not seem to be a commonly agreed number of these, unlike the square shafts which nearly always have five). Examples include those at Mount Stuart [7], Leven, and Tongue [8].

Lectern-shaped sundials are even odder, consisting of a pedestal or shaft on which is an elaborately carved and hollowed stone containing several sundials, the whole *ensemble* bearing a resemblance to a lectern or elaborate music-stand with a sloping top in the equatorial plane, usually with a star on top. These dials (also known as Masonic sundials) were said by Thomas Ross to be based on the form of Peter Apian of Ingolstadt's *Torquetum*, an instrument invented in the sixteenth century for calculating the positions of the sun, moon, and stars. Apian's design was published in his *Book on Instruments* of 1533. This similarity must be regarded as superficial, however, as the *Torquetum* is mobile, unlike the massive, heavy lecterns of masonry. Good examples from Woodhouselee (Midlothian) [9], and Neidpath Castle, Peebleshire [10], have been catalogued by a number of writers. At Lamancha House, Peebleshire [11], an extraordinary lectern-sundial was placed on a capital in the form of a wicker-work basket filled with fruit; the basket resembles an Egyptian bell-capital, but it may also have allusions to the 'net-work' and 'pomegranates' of the 'chapters' of the Solomonic Temple.

A further variant is the facet-headed dial, polyhedral or extremely irregular, set on a baluster that is usually spiral or twisted [12]. This spiral form, as will be described below, has strong Masonic connotations, and is associated with the Solomonic Temple as well. One of the most complicated—so irregular that no two sections through it would be alike—was at Haddington, and should be compared with the design in the Foundation of the Royal Order print [see 4].

Why were such extraordinary and complex objects created in such numbers in a land not renowned for its clear skies? The Architect/mathematician/astronomer/diallist derives from Renaissance Vitruvian ideals, and it is probable that working Masons designed these sundials both to show off their practical skills as craftsmen, and to suggest their acquaintance with the higher learning and their Craft's guardianship of complex truths, knowledge, sciences, and mysteries. The connection between the Craft, the Heavens, the Earth, the Firmament, and the

10 *Lectern-shaped sundial from Neidpath Castle. From M & R, p426 (A).*

11 *Lectern-shaped sundial from Lamancha House. From M & R, p430 (A).*

way in which advanced ideas, knowledge of complex instruments, and enlightenment were communicated to craftsmen, embraces a vast series of notions of co-operation, fellowship, mystical and scientific themes, and the importance of the Master-Mason-cum-Architect as a Renaissance *Uomo Universale*.[48]

Yet the whole idea of a petrified astronomical instrument is itself bizarre, but can make more sense if seen in the light of Schaw's activities, those of Dickson, and other matters discussed above. When the Calvinist ethic of abhorring decoration and demanding a function for it is considered, this may also have contributed to the genesis of these strange objects. There seems to be little doubt that the sundials had a far greater significance than the merely functional one of telling the time, for in their complexity and multiplicity of facets and dials they suggest a welding together of a variety of forms and shapes symbolically implying the healing of the schisms in Christendom, and encapsulating the desire for an all-embracing and benevolent enlightenment that could repair the disasters of religious difference, superstition, intolerance, and cruelty. Needles, hearts, and stars which feature in so many sundials suggest not only the influence of the stars on the fate of Man, but Masonic and Marian imagery. The compass needle, for example, has associations with the Stella Maris, and hence is both Marian and Isiac.

Doctor Stevenson, in his recent study of Scottish Freemasonry of 1988 cited in the footnotes and bibliography of this book, sheds new light on Schaw and others, identifies these sundials as demonstrating connections between Masons, mathematicians, astronomers, and ideas, and places events in Scotland firmly in the forefront of Masonic history. His book is indispensable, for he develops various themes previously discussed by Doctor Yates, and takes those clearly within Masonic history. Significantly, although sundials ceased to be fashionable in Scotland around 1750, it is precisely from that period that elaborate dials became popular on the European Continent: it was then that Continental Freemasonry developed and became widespread. That such sundials are Masonic cannot be doubted, for they recur in numbers in the Netherlands and in Central Europe during the phenomenal rise of Freemasonry in the Age of the Enlightenment. Some spectacular sundials have been recorded in Alsace and in Hungary. E. Zinner, R. R. J. Rohr, M. Neumann, and others have noted many examples.

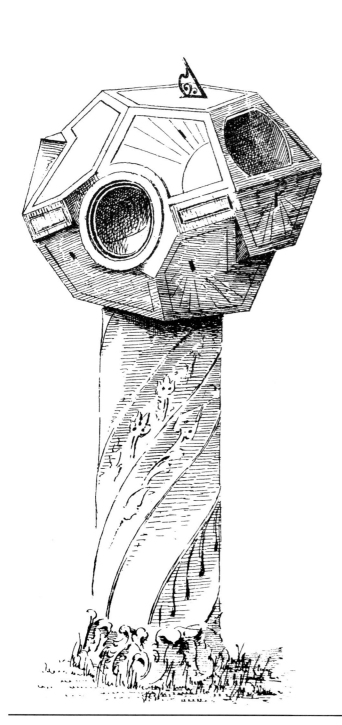

12 *Multi-faceted dial from Haddington. Cf. 4. Note the spiral form of the pedestal. From M & R, p466 (A).*

Scotland, England, Jacobites and Hanoverians

The huge changes inherent in the Reformation not only altered features familiar in medieval life, such as observances by Guilds and Fraternities during religious festivals, but created a void in which new forms of ceremony and ritual could be developed in the secrecy of meetings such as the Lodges. The enormous impact of the English Revolution of the 1640s and 1650s clearly left ideas of republicanism and radicalism that had a considerable effect throughout the eighteenth century, especially through the Netherlands. The Scientific Revolution that began with Copernicus had reached new heights with the publication of Newton's *Philosophiae Naturalis Principia Mathematica* in 1687, a work that had the profoundest effects on the Enlightenment, and especially on the French *philosophes*. Radicals of the eighteenth century learned from the Newtonian Revolution a new reverence for Nature, but the move to disengage the clergy and established Churches from Government that had begun with the English Revolution soon became a part of Continental radicalism. Although there was an undercurrent of English republicanism in the eighteenth century, many shied away from this (with memories of the Commonwealth): Newton and Boyle, for example, chose a liberal and moderate undogmatic type of Christianity in preference to the radicalism of the Puritan sectaries.

Freemasonry in England, firmly associated with Whiggery from 1717, provided a social institution that could promote cultural, political, and undogmatic notions. Members of the Craft would acknowledge the God of the new science, the Great Architect, who was no longer a figure of rage, vengeance, and wrath, but the embodiment of Order, Measurement and Stability: the Great Architect was a Creator, benevolent, truthful, full of grave wisdom, and part of the natural order of things.

During the early part of the eighteenth century organized Freemasonry became widespread in both the British Isles and on the Continent. This spread is closely connected with the rise of the Whig oligarchy and with the growth of British power. Freemasonry was fashionable in the Netherlands and in the Holy Roman Empire (notably in Austria), which is not surprising, for both were allies of Britain in the power-struggle with France, and both were aware of British prosperity, of the remarkable constitutional structure, and of the new stability in Britain. That Freemasonry was intensely political can hardly be doubted. The Craft may have been brought to Vienna in the wake of Prince Eugen of Savoy, the great military commander and ally of Britain, who had many Freemasons in his entourage. The Duke of Lorraine, Francis, later to become Emperor, was initiated as a Freemason at Houghton Hall in Norfolk, Walpole's estate in 1731. At his Coronation in 1745 it seems that a Masonic ceremony was held, and many Netherlanders were initiated.[49]

In England during the eighteenth century Freemasonry was approximately Protestant, and was not seen as posing any threat to the established Church or to the State: on the contrary, it tended to support both. Yet on the Continent Freemasonry was often denounced as subversive, especially where the Roman Catholic Church was concerned, and it was also perceived as republican and radical. The reasons for this are clear: Freemasonry on the Continent tended to be supported by those of a liberal bent who admired England and English constitutions, who revered Newton and his philosophies, and who abhorred absolutism and the clerical and intellectual stranglehold on the old régimes. It was this precise connection with Protestantism and with anti-absolutism (spelling a threat to both Church and Divinely-Ordained Monarchy) that condemned Continental Freemasonry in the eyes of the Church.

Freemasonry claimed a link with the mysteries of Antiquity, but it clearly was also a link with Renaissance Hermeticism, Newtonian Science, and the Guilds of the past. With its aprons, tools, and other emblems, it evoked a world of the noble craftsman, the dignity of labour, and the creation of noble Architecture. It also broke down social barriers, for within the Lodge the aristocrat hob-nobbed with the Third Estate, and, if the aprons and tools were anything to go by, would soon be rubbing shoulders with artisans in the confines of the Lodge. An easy socializing that had been a feature of English custom thus spread to the Continent, and threatened the rigid stratification of society. In fact, Freemasonry portended a social revolution of Continental import. Thus Freemasonry on the Continent began to be seen as subversive, quite unlike its parent organization. Sundials in the Netherlands and in Central Europe are a memorial to the spread of British Freemasonry among her Continental allies in the military struggles with France, the epitome of absolutist monarchy.

Yet from the end of the sixteenth century Freemasonry in Scotland seems to have been closely associated with the House of Stuart, and throughout the seventeenth and the first half of the eighteenth centuries this link was maintained. In fact Freemasonry in France (and where there were emigrés from Scotland and Ireland after the Williamite Wars, the 1715 Rebellion, and the events of 1745–6 which put paid to the Stuart Restoration hopes) was strongly Jacobite in its leanings. Only when the Jacobite cause was finally lost did this connection become loose and die away. The association with the Hanoverian camp and therefore with Whiggery coincides with the creation of Grand Lodge in 1717. This centralization is probably due to one very important reason, and that is the state of the country after the accession of the Elector George Lewis of Hanover to the Throne in 1714 and the Rebellion of 1715, which unquestionably involved many Jacobite Freemasons. There was a clear need to control the Craft, to purge it of any taint of Jacobite sympathy, in order to avoid trouble, or even persecution. The result was an overt show of allegiance to the House of Hanover. The Whigs, quite clearly, determined to set up a powerful Masonic organization which would rival the Jacobite Masonic network, and so the Three Degrees of Craft Freemasonry were placed firmly under the control of Grand Lodge. Higher Degrees seem to have been exclusively Jacobite until after 1745; then, the Higher Degrees, having been purged of Jacobite elements, and the danger of a Jacobite Restoration having passed, were adopted by English Freemasonry. Eventually the organizations responsible for the Craft became United Grand Lodge in the nineteenth century.

The Effect on the Design of Early Lodges

Masonic imagery, as will now be clear, is varied, catholic, and curious. It is worth reflecting on how much of the above affected the design of Masonic Lodges, for many Lodges met in buildings used for other purposes. To some extent, therefore, Freemasons had to set up their emblems and images in rooms acquired for meetings and so the décor was of a temporary nature, indicating perhaps a Lodge of the imagination, with objects and signs placed in certain positions as an aid to remembering ritual, secrets, and the Mason Word. Lodges, in a sense, therefore, were places where the Hermetic Art of Memory could be practised.

It is also clear from Masonic rituals and catechisms that there was an Ideal Lodge, a symbolic building, that Freemasons shared in imagination. Seventeenth-century meetings in hired rooms involved the markings of plans of this imaginary Lodge on floors, and there also seem to have been cloths marked with positions which were laid on floors for specific ceremonies. Lodges of the mind contained the grave of the Master Hiram in a trough under the west window looking to the east, and this grave contained a secret or a potential substitute secret.

Jachin and Boaz, as well as being associated with the Two Pillars enshrining knowledge of Masonic Legend, with the Temple of Solomon, and with Biblical refer-

ences to earth and heaven supported on pillars (the probable origin of the image of two columns with spheres on top), were also identified with the Pillars of Hercules at the Straits of Gibraltar, which stood at the *end* of the world in the Middle Ages, but signified the *gateway to the New World* in Renaissance times, with ideas of endless expansion, wealth, knowledge, and a triumphal development of European societies. *Non Plus Ultra*, in fact, had become *Plus Ultra*, and recurs in devices of the Holy Roman Emperor himself, of Queen Elizabeth, of the Kings of France, and of many other Renaissance figures.[50] In Masonic thought, therefore, the Two Pillars signified the entrance to the Temple/Lodge not only as a memory of the Temple in Jerusalem, as a reminder of the seeking, finding, and keeping of lost wisdom, but also as a mark of the ending of an old world or existence and the moving from a known world to a new one (in many senses).[51] As will be seen, the Two Pillars played an enormously important part in Masonic iconography, art, and Architecture, but they were also common and popular emblems during the sixteenth century, as Doctor Yates and others have demonstrated. They were also to recur in one of the grandest of Imperial Baroque Churches in Central Europe.

The Ideal Lodge of the seventeenth century was orientated east–west, contained the Two Pillars by reference to the names Jachin and Boaz, and held the grave of Hiram, the Architect: for was not the first Lodge situated in the portico of the Temple? The work of Freemasons in the Lodge was mystical, and involved the Building of the Temple, or the reconstruction of a lost Ideal Community in a setting worthy of it, where the Architect and the Craftsmen mixed freely and social distinction was broken down from the highest echelons of society to the lowest. This high/low progression idea, according to Doctor Stevenson, may possibly explain the apparently nonsensical *mahabyn/matchpin/marrowbone* of the Hiramic Legend, for an Entered Apprentice in the Catechisms was 'in the "hall"', which we can interpret as follows. If the 'hall' is the Lodge (*Mahal*, an Urdu [Arabic] word meaning private apartments or lodgings, or a palace), and *Ben* (Middle English *Binne*, related to *Bin*, or *Binnan*, or Binnen), meaning within, towards the inner part, or into the chamber from the kitchen (e.g. *but-and-ben*, meaning the outer and inner apartments of a house), then the Masonic connotations are clear. The Master had access to the far, innermost chamber (*Far Ben*), and his word therefore suggests his privilege. Doctor Stevenson[52] proposes a slightly different meaning by which words exchanged were reminders in architectural terms that the Fellowship of Freemasonry overcame social distinctions.

The Mason Word appears to have been two words,

and was partly mnemonic of the secret knowledge and wisdom, and partly an indication that the Word, with a capital W, was like the Biblical Word, or the Word of God, imbued with special significance and meaning. If Jachin and Boaz sufficed by name as mnemonics of the Pillars (either the Solomonic/Hiram Pillars or the Two Pillars of even greater antiquity in legend by which the Word, in the sense of essential esoteric knowledge, was preserved) for Apprentices and Higher Grades, it is clear that at some time in the seventeenth century separate signs for recognition (grips or handshakes) were evolved for Fellow Crafts and Masters,[53] so that three distinct Grades or Degrees developed, possibly as a result of English Freemasons embracing Scottish rites, but more likely because the three Grades or Degrees actually developed in Scotland by the end of the seventeenth century.[54]

Mahabyn, however, may have another, even more immediate, significance associated with the binding agency of Freemasonry: it may relate to lime as in mortar, for is not one of the tools associated with a Master a trowel? This matter is explained in the Glossary of the present work under *Lime*, *Mahabyn*, *Mortar*, and *Tree*.

Early rituals point not to two, but to Three Pillars, supporting Wisdom, Strength, and Beauty, and reminding Masons of Solomon (who caused the Temple to be built), of Hiram, King of Tyre (who gave men and materials), and of the other Hiram (who built and adorned the Temple); the latter is usually, and erroneously, referred to as Hiram Abiff. Wisdom/Solomon/the Master is represented by the Ionic Order; Strength/King Hiram/the Senior Warden is represented by the Doric, and Beauty/Hiram the Master/Builder/Junior Warden is represented by the Corinthian. These 'Warden's Columns' are also associated with floor candelabra, and were sometimes themselves the candleholders.[55] Pillars also support hour-glasses (passing time and the transitory nature of life), and sometimes carry globes (or interpreted as two superimposed lavers, or bowls, sometimes as Heaven and Earth, but more probably derived from sixteenth-century representations of Solomon's Temple showing globes on top of Jachin and Boaz). So, there seem to have been *three* sets of the Two Pillars: the Pillars used to record knowledge and secrets; the Solomonic Temple Pillars of Hiram; and the Pillars of Hercules (the latter common emblematic devices of the Renaissance period). In addition, however, there were a Doric, Ionic, and Corinthian Column, and some or all of these got confused at some time or another.

A Lodge was the place (a room or a building) in which Freemasons met, but it was also the society, or body of Freemasons itself, and it was the meeting of that body. It has previously been noted that a Lodge was the building set aside for the use of Masons in a building site, and was often the workshop, refectory, meeting-room, and dormitory rolled in one. Every Lodge of Speculative Masonry has a name and number, and the number indicates precedence.

Every new Lodge has to be constituted, and opened in three degrees. The officer scatters corn (plenty), pours wine (joy and cheer), pours oil (peace and concord), and sprinkles salt (fidelity and friendship) before dedicating the Lodge. The Chaplain takes a censer three times around the Lodge and offers prayers. Three candles and a box containing the warrant and constitutions have also played their parts in the legitimacy of a Lodge. Lodges have not met in private houses for many years, presumably for purposes of secrecy.[56]

Lodges were orientated east–west, with the Master's place at the east (as opposed to the Temple, where the Holy Place was in the west), and so followed ecclesiastical practice. The east was associated with the sun, with light, and with life: so, as the sun rises, the Master in the east instructs the Lodge in the Craft, symbolizing enlightenment.

Some early Lodges were not always 'oblong squares', and some seem to have been triangular, while others were cruciform.[57] This is not to say that the actual rooms or buildings were triangular or cruciform, but that the imaginary or remembered Lodge was marked on floors to plans of those shapes. It is known that Brethren were not regarded as being in the Lodge until they had stepped within the chalked or otherwise defined limits.

The Canongate Kilwinning Lodge plan was rectangular: the Master was at the east; the Senior and Junior Wardens in the west, with triangular pedestals themselves set at the points of a triangle; the Secretary was on the Master's left, and the Treasurer on his right, while positions were defined for the two standard-bearers and the Bible Bearer, and for the Master of Ceremonies (on the Master's left) and Senior Deacon (on the Master's right). The Junior Deacon was positioned near the Senior Warden, and the Inner Guard near the Junior Warden.[58] The Brethren were seated along the sides of the Lodge in lines between the positions of the Treasurer and Senior Warden and Brethren, the Secretary and the Junior Warden. Two large pillars stood on either side of the long axis marking the entrance to the Lodge inside the room enclosure. In the centre, half way between the pillars and the Master, was the altar, a reminder of the Temple, of the injunction to build altars in the Bible, and the need to have a focus, a table, a mnemonic of many things. A Lodge itself was regarded as an Ark, or repository of wisdom and secrets, but many Lodges had Arks, or boxes containing the Warrant, Regalia, and so forth; in the case of travelling Lodges (for example those connected with the Army) Arks were doubly necessary. The Ark, in another sense, of course, was Noah's.

Candles were symbols of spiritual light or illumination, and have connotations with consecration, gratitude, and the keeping of promises. Medieval Craft-Guilds, as has been mentioned, maintained altars in churches and kept them well supplied with candles. Three candles have a clear religious significance (the Trinity, etc.), but they also can suggest silence and secrecy, as in *Tace*, the Latin for 'Be Silent', 'Trust none of them for they are all Thieves, but Tace is Latin for a Candle',[59] and '"*Tace*, Madam", answered Murphy, "is Latin for a candle; I commend your prudence."'[60] This curious phrase is a humourously veiled hint to keep silent.[61] Candles were therefore reminders of Masonic secrecy, and the three candlesticks were often arranged to stand on the points of a triangle. (In an eighteenth-century plan two points are set to form a parallel line with the north wall of the Lodge, while the 'apex' points south. In the same plan three steps for the First, Second, and Third Degrees are shown to the West, while the Master and Bible are placed within a triangular form to the east.) The three candles also represent the Volume of the Sacred Law, the Square, and the Compasses (the Greater Lights), while the Lesser Lights were the candles of the Master and Wardens.

Plans of Lodges [see 2, 13] dating from the eighteenth century show typical layouts. These have three steps (one for the First Degree [or Entered Apprentice, kneeling with the left knee], one for the Second Degree [or Fellow Craft, kneeling with the right knee], and one for the Third Degree [or Master, kneeling with both knees]), three candlesticks, as previously described, and the Master's place at the east end. Other illustrations from eighteenth-century exposures of the Craft show Masonic activities on floor-drawings, cloths, or carpets [14–20]. A curious feature of these publications is not only the tendency for wholesale copying, but the fact that many of the plates are actually mirror-images of earlier plates, and thus give a false view (left and right becoming confused). Whether this was deliberate obfuscation or (more likely) expediency caused by the processes of copying engravings is difficult to assess.

Straight or mirror-image, however, many of these 'exposures' feature tracing-boards. (A word or two of explanation concerning these terms is necessary here.) A *tracing-board* is an emblem of the drawing- or tracing-board of the medieval Masons on which plans and details were drawn. A tracing-board of operative Masons was a board on which parchment might be fixed, or it might be a flat stone or slate on which drawings might be made, or it might even be the floor itself on which the Master-Mason would lay out details to be made by the

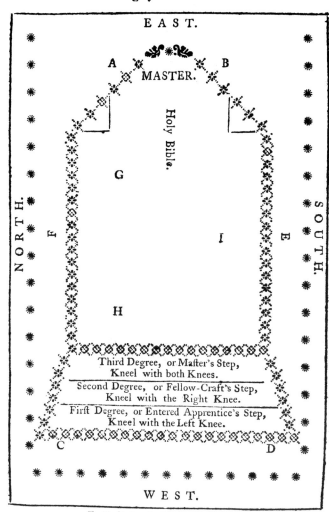

PLAN of the DRAWING on the FLOOR at the making of a MASON.

EXPLANATION.
A Senior Deacon, with a black Rod.
B Paſt-Maſter, with the Sun and Compaſſes, and a String of Cords.
C Senior Warden, with the Level, and a Column in his Hand.
D Junior Deacon, with a black Rod.
E Junior Warden, with a Column in his Hand.
F The Secretary, with Crofs Pens.
G H I Candles.
✳ Maſons ſtanding round at the Ceremony.

13 *Masonic Lodge layout from* Jachin and Boaz, *published in London in 1776. This is a version of a diagram in* The Free Mason stripped Naked: or, the whole Art and Mystery of Free-Masonry, Made Plain and Easy to all Capacities, *by Charles Warren, published in Dublin (n.d.)* (UGLE).

14 *Assembly of Freemasons for the Reception of Apprentices. The apprentice enters on the left, his breast bare, blindfolded, with shoelaces undone and knee exposed. Note the Grand Master seated and the Brethren with aprons. On the floor is a cloth with Jachin and Boaz, the seven steps leading to the Temple, the Mosaic Pavement, the west window, the flaming star, the east window, the indented tuft (or tessellated border), the sun, the perpendicular, and other emblems. From Plate I of Bernigeroth (UGLE).*

15 *Reception of Apprentice. The Brethren are in position around the cloth; the candidate kneels on the stool, and swears with his hand on the Bible never to reveal the mysteries of Freemasonry. This appears to be a mirror-image of an earlier plate, which shows the candidate kneeling with his* left *knee, probably reflecting techniques of copying images on engraved plates. From Plate 2 of Bernigeroth (UGLE).*

16 *Lodge assembled for the reception of Master-Masons. The Grand Master is seated, and the lights are tripled. Note the floor-cloth design. From Plate 3 of Bernigeroth (UGLE).*

15

16

17

18

19

17 *Assembly of Freemasons for the Reception of Master-Masons. The Grand Master sits beneath a canopy. The new member or member-elect is the figure second from the right with the guardian's (or watcher's) sword pointing at his breast. The figure beneath the covering on the left is a candidate to whom the Grand Master has not yet bestowed the accolade. From Plate 4 of Bernigeroth* (UGLE).

18 *Assembly of Freemasons for the Reception of members to the Degree of Master-Mason. On the right are three hooded seated figures (recipients who have not yet received the accolade). The candidate is being laid on the coffin as a symbol of his death before Enlightenment and new life. From Plate 5 of Bernigeroth (UGLE).*

19 *The next stage of initiation. The candidate lies on the 'coffin' or grave on the Lodge, his face covered by a linen the colour of blood, while the Brethren point their swords at his body. The other candidates lie covered on the right. From Plate 6 of Bernigeroth* (UGLE).

craftsmen.[62] Tracing-boards, then, were not necessarily boards on which a semi-transparent skin or paper might be placed for tracing purposes: tracing meant more than copying, and, in fact, signified the process of designing, devising, detailing, drawing, or planning. The root of the term is the Latin *Tractus*, meaning a drawing or a track.[63] Gothic 'tracery' is derived from this, and indeed had to be set out on large surfaces for full-size detailing, so the floor became a tracing-board for such designs. It is important to realize that medieval drawings had to be accurate: the setting out of a vast Second-Pointed piece of window tracery, or the complex geometry of a lierne vault, need precise drawings to make them possible at all. Records survive to show that considerable quantities of skins were used to make the full-size working drawings for a number of major buildings such as the cathedral at Exeter.[64]

The tracing-board of speculative Freemasonry developed as an emblem. The process seems to have been as set out below. Early in the history of speculative (i.e. non-operative) Freemasonry, it seems to have been usual to trace out the form of the Lodge on the floor of the room in which the meeting took place. The necessity of chalking or otherwise marking up an area and then of erasing the marks proved troublesome and cumbersome. Use of chalk, charcoal, and clay to mark out (or trace) the Lodge had symbolic connotations: chalk represented freedom, for it was free for the use of Man, left a trace, yet could be erased; charcoal was fervent, able to destroy or change metal; while clay was zealous, representing the earth and the grave. Such materials must have been difficult to apply and even worse to remove, especially where it was necessary to delete all traces in borrowed premises such as rooms in inns or private houses. Drawings of Lodge layouts were often made with chalk, stone-blue (a compound of indigo with starch or whiting, used by laundresses), and charcoal mixed, and one of the first tasks of a newly-initiated Freemason was to take a mop and clean the tracing until nothing remained.[65]

Various designs, including the Mosaic Pavement, or chequerboard-pattern (signifying something upon which the Freemasons drew ground draughts, or draughted a symbolic building, or representing the chequered existence of Man); the Laced or Indented Tuft (called *La Houpe Dentelée* or *Die Schnur von starken Faden* [the rope or cord of strong thread] with tassels, representing the four cardinal Virtues); Masonic tools and instruments; the tomb of Hiram; and others were included. Clearly the trouble taken to trace such patterns (and clean them up afterwards) must have been considerable, and in due course (apparently in the early part of the eighteenth century) cloths with the various emblems and

20 *The Grand Master raises the candidate from his symbolic death while granting the Mason Word. From Plate 7 of Bernigeroth* (UGLE).

plans of Lodges painted on them were introduced as floor-cloths or even carpets. Lodges of the Three Degrees required different cloths [21]: the latter appear to have been of painted canvas and cannot have had a long life. Consequently the floor-cloths were translated to the status of table-cloths, or even hung on walls. As a wall-diagram the tracing-board became the Lodge Board, containing a composite set of emblems, and its origins became obscured. The floor-cloth (used either on the floor, on a table, or placed on a wooden roller and suspended from a wall) seems to have been called such

until around 1800, when the tracing-board (sometimes the framed or suspended floor-cloth) came into general use.

The tracing-board of speculative Freemasonry is an emblem, and is now remote from the floor-cloths, carpets, and practical drawing-boards of yesteryear. In French Masonic literature the *Planche à Tracer* is sometimes called *tracé*, or outline, or layout. Occasionally, as on some French representations of layouts, tracing-boards in the original operative sense are seen, with pin-pricks representing the outline of the tracing.[66]

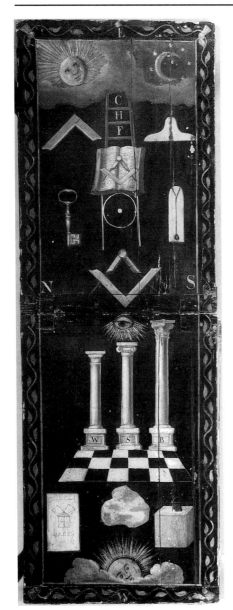

21 *A set of English tracing-boards of early nineteenth-century date showing:* (left) *the three Orders (Doric, Ionic, and Corinthian) and many Masonic attributes,—note that Ionic is incorrectly identified with Strength instead of Wisdom;* (centre) *Jachin and Boaz surmounted by globes, with the winding stair leading to a chequer (so-called Mosaic) pavement and a canopied aedicule supported on four columns; and* (right) *the coffin, various Masonic emblems, with the acacia plant* (UGLE).

S. Fokke inv. et fec. 1746.

LES
FRANCS-MAÇONS
ECRASÉS.

SUITE

DU LIVRE INTITULÉ

L'ORDRE DES FRANCS-MAÇONS

TRAHI.

TRADUIT DU LATIN.

A AMSTERDAM,

M. DCC. XLVII.

22 *Frontispiece and title-page of Larudan, designed and engraved by S. Fokke. The title means 'The Freemasons ruined', and the picture shows a Lodge falling down, complete with Masonic emblems. This was one of the most celebrated of the French 'exposures' (UGLE).*

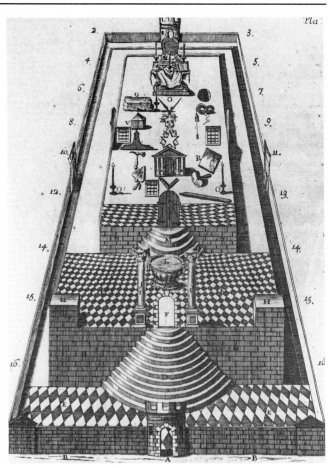

23 *Plate I from Larudan. It purports to show a Lodge or a layout for the Reception of an Apprentice* (UGLE).

24 *Lodge layout or floor-cloth for the Reception of a 'Compagnon' Mason. Plate II from Larudan. The remarkable resemblance to sixteenth-century depictions of the Temple of Solomon should be immediately apparent* (UGLE).

25 *Lodge layout or floor-cloth for the Reception of a Master-Mason. Plate IV from Larudan. Note the triple lights, the acacia bush, the grave, and other Masonic emblems. Again, the resemblance to the Solomonic Temple should be noted* (UGLE).

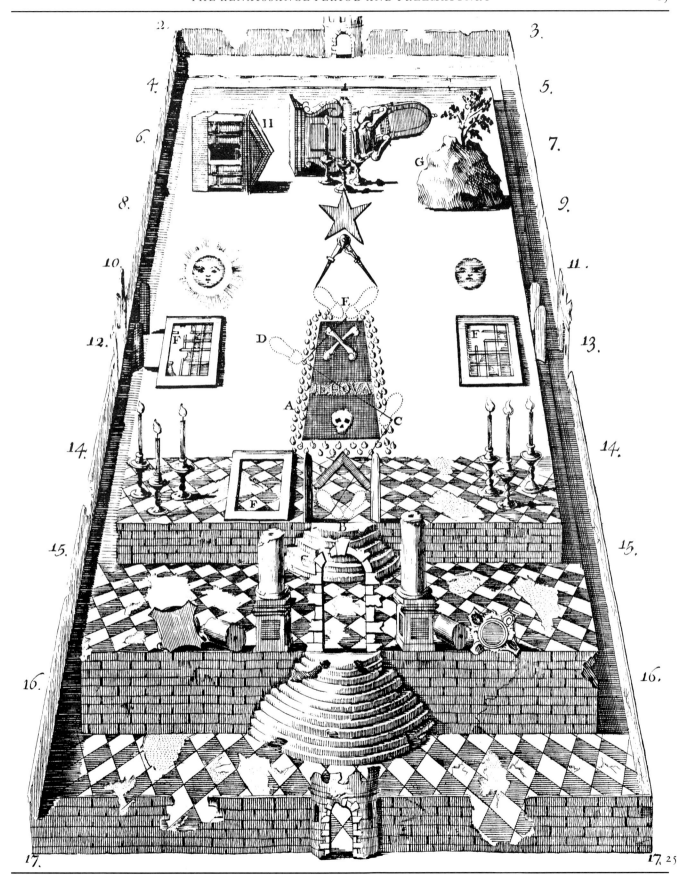

L A D E S O L A T I O N .
DES ENTREPRENEURS .
MODERNES .
DU TEMPLE DE JERUSALEM .

NOUVEAU CATECHISME

DES FRANCS-MAÇONS.

CONTENANT tous les Myſtères de la Maçonnerie, épars & obmis dans l'ancien Catéchiſme, dans le Livre intitulé le *Secret des Francs-Maçons*, &c. Et dans celui qui a pour titre, *le Sceau rompu*, &c. Diviſés en neuf Chapitres, précédés de l'Hiſtoire d'*Adoniram*, Architecte du Temple de Salomon; avec de nouveaux deſſeins des Loges de l'Aprentif-Compagnon, & du Maître.

Dédié au beau Sexe.

TROISIE'ME EDITION,

Revüë, corrigée & augmentée des Obſervations de l'Auteur ſur l'*Hiſtoire des Francs-Maçons*, d'un Extrait critique de l'*Anti-Maçon*, de deux Lettres, & d'une Conſultation ſur le même ſujet, enrichie de Figures en Taille douce.

Prix 4 liv. en blanc.

par L. Travenol

A JERUSALEM,

Chez PIERRE MORTIER, ruë des Maçons au Niveau d'or, *entre l'Equère & le Compas.*

M.CCCC.XL. Depuis le Déluge.

Avec Approbation & Privilége du Roi Salomon.

During the eighteenth century several 'exposures' of Masonic activities and 'secrets' were published, many of them of French origin, and most of them dependent upon each other, even to the extent of mirror-imaging the plates, as has been noted above. One of the most remarkable of these exposés was *Les Francs-Maçons Écrasés*, published following a work entitled *L'Ordre des Francs-Maçons Trahi*, and supposedly translated from the Latin. *Les Francs-Maçons Écrasés* was by the Abbé Larudan, and the frontispiece showed the 'ruin' of a Masonic Lodge [22]. The same volume depicted layouts of the Lodges that were obviously derived from sixteenth-century reconstructions of Solomon's Temple [23–25], complete with Jachin and Boaz, chequered floors, steps, lights, compasses, and other familiar emblems.

Another important 'exposure' was that of 'L. Gabanon', pseudonym of Louis Travenol, whose *Nouveau Catéchisme des Francs-Maçons* appeared in several

26 *Frontispiece and title-page of Travenol. Note the Masons in their aprons. The Angel of Fame has floor-cloths or tracing-boards as banners on his trumpets. This was an important French 'exposure' of Freemasonry (UGLE).*

27 *Reception of Apprentices from Travenol. Note the floor-cloth (UGLE).*

29 *Reception of Master-Masons from Travenol. Note the candidate, the floor-cloth with 'tears', the triple lights, and the skull* (UGLE).

30 *Dinner for Freemasons, from Travenol* (UGLE).

28 (opposite) *Reception of 'Compagnons' from Travenol. Note the floorcloth* (UGLE).

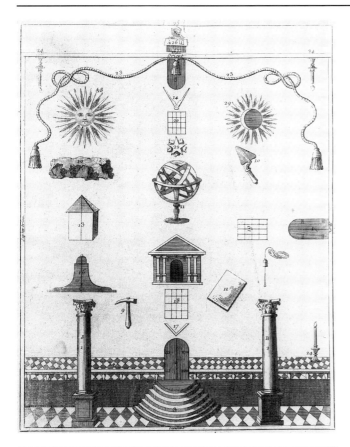

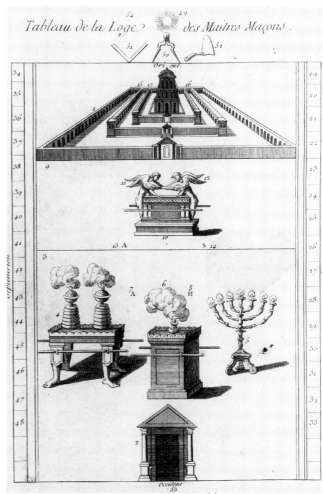

32 *True Plan of a Lodge for the Reception of an 'Apprentif-Compagnon', from Travenol, showing Jachin and Boaz; (3) the steps to the Temple; (4) the Mosaic Pavement; (5) the western gate; (6) the gate to the interior chambers; (7) the southern gate; (8) the eastern gate; (9) the hammer; (10) the trowel; (11) the tracing-board or table with outlines of profiles; (12) the uncut stone; (13) the cubic stone with pyramid; (14) the compasses; (15) the plumb; (16) the level; (17) the square; (18, 19, 20) the western, southern, and eastern lights; (21) the globe; (22) the flaming star; (23) the* houpe dentelée; *(24) the three lights; (25) the seat of the Grand-Master; (26) altar; (27) the stool; (28) the sun; (29) the moon* (UGLE).

33 *Plate from Travenol showing a Lodge of Master-Masons with the Temple of Solomon (top), the Ark (centre), altar, candelabrum, and portal. Cf. 50* (UGLE).

31 *Plan of a Lodge of 'Apprentif-Compagnons' from Travenol. Note Jachin and Boaz, the steps, the architectural centrepiece, and the Masonic emblems* (UGLE).

LES SECRETS

DE

L'ORDRE

DES

FRANCS-MAÇONS,

Dévoilés & mis au jour

PAR MONSIEUR P***

Nil est adeò absconditum quod non tandem reveletur.

PREMIERE PARTIE

A AMSTERDAM.

MDCCXLV.

34 *Frontispiece and title-page showing a candidate for the Degree of Apprentice being blindfolded, from Pérau (UGLE).*

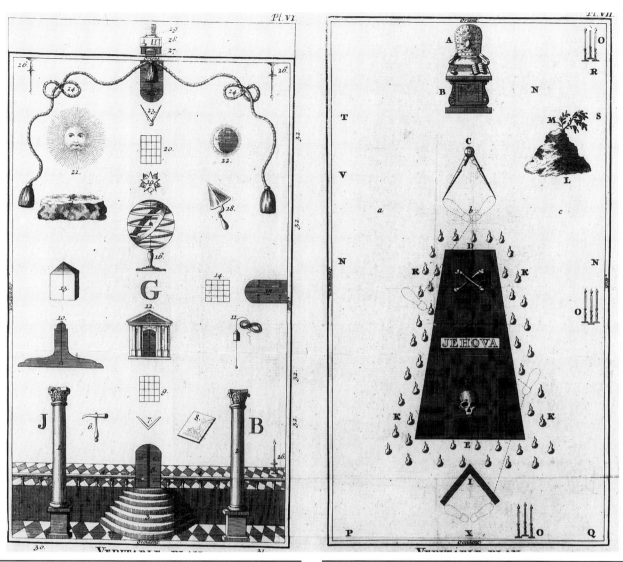

35a *A true plan of a Lodge for the Reception of 'Apprentif-Compagnon'. (1) Jachin (Wisdom); (2) Boaz (Beauty); (3) the Seven Steps to ascend the Temple; (4) the Mosaic Pavement; (5) the western gate; (6) the Masons' hammer or mallet; (7) the square; (8) the floor to be delineated upon (tracing-board); (9) the west window; (10) the level; (11) the perpendicular, or plumb-line; (12) the portal of the interior chamber; (13) the pointed cubical stone (i.e. pyramid on cube); (14) the south window; (15) the south door; (16) the sphere; (17) the rough stone; (18) the trowel; (19) the flaming star; (20) the east window; (21) the sun; (22) the moon; (23) the compass; (24) the indented tuft; (25) the east door; (26) the three lights; (27) the stool; (28) the table; (29) the Grand Master's chair; (30) the Senior Warden's chair; (31) the Junior Warden's chair; (32) the three Masters' seats; (33) the three Fellow-Crafts' seats (except the last Member received); (34) the Junior Warden's plumb-line. From Pérau (UGLE).*

35b *A true plan of a Lodge for the Reception of a Master. (A) the Grand Master's seat; (B) the altar with Bible and mallet; (C) the compass; (D, E) the coffin; (F) bones across; (G) the ancient word of the masters; (H) a death's head; (I) the rule; (K) three tears, or guttes; (L) a mountain; (M) a branch of acacia; (N) three Brethren holding rolls of paper; (O) the nine lights placed three by three; (P) the Senior Warden; (Q) the Junior Warden; (R) the Speaker; (S) the Brother Visitors; (T) the Secretary; (V) the Treasurer; (X) the Receiver. The positions marked a, b, and c are whence the sun, flaming star, and moon are placed on some cloths, but this custom seems to have been mostly used for the reception of Apprentices and Fellow Crafts. From Pérau (UGLE).*

36 *Frontispiece and title-page of Pérau's* Les Secrets de L'Ordre des Francs-Maçons Dévoilés & mis au jour par Monsieur P*** *(Amsterdam 1745), showing the Grand Master 'raising' a new Master-Mason* (UGLE).

editions in the 1740s [26]. Travenol also included some interesting plates in his *Catéchisme*, comprising a Reception of Apprentices [27], a Reception of 'Compagnons' [28], a Reception of Masters [29], a dinner for Free-masons [30], a plan of a Lodge of an 'Apprentif-Compagnon' [31], a True Plan of a Lodge for the Reception of an 'Apprentif-Compagnon' [32], and a Plan of a Lodge of Master-Masons [33].

Similar illustrations embellished *L'Ordre des Francs-Maçons Trahi, et Le Secret des Mopses Révélé*, included in the Abbé Gabriel-Louis Pérau's *Les Secrets de L'Ordre des Francs-Maçons Dévoilés & mis au jour*, published in Amsterdam in 1742 [34]. Pérau's book shows 'true plans' of Lodges for the Receptions of both 'Apprentif-Compagnons' and Master-Mason [35]. Pérau's second part of *Les Secrets de L'Ordre des Francs-Maçons Dévoilés & mis au jour par Monsieur P**** (Amsterdam, 1745) shows the Grand-Master 'raising' a new Master-Mason from the 'dead' [36] as well as plans of Lodges [37].

Pérau also produced *Le Secret de la Société des Mopses Dévoilé & mis au jour par Monsieur P**** published in

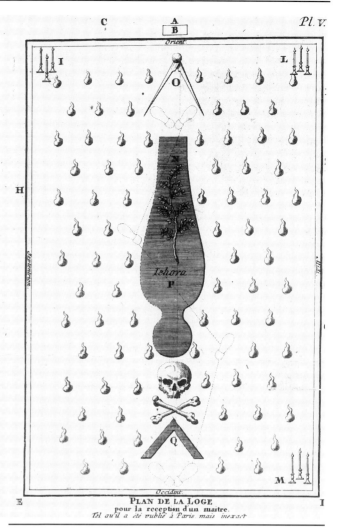

Amsterdam in 1745 [38]. The plan of a Lodge of Mopses differs from other tracing-boards or floor-cloths previously described [39].

One of the most attractive and comprehensive of illustrations (as far as Masonic emblems are concerned) is the frontispiece [40] of *Jachin and Boaz*, published in London in 1776, a volume that also contains a diagram of a Lodge layout [see 13]. In fact, the historian of Freemasonry can delve deeply into the literature of eighteenth-century Freemasonry, and find there much of delight, both visually and intellectually. One of the keys to the Enlightenment can be found among seemingly esoteric publications, yet the unclosed mind and the unclouded eye will have no difficulty in recognizing themes from sixteenth-century representations of the Temple of Solomon to the sweetest gardens of the European revolution in sensibility.

37a *Plan of a Lodge for the Reception of an Apprentice. This design purports to be correct, but is not. (1) Jachin; (2) Boaz; (3) seven steps to enter the Temple; (4) Mosaic Pavement; (5) west window; (6) tracing-board for the Masters; (7) flaming star; (8) south window; (9) plumb or perpendicular; (10) east window; (11) level; (12) unhewn stone; (13) square; (14) cubic stone, with point (pyramid); (15) indented tuft; (A) Grand-Master; (B) First Inspector, Watcher, or Guardian; (C) Second Watcher; (D) altar; (E) foot-stool; (F, G, H) the three lights. In this, as in other French designs, Jachin is associated with strength, and Boaz with wisdom. From Plate IV of Pérau (UGLE).*

37b *Inexact plan of a Lodge for the Reception of a Master. Note the acacia on the coffin, the position of the skull and crossbones, and the liberal scattering of tears, or gutters (incorrectly described as 'gutters' in some documents). From Plate V of Pérau (UGLE).*

38 *Frontispiece and title-page of* Le Secret de la Société des
Mopses Dévoilé. *The frontispiece shows the Reception of a
female Apprentice into a Lodge of* Mopses. *The* Mopses
(from the German Mops, *meaning a pug-dog) kept alive ideas
of private association in Germany, and originated in response to
the Papal Bull of 1738 against Freemasonry. It was an
androgynous society founded in 1740, and the name is taken from
that of a pug or a young mastiff-type of dog with a pug-like face,
noted for its courage and faithfulness. The Order admitted
women to all its offices except that of Grand Master, which was
held for life. There was, however a 'Grand Mistress', and the
male and female heads of the Order alternately assumed for six
months each the supreme activity of the Order. As the plate
comes from* L'Ordre des Francs-Maçons Trahi *(Betrayed),*
et Le Secret de la Société des Mopses Dévoilé
*(Amsterdam 1745), the widely believed claim that women were
admitted only after 1776 is clearly incorrect, for the Grand
Mistress is seated, and a woman Apprentice is being initiated
(although the rite of initiation appears to be less than savoury,
and is probably scurrilous) from Pérau (UGLE).*

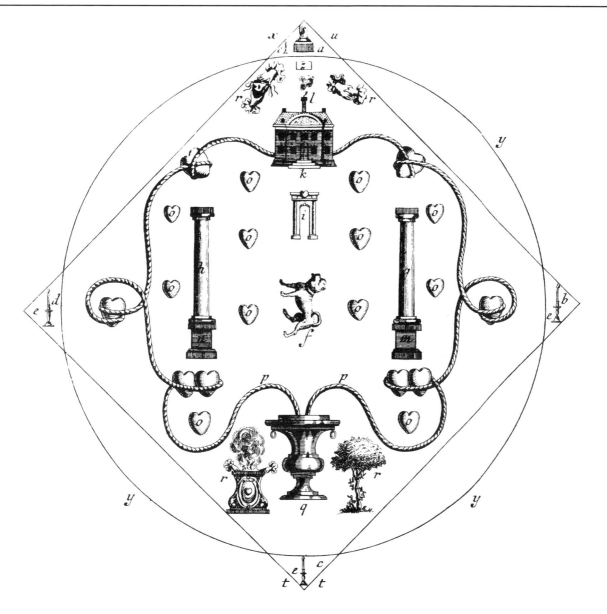

39 *Plan of a Lodge of the Order of Mopses. (a) east;
(b) south; (c) west; (d) north and seven stars; (e) four lights;
(f) Mopse (pug-dog or young mastiff* = doguin *in French* =
Mops *in German) representing courage and faithfulness;
(g) fidelity; (h) friendship; (i) door to the palace of love;
(k) palace of love; (l) chimney to eternity; (m) sincerity;
(n) constancy; (o) four scattered hearts; (p) strand of rope
indicating kindness, courtesy, and free-will, linking the hearts;
(q) vase of reason from which flows the strand; (r) four
symbols of friendship; (s) Master of the Lodge, or Grand
Mopse, seated before the table; (t) watchers or guardians;
(u) officers and officials; (v, y) Brothers and four Sisters,
placed informally around the circle and square; (z) position in
many Lodges where the candidate was elevated in the air while
the eyes were bandaged. From Plate VIII of Pérau (UGLE).*

VIDE, AUDE, TACE.
5776.

Published according to Act of Parliament Aug.st 30. 1776. by W. Nicoll.

40 *Frontispiece of* Jachin and Boaz *published in London in 1776* (UGLE).

CHAPTER 4

THE GREAT PROTOTYPE

Introduction: The Jewish Temple; Representations of the Temple; Fischer von Erlach; The Case of the Karlskirche; The Spiral Columns

And the king commanded, and they brought great stones, costly stones,
and hewed stones, to lay the foundation of the house.

And Solomon's builders and Hiram's builders did hew *them*,
and the stonesquarers: so they prepared timber and stone to build the house

I Kings 5, 17, 18

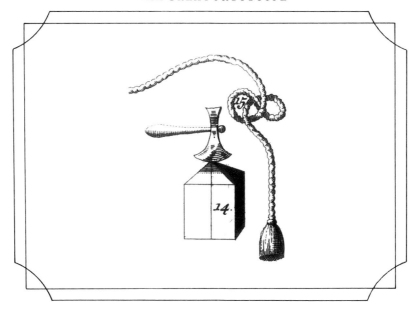

Introduction: the Jewish Temple

The Jewish so-called 'Temple' (*templum* means an area, demarcated and consecrated by the augurs for the taking of auspices, set apart, or used for sacred purposes; it can mean an area of sky or land, heaven or earth, or both, as well as a building consecrated to a deity or deities) had a strong axis leading from the entrance to the Holy of Holies and the Ark of the Covenant, and did not contain a cult statue: it therefore differed from most pagan temples. Solomon's Temple consisted of a porch, the House, and the Holy of Holies. This was built some thousand years before Christ, restored or rebuilt by Zerubbabel around 500BC, and the Third Temple, apparently a magnificent structure, was built by Herod I only to be destroyed in AD70.[1] Freemasonry has revered the Temple as a symbol of what has been lost, as an ideal, as the model for the Lodge, and as an inspiration of what might be reconstructed. The Knights Templars also held Solomon's Temple in considerable reverence, and it is difficult to accept that there was no connection between Freemasonry and the Templars, although the evidence is obscure, not surprisingly.

Representations of the Temple

Illustrations showing the Temple in Classical Antiquity tend to depict aediculated forms or the entrance portico of what are clearly Classical compositions, and do not concern us here.[2] Things get more interesting from the point of view of this study with the medieval period, for both the twelfth-century Synagogue of Worms and the Cathedral of Würzburg had columns that were inscribed and which suggest Jachin and Boaz [see 3]. There were, therefore, definite allusions to the Solomonic Temple in Jerusalem, in both a synagogue and in a great Christian church: the exotic forms adopted, with serpentine carvings, look forward to twisted barley-sugar or wreathed columns of later times. Similar knots can be found in two shafts of the Broleto at Como. Twelfth-century plans attributed to Moses Ben Maimon (1135–1204) show the Temple in Jerusalem, its surroundings, and much detail, and were prepared to illustrate the Commentaries on the Mishnah [41]. Moses Ben Maimon (better known, perhaps, as Maimonides) was a singularly important figure as an interpreter of the Jewish Code of Laws, and was the author of the *Mishnah Torah*, or code of Maimonides.[3] The extraordinary plan of the Temple in Jerusalem has captions in Hebrew, even

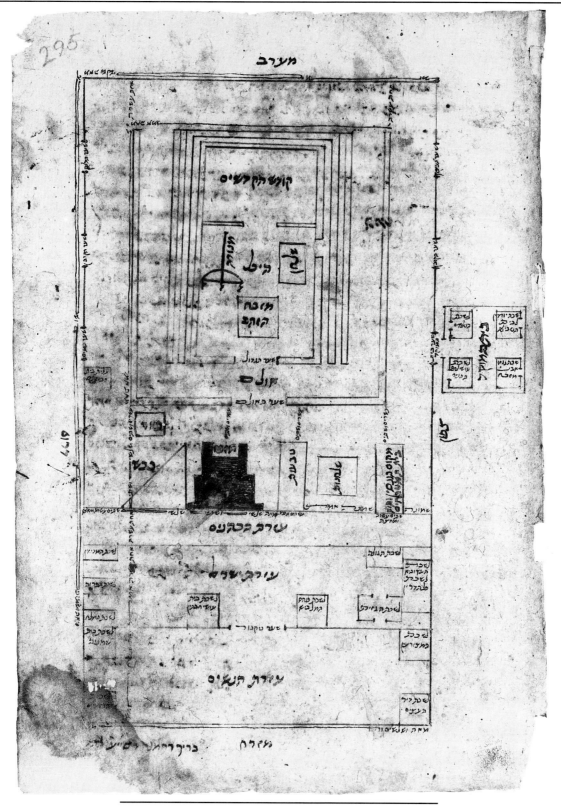

41 *Moses Ben Maimon's plan of the Temple, a twelfth-century version based on* Mishnah (BO. MS. Pococke. 295. fol 295 R).

though the main part of the text is in Arabic. Maimonides's Code was translated into Latin by Louis Compiègne de Veil as *De Cultu Divino, ex Mosis Majemonidae secunda Lege seu Manu Forti Liber VIII* . . . published in Paris in 1678, and reprinted in *Fasciculus sextus Opisculorum quae ad historiam ac philologiam sacram spectant* in Rotterdam in 1696. Another Rotterdam version has a slightly different title: *De Cultu divino ex R. Majemonidae secundae legis, seu manus fortis libro VIII*.

Maimonides's illustrations [41] and those of Richard of St Victor (d.1173) attempt to reconstruct the Temple, including the waters gushing from under the buildings. Richard of St Victor, in his *De Templo Salomonis ad litteram* and in his *De Aedificia Ezechielis*, occasionally called *In Visionem Ezechielis*, went into the problem at length: his plan has a distinct vestibule, the Temple with altar in the centre, and the Holy of Holies beyond. These versions show highly organized buildings, and have a pronounced architectonic quality. In the case of Richard of St Victor he was among the very first to attempt explanations of the sense of the Scriptures, and he was the first to provide drawings (a plan, with three views showing, as would be expected of the period, a Romanesque building). Reproductions of these were printed in Richard's *Opera Omnia*, published in Paris in 1518, in Lyons in 1534, in Venice in 1592, and later in 1650.

Of course there are notorious problems facing the draughtsman who has to work from description alone. The case of the Mausoleum at Halicarnassus is typical and celebrated, for although we have bits of that great Hellenistic building, know much about Greek Architecture, and have a description from Pliny, the variations of interpretation have been many.[4] The difficulties with the Solomonic Temple are compounded by the difference between the account of the building in *I Kings* 6,7 and that in *II Chronicles* 3,4 not to mention the fact that we do not know nearly as much about Jewish Architecture before the Graeco-Roman ascendancy as we do about the Classical language of Architecture. Certain commentators, including Moses Ben Maimon, thought that the Second Temple (that of Zerubbabel, reported in *Ezra*) was largely a rebuild of the Solomonic Temple with additions from the Ezekiel account.

The late thirteenth- and early fourteenth-century Franciscan, Nicolaus de Lyra (1270–1349), acquired his reputation by interpreting the Temple in his *Postilla litteralis* and *Postilla mystica seu moralis*; it is clear he knew Maimonides and other Jewish and Christian sources, but his great importance lies in his attempts to illustrate the complete Temple complex.[5] Moses Ben Maimon's diagram of the Temple seems to have been the model for Nicolaus de Lyra's clear plan, although de Lyra goes into much greater detail, showing a symmetrical ramp to the

altar, columns *in antis*, and a highly organized architectonic arrangement of elements.[6] De Lyra's *Postillae* were printed with all the illustrations in the edition of the Bible published by Anton Koberger as *Postillae super Biblia cum additionibus Pauli Burgensis* in Nürnberg in 1481, 1485, and 1493; other early printed editions include those of Basel (1498 and 1502), Venice (1489 and 1588), and Lyons (1502). The *Postillae* illustrations were not only based on Biblical sources, but were much admired for their quality.[7] Koberger's ground-plan of the Temple is only one of several versions of de Lyra's images, and his woodcuts follow original illustrations in manuscript quite closely [42].

It is perhaps significant to record that Calvin used the term 'temple' to designate churches devoted to his cause, not only to differentiate Calvinist churches from those of other denominations, but to emphasize the Biblical roots of Protestant faith in that he saw his own ministry as a continuation of ancient pre-Roman-Catholic priesthood. By the time of Diderot's *Encyclopédie* in the eighteenth century the French regarded the words 'temple' and 'church' as synonymous, but 'church' was not necessarily applied to Protestant places of worship: in other words a 'church' was not always Protestant, but a 'temple' was if used to describe a Christian place of worship. This fact is very significant when we consider the honours accorded to the Protestants and to Protestantism in Masonic circles in Roman–Catholic countries during the Enlightenment.

Just as the Renaissance turned to Antiquity, so did the Reformation turn to Biblical sources for 'truth' and *Ur-texts*. Franciscus Vatablus (or François Vatable), held a Chair in Hebrew at the Collège de France, and died in Paris in 1547. He appears to have had Protestant leanings, for he was denounced for heresies at one stage, and indeed seems to have had contact, direct or indirect, with Ulrich Zwingli, the Protestant theologian.

Robert Estienne, the publisher, produced an edition of the Bible in 1540 to which he added Vatablus's commentaries that included chapters on Ezekiel together with Vatablus's woodcuts of the Temple (these woodcuts subsequently reappeared in other editions, notably the *Biblia Sacra* of 1573 published in Paris). Variants recur in a 1567 Bible brought out by François Perrin and

42 *Plan of the Temple and precincts in Jerusalem. From Nicolaus de Lyra,* Prologus Primus . . . fratris Nicolai de Lira in testamentum vetus, et . . . Explicit postilla . . . *printed by Koburger, or Koberger, in Nürnberg in 1481* (BL. IC. 7206).

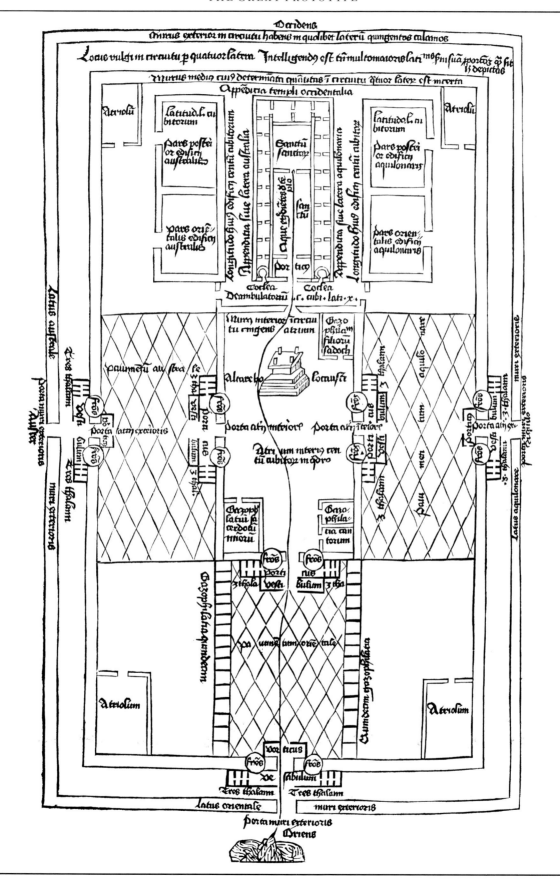

43 *Version of Franciscus Vatablus's (François Vatable)
designs for the Temple of Solomon (which originally appeared
in the Estienne Bible published in Paris in 1540), from the
edition published in Venice in 1648. Similar illustrations were
printed in the François Perrin/Antoine Vincent Bible of 1567,
and there were many other close copies made over the years. Note
the fact that the roof is removed* (left) *to permit the Ark and
Cherubim to be seen. Jachin and Boaz, with globular*
chapiters, *stand in front of the main façade. The view of the
Temple with courts and altar bears a strong resemblance to the
illustrations of Masonic Lodges published in the 'exposures' of
the eighteenth century (cf. 24, 25, for example) (UGLE).*

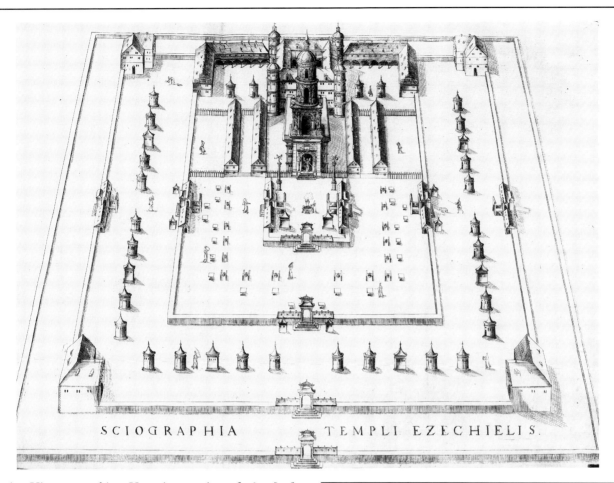

SCIOGRAPHIA   TEMPLI EZECHIELIS.

Antoine Vincent, and in a Venetian version of 1648 [43]. Not only is the Temple shown with the roof off so that the Ark could be depicted, but Jachin and Boaz are indicated with globes on top as 'chapiters'. Now these illustrations are very significant, for the details are proto-Masonic, while the method of illustration and present-ation seem to herald later illustrations of Freemasons' Lodges.

The Vatablus woodcuts appeared again in the editions of the Bible published by Estienne in 1545 and 1546, and in another published in Geneva in 1557; they were also used by Jean de Tournes in a French Bible of 1551 published in Lyons, and in a Frankfurt-am-Main Bible of 1571. Another Geneva edition by Estienne of 1560 (this time a translation) also included an aerial view of the Temple with a key.

Matthias Hafenreffer (1561–1619) produced a *Templum Ezechielis* in Tübingen in 1613 [44] based on an axial scheme with Solomon's Palace situated behind the Temple. Hafenreffer was a Protestant who favoured an ordered axial arrangement for his 'reconstruction' based on Ezekiel, but he clearly knew Vatablus's work, for he used one of his designs in his own book.

Further plans of the Solomonic and Ezekiel Temples

were published, notably by Sebastian Châtillon in his Bible published in Basel in 1551 with subsequent editions. Hector Pinto in his *In Ezechielem Prophetam commentaria*, published in Salamanca in 1568, merges various ideas, including those of Richard of St Victor and of Hugh of St Cher's *Postillae in sacram scripturam . . .* printed in the Basel Bible of 1498. Benedictus Arias Montano, in his *Exemplar*, published in Antwerp in 1572 in the Antwerp Polyglot Bible, included three illus-trations of the Temple which were subsequently reprinted in Leyden in 1593, in London in 1660, and in Amsterdam in 1698. He included much material from the *Middoth*,[8] and clearly considered all three Jewish Temples (those of Solomon, Zerubbabel, and Herod) as real, rather than symbolic, ideal, or visionary buildings.

While Protestants had certainly concerned themselves with matters relating to the Temple, investigation of the

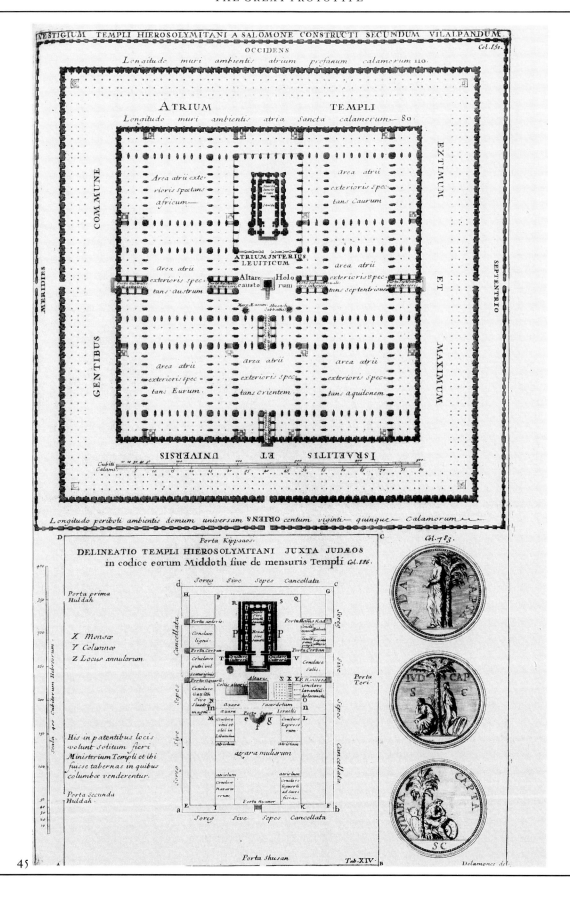

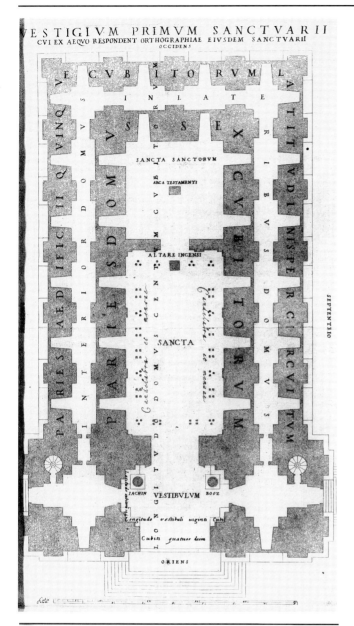

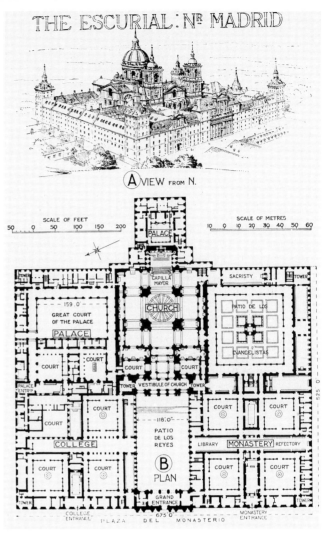

47 *The Escurial (Escorial), near Madrid, showing the plan and a view from the north. The plan has certain close affinities with Villalpando's interpretation of the Temple in Jerusalem. From Sir Banister Fletcher's* A History of Architecture on the Comparative Method *(London, 1954), p759 (R.I.B.A. British Architectural Library)*

46 *Detail of the plan of the Temple by Villalpando showing the porch and Jachin and Boaz, from his* De Postrema . . . *(UGLE).*

45 *Plan of the Temple and its precincts in Jerusalem by Juan Bautista Villalpando from his* De Postrema Ezechielis Prophetae Visione, *published in Rome in 1631. The highly regular plan should be noted. This version of Villalpando's Temple is from Plate XIV of Lamy. As well as Villalpando's plan this plate shows (bottom) a plan based on* Middoth: *note the wide front of the Temple, similar to the version proposed by Perrault (BL. 691. k. 15).*

subject received a considerable boost when the Jesuits Hieronymo Prado and Juan Bautista Villalpando produced their *In Ezechielem Explanationes et Apparatus Urbis ac Templi Hierosolymitani, commentariis et imaginibus illustratus* in Rome from 1596 to 1631. The illustrations in the volume entitled *De Postrema Ezechielis Prophetae Visione* (Rome, 1631) showed the Temple with a highly organized plan and elevations of considerable grandeur; in fact, they were certainly a cut above any earlier designs, but they assumed that the Temples of *Chronicles, Kings,* and *Ezekiel* were one and the same, and that the Herodian Temple was a myth [45, 46]. Villalpando insisted on the claim that the Solomonic Temple was designed by God, was therefore perfect, and was the great forerunner of the Christian church: the idea that the Architects of the Temple had been divinely inspired, and that Classical Orders derived from the Temple, and therefore from God, was firmly planted. Furthermore, Villalpando proposed that only by producing accurate architectural drawings of the Temple could the essence of the prophetic visions in the Bible be understood: this seems to be an allusion to the Art of Memory, in a somewhat roundabout way.

The odd thing about Villalpando's version of the Temple is that it is more a grandiose Renaissance building than a reconstruction based on historical analysis. Villalpando's Temple was a stunning image *in Renaissance terms* of the Architecture which he imagined God had created: not only the forms and proportions, but the Orders of Architecture, were designed from the divinely inspired Order of the Temple. He connected Classicism, Vitruvius, and Holy Writ in an attempt to demonstrate that Christian Revelation and Classical Antiquity were compatible, and there are indications that the whole process of disentangling an Architecture from the clues in the Bible was seen in similar terms to proceeding through a labyrinth. It is interesting that the descriptions in Ezekiel were called *mysteriorum Dei labyrinthum* by St Jerome himself in his *Commentariorum in Ezechielem Prophetam*, while allegorical meanings were also the concern of St Gregory in *Homiliarum in Ezechielem*, of Bede in *De Templo Salomonis*, and of other early commentators.[9] Themes recur, merge, and overlap.

Villalpando's plan resembles that of the Escorial Palace, near Madrid [47], designed by Juan Bautista de Toledo and Juan de Herrera for King Philip II, and which again has a curious iconography, discussed at length by René Taylor elsewhere.[10] In the Escorial ideas of the Temple, the tomb, the monastery, the palace, and the pattern combine with symbols of martyrdom, with the Signs of the Zodiac, and with Hermetic-Alchemical-Astrological ideas. The religious and mystical nature of the King, his ascetic habits, his devotional routine, his

interest in relics (he had a vast collection amassed not only from piety, but for reasons of belief in their beneficent and medicinal qualities), and the various uses of the Escorial (including that of mausoleum for the Catholic monarchs of Spain) all found a place on the extraordinary building. Even the angle-towers of the Escorial and the form of the plan have been suggested to represent the bases and design of the grid-iron on which St Laurence suffered his martyrdom (Pope Gregory XIII presented a pot full of the melted fat of St Laurence to the King of Spain, which may help to explain this complicated allusion).[11]

Herrera himself is known to have been a Lullist, that is influenced by Ramón Lull (1232–c.1316), who was a mystic, philosopher, and who sought to unite Roman Catholic, Jew, and Moslem by means of their common philosophical, mystical, and scientific beliefs. Lull was a Christian Cabbalist, and some of his ideas permeated Renaissance Neoplatonism.[12] Herrera himself owned a large collection of Hermetic writings, and had taught Villalpando. Both Juan Bautista de Toledo and Herrera were involved in astrological investigations, and in studies of the occult, and it seems obvious that the Escorial designs may have influenced Villalpando for the illustrations of the Temple in his *In Ezechielem Explanationes*. Through Herrera and other influences Villalpando was steeped in Vitruvian ideas, and was concerned to interpret descriptions in *Chronicles* and in *Ezekiel* as part of a syncretic Biblical/Christian/Architectural study.

It also must be considered whether or not the Escorial was itself influenced by descriptions of the Temple: from the complexities of intermingled iconographies prevalent at the time it would seem highly probable. The Escorial was certainly influenced by Lullism, by Vitruvian patterns, and by ideas concerning the order and harmony of the universe. It is a design so full of astrological, magical, religious, geometrical, and other allusions that it cannot be discussed at length here. René Taylor[13] covers the Hermetic and other aspects in considerable detail and with enormous erudition [47].

If the Escorial was based on the Temple, then Philip of Spain was identified with Solomon himself, and indeed that was so, for Fray José de Sigüenza, in his *Tercera parte de la Historia de la Orden de San Geronimo*, published in Madrid in 1605, refers to the new Temple of Solomon and to the fact that Philip attempted to imitate Solomon in his works.[14] Villalpando's Temple, like Herrera's Escorial, was a symbol of the Almighty's creation, and held within it systems of hierarchy and of universal order. Its connection with the design of the Escorial is interesting, for that curious pile has strong astrological allusions, and mixes Hermetic, Solomonic, Christian, Jewish, and other symbols and connections with ideas of

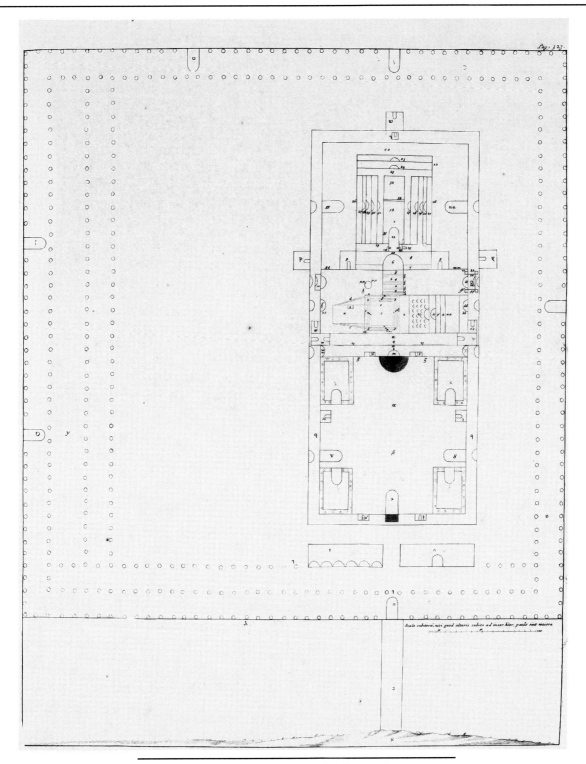

48 *Plan of the Temple and its court by Constantinus*
L'Empereur from Part 5 of Guglielmus Surenhusius's
Mishnah sive Legum Mischnicarum liber qui inscribitur
Ordo Sacrorum, etc . . . *(Amsterdam, 1702). This is based*
on Moses Ben Maimon, and the parallels with designs for
Lodges will be clear (BL. 15c. 7–12).

De binnenhof des Tempels, met het altaar, en de koperе kolommen.   Inwying van Salomons Tempel.

49 *The inner courtyard of the Temple in Jerusalem with the Temple façade, altar, and the two columns of brass, from* Histoire les Plus Remarquables de l'Ancien et du Nouveau Testament, *by J. Cóvens and C. Mortier (Amsterdam, 1732). This plate, by Jan Luyken, is from the French version of* Afbeeldingen der merkwaardigste Geschiedenissen van het Oude en Nieuwe Testament *published in 1729. The Temple is based on the version in Villalpando's work, except that it also has Jachin and Boaz, which signify the Solomonic rather than the later Temple. The plate also shows the Ark with Cherubims in the Holy of Holies, the altar, and the 'molten sea' carried on two rows of oxen* (UGLE).

harmony, organization, syncretism, and Vitruvian architecture. In this respect it is a very interesting problem to compare attempts to recreate the Solomonic Temple as the palace-cum-church of a Catholic monarch with an eighteenth-century church of enormous verve and Baroque swagger in which ideas of Imperial grandeur mingle with allusions to Antiquity and to the Temple: this will be discussed shortly.

The impact of Villalpando's images was enormous, and had a profound influence on many interpreters, including Surenhusius, although the latter's *Mishnah* included a version of the Temple plan [48] that owes more to Maimonides than to Villalpando. The elevational treatment of the buildings, however, is derived from Villalpando, while the early eighteenth-century plates by Jan Luyken [49] are also strongly influenced by the earlier images. Matthaeus Merian the Elder (1593–1650) produced an extraordinary version in his *Icones Bibliae*, which, like the Escorial and Hafenreffer's vision, is a unified composition [50]. No less a figure than Sir Isaac Newton devoted *A Description of the Temple of Solomon* to a study of the measurements of the Temple which was published in 1728 in *Chronology of Ancient Kingdoms Amended*; it contains a plan of the Temple symmetrically arranged. It is extraordinary to consider

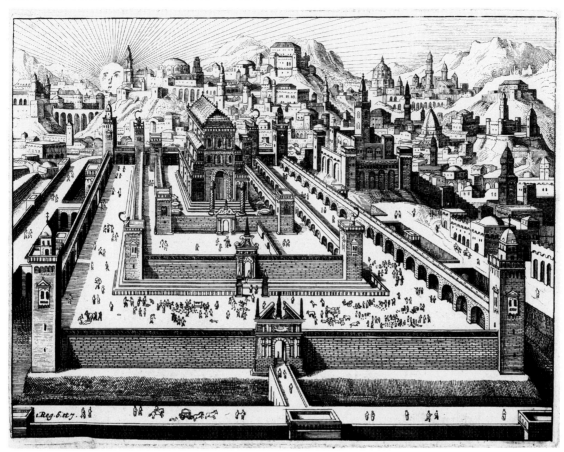

the attitudes of Newton, the hero of the Enlightenment, for his stance on architectural history was based more on his Unitarian and anti-Papist principles than on reason. The book attempts to determine the dates of events in Antiquity from astronomical considerations, and mixes mythological and historical happenings.

Newton's volume had a profound influence on John Wood Snr (also Unitarian and anti-Papist), the man who brought Palladianism to Bath, Bristol, and Liverpool, and author of *The Origin of Building: or, the Plagiarism of the Heathens Detected*, published in Bath in 1741. Wood was obsessed by Masonic symbolism and by mystic considerations. He saw Solomon's Temple as a hieroglyph of Jewish history, and built up the importance of Jewish planning and Architecture in preference to Vitruvian writings, of which he was profoundly suspicious, because Vitruvius was a 'pagan' and, in Wood's view, had plagiarized Jewish ideas. In *The Origin of Building* Wood speaks of Lodges being dug in the mountains, and of rocks as symbols of soundness and the foundations of wisdom. Wood wallowed in Celtic prehistory, and was himself a Freemason who believed the Orders were divinely ordained and first used in the Temple of Solomon.

He saw Bath as a place with temples to the sun and

50 *View of the Temple in Jerusalem by Matthias Merian, from his* Icones Bibliae. *This copy is from a scrapbook collection of engravings at Freemasons' Hall assembled by Antoine-Louis Moret and entitled* Recueil de vignettes religieuses et maçonniques . . . (UGLE).

moon, the capital of the Ancient Britons, and as Troy. The new city, with its square, terrace, crescent, forum, and circus, was, in fact, a series of mystical symbols, clothed in Classical Orders that were not Graeco-Roman but Divine. Royal Crescent was connected with the crescent-moon of Isis-Minerva-Diana-Onca, and King's Circus was a mixture of an Ancient British Temple of the Sun and the Zerubbabel Temple in Jerusalem (an idea derived from the circular visions of the Temple promoted by the Dome of the Rock, the Church of the Holy Sepulchre, Templar churches, and illustrations of the Temple as circular Pantheons by Heemskerck and others). In this book is a plan of King Solomon's Temple [51] that seems to show a rigidly symmetrical scheme owing more to Classical Antiquity and to Newton than to the plans of Constantin L'Empereur or Maimonides.

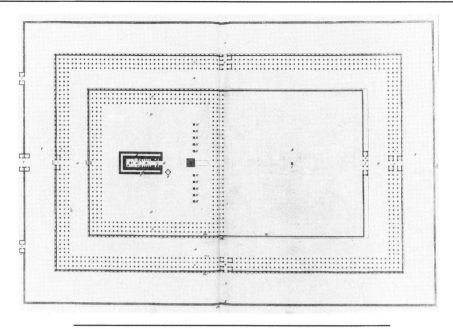

51 *Plan of the Temple in Jerusalem and its precincts by John Wood, from Plates 24 and 25 of his* The Origin of Building: or, the Plagiarism of the Heathens Detected *(Bath, 1741)* (UGLE).

52

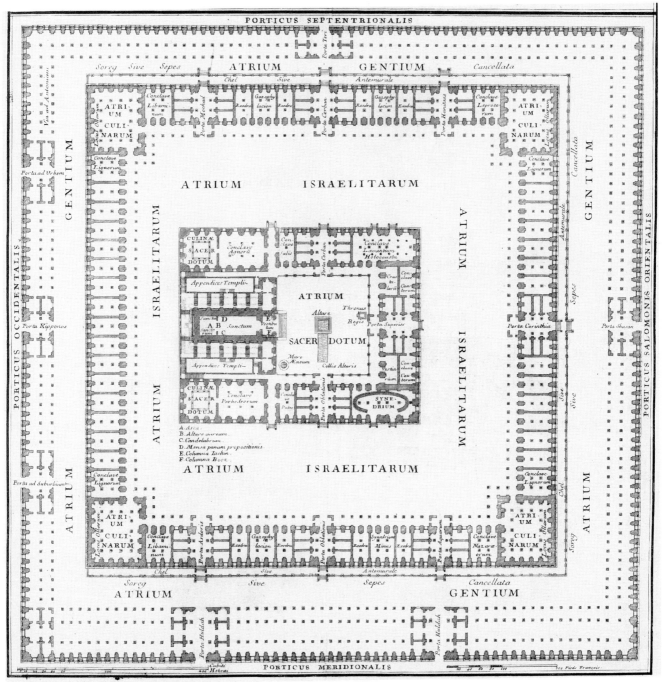

52 *Plate X from Lamy. This Sublime reconstruction of the Temple in Jerusalem has overtones of Fischer von Erlach, and anticipates Boullée* (BL. 691. k. 15).

53 *Plate XII from Lamy. The plan of the Temple in Jerusalem differs from the influential work of Villalpando; indeed Lamy had little regard for Villalpando, and returned to* Chronicles *for his sources as well as to the* Mishnah. *Jachin and Boaz are shown in the Temple vestibule* (BL. 691. k. 15).

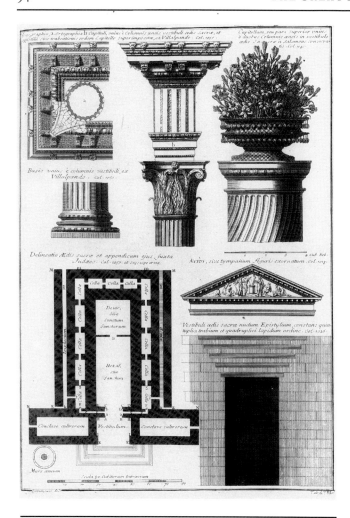

54 *Plate XVIII from Lamy. Details of Lamy's reconstruction of the Temple, showing the 'chapiters', a plan of the Temple, and certain comparisons with Villalpando's work. Note the spiral fluting of the column* (BL. 691. k. 15).

Yet, if Vitruvian ideas and Classical Architecture derived from the Temple of Solomon and from God, this was hardly surprising. Classical Architecture, anticipated in Biblical times, with the Classical orders Divinely inspired, was also the theme of Villalpando's thesis in his commentaries on Ezekiel. What was the reason for this? It was clearly to free Classical Architecture from the stigma of pagan origins and thus enable it to be used in Christian churches and in Christian cities (whether Roman Catholic or Protestant). Wood constructed a Classical church within the ruined nave of Llandaff Cathedral in 1734–52 (demolished 1850), which was a hypothetical reconstruction of the inner court of the Solomonic Temple. The masonry of Llandaff's choir was

to Wood Romano-Christian, and thus a direct descendant of the Temple built by Hiram using proportions and measurements that had esoteric and Divine symbolism. According to Wood, Bath Abbey had the dimensions of Noah's Ark, of the Tabernacle, and of Solomon's Temple. These matters are discussed further in Mowl and Earnshaw's recent work (see Bibliography).

More extraordinary because of the stripped-down, primitivist, and forward-looking plates, was Bernard Lamy's *De Tabernaculo Foederis, de Sancta Civitate Jerusalem et de Templo EJUS*, published in Paris in 1720, which depicts a vast stepped platform on a scale worthy of Boullée, while the Temple itself is a severe almost Neoclassical design [see 45, 52, 55]. The wide vestibule and Ledoux-like character of the building point to the Karlskirche and to Chaux, both, as we will see, with strong Masonic connections. There are certain stylistic similarities to Perrault's treatment of the same theme in Compiègne de Veil's *De Cultu Divino . . .*

Fischer von Erlach

It is clear from published sources alone that during the sixteenth-, seventeenth-, and early eighteenth-century periods Jewish, Catholic, Protestant, and other traditions influenced each other, mingling with Hermetic, symbolic, and many other themes at the same time.[15] We have noted the curious coming together of ideas in the Palace of a Roman–Catholic King at the Escorial, but there is another great masterpiece of Catholic Architecture that has overt Temple and Masonic themes.

Johann Bernhard Fischer von Erlach (1656–1723) met the scholarly Jesuit Athanasius Kircher (1602–80) in Rome.[16] Kircher was one of the first to attempt serious studies of Egyptian and Egyptianizing artefacts in Rome, and himself owned a vast collection of such objects. Fischer absorbed many theories while in Rome, as well as acquiring a thorough grounding in the Architecture of Italy and France. His *Entwurff Einer Historischen Architektur* of 1721, however, contains interpretations of Egyptian Architecture that owe more to imagination than to fact, and indeed had an influence on later Architects such as Boullée, whose vast pyramids with ramps up the sides are clearly derived from Fischer's plates. Fischer believed that Classical Architecture derived from the Temple of Solomon [56], and this Masonic idea was further expanded in his work by tracing the development of Architecture in Ancient Egypt, Persia, Greece, and in non-European countries. Fischer clearly knew his written sources well, and gives chapter and verse for them (his versions of the Temple of Solomon are based on Villalpando). Where possible, he tried to get drawings of buildings or of ruins, and this helped him to achieve

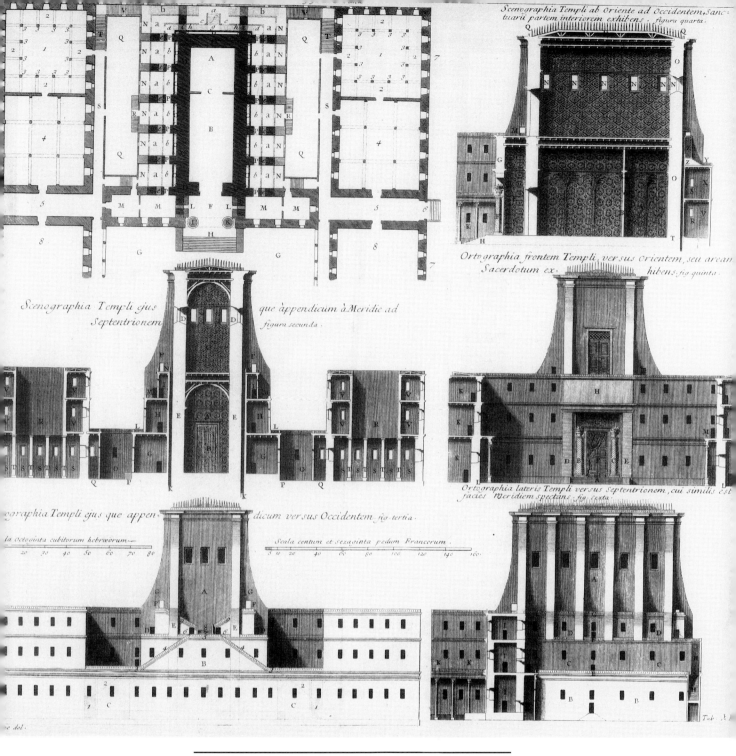

Scenographia Templi ab Oriente ad Occidentem, Sanctuarii partem interiorem exhibens. figura quarta.

Ortographia frontem Templi, versus Orientem, seu aream Sacerdotum ex- hibens, fig. quinta.

Scenographia Templi ejus que àppendicum àMeridie ad Septentrionem, figura secunda.

Ortographia lateris Templi versus Septentrionem, cui similis est facies Meridiem spectans, fig. sexta.

ographia Templi ejus que appen- dicum versus Occidentem, fig. tertia.

Scala octoginta cubitorum hebræorum
20 30 40 50 60 70 80

Scala centum et sexaginta pedum Francorum.
5 10 20 40 60 80 100 120 140 160

55 *Plate XIX from Lamy. The extraordinary details of the Temple, showing the severe proto-Neoclassical style. The plan (top)* and elevation (middle right) *show Jachin and Boaz in the vestibule with their spiral flutings and 'chapiters' (see 54)* (BL. 691. k. 15).

some accuracy. He was acquainted with the philosophy of Leibnitz and derived from it his own theocentric ideas of the world, where God was the greatest of all Architects (a significantly Masonic and Isiac notion).

His enthusiasm for Antiquity was perhaps fired by the antiquarians he had met at the Court of Queen Christina, and his cosmopolitan circle of friends included many in Protestant Northern Europe. It is more than likely that he met Christopher Wren when he visited London in 1704, and it is most unlikely that he avoided all contact with Freemasonry, for indeed some of the ideas expressed in his *Entwurff*, and especially his looking back to the Temple of Solomon and to Egypt, might suggest that he was a Freemason himself. It will be recalled that there were many Freemasons in Prince Eugen's entourage, and that Freemasonry seems to have reached Vienna through Masonic influences in the Netherlands. Fischer's use of architectural elements was eclectic in the extreme: one has only to analyse the brilliant Karlskirche in Vienna to find many strands [57–60].

The Case of the Karlskirche

The Emperor Charles VI (1711–40) vowed in 1713 to build a great church to deliver the city of Vienna from the Plague. It was to be dedicated to the Emperor's Patron Saint, St Charles Borromeo, and was to be a memorial to the last Habsburg King of Spain and to the dream of uniting the Crowns of the Empire and of Spain, as Charles V had done. The Karlskirche draws elements from several sources which Fischer harmonized in one composition. The Temple in Jerusalem is well to the fore, as would be expected from one who believed that it was the basis from which Architecture itself developed, but it is alluded to in an astonishing way: two massive columns [58] on either side of the great prostyle hexastyle Corinthian portico look like Trajanic columns, but they carry on their spirals reliefs representing scenes from St Charles Borromeo's life and the miracles he performed after his death.[17] These columns were also the Emperor's own emblem, inherited from Charles V, who had adopted the Pillars of Hercules (discussed above) to symbolize the *Plus Ultra*, or more beyond, of his great Empire: the 'Pillars' therefore carry the Crown of Spain flanked by the eagles of the Holy Roman Empire. The deeds of St Charles also allude to the *Constantia Et Fortitudo* of the Emperor Charles VI: Leibnitz had proposed that ancestors and namesakes of the Emperor should also be celebrated, and their deeds represented on the shafts of the columns, but this was not realized.[18] The columns also allude to Jachin and Boaz, and so the Temple, and their spirals are not only Trajanic, but Masonic and Solomonic, as will be made clear in this study.

TA:II

56 *Fischer von Erlach's version of Villalpando's Temple of Solomon from* Entwurff (SJSM).

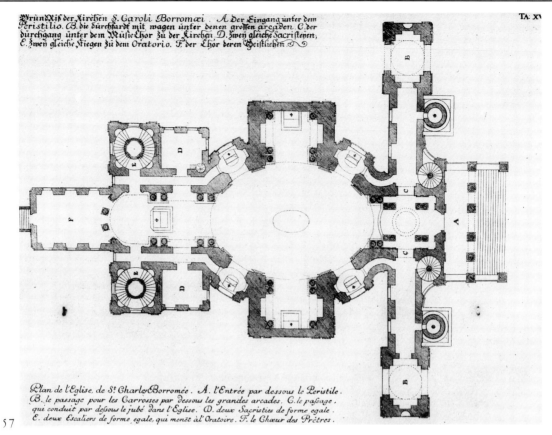

Plan de l'Eglise, de St Charles Borromée. A. l'Entrée par dessous le Peristile.
B. le passage pour les Carrosses par dessous les grandes arcades. C. le passage.
qui conduit par dessous le jubé dans l'Eglise. D. deux Sacristies de forme egale.
E. deux Escaliers de forme egale, qui menet àl'Oratoire. F. le Chœur des Prêtres.

57

58

59

60

57–60
57 *Plan;* **58** *prospect or liturgical west front;* **59** *side (liturgical south) elevation, and* **60** *east-west section of the Karlskirche, Vienna, from* Entwurff. *This extraordinary building employs the concave front flanked by Baroque towers and dominant dome of Borromini's Santa Agnese in Agone in Rome, but applies a prostyle portico in the Antique manner of the Pantheon, together with two spiral columns (which allude to Antiquity through the Trajanic model, to the deeds of Saint*

Carl Borromeo, to the Pillars of Hercules, to the Imperial theme of plus ultra, *to Jachin and Boaz, and to the Solomonic Temple). The long narrow passage linking the towers is a clear reference to the porch or vestibule of the Temple in Jerusalem, and indicates that Fischer von Erlach probably knew some of the illustrations to the Code of Maimonides. The Karlskirche is an extraordinary synthesis of Baroque, Borrominiesque, Biblical, Imperial, Antique, Talmudic, and iconographical themes all in one building (SJSM).*

Titus habens Solymas, flammis radicitus vrit et templum donis opulentum & numine summ

61 *Martin van Heemskerck's version of the destruction of the Temple of Solomon in Jerusalem in an engraving by Philip Galle. Note the Two 'Pillars', the twisted 'barley-sugar' columns* in antis *of the porch, and the domed form of the building* (Bild-Archiv der Österreichischen Nationalbibliothek, Vienna).

The great portico, reminiscent of Antiquity, with the dome behind, recalls the Roman Pantheon, but also derives from images of the Temple as a domed form with the Two Pillars standing in front of the steps, as in Martin van Heemskerck's drawing of the Temple of Jerusalem. Van Heemskerck used Corinthian columns for the Two Pillars, but twisted 'barley-sugar' types for the portico of the Temple itself [61]. The allusion is further reinforced by Leon Battista Alberti's constant references to temples in his *De re aedificatoria*: temples to the sun should be circular, while the temple of Vesta should be like a ball, he observed, and he calls all places of worship 'temples'. The circular form of the church of the Holy Sepulchre in Jerusalem and the circular Templar churches modelled on it and on the so-called Dome of the Rock (which was used as a church by the Templars and which stood on the great rock associated with the Temple) had potent symbolic, allusory, and visual properties. Other important circular or polygonal structures include the great church at Aachen built by Charlemagne, San Stefano Rotondo in Rome, and many Renaissance and Baroque designs (many of which never got off the drawing-board). This important connection between the Dome of the Rock, the church of the Holy Sepulchre, Templar churches in London, and round churches (Cambridge, Ludlow Castle, and the Holy Sepulchre in Northampton are but three examples) must be stressed, for ideas of round churches persisted as holy places for Orders and Brotherhoods: Montsalvat in *Parsifal* is one example, and there were others. Round forms suggest wholeness, completeness, and the protection of the outer circumference; they are apposite to Closed Orders or to meeting-places, as is amply demonstrated by the polygonal plans of so many English

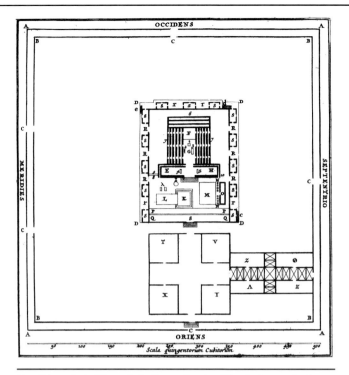

62 *Plan of the Temple in Jerusalem by Claude Perrault, from Maimonides. Note the extremely wide vestibule* (BL. 3129. aa. 20).

63 *Elevations of the Temple in Jerusalem by Claude Perrault, from Maimonides. Note the primitivist pylon-like front to the Temple, heralding Neoclassical stripped simplicity of more than a century later* (BL. 3129. aa. 20).

Chapter Houses. The circular form of the Roman Pantheon and that of the cathedral at Aachen both suggested Imperial connotations with Antiquity and with the beginnings of the Holy Roman Empire itself.

The Temple allusion of the Karlskirche is reinforced by the statues of Church and Synagogue placed on either side of the steps leading to the portico, and the reference to Roman Antiquity is further emphasized by the resemblance of the pedimented portico of the Karls-kirche to that of the Temple of Concordia that stood in the *Forum Romanum*. Within the tympanum is sculpture depicting Vienna's deliverance from the Plague as a result of St Charles's intervention, while at the apex of the pediment is a statue of the Saint as Intercessor for Mankind, and therefore embodying one of the Three Theological Virtues, namely Charity. The other two Virtues, Faith and Hope, stand on top of the towers [see 58]. The precedents of Hagia Sophia in Constantinople and of St Peter's in Rome also played their parts.

Fischer was also influenced by Mansart's *Église des Minimes* and the *Dôme des Invalides* in Paris, but there is another precedent that is quite clear: Borromini's church of Santa Agnese in Agone in the Piazza Navona in Rome, with its concave front, flanking towers, and dome. Fischer himself had experimented with a concave front earlier in Salzburg, at the Dreifaltigkeitskirche, com-pleted in 1702. The composition is similar, and the elliptical plan of the great dome derives from Roman Baroque precedents, notably the work of Borromini. Certain echoes of Wren's work at St Paul's also occur, but the influence of Borromini is stronger. Fischer's eclectic composition glorified the Emperor as a second Solomon and as the successor to the Roman Emperors (an idea we have already encountered at the Escorial, and in reference to Aachen and the Pantheon in Rome), and this complex iconographical notion was fully understood by contemporaries.[19]

There is another odd aspect of the plan that seems to have escaped commentators: the very wide front, with its terminating tower-pavilions and passages to which the Two Pillars are attached is strange in the extreme. Why is

it like that? A probable explanation is that the porch of the Temple was wider by thirty Cubits than the House proper behind it, and resembled a bema or transept,[20] according to *Mishnah* 7 of *Middoth* 4. This wide porch is shown [62,63] in Claude Perrault's illustration of the Temple from the *Mishnah Torah*, or Code of Maimonides, translated into Latin by Louis Compiègne de Veil, and published in Paris in 1678. Perrault showed a stark, blank wall with a vast entrance-door reminiscent of the Neoclassicists' work of a century and more later, but Perrault's drawing shows something else: the vast porch could become two Egyptian pylons with very little alteration. Thus the wide porch had Egyptianizing connotations that would have been obvious to those Architects working at the end of the eighteenth and beginning of the nineteenth centuries when the great Egyptological publications came out [63]. A further device is found inside the church (which on plan and elevation has certain phallic properties): this is the equilateral triangle with the sign of Yahweh set in a burst of radiant light. Thus the Karlskirche contains within its composition and iconography many features familiar in Masonic design, and it is an astonishing, fascinating, and remarkable building.

The Spiral Columns

One more point needs to be made concerning the Karlskirche and the two 'Trajanic' or 'Hercules' columns. The spiral form has itself Solomonic conno-tations, for the twisted, barley-sugar, or spiral column was illustrated by a number of artists in representations of the Temple. Heemskerck used twisted columns [see 61] as did Jean Foucquet in the *Antiquités Judaïques* illustrations now in the Bibliothèque Nationale in Paris. Raphael also used twisted columns in the cartoon showing the Healing of the Lame at the Beautiful Gate now in the Victoria and Albert Museum in London. Bernini also used twisted columns in his *Baldacchino* in St Peter's, Rome, but these were allusions to the twisted columns, some of which were supposedly looted from the Temple,[21] that adorned the Constantinian basilica. Indeed, the basilica had twelve spiral columns in the sanctuary over the tomb of St Peter, so they were part of a monument with a prestige unmatched anywhere else in Western Christendom.[22] It is clear that the twisted 'Solomonic' form was seen as exotic, eastern, Biblical, sacred, and associated with holy places, which explains why it recurs in Romanesque columns and piers, and in the Baroque period, notably on altarpieces and in canopies over altars.

A variant is the column with vines twined around, or the column around which serpents twisted. Ribart de

64 *Plate II of Ribart, showing the garlanded spiral form of the proposed French Order, based on the spirals associated with Continental Lodges, with the Temple, and with Antiquity. (Top) Type of the French Order showing its origin, and (bottom) the French Order Developed, showing the triple columns used in an arcade and the triple, garlanded columns in the circular temple* (Butler Library, Columbia University in the City of New York).

MONUMENT FRANÇOIS OU NATIONAL

Chamoust's *L'Ordre François trouvé dans la Nature* of 1783 proposes a 'French Order' in which plants twine around the shafts of columns, and where nature is the begetter of the Order, an idea derived from Laugier and others [64,65]. Of course the spiral garland or snake wound round pillars suggests the forms found in circular labyrinths, just as the Greek-key forms derived from square labyrinths. Serpents are associated with wisdom (very Isiac), while in a circular form, that is with their tails in their mouths, they symbolize eternity or everlasting life. The *caduceus* of Hermes, with its twining serpents, was an enchanter's wand, producing prosperity and wealth, but it also signified influences over the living and the dead. Asclepius, who could heal, and even resurrect the dead, is associated with snakes, the symbols of rejuvenation and prophecy, which are often depicted twined around his staff. Incubation-cures were sought in the temples of Asclepius, who later became identified with Serapis, the Graeco-Roman version of Osiris (incubation involved sleeping within temple precincts, or in special rooms in the temple compound set aside for the purpose).

The Masonic overtones that are clear in the Karlskirche and in Ribart's publication became startling in the eighteenth century, and it was in France that some of the most interesting Masonic Architecture developed. We first need to look briefly at certain events in Britain, however, before we turn to France.

65 *Plate III from Ribart, showing the triple form of the French Order, that is three columns on a triangular base. This triangular base, three columns, and the spirals, make the French Order indubitably Masonic* (BL. CUP. 22. s. 14).

CHAPTER 5

MASONIC DESIGN AND ARCHITECTURE

**Introduction; Eighteenth-Century Certificates and
Grand Lodge in London; Freemasonry in Europe; Freemasonry
and Neoclassicism; Freemasonry and Egyptian
Elements in Neoclassical Architecture; Antoine-Chrysostôme
Quatremère de Quincy; Freemasonry becomes Overt**

Taking all the available evidence into account, we are satisfied
that the inception and establishment of Grand Lodge in 1716 or 1717
was not a pure invention of Anderson.

Douglas Knoop and G. P. Jones
The Genesis of Freemasonry
Manchester, 1949, p168

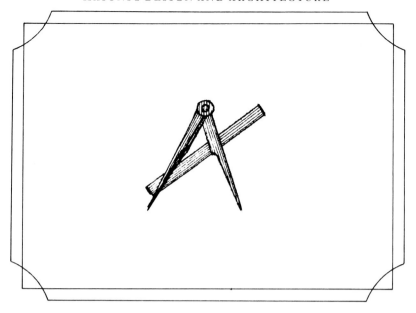

Introduction

To be an Accepted Mason became socially respectable by the end of the seventeenth century in England, although gentlemen in Scotland had been joining Masonic Lodges much earlier. Lodges developed into social and convivial societies, and, by the second decade of the eighteenth century, four London Lodges united to form a Grand Lodge with the objects of promoting benevolence and brotherly sentiments, and of giving help to Brethren (although it also seems to have been formed to purge Freemasons of Jacobite tendencies after the 1715 Rebellion, and to consolidate English Freemasonry in the Whig and Hanoverian cause). This London Grand Lodge was the progenitor of other Lodges at home and abroad, and from 1717 it began to regulate the constitutions of the various groups in existence. In 1721 Dr James Anderson was appointed to oversee the production of a *Book of Constitutions* [66] to contain the history, charges, regulations, and Master's Song which duly appeared in 1723.[1]

The Masonic literature is endless[2] on the subject of the regulations, who was a Mason and who was not, and readers who wish to delve into it have plenty of sources to examine. Knoop and Jones on the *Genesis of Freemasonry* and Bernard E. Jones's *Guide and Compendium* should satisfy the most voracious appetites. It is beyond the scope of the present work to go over all that ground again: visual and architectural aspects are the topics with which this book is concerned.

Eighteenth-century certificates and Grand Lodge in London

Eighteenth-century Masonic certificates and printed summonses (in themselves a major study) are often embellished with emblems and motifs, including the Tuscan, Doric, Ionic, and Corinthian Orders of Architecture. A summons of the West India & American Lodge of the Most Ancient & Honourable Society of Free & Accepted Masons of 1760 shows pairs of columns of Corinthian, Tuscan, and Ionic Orders on which stand the Theological and Cardinal Virtues [67]. Other summonses feature various familiar Masonic motifs [68,69]. The three sets of columns of three Orders derive from mixing some of the associations of columns and pillars outlined above with ideas of Strength, Wisdom, and Beauty: Doric for Strength, Ionic for Wisdom, and Corinthian for Beauty seem to have been the allusions. On occasion Masonic certificates and summonses will show two columns (Jachin and Boaz) of two different Orders, each supporting a globe, the iconography of which has previously been discussed. With Wisdom on one side and Beauty on the other, the original associations of Jachin and Boaz become obscured. The problem here is that Palladian and Rococo sensibilities tended to be removed from the intensities of Renaissance-Hermetic ideas, and there is a general watering-down and confusion of symbol and emblem, although the objects themselves are often of great beauty and are finely crafted.

As many of these interesting summons cards make

66 *Frontispiece of* The Constitutions of the Free-Masons *published in London in 1723. This appears to have been the first printed constitution of any speculative Masonic body (i.e. the Premier Grand Lodge of England, founded 1717). Note the proof of Euclid's forty-seventh proposition on the pavement and the Five Orders of Architecture* (UGLE).

67 *A Summons to attend the duties of the West India &*
American Lodge of the Most Ancient & Honourable Society
of Free & Accepted Masons at the Queen's Arms Tavern in
St Paul's Churchyard, 1760. Note the Corinthian, Tuscan,
and Ionic Orders of Architecture: in Masonic iconography
Doric is equated with strength, Ionic with wisdom, and
Corinthian with beauty. On the left are the Three Theological
Virtues of (from left) Charity (with children), Hope (with
Anchor), and Faith (with book), while on the right (from the
left) are Fortitude and Wisdom as Minerva, Strength as
Hercules, and Beauty as Venus (presumably). Other Virtues
in Masonry are Prudence, Temperance, and Justice, while
Initiates are taught the importance of Secrecy, Fidelity, and
Obedience. Note the palm-trees as Nilotic motifs, an allusion
to Egypt (GLCL).

68 *A Summons to attend the duties of the Lodge of Unity at*
the Horn Tavern, Doctor's Commons, St Paul's, of 1813.
Like that of the West India and American Lodge there are
three Orders and an arch. The figure of Charity has acquired an
Egyptian head-dress, and the chequered floor is Masonic,
consisting of a multiplicity of squares, symbolizing the chequered
life of man, and alluding to crafted floors of Antiquity. The
Nilotic theme is emphasized by the cornucopia (a symbol of Isis
and the fecundity associated with the flooding of the Nile).
Beehives represent industry, and, of course, the ability to build
crafted structures of great complexity. It has been claimed that
the beehive fell from favour because it was adopted by the
Jacobites as an emblem of their continuing potency after 1745,
but this is clearly nonsense from its adoption by a City of
London Lodge, which would have been anything but Jacobite.
Beehives represent immortality, and, of course, are associated
with the Virgin Mary and with Isis, with Christ the aethereal,
and with sovereignty (GLCL).

69 *A Summons to attend the Lodge of Harmony. There are three steps (the Three Grades), the chequered floor, Faith (left), Hope (right), and Charity (above). The Two Columns (one Ionic and one Corinthian) have globes on top, clearly derived from sixteenth-century views of the Temple, and owing nothing to Jewish Antiquity, but much to Rome, where a column with globe was preserved. The All-Seeing Eye is a symbol of the Deity.*

The Ladder is that of Jacob as a symbol of moral, intellectual, and spiritual progress: the number of rungs was usually depicted as seven, representing Temperance, Fortitude, Prudence, Justice, Faith, Hope, and Charity. There are also Seven Stars or Planets, a roughly hewn block of masonry, Masonic tools and instruments, and a recurring theme of three (GLCL)

clear, Freemasons generally met in taverns during the eighteenth century, for only gradually did Lodges acquire property as permanent venues for meetings. The Grand Lodge in London built its splendid Freemasons' Hall in Queen Street, Lincoln's Inn Fields, in 1775–6 to designs by Thomas Sandby (1721–89), probably the latter's finest architectural work. The great Hall, with its Order of Roman Doric, elegant lunettes, and elaborate ceiling [70, 71], was the setting for many of the most important meetings that led eventually to the abolition of slavery, to the establishment of the first attempts to improve the conditions of the urban poor, and to other significant reforms of the first decades of the nineteenth century. An extraordinary illustration by Cipriani and Sandby shows the interior of the hall with various allegorical Masonic figures in attendance [71]. In Cipriani's illustration, where the reality of the Hall is mixed with Masonic emblems, the two globes are set on the table with compasses, a trowel and other paraphernalia. In this respect it is interesting to note the block of stone suspended on a tripod, for this is not just a block of stone but represents earth, the heaviest and most inert of the four alchemical elements. Earth is the foundation of the material selected by God from which Mankind can be fashioned in His image; but a block is something more when it becomes a cube, for a cube, as one of the basic forms of Geometry, is derived from the square, is equated with earth, and is a hieroglyph in Hermetic terms of the Divine Will. The cube appears in the ceiling of the choir of the church in the Escorial, and on it God the Father and the Son rest their feet.

Sandby's building was reconstructed to designs by F. P. Cockerell in 1864–6, although Sandby's interior of the Hall was restored. It was damaged by fire in 1883 (after which it was restored by Horace Jones), and it was finally demolished in the 1930s. Sir John Soane added a Council Chamber to the Hall in 1828 which was demolished in 1864. This Mannerist interpretation of a stripped Neoclassical style, with the shallow dome, high-level lighting, and segmental arches may still be appreciated from the fine drawings that survive in Sir John Soane's Museum [72]. Soane also proposed certain alterations to Sandby's Great Hall, involving the removal of the organ and the insertion of typical Soanesque segmental arches between Sandby's robust piers. His work for Freemasons' Hall included some interesting designs for furnishings [73].

Once Grand Lodge became established in 1716 and

70 *Freemasons' Hall, by Thomas Sandby, in 1900* (RCHME BB 71/4486).

71 *Freemasons' Hall, Queen Street, Lincoln's Inn Fields, of
1775–6, designed by Thomas Sandby (1721–98). Allegorical
print by Cipriani and Sandby showing the interior of the Hall
with Masonic figures in attendance. At the top is Truth
(sometimes identified as Prudence), with her mirror reflecting
its rays on diverse ornaments of the Hall, as well as on the
globes, Masonic instruments, and furniture. Truth is attended
by the Three Theological Virtues, Charity (left), Hope (with
Anchor), and Faith (with Book and Chalice from which shines
the Cross), while the Genius of Freemasonry, commissioned by
Truth and her attendants, is descending into the Hall bearing a
lighted torch in his right hand and carrying on his left arm the
ribbon with a pendant medal with which the Grand Master will
be invested in token of the divine approbation of a building
sacred to Charity and Benevolence (GLCL).*

72 *The Council Chamber, Freemasons' Hall, London, by Sir John Soane, from a painting in Sir John Soane's Museum* (SJSM)

1717 and some sort of coherent official histories began to be prepared, various claims that historical and mythical personages had been connected with Freemasonry were made. Nimrod, Solomon, William of Wykeham, Henry Chichele, Cardinal Wolsey, and Inigo Jones were identified as of Masonic importance, either as patrons or as 'operative' Masters.[3] Anderson, as editor of the *Book of Constitutions*, was fairly liberal in his bestowal of titles or Masonic connections to numerous people, including Sir Christopher Wren, about whose Masonic associations there is some doubt,[4] in spite of Aubrey's *Natural History of Wiltshire* which claims that Wren was adopted as a Brother on 18 May 1691. And yet every claim cannot be dismissed completely for, as we have seen, there is no question that the Solomonic Temple exercised a powerful influence on the minds of men, and was closely tied in with Hermetic and other ideas prevalent during the Renaissance period. Solomon, as an important figure in the building of the Temple, as a begetter of the Escorial and, indirectly, in the genesis of the Karlskirche, actually *has* some sort of claim to be significant in Masonic terms, indeed probably the strongest after Imhotep himself. It must not be forgotten that Solomon 'went after Ashtoreth the goddess of the Zidonians and after Milcom the abomination of the Ammonites' in *I Kings* 11, 5, and 'builded for Ashtoreth the abomination of the Zidonians, and for Chemosh the abomination of the

Moabites' high places' in *II Kings* 23, 13. Ashtoreth was also invoked as Astarte of Sidon, the Great Mother, Mother of the Gods; with Ascalon the Syrophoenician goddess; with Ishtar the Babylonian and Assyrian; and with the pancosmic goddess Isis, who is referred to on inscriptions as Astarte in Delos. Solomon therefore venerated Isis in one of her many guises: the connection of the Temple, Solomon, and the Egyptian-Isiac mysteries is not as tenuous as it might seem.

Begemann, however, that splendidly suspicious old German, was highly doubtful of most of Anderson's work, and attempted to sift fact from what he clearly decided was unreliable fiction. The important point is that Grand Lodge assembled, was constituted, and elected a Grand Master on the Feast of St John the Baptist, 1717; that the regulations or statements of Masons' customs were modernized in the eighteenth century; and that Freemasonry in its Speculative or Accepted form became fashionable throughout Europe and America from the 1720s. St John, the Messenger, is

73 *Design by Soane for furnishing for Freemasons' Hall. Note the triangular form and the use of the three Orders of Architecture (with corresponding entablatures), and typical Soanesque capping using the segmental arch associated with Isis (SJSM).*

connected with Hermes, Anubis, and Thoth, Keeper of the Sacred Name, and St John was the Saint whose name was associated with Freemasonry thereafter.

Freemasonry in Europe

In the centuries before 1717 there had been secret systems for the binding of men together for some common purpose. There seems to have been a considerable movement of Rosicrucians on the Protestant side in the seventeenth century, while the Jesuits appear to have employed some of the techniques of the Rosicrucians in the opposing camp.[5] Something of differing interests lingered in Freemasonry: in 1688 the Royalists in Britain were divided, and certain Jacobite Freemasons took the Craft abroad with them, establishing Lodges in which the Stuart cause was promoted. Freemasonry in England itself abandoned the Stuarts and became Hanoverian, and it is from this period that Freemasonry was established on a settled basis, undergoing a considerable metamorphosis in that it became almost entirely Speculative: in the process the connection between Architecture and craftsmen-operative-Masons was weakened. The many secret societies that existed in the seventeenth century could, in fact, be employed by any cause, and the establishment of Grand Lodge and the 'gelling' of a ritual and constitution mark a point when Freemasonry in England was reformed, registered, and cleansed of Jacobite intrigue. Essential to this was the removal of antagonisms arising from differences of religion, rank, and interest: concord, fraternity, and tolerance were to be encouraged.

Freemasonry, indeed, with its Great Architect, reverence for natural order, and connections with Newtonian figures and with Whiggery, encouraged a form or religiosity, but it was protean, undogmatic, and liberal. For this very reason it was to incur the displeasure of the Roman Church, while the fact of its essential Protestantism was hardly to endear it to that Church. While some Continental Lodges appear to have grown from formations by exiled Jacobites (it will be remembered that Freemasonry had been very strong in Scotland more than a century earlier), the spread of Freemasonry is not unconnected with British influence among her allies, notably in the Netherlands and in the Holy Empire of the German Nation. Certainly within the life of the Lodges there was a climate of opinion that admired British institutions, British order, liberalism, science, and undogmatic stance in matters of religion. It is no accident that Protestants were to be commemorated in Masonic circles on the Continent, notably at Maupertuis, in the grave of Court de Gébelin, and even in a chorale in *Die Zauberflöte*, on which topics more will be said anon. The very fact of Freemasonry's associations with religious toleration was enough to condemn it in the eyes of the Roman Catholic Church, while its overt admiration for Protestantism and for an increasingly protean type of religious belief was bound to lead to trouble.

It is all the more interesting to consider Austrian Freemasonry in this light, for Francis, Duke of Lorraine, and husband of the Empress Maria Theresia, had become a Brother of the Craft at Walpole's Houghton Hall in 1731, and seems to have remained a devoted Freemason, despite his wife's disapproval and devout Roman Catholicism.[6] As has been mentioned earlier, Prince Eugen of Savoy's circle was full of Freemasons who had been initiated in the Netherlands, and who were in close touch with British Freemasons during the wars with France. A Lodge had been founded in The Hague as early as 1710, and many brethren were Huguenot refugees involved in the book trade and in publishing. Huguenots were also numerous in London and Berlin, where they played a considerable part in commercial and intellectual life. Most importantly, however, their experiences at the hands of absolutist monarchies and Roman Catholics in their native land led many of them to start to question Christian doctrine.

Masonic Lodges offered a tolerant milieu for such dissenters, and the undogmatic nature of Freemasonry embraced men of many beliefs. All could survive and co-exist. The point about Freemasonry was that it offered a secret clubbable body to meet, and enlightened ideas could be floated without fear. Opponents of absolutism and sceptics in matters or religious dogma found in Freemasonry a club to which they could belong, and what is more it was an international club, and growing daily. By this very internationalism it posed a threat to absolutism and to the Roman Church.

Prince Eugen of Savoy's library had a very large collection of work by Bruno, and his Court in The Hague had been a centre for all manner of libertarians, free-thinkers, and even radicals;[7] his circle in Vienna was also remarkable for its liberal content, and his own interests (if his intact collection of books in Vienna is anything to go by) included all the late-Renaissance neo-pagans, with Bruno well to the fore. The Prince's Belvedere Palace in Vienna, designed by Fischer von Erlach's great rival Lukas von Hildebrandt, is a Baroque masterpiece, but, in its strangely oriental roofs, seems to have an affinity with the Saxon Schloss Pillnitz and with other eclectic tendencies of the eighteenth century that are associated with the Enlightenment and with advanced ideas.

Universalism, tolerance, interest in the writings of people the Church regarded as heretics, and borrowing from exotic cultures including China, were features of the Enlightenment and of the tastes of those eighteenth-century figures who were also to embrace Freemasonry. The connection of Freemasonry with Architecture has been stressed, but what is even more startling is that in the eighteenth century certain stylistic aspects were also closely interwoven with the Craft. Mention has been made of the importance of Scotland in the history of speculative Freemasonry: the Craft, through Schaw and others, was also closely connected with the House of Stuart, so much so that it became known as the Royal Art. The reign of King James I and VI saw the rise of Inigo Jones, whose championing of the Italian Renaissance style of Architecture based on the work of Andrea Palladio introduced some remarkable modern buildings to a Britain used to a somewhat clumsy and over-elaborate Architecture derived from Northern Europe. Jones's Palladianism did not take root after the fall of the monarchy, for it was too deeply associated with the Stuart cause. When Lord Burlington and his circle revived an interest in Jones in the eighteenth century, however, and the Palladian Style became *de rigueur* for the country houses of the Whig oligarchy as well as for many public buildings, not only was that style associated with a Royalist cause, but it was almost a deliberate attempt to show that the Hanoverian Succession followed naturally from the House of Stuart, and that an approved style of the first half of the seventeenth century was once more reinstated. Thus continuity and assurance were achieved, but this time the associations were with the Whigs and with Freemasonry.[8] Walpole's Houghton is a case in point. Later, Wörlitz in Saxony was to acquire a *Schloss* of impeccable Palladian proportions set in a garden of allusions.

This is not to underestimate the legacy of English republicanism, passed to the Continental Lodges through the Netherlands, which eventually found its way to France, and burst forth at the end of the eighteenth century. After the Restoration of the Stuart Monarchy republicanism went underground, but it did not die, and found fertile soil in the Netherlands, which, in any case, had a Protestant republican tradition.

So there are three distinct strands in Freemasonry: the Royalist Stuart legitimist strand; the moderate Whig strand and its loyalty to the House of Hanover; and the republican strand that was more radical and that certainly had a powerful effect on the Lodges of France and the Low Countries. Even in the Roman Catholic countries the Lodges were the meeting places for those of advanced opinion, interested in science and in natural phenomena, and probably more involved in improving the lot of Mankind by rational means than in religion in any organized sense. Protestantism was seen as a first phase in the breaking of the power of the Clergy and the Church, so Protestant heroes (like Admiral Coligny) were remembered with respect as the great forerunners of the Enlightenment. The Freemasons of Europe tended to be sceptics, even secular in their opinions, aware of aspects of the Great Architect's creation in themselves as part of the natural order of things, but eschewing the supernatural and the intervention of Providence.

There were other remarkable aspects of endeavour in Europe that have distinct Masonic associations. One was the design of gardens, based on English exemplars, which became fashionable in France, Germany, and elsewhere. The garden of associations, with poetic elements, allusions, and 'natural' aspects was to give birth to the cemetery movement, and this will be discussed later. The other great British export to the Continent was the encyclopaedia. The first encyclopaedia of the eighteenth century was Ephraim Chambers's *Cyclopaedia*, published in London in 1728. Chambers was an associate of James Anderson, and was among the commoners in the leadership of Grand Lodge. The *Cyclopaedia* reflected the Masonic desire for knowledge, to encourage learning, and to establish facts. The publication of this great work was assisted by a number of Freemasons, including John Senex, and the *Cyclopaedia* helped to disseminate Newtonian ideas. It also, very significantly, carried an account of British Freemasonry which was copied by many Continental sources.

Chambers's work inspired that great achievement of the Enlightenment, the *Encylopédie* of Diderot and d'Alembert, published from 1751. The *Encyclopédie* was to be a revision of Chambers's work, but soon took on a flavour of its own and became very much more comprehensive. The many contributors included almost everyone of any note in intellectual circles in France at the time. Diderot commissioned a frontispiece from the Freemason C.-N. Cochin, who used Masonic symbolism for the design. Even the first volumes of the *Encyclopédie* were adorned with emblems of Wisdom and Light, but the main connection between Diderot's work and Freemasonry is through the contributors who had contacts with Huguenot exiles in the Netherlands, and through the publisher Marc-Michel Rey, who seems to have had financial and distributory interests in the *Encyclopédie*. The radicals of the Netherlands assisted Rey to become the most distinguished publisher of the whole Enlightenment: Rey handled work by Rousseau and Baron d'Holbach, among others, and his circle in Amsterdam contained many Freemasons. It is through Rey and the Abbé Claude Yvon and his colleague, the Abbé Jean Martin de Prades (both of whom had to flee from France to the Netherlands in 1752 on account of their robust materialistic and rational views), that there are connections between the *Encyclopédie* and Freemason-

ry. Yvon himself was a Freemason, and de Prades corresponded with a number of active Freemasons. There can be no question that encyclopaedism had close connections with the Craft, and that the approach to intellectual endeavour implicit in the collation of information was fostered by Freemasons. Yvon was a contributor to the *Encyclopédie*, and seems to have inserted a flavour of materialism and rationalism into articles dealing with the soul, polytheism, and other weighty matters.[9]

Masonic Lodges are known to have been formed in 1721 at Mons, in 1725 in Paris, in 1731 in The Hague, and elsewhere, and several received their warrants from The Grand Lodge of England, except The Grand Lodge of Paris, which did not get its warrant until 1743, probably because its leading lights were Jacobites. The Grand Lodge of Paris was initially not bound by English Freemasonry, and probably became associated with a revival of interest in the Knights Templars in an attempt to develop a history of Masonic lore going back to the Crusades and to the Holy Land (and therefore to the Temple itself). Such an association, of course, was unpalatable to the Roman Catholic Church, and in 1738 Pope Clement XII (Pontiff 1730–40) issued the Bull *In Eminenti*: on 28 April, the first Papal condemnation of Freemasonry was issued, attacking its naturalistic bias, its demand for secret oaths, its religious indifferentism, and its possible threat to Church and State. Thenceforth Roman Catholics who joined or participated in the Craft ran the risk of being excommunicated.

In spite of this, Freemasonry prospered on the Continent, and acquired new and ever more exotic Degrees. From the 1730s onwards Continental and British Freemasonry tended to become distinct in their differences, notably in relation to the ecclesiastical and secular authorities, for in Britain the Craft was associated with Whiggery, but on the Continent, especially in the Roman Catholic countries, Freemasonry tended to become a vehicle for the dissemination of ideas not exactly palatable to reactionary forces. Certainly in France the Craft was seen as deriving from crusading chivalry, from Ancient Egyptian mysteries, and possibly from the Templars. In 1756 attempts were made to bring the Grand Lodge of France closer to British Craft Masonry, but violent rivalry between it and more arcane elements led the Government to intervene and close down Grand Lodge. In 1772 the Grand Orient was established with the Duc de Chartres as Grand Master, and the Grand Lodge united with it: thereafter French Freemasonry seems to have been a vehicle for intrigue, political activism, and, ultimately, the most noble ideas of the Enlightenment itself.

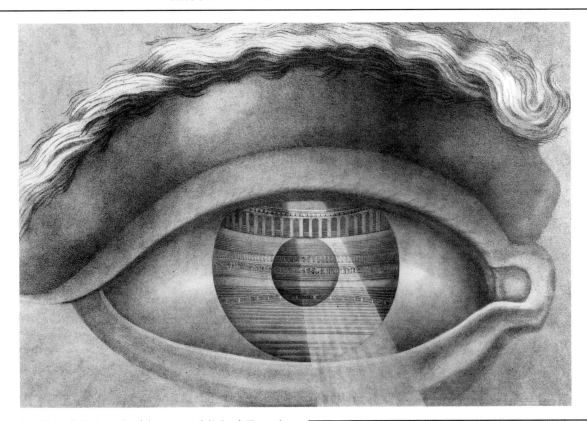

74 *The All-Seeing Eye and the Theatre at Besançon by C.-N. Ledoux, an unquestionably Masonic allusion, with certain overtones after Alberti. From* L'Architecture (SJSM).

Once the Grand Orient had been established French Freemasonry tended to go its own way, although 'English' rites were used in Scandinavia, the Netherlands, the Holy Roman Empire, and elsewhere. By 1780, in spite of Papal Bulls and harrassment by the authorities, there were some 82 Lodges in Paris,[10] in addition to which were military Lodges, women's Lodges, and schismatics of various kinds.[11]

As in England, French Freemasons did not at first have purpose-built Lodges, and met in private houses, restaurants, or inns. Police raids seem to have broken up many a convivial gathering, but generally the costumes, tools, emblems, décor, and other paraphernalia had to be carted around for use by Lodges when and where required. Chequered carpets, candlesticks, and other objects were used to provide the 'sets' for ceremonies, while floor-drawings defined the areas for rituals.[12] These plans, of course, were representations of Solomon's Temple, and were designed to show the route of initiation as well as the positions of main elements. They are distantly related in idea with the ancient labyrinths in cathedral floors [see 5, 6] or in turf (Chartres in France and Wing in Rutland) that were routes for pilgrims to progress while in prayer, taking wrong turnings, until eventually Paradise is reached: labyrinths, as previously described, were also allegories of the journey through life. Masons were seeking the origins of the Craft in the still centre of their Lodges, which were

drawn apart from the rest of the world and shielded from prying eyes; in the Lodge and its emblems Masons sought the memory of beginnings and of the Temple itself. The Lodge therefore was, with its iconography, a mnemonic of the Temple, and was itself a Temple to the Art of Memory.

By the 1760s the typology of French Lodges had become clear. The utilitarian parts of the building were at the lowest level, and the rooms of the Lodge were disposed in series: the first room was dark, with two small chambers for candidates (the parallel with Graeco-Roman Isiac rites is clear); the second part was for purification, washing, etc. (again the parallel with Isiac initiations in the Graeco-Roman world is obvious); then the main hall of the Lodge for ceremonies was disposed with space for initiation. Then came the banqueting or dining room,[13] where convivial activities would follow the more serious rites of initiation. Needless to say, the exteriors of buildings used as Lodges were very discreet, and gave no sign of the purposes or activities within.

The need to keep and store archives, records, and books in Lodges led to the provision of rooms for such purposes, and by the 1780s separate rooms appear to have been regarded as ideal for the three Grades of Initiation.[14] Proportions of the Lodges were often based on the measurements given of the Solomonic Temple, while the Two Pillars marked the entrance to the space of the Lodge, and the east, or Orient, was given lavish décor to mark its importance (although, as has been made clear, the orientation of the Temple was the other way round).

In French Freemasonry the allegorical and metaphorical aspects appear to have been invested with greater significance than in eighteenth-century England. Architectural history was equated with the development of society, and Architecture was seen as a means of establishing a just and ordered system. Continental Freemasonry proposed that exemplars and basic theories of Architecture and society were inextricably linked. Order and Geometry were therefore associated with the structure of society, and especially with a lost ideal of society: the Temple was the greatest achievement of Architecture and ancient society, and so the preliminaries to a purification of society and a reconstruction of the lost or submerged values of that ancient society were achievable by reconstructing the Temple in hundreds of locations and thousands of minds. It is a remarkable idea, and very important in an understanding of an aspect of the Enlightenment not often aired in Britain; yet, as has been described above, it was not new, for it was there in Renaissance times and earlier.

Freemasons sought a return to simple, primitive, elemental truths, and a reconstruction of a noble, unfalse, altruistic progress from those truths along the civilized paths of architectural history in which the language of the Orders, the Temple of Solomon, and Reason would play their parts. Freemasons desired to rebuild a moral edifice, no less, as an exemplar of what was noble and splendid and true in the first ages of the world, and within it they tried to conserve the ecumenical catholicity of the Masonic Tradition as a way forward to progress and benevolent development of the whole of Mankind. Freemasons saw themselves as endeavouring to reconstruct the dissipated parts of the Temple, to seek again the original proportions in all their purity, and to re-establish a hierarchy of ornament harmonious with the structure.

There are thus similarities to the ambitions of King Philip II in building the Escorial, and to many earlier ideas and theories discussed above. The staggering point with which to come to terms is that so many syncretic threads from Antiquity, and especially from the Graeco-Roman world, survived to play such a significant rôle in the last half millennium.

Freemasonry and Neoclassicism

The search for simplicity, of course, is associated with Laugier's theories in his *Essay on Architecture* of 1753, and with a general Neoclassical desire for the primitive, the original, and the simple that was such a feature of the time. Claude-Nicolas Ledoux (1735–1806), in his *L'Architecture Considérée sous le Rapport de L'Art, des Moeurs et de la Législation*,[15] proposed several designs that are interesting from the point of view of this study, for Ledoux was involved with Masonic and crypto-Masonic cults. William Beckford met Ledoux in 1784 and was somewhat put out by an occult meeting at the French Architect's house:[16] it would seem that Ledoux was more involved in the type of heretical Masonry of Cagliostro, discussed below. A drawing of an eye [74], with the theatre at Besançon reflected in the pupil, published in Ledoux's book recalls Alberti's device, the winged eye, and was probably inspired by Masonic emblems, including the All-Seeing Eye. Ledoux used blank walls, removed ornament, and simplified architectural form. In his book, the possibilities of stereometrically pure pyramidal forms are exploited, as in his celebrated gun-foundry for an Industrial City near Chaux, where Ledoux reduced the factory to a pure, geometrical, architectural expression. A comparison with the Escorial, with its corner towers, and its astrological and symbolic allusions, not least its connection with the grid-iron of St Laurence, is hard to avoid, for the pyramids at the corners could easily be the supports for such a grid [75, 76].

Ledoux's designs for Arc and Senans saltworks and for his ideal town of Chaux (which means 'lime', significantly) demonstrate his search for primitive simplicity in Classical Architecture, a totality and wholeness of vision (as in the elliptical town plan of Chaux), and a harmonious relationship of buildings to function, expression, and to each other. His *Barrières* of Paris, or customs posts (of which only four of the fifty-plus survive), were masterworks of Neoclassical simplicity and understatement: Beckford said that from their massive, sepulchral character, they looked more like the entrances to a necropolis rather than to a 'city so damnably alive as this confounded capital'.[17] At the Barrière du Trône Ledoux designed not only two severe

---

75 *Plan, elevation, and section of C.-N. Ledoux's* Forge à Canons *from his* L'Architecture. *Note the rigid grid-iron plan and use of pyramids. The form recalls Juan de Herrera's Escorial and various versions of the Temple complex in Jerusalem, notably that of* Vallalpando *(SJSM).*

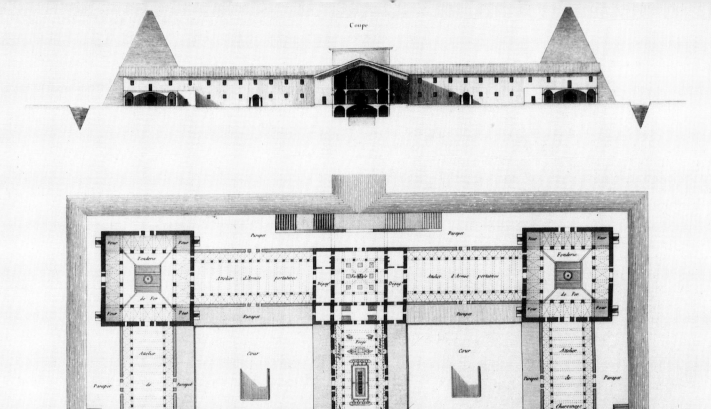

Coupe

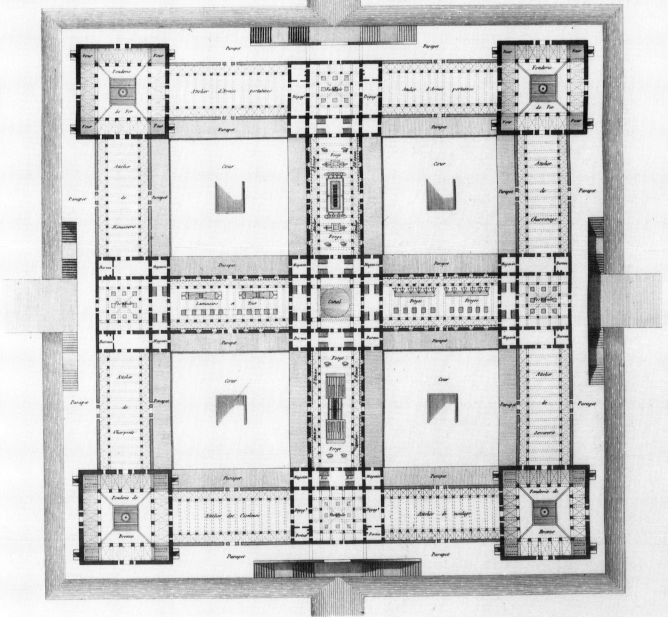

Elevation

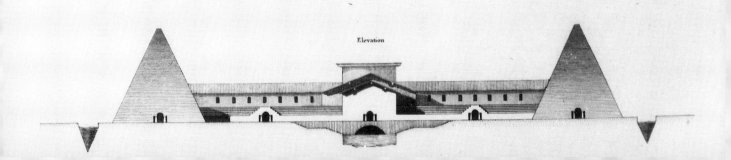

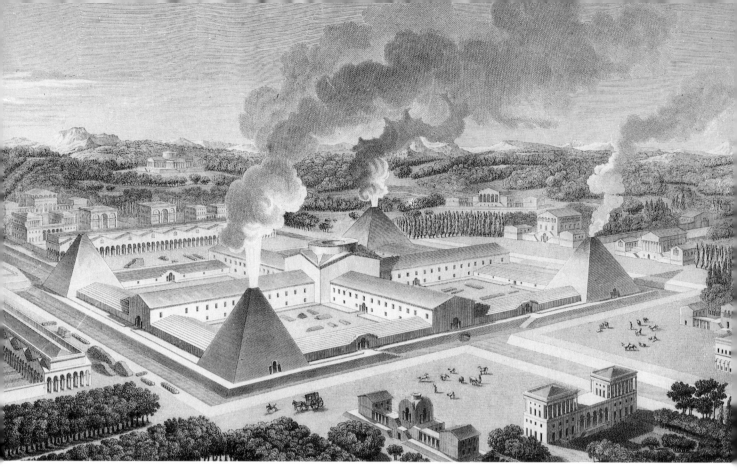

pavilions, but two free-standing columns on tough
pedimented bases: these columns suggest the Pillars of
Hercules, the world beyond and within, and the Two
Pillars of Masonic legend based on the Solomonic
Temple.

As we have seen, the Two Pillars, wide vestibule-like
front, and domed space behind with Holy of Holies to
the east were used by Fischer von Erlach for his
Karlskirche in Vienna, and the Pantheon type mixed
with Graeco-Roman and Jewish Temple found its way
into French Masonic design [77]. The Primitive Hut, as
an ideal, became associated with nobility through Rous-
seauesque ideas, and with Adam, who gained his
knowledge from the Great Architect Himself, trans-
forming the Primitive Hut into a place with geometrical
proportions. Hence Adam became the first Mason, the
first natural 'primitive' man, and the author of the
exemplar of the Primitive Hut. Ideals of Classical
Primitivism that came to fruition in the toughest works
of the Neoclassical period were associated, however
tentatively on the surface, with Freemasonry. Architects
and Freemasons were seen as the representatives and
interpreters of the Great Architect of the Universe, and
so the contributions of the Architect in producing
civilized, primitive, stripped-down Classical buildings
were not without significance as Masonic Architecture.

Many Architects and architectural theorists working
in Paris alone in the 1770s and 1780s were known
Freemasons, including Quatremère de Quincy, A.-L.-T.
Vaudoyer, A.-T. Brongniart, Vaudoyer, J.-B. de Puisi-
eux (who assisted Soufflot in the building of Ste
Geneviève and author of the indubitably Masonic
Éléments et traité de géométrie published in Paris in 1765),
and de Wailly. É.-L. Boullée, C.-N. Ledoux, and J.-J.
Lequeu seem to have been profoundly influenced by the
notion that architectural design and theory could be
harnessed to the creation of political and social change,
and used elements of design already given new meanings. Late eighteenth-century French designers had a
vast vocabulary of Masonic and quasi-Masonic emblems,
images, and allusions on which to draw, most of it
familiar to the public.[18] There is no evidence that Boullée
himself was a Mason, but Ledoux was a member of an
associated occultist body, and Lequeu was clearly
steeped in Masonic ideas. Laurent Bordelon's *La Coterie
des Anti-Façonniers*, published in Paris in 1716, described
groups of people in their sphere-shaped 'lodges': Ledoux
proposed a spherical lodge for Maupertuis in the 1780s
and a spherical centre for the cemetery at Chaux [78, 79],
while Boullée designed a spherical cenotaph for Newton

78 *Ledoux's extraordinary elevation of the Cemetery at Chaux, showing his use of spheres. From* L'Architecture (SJSM).

77 *Engraving from* Le Régulateur du Maçon *of 1801 showing a Pantheon structure on a base of seven steps, with G in blazing star, Masonic tools, a beehive, the seven stars, sun and moon, and pyramid on cube. Note the cord, or 'tessellated border', known as* La houpe dentelée, *or die Schnur von starken Faden: this cord is intertwined with knots, and has a tassel at each end. A cord of strong threads with lovers' knots alludes to the care of Providence, which surrounds and keeps Freemasons within its protection. According to French ritual, the cord is intended to remind Freemasons that the Brotherhood surrounds the earth, and that distance does not relax the bonds: it is an emblem of the fraternal bond by which Freemasons are united. The cord should consist of sixty threads or yarns, because no Lodge (according to ancient statutes) was supposed to have more than sixty members. Four tassels were necessary to complete the symbolism of the Four Cardinal Virtues, but two are often found in French and German designs. 'Tessellated', of course, suggests the small stones used in a mosaic pavement, but the 'tessellated border' of Freemasonry seems to mean a cord of black and white threads, decorated with tassels, surrounding the tracing-board of the First Degree (which is a representation of the Lodge): it signifies the mystic tie binding the Craft (wherever dispersed), into one band of Brotherhood. The cord may also allude to the halter of ancient mysteries by which a candidate was led to initiation* (A).

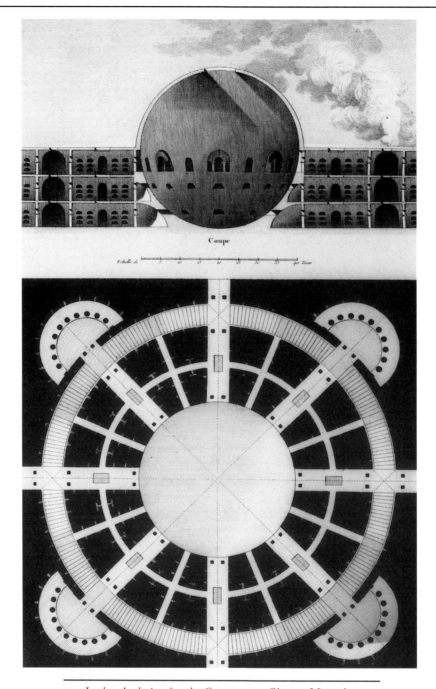

Coupe

Echelle de

79 *Ledoux's design for the Cemetery at Chaux. Note the severe stereometrically pure forms and the central sphere (a favourite theme of French Neoclassical designers imbued with Masonic ideas). From* L'Architecture *(SJSM).*

80 *Elevation of Boullée's cenotaph to Newton. The pure form of the sphere sits in the 'cup' of concentric drums with rings of evergreen trees. Note the monumental stairs and simple, stereometrically pure forms. The debt to Roman Imperial mausolea is clear (BN. CE. HA57, No. 7).*

81 *Section through Boullée's cenotaph to Newton. A blazing globe set in the centre suggests day and the sun as well as illumination in the sense of Enlightenment and the explanation of the mysteries of Nature (BN. CE. HA57, No. 9).*

82 *Section through Boullée's cenotaph to Newton of 1784. The rings of cypress trees, the sarcophagus-shaped cenotaph, and the stereometrically pure forms should be noted. The sphere is pierced to allow light in to suggest the position of the stars. Here Neoclassical concerns with clarity and simplicity merge with megalomaniac scale (after Piranesi), and the Architecture of Imperial Roman mausolea (BN. CE. HA57, No. 8).*

[80–82]. It appears that Laugier himself had direct Masonic connections, for he is credited with a poem in defence of the Craft against the Papal denunciations of 1738 and 1751 which was published in 1779 and again in Grandidier's *Essays on Strasbourg Cathedral*, published in 1782. Laugier seems to have equated the primitive with the natural, and the polite with aspects of exemplars with which Masonic writings were also concerned. What is important is that one of the most significant seminal works of Neoclassicism was written by a defender of Freemasonry, and who had known links with the Craft.[19]

It is also significant that Quatremère de Quincy was a Freemason, for his scholarly studies of Ancient Egyptian Architecture were carried out before Denon and before the work of the Commission (based on the Napoleonic investigations of Egyptian architecture) appeared; as Professor Anthony Vidler notes, Quatremère de Quincy 'exhibited all the characteristics of one who was influenced by his Masonic affiliations'.[20]

Piranesi[21] had insisted that the hardness and simplicity of Egyptian Architecture were not due to ignorance but were deliberate expressions. The taste of his day saw non-naturalistic styles as primitive or inferior, but Piranesi knew that Egyptian art was highly sophisiticated, and had tremendous possibilities for future designers in an age dominated by the tyranny of Good Taste. Johann Gottfried Herder (1744–1803) was one of the first in the eighteenth century to point out what Egyptian art might contribute to the period. Herder noted that the first great monuments in the world were those of Egypt, and that lasting buildings, using squares, triangles, and points, became the pyramids or obelisks. Impressions of permanence, without recourse to ornament, were achieved by the Ancient Egyptians, and Herder realized the possibilities of a stark, simple Architecture, a severe expression of basic form, in the exemplars of Ancient Egypt. Gould classified Herder, who was a profound influence on Goethe, as a 'writer of the Craft',[22] and indeed his work contains much overt Masonic material. His memorial in Weimar has the motto 'Light, Love, Life' within a frame of a serpent eating its tail; behind the serpent's head is a blazing sun, and in the centre of the circle are Alpha and Omega.

Freemasonry and Egyptian Elements in Neoclassical Architecture

The importance of Freemasonry in the history of Neoclassical Architecture is considerable, especially where the Egyptian Revival elements are concerned. The idea of Egypt as a source of knowledge of building and of all wisdom enshrouded in the Hermetic mysteries was well known to Freemasonry. The Craft of Masonry itself was traced to Egypt, the Israelites were supposed to have learned the skills of building in stone from the Egyptians (and, as we have seen, another version has it that Abraham passed on secrets to the Egyptians), and there was a close connection between the story of captivity in Egypt, the use of the Cubit as a unit of measurement, and the legends of the Craft and the Solomonic Temple. In most of the legends Masonry, as the Craft involved with Geometry, building with stone, measurement, and the creation of Architecture, was also the guardian of sacred esoteric knowledge passed to Mankind from the Creator.

Freemasonry in the latter half of the eighteenth century reflected many of the philosophical, moral, political, artistic, and intellectual currents of the Enlightenment. Liberalism and progressive notions were implicit in Masonic ideals of the Brotherhood of Man, and Continental Freemasons seem to have held little brief for the Roman Catholic hierarchy and its most reactionary pronouncements: indeed many of the condemnations, threats, and Bulls seem to have had little effect during the apogee of the Enlightenment.

A ceremonial setting using motifs from Ancient Egypt would seem to be logical, given Masonic belief in Egypt as the source of skill and wisdom, yet an Egyptianizing theme in Freemasonry does not appear to have surfaced much before 1750. Although overt Egyptian décor was used to great effect in the Chapter Room of the Supreme Grand Royal Arch Chapter of Scotland in 1901, [Colour Plate XI], and in Freemasons' Hall in Dublin, eighteenth-century British Lodges do not appear to have embraced the Egyptian style with much enthusiasm. Continental Lodges, however, notably those in France and in Central Europe, acquired certain Egyptian features.

The main influences in this transformation were Count Alessandro Cagliostro (1743–95) and Carl Friedrich Köppen. Cagliostro's supposed real name was Guiseppe Balsamo, and he appears to have been an unscrupulous charlatan. He passed a dissolute and criminal youth, and is supposed to have studied alchemy in the east. In Europe he peddled drugs and potions, and became a Mason in London in 1777. He later became Grand Master of a Lodge in Paris to which a temple of Isis was attached, and claimed to be Deputy of the 'Grand Kophta' who had not been seen by anyone. In 1785 Cagliostro was implicated in the 'affair of the diamond necklace', in which Jeanne de St Rémy de Valois obtained possession of a diamond necklace by duping Cardinal de Rohan, and although Cagliostro was acquitted, he was imprisoned in connection with other frauds. British Freemasons regarded Cagliostro and his 'Egyptian' rites as fraudulent, but nevertheless his rituals were speedily adopted in some French and German Lodges. Köppen published a curious work on the rites of initiation of Egyptian priests in 1778, and this work became influential in Continental circles of the Craft.[23]

It is clear from typical standard designs for Masonic Certificates for Lodges under the Grand Orient of France that the Egyptian element was well to the fore. Pyramids, Egyptian columns, palm trees, sphinxes, and Egyptian Isis or Hathor-headed capitals are much in evidence [83–85]. A French Master-Masons's apron of c.1800, printed from an engraved plate, shows Egyptian features, with busts of Cambacérès, Pro-Grand Master of the Grand Orient, and Napoléon. While the design clearly owes something to the Egyptian campaign of Napoléon, the Masonic elements are clear [86]. From the description of the 'Egyptian' rites it seems that they derived from Isiac ceremonies in Ancient Egypt, but especially in the Graeco-Roman World. An Antique pavement of mosaic from Antioch, for example, shows the *Mors Voluntaria* when the initiate goes fearlessly towards the unsheathed sword, the important moment of initiation in the House of the Mysteries of Isis. The idea of a trial, even a voluntary death, where faith triumphs, has its parallels in Masonic literature, Isiac ritual, and Christian martyrology.

As the theories of Laugier and Herder, the influence of Piranesi, and the rediscovery of the Antique, first of Roman (given a further impetus by the rediscovery of Herculaneum and Pompeii), then of Greek, and finally of Egyptian examples, drew Architects and designers away from the frivolities of the Rococo to a more severe expression, clear geometrical shapes were exploited. The frontiers of taste were pushed further towards ever-greater ruggedness, massiveness, and primitiveness, and the search for simplicity led naturally to Egyptian exemplars.

Young French Architects began to experiment with huge forms, simple massing, and symmetry in the Academies of Paris and Rome, using public buildings, monuments, cemeteries, and vast civic structures as their subjects. Étienne-Louis Boullée (1728–99) was the visionary Architect and leader of a whole generation of Architects who experimented with unadorned walls, simple forms, and a massive megalomaniac scale derived from Piranesi's views of Rome and other drawings.

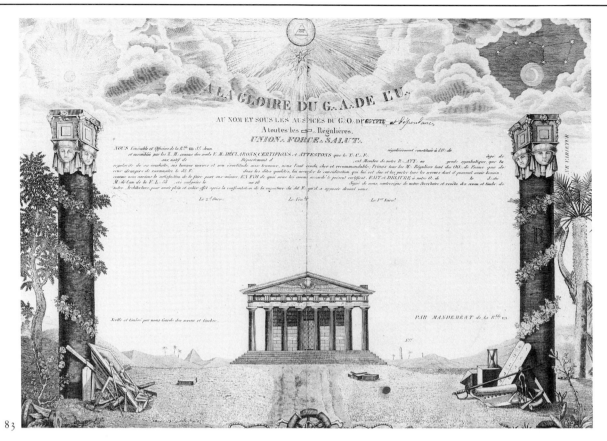

83

84

85 *A design for a Masonic certificate for Lodges under the Grand Orient of France, from a nineteenth-century printer's sample-book. Note the pyramids, palm trees, Masonic tools, Egyptian Architecture, and figure of Charity, with Ancient of Days. Note the rock-work cavern with cave on the left (UGLE).*

83 *A design for a Masonic certificate for Lodges under the Grand Orient of Egypt and dependencies, from a nineteenth-century printer's sample-book. On the left is Jachin and on the right Boaz, both with Hathor-headed columns. Note the pyramid,, obelisk, Nilotic trees, elephant, and Doric temple with winged disc with uraei in the tympanum. Of particular interest is the way in which the columns are entwined with flowers and foliage arranged as spirals, indicative of the Masonic significance given to spiral columns: these spirals recall Ribart de Chamoust's French Order illustrated in 64 and 65 (UGLE).*

84 *A design for a Masonic certificate for Lodges under the Grand Orient of France, from a nineteenth-century printer's sample-book. Jachin and Boaz have acquired pomegranates in the form of Isiac lotus-crowns. Other features include the sphinx with Ankh, Masonic tools, pyramid, Nilotic plants, Isiac fountain, boy with inverted torch symbolizing the extinguishing of life, winged boy with serpent twined around a club (resurrection, Harpocrates/Horus, and silence), Serapis/Osiris, and three-headed serpent holding the key, crown, and sword. Note the sarcophagus in the rock-work cave (UGLE).*

86 *French Master-Mason's apron of* c.1800 *printed from an
engraved plate. The busts on Jachin ((left) and Boaz (right)
are of Jean-Jacques-Régis Cambacérès, Duc de Parma, Pro-
Grand-Master of the Grand Orient, and Napoléon (right)
respectively. Note how Jachin and Boaz are entwined with
spirals of flowers, and the Egyptian temple, obelisk, pyramid,
pylons, and chequerboard Masonic floor* (UGLE).

Comt on ediﬁa la tour de babiloine. et le langueg fuit mue en. lx. xij. langueges. et les auges la deﬁceurit.

I *The Building of the Tower of Babel, showing Masons preparing stone, hoisting blocks into position, and working on the flimsy cantilevered scaffolding at the top. The Angels of Heaven are distorting the speech of the men so that they start fighting, fall to their deaths, and the Tower falls with them. On the left is the Lodge in which the Masons are preparing lime-mortar which is then carried on hods on the shoulders of the hod-carriers. A fifteenth-century illumination from the Duke of Bedford's* Book of Hours *(BL. Add. 18850, fol. 17v. Y850611).*

II *The Duchesse de Roussillon visiting the building-site of the great Abbey of the Sainte-Madeleine in Vézelay and viewing the walls being built of dressed stone bedded in lime-mortar, as depicted in a fifteenth-century French miniature in L'Histoire de Charles Martel. Note the trowels. The tops of unfinished walls are protected against the elements by means of temporary coverings of straw. The timber structure on the right is the Masons' Lodge, where stone is being prepared ready for carriage to the church, and in front of the Lodge is the Master-Mason with staff supervising the mixing of the mortar (Copyright Bibliothèque Royale Albert 1er, Bruxelles, MS 6 fol. 554 verso).*

III *The rebuilding of the Basilica of Saint-Denis as shown in a fifteenth-century illuminated MS. To the left are the King and the Abbot (supposedly King Dagobert and the seventh-century Abbot; but, with the unmistakably Gothic form of the Basilica, the process of syncretism also identifies the figures with Kings Louis VI and VII and the famous Abbot Suger of the twelfth century). The Master-Mason is very dashing (the figure on the left with a feather in his cap). To the right is the Lodge where stone is being dressed, squared, and carved. Note the Masons' mallets, chisels, square, and the lime-mortar being carried (BN. Ms. fr. 2609. fol. 60v).*

*IV   Interior of a Viennese Masonic Lodge in c.1790. The
central figure in the foreground (the Master of
Ceremonies) is, according to Professor Robbins Landon,
Prince Nicolaus Esterházy. At least three events seem to be
happening at once, so it is a composite picture, depicting
not a realistic view of one occasion, but a syncretic record
of several. The columns entwined recall the Solomonic
twisted columns and the winding stair, and, with their
serpentine décor, suggest a Masonic setting. The rainbow,
as the sign of Hope, and the sun, suggest Crowned Hope, so
the Lodge is probably* Zur (neu) gekrönten Hoffnung. *The
Master (Johann, Count Esterházy, and Imperial and
Royal Chamberlain) is shown with the gavel. The seated
figure on the extreme right is the unmistakable figure of
Wolfgang Amadeus Mozart, who seems to be in ebullient
spirits, making a jest with the cleric beside him. Note the
three lights on the triangle,* Hermes with caduceus, *and
the various Masonic implements and symbols*
(Historisches Museum der Stadt Wien I.N.47.527).

V   *Painting by Stewart Watson showing the Inauguration of Robert Burns as Poet Laureate of the Lodge Canongate Kilwinning, Edinburgh, in 1787* (The Grand Lodge of Scotland).

VI   *Schinkel's design for Act I, Scene 6 of* Die Zauberflöte *in the 1816 production of the opera at the Königliche Schauspiele-Opernhaus, Berlin, showing a dark vault in the form of a hemi-dome, indicated by stars that follow the lines of 'ribs' terminating in an 'oculus' like that of the Pantheon in Rome. In the centre is the Queen of the Night standing on her crescent-moon, an extraordinary image that recalls the Immaculata from Baroque and Rococo ceilings; the Isiac and Marian allusions are clear, and the identification in such a startling manner by Schinkel of the Queen with the Immaculata points to an important aspect of* Die Zauberflöte. *The Queen and her allies represent the Roman Catholic Church;* Dieses Weib dünkt sich gross, hofft durch Blendwerk und Aberglauben das Volk zu berücken und unsern festen Tempelbau zu zerstören *(This woman thinks much of herself, and hopes by trickery and superstition to ensnare the people and to destroy our safe and strongly-built Temple), as Sarastro puts it. Carl Friedrich Thiele's published version was based on Schinkel's original project (Schinkel Museum SM XXII c/121), from Thiele (BL. 1899. c. 5).*

VII   *Schinkel's design for Act I, Scene 15 of* Die Zauberflöte *in the 1816 Berlin production at the Königliche Schauspiele-Opernhaus, showing the forecourt to Sarastro's palace with a tropical landscape in the background. The three portals lead to Wisdom, Reason, and Nature, but are contained within a unified building in which Osiris presides over the central portal (Wisdom); a male priest with hieroglyphical tablet (derived from Piranesi's designs) is over the portal of Reason; and a goat is set above the portal of Nature. The sources for the design appear to be Piranesi's* Diverse maniere…, *Denon's* Voyage, *and Alexander von Humboldt's account of his journey to South America. Carl Friedrich Thiele's version was based on Schinkel's original project (Schinkel Museum SM XXII c/118), from Thiele (BL. 1899. c. 5).*

VIII Schinkel's design for Act II, Scene 1 of Die Zauberflöte *in the 1816 Berlin production at the* Königliche Schauspiele-Opernhaus, *showing the luxuriantly tropical flavour of the Nilotic landscape or 'Palmenwalde'. In the centre is a distant view of a Philae-like complex of Egyptian temples dedicated to Isis. The sources may be Humboldt's travels and Denon's* Voyage . . . *Carl Friedrich Thiele's version of Schinkel's original project (Schinkel Museum SM TH XX) from Thiele* (BL. 1899. c. 5).

IX Schinkel's design for Act II, Scene 20 of Die Zauberflöte *in the 1816 Berlin production at the* Königliche Schauspiele-Opernhaus, *showing the interior of a strange vault with massive piers and primitivist structure. Note the statues of mummified figures. Sources seem to have been descriptions of the Viennese production of 1791 and Denon's study of the interior of the temple of Apollinopolis. From Thiele: this version of Schinkel's original project (Schinkel Museum SM Th XXIII) was made by Friedrich Jügel* (BL. 1899. c. 5).

X Section perpendiculaire d'un souterrain de la maison Gothique, au droit de la ligne milieu, en la largeur des mamelons et suivant la pente de la montagne. *J.-J. Lequeu's version of the Trials by Fire, Water, and Air, based on* Séthos. *Above the Gate of the Intrepid is painted the inscription 'He who follows this path alone and without looking behind him' (Orpheus Legend), 'will be purified by Fire and Air; and if he strives to conquer the dread of Death he will emerge from the underworld, and will behold the light once more, and will be worthy to be admitted into the company of wise men and men of valour'. On the left is a shaft leading from the Great Pyramid, then a warning inscription, the three-headed dog Cerberus, then passages with corbelled vaults (based on Piranesi's designs in* Diverse Maniere . . .), *then a huge kiln-like furnace for the Trial by Fire (complete with instruments of torture), then three bays of corbelled vault* à la *Piranesi, then the chamber for the Trial by Water. Finally, the third stage of initiation, the Trial by Air, is reached, and the initiate is hoisted to the presence of Wisdom and the brimming cup of Oblivion and the cup of Memory. This could easily be a set for* Die Zauberflöte. (BN. CE. AC, 1. plate 61, fig. 156).

XI   The Chapter Room at 78 Queen Street, Edinburgh, for the Supreme Grand Royal Arch Chapter of Scotland, designed by Peter Henderson and built in 1901. The Royal Arch Halls are shown in an exhibition drawing (pencil and watercolour) by Robert F. Sherar, 1901. The use of Egyptian motifs extended to the carpets and furniture. The Building News of 26 July 1901 (p105) noted that the 'chapter-room is in the style of an ancient Egyptian Temple ... It has been suggested that (the figure decoration) should represent the story of Isis and Osiris ... or be simply reproductions from the Book of the Dead ... The ceiling is carried on timber trusses, the details of which are Assyrian in style. The upholstery of the seats is a deep crimson, and forms a sort of dado all round ... The capitals of the large columns and the ceiling over the dais are in brilliant colours after the style of a peacock's tail' (RCAHMS).

87 Cénotaphe dans le genre Égyptien *by Boullée. This ramped form of pyramid derives from Fischer von Erlach's Plate XI in his* Entwurff . . . *In spite of its title* 'Cénotaphe' *the building is clearly a cemetery or a centre for cults, to judge from the processions going up and down the gigantic ramps* (BN. CE. HA55, No. 26).

Boullée's designs for cenotaphs and cemeteries show buildings in which Egyptian motifs play no small part [87]: huge blank walls emphasize the terror and finality of death, expressive of Boullée's ideas of an Architecture suggestive of its purpose, and were designed as Temples of Death, intended to chill the heart. Such buildings were to withstand the ravages of time, to be perfectly symmetrical, and included huge Neoclassical sarcophagi (which became enormous buildings themselves), pyramids, and funerary triumphal arches. By cutting all ornament to the very minimum, Boullée gave his buildings an immutable character. Cone-shaped cenotaphs incorporating ideas based on both domes and pyramids, with obelisks and cypresses much in evidence; monuments with flat surfaces, bare and unadorned, the decoration consisting of a play of shadows; and gloomy, terrifying images incorporating abstractions and paraphrases recur in his work. Terror and desolation, finality, stillness, and monumentality can be found in plenty in Boullée's designs.

Antoine-Chrysostôme Quatremère de Quincy

A major influence on the young French Architects was Antoine-Chrysostôme Quatremère de Quincy (1755–1849), whose prize essay submitted to the Académie des Inscriptions et Belles-Lettres in 1785 is likely to have been known to Boullée and others, although it was not published in Paris until 1803 as *De L'Architecture Égyptienne, Considérée Dans son origine ses principes et son goût, et comparée Sous les mêmes rapports à l'Architecture Grecque.* He dwelt on the massiveness and brooding grandeur of Egyptian Architecture, and granted that Egyptian Architecture contained much that was admirable: the pyramids were rightly objects worthy of respect, while the architectural arrangement of temples gave an impression of greatness. The illustrations by Gaitte in Quatremère de Quincy's work show architectural detail in reasonably correct form [88–90]. As has been noted, Quatremère de Quincy was not only a Freemason, but was very powerfully influenced by his Masonic convictions.

Freemasonry becomes Overt

After Ledoux had remodelled the château at Maupertuis for the Marquis de Montesquiou (an influential and important Freemason), Alexandre-Théodore Brongniart designed the ruined pyramid in the gardens with its recess on one side containing a Doric portico supporting the segmental pediment [91]. This dominated the lake in the garden known as the Élysée (where Montesquiou held Masonic meetings), and symbolized Antiquity; the

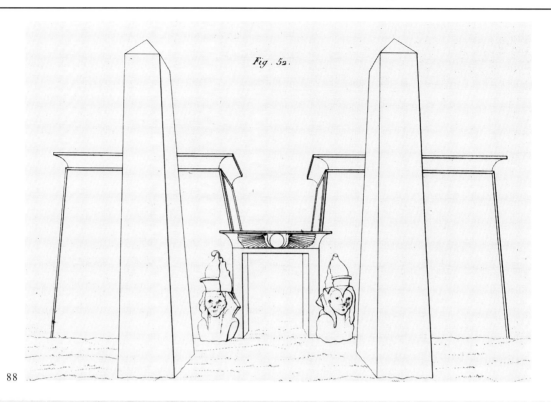

Fig. 52.

88

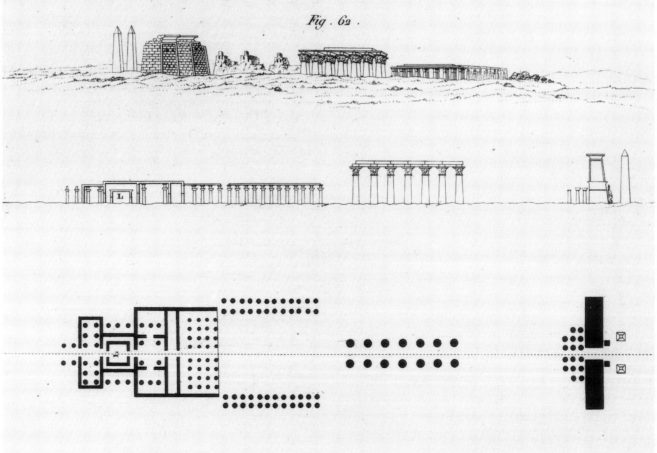

Fig. 62.

89

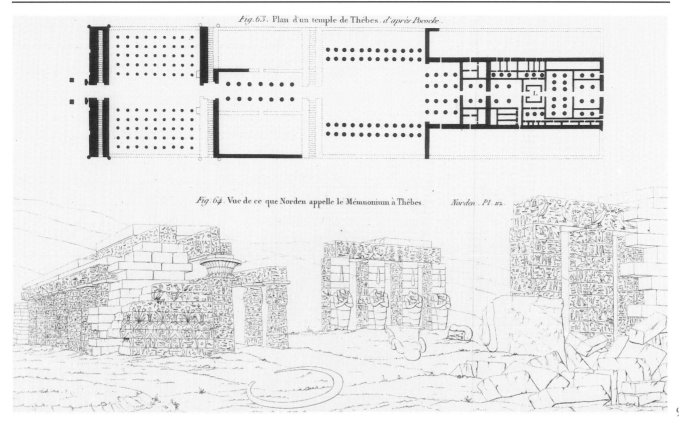

Fig. 63. Plan d'un temple de Thèbes. d'après Pococke.

Fig. 64. Vue de ce que Norden appelle le Mémnonium à Thèbes. *Norden. Pl. 112.*

90

90 *Egyptian temple, from Quincy, showing the clearly defined axial route (after Pococke) and a view of ruins at Thebes (after Norden). Illustration by Gaitte (SJSM).*

88 *Engraving by Gaitte of the entrance to the temple at Thebes with pylons, obelisks, winged globe in the coved cornice, and two colossal heads. The similarity to the Jachin-Boaz iconography of Masonic work is clear, and explains much of why Egyptian design was embraced by the Freemasons. From Quincy (SJSM).*

89 *Egyptian temple. Engraving by Gaitte, from Quincy, showing the pronounced axial routes, with pylons, obelisks, colonnades, courts, and inner parts. Such a route had its parallels in Terrasson's work and in the Lodge of Ledoux which William Beckford visited (SJSM).*

Isiac segmental pediment also emphasized the Egyptian and Masonic connotations through its similarities with the crescent-moon, the bow, and the pediments of temples in the Graeco-Roman world that was devoted to Nilotic deities, such as the great Isaeum Campense in Rome itself, which contained segmental pediments.

Another series of garden pavilions and Egyptian ornaments was built at the park at Étupes to designs by J.-B. Kléber (1753–1800) for the Prince de Montbéliard in 1787; the ensemble included an Egyptian island, perhaps suggested by the Isiac buildings at Philae. (Kléber, curiously, was assassinated in Egypt towards the end of the Napoléonic campaign.) The pyramid erected in the Parc Monceau in Paris by Carmontelle in the 1770s is steeply pitched, owing more to the pyramid of Cestius in Rome than to the Royal tombs of Gizeh. The Monceau pyramid has a primitive blocky entrance flanked by Egyptianizing figures, and typifies the Enlightenment's passion for simplicity, sturdiness, and elemental geometrical forms [92]. Masonic connections are clear, for the Parc Monceau was laid out for the Anglophile Duc de Chartres, Grand Master (installed 22 October 1773) of the Grand Orient, later the Duc d'Orléans (from 1785) and First Prince of the Blood, and later still Philippe-Égalité of the Revolution. Freemasonry in France was very highly connected, and the influence on Architecture was clear.

Masonic activities in Paris sometimes became overt and public, and the Order prospered throughout France, gaining members in droves under the leadership of the Grand Orient. Freemasonry from the 1770s was popular, and appealed to a wide cross-section of French society. The Grand Orient acquired the former Jesuit Novitiate as its headquarters in the Faubourg Saint-Germain in 1774, and work began on the conversion to designs by Pierre Poncet. Rooms were arranged in series, the first being hung with flowered patterns on cloth, the second decorated in watered blue and white, and the third (the main hall) had a blue ceiling, a double row of benches, triangular tables, and two columns of pure metal with capitals carrying clusters of stars.[24] The Orient itself had a platform with a throne, and beyond was the banqueting hall, decorated in blue and red, with a blue ceiling, and with a platform and chair for the Grand Master. According to the *État du G∴O∴ de France*[25] the front of the Lodge was decorated for one grand festival with an 'illumination' of Gothic architecture, eight twisted (presumably barley-sugar) columns, and obelisks in between. So by 1776 the spiral column and Egyptian features were becoming common features of Masonic décor, mingling ideas of the Temple with elements from Ancient Egypt. Another splendid occasion for the Grand Orient was the initiation of Voltaire in 1778 into the Lodge Nine Sisters,

91 *The ruined pyramid by Brongniart at Maupertuis. Note the Doric columns carrying the segmental pediment (a form associated with Isiac cults). On the left is the cenotaph in memory of Admiral Gaspard de Coligny, the Protestant murdered on St Bartholemew's Day 1572. From Laborde. The design was by Constant Bourgeois and the engraving by Athenas femme Massarel* (Dumbarton Oaks, Trustees for Harvard University).

92 *Pyramid in the Wood of Tombs, Parc Monceau, Paris, erected for the Duc de Chartres, Grand Master of the Grand Orient. Note the primitivist entrance (A).*

in the presence of Benjamin Franklin and the Count Stroganoff of Russia.[26]

Only a few months later, on the death of Voltaire, the Temple was transformed into a Lodge of Sorrows, was lavishly dressed with black cloth, and acquired a temporary cenotaph in the form of a pyramid on steps, as well as three broken columns, symbolizing the cutting off of life. The latter became common funerary monuments in the nineteenth-century cemetery, but Bernard Jones states[27]

93 *French Lodge design for Reception of a Master-Mason. This lushly eerie setting has reminders of mortality, the grave, the acacia, Jachin and Boaz, and other familiar elements, but the drapes with pear-shaped* guttes, *or tears, give it an overpowering quality. From* Le Régulateur du Maçon, *Paris, 1801. It appears that Continental examples of the Lodge of Sorrows for deceased Brethren had similar décor* (A).

that although the design of a charity-box produced at each Lodge meeting is symbolic of death and is in the form of a broken column, this has no Masonic significance, 'having been copied from memorial monuments of a design common to the period of its adoption', the early 1800s. With respect, Jones appears to be incorrect, for the broken columns were in use in French Lodges at least as early as 1778, and were displayed in the *Pompes Funèbres* associated with the deaths of Brethren. However, *The Royal Masonic Cyclopaedia*[28] states that in Freemasonry 'the Broken Column is the emblem of the fall or death of one of the chief supporters of the Craft'.

The 'catch' of Voltaire's initiation led to many more recruits to the Order, and by 1780 it is clear, what with publicity, denunciations from the Church, and many works of Masonic scholarship, anecdote, and exposure, that Freemasonry and its activities in France were hardly secret any more; in fact the amount of Masonic publications is daunting to the student of the period [93].

At some time in the 1770s French Freemasonry was bedevilled by a series of defections, by the establishment of quasi-Masonic societies, and by the attractions of mystical, occultist, and other rites. The trouble with Reason was that eventually it reasoned Reason out of existence, and the replacement of the Church and its teachings by 'rational' ethical systems left the need for mystery, belief, and miracles unsatisfied. Mesmer, with his theories of magnetism, Cagliostro with his Egyptian rites, and the secret underground infiltration of many societies by the *Illuminati* of Bavaria were manifestations of disturbing undercurrents, but the grotesque, the sensational, the irrational, and the terrible offered some attractions to a society weary of Progress, Reason, and Science. Cagliostro's rites required special and complex scenery so that the Trials by Fire, Water, and Air could take place. Before the Architecture of these Lodges can be described, we must turn to a consideration of one of the seminal works of Continental Freemasonry.

CHAPTER 6

SÉTHOS AND THE EGYPTIAN RITES

**The Literary Forerunner; *Thamos*; Mozart and Freemasonry;
Die Zauberflöte: Masonic Opera; The Stage-sets and
Egyptian Architecture; Jean-Jacques Lequeu**

O Isis und Osiris, schenket
Der Weisheit Geist dem neuen Paar!
Die ihr den Schritt der Wand'rer lenket,
Stärkt mit Geduld sie in Gefahr.

Lasst sie der Prüfung Früchte sehen;
Doch sollten sie zu Grabe gehen,
So lohnt der Tugend kühnen Lauf,
Nehmt sie in euren Wohnsitz auf.
    Die Zauberflöte, Act II, Scene I

('O Isis and Osiris bestow
the Spirit of Wisdom on this young pair!
You who guide the traveller's pace,
grant strength with patience in time of peril.

Give them the rewards of their Trial,
Yet should they enter the tomb,
grant honour to Virtue's brave action,
and accept them in their dwelling-place.')
    The Magic Flute, Act II, Scene I

The Literary Forerunner

It is clear that, among the many intellectual forces at work during the eighteenth century of our era (based firmly in a veneration and even apotheosis of Nature and Mankind), none was of such fundamental significance as Freemasonry, for it embraced humanitarian teaching, a system of codes of behaviour and of philosophy illustrated with symbols, and it was available to all men, regardless of class and creed (at least theoretically), in a coherent organization where associations of Brethren could meet in good fellowship for discussions, instruction, and conviviality.

Freemasonry taught that beyond a gloomy and materialistic world lay a new light-filled place towards which Mankind should strive, and that it was imperative that all men should seek to build a Temple of Humanity in which all valuable knowledge would be enshrined, and where the lost past would be remembered. Not surprisingly, many Masonic ideas were expressed in poetry, prose, and in music. The Grand Duke Carl August of Weimar's circle was concerned with noble ideas of reconciliation by means of harmony. Works by Kleist, Klopstock, Wieland, Lessing, Pope, Sterne, Swift, Beaumarchais, the Encyclopédists, Henri Beyle (Stendhal), Goethe, and

Herder are steeped in Enlightenment-Masonic notions. Bode and Illuminatist musical circles spread these ideas, and it is no exaggeration to claim that Europe (and America) became infused with a new hopefulness concerning Man's relations with Nature and Creation, where Reason would triumph, with Beauty and Strength. A new equipoise would replace the darkness of superstition and of capricious tyranny.

One of the greatest of all creations in which Freemasonry is central is unquestionably Mozart's *Die Zauberflöte*. While there had been Masonic operas before, including Jean-Philippe Rameau's *Zoroastre* of 1749 with libretto by Cahusac, and Johann Gottlieb Naumann's (also a Mason) *Osiride* of 1781 with libretto by Mazzolà (Lorenzo da Ponte may also have contributed), the most important forerunner as far as the Anglophile Mozart was concerned is a long work that enjoyed considerable popularity from the time it was first published.

In 1731 the Abbé Jean Terrasson (1670–1750) published his *Séthos, histoire ou vie tirée des monumens anecdotes de l'ancienne Égypte. Traduite d'un manuscrit grec*. This very long book, by a man who had translated Diodorus Siculus into French, concerns Séthos, an Egyptian Prince, who was initiated into ancient mysteries, and who, after many travels and adventures, retired to a temple of initiates. English[1] and German translations appeared in 1732, an Italian version in 1734, and another German edition in 1777. The book was much read in Masonic circles, and was cited by some French historians as if it were a standard work on ancient Egyptian mysteries. Thomas Moore's romance *The Epicurean* of 1827 contains ideas borrowed from *Séthos*, and the connection between *Séthos* and *Die Zauberflöte* was first noticed by Thomas Love Peacock in a review of *The Epicurean*. Like other works of the period, Terrasson's book is Rococo, in the sense of its central idea being dressed up in 'exotic' garments. Yet the description of the Isiac mysteries in *Séthos* is very long and detailed, and throughout the book Egypt is regarded as the fount of wisdom and of the Hermetic Tradition.

Séthos is set in the Egypt of Antiquity, and the Prince undergoes various trials for his initiation into the mysteries of Isis. In mythology Isis and Osiris, husband and wife, sister and brother, are mostly venerated together, but, after the murder of Osiris and his dismemberment, Isis put his body together again, although she was unable to locate his generative organs, so she gave birth to Horus/Harpocrates by parthenogenesis. The mysteries were those of Isis alone, although even in Graeco-Roman Egyptian cults Serapis/Osiris and Isis were often venerated in different parts of the same temple complexes.

In *Séthos* various Enlightenment notions are well to the fore, including disapproval of the arbitrary (and therefore illegitimate) use of power by princes. Terrasson's initiates into the Isiac mysteries even have the right to sit in judgement on dead princes to establish if their acts in life were benevolent or not: if they were not, the bodies were denied the rites of burial, and this denial, according to Terrasson, was sufficient to keep the ancient Kings within the rule of dispassionate law.[2] Séthos, once he has passed his various trials, has his hereditary claims to authority confirmed by his merits,[3] so the initiation into the Isiac mysteries makes him part of a body of men all of whom have passed various tests, and all of whom are distinguished by moral and intellectual excellence. Terrasson's initiates never tell lies, but they never reveal secrets either, just as Apuleius, in the *Golden Ass*, ends his book with an initiation into the mysteries of Isis, yet leaves his readers in some confusion about what the initiation rites or mysteries actually were. This tradition of letting on there were secrets yet concealing them is of considerable antiquity; it certainly existed in the Graeco-Roman world and presumably in even earlier civilizations. *Séthos* has copious references to authorities of Antiquity, and the book was so steeped in Classical learning that it acquired a status rather more august than might be imagined.

Thamos

The playwright Tobias Philipp Freiherr von Gebler (1726–86), also a Freemason, who knew Lessing and Wieland as well as other Masonic authors, wrote the text of *Thamos, König in Ägypten*, given in Salzburg in 1773 with specially composed music (K 345) by the young Wolfgang Amadeus Mozart, who thus came into contact with mystical ideas of initiation, Hermetic religion, and Freemasonry. Mozart's impressive and solemn music (comparable with severe Neoclassical designs of the period) was later re-cast and expanded for a new production (with Egyptianizing sets) given by the troupe of Emanuel Schikaneder in Salzburg in 1779, It is with Mozart that Masonic art reaches the highest levels, not least in his works with a pronounced Egyptian flavour.

Otto Jahn observed of the choral writing in *Thamos* that it is grander, more free, and more imposing than that of any of the Masses of the period, and pointed out that a 'solemn act of worship was represented' on the stage; he also noted that the 'expression of reverence to the Supreme Being was heightened in effect by the Egyptian surroundings'.[4]

'Egyptian' theatrical sets, designed with varying attention to historical accuracy, became fashionable in the last third of the eighteenth century, a fact not unconnected with the influence of Freemasonry. With *Thamos* Egyptianizing stage-sets were designed for a production north of the Alps, probably influenced by the stage designs of Tesi of the previous decade.

Mozart and Freemasonry

Mozart was initiated a Freemason in December 1784, and joined the Lodge *Zur Wohltätigkeit* (Beneficence), which met within the rooms of the more powerful Lodge *Zur wahren Eintracht* (True Concord). Freemasonry was established in Austria in 1742, having been given fashionable status not only because of the fact that it had been embraced by France and England, but because Francis Stephen, Duke of Lorraine, husband of Archduchess Maria Theresia, was a Mason, having been initiated, as previously described, at Houghton Hall. The Papal Bull of 1738, which denounced Freemasonry, seems to have been ignored in the Holy Roman Empire, apparently because the Duke persuaded the Emperor Charles VI to avoid persecuting the Craft.[5]

The Kaiser, of course, had directed the building of the Karlskirche [see 57–60] to designs by Fischer von Erlach which, as we have seen, contains many Masonic allusions. The protection given to the Craft, therefore, may have been less due to Francis Stephen's intervention than to a covert appreciation by the Emperor of Freemasonry, its iconography, and its importance in the development of mnemonic techniques to preserve history, legend, and the lost buildings of Antiquity. It must be remembered that there had been a strong thread of mysticism in Habsburg history, not least in the concerns of Rudolph II, Charles V, and, of course, the Spanish connections and the Escorial. We have already established a Masonic connection through Prince Eugen of Savoy and his circle in the Netherlands and in Vienna.

Austrian Lodges followed the English rites and the 'Ancient Landmarks', but under Kaiser Joseph II a decree was passed that prohibited submission of any spiritual or secular order to foreign influences, so in 1784 the *Grosse Landesloge von Österreich*[6] was formed and constituted. It is clear that Freemasonry was a focus for Austria's intelligentsia, and that the important Lodges had Brethren who were eminent in all branches of life. The Lodges were also significant in that many of the Brethren had 'advanced' opinions, and were well aware of the problems likely to develop if the colossal gaps between rich and poor were perpetuated. The prevailing opinion among Freemasons was that through Enlightenment, education, knowledge, reason, and nature, Society as a whole could be improved, would be raised in tone, and could benefit everyone, not least the lower orders.

Mozart's father joined the Craft in 1785, and Wolfgang's friend Haydn had become an Entered Apprentice in the same year. W. A. Mozart was devoted to Freemasonry, and clearly found in the Craft satisfaction regarding basic philosophical attitudes to death and existence. His Masonic music, including the cantata *Dir, Seele des Weltalls* (K 429), *Die Ihr Einem Neuen Grade* (K 468), *Die Maurerfreude* (K 471) [94], *Zerfliesset Heut', Geliebter Brüder* (K 483), *Ihr Unsre Neuen Leiter* (K 484), *Die Ihr des Unermesslichen Weltalls Schöpfer Ehrt* (K 619), (with libretto by Franz Heinrich Ziegenhagen, who was strongly influenced by Rousseau and the Encyclopédists, and who was interested in the reform of religion, in the study of relationships of Man and Nature, and who advocated religious tolerance), *Laut verkünde unsre Freude* (K 623), and *Lass uns mit geschlungen Händen* (K 623a), is often among the most deeply affecting he ever wrote, but two Masonic works stand out for their extraordinary invention and power: the *Maurerische Trauermusik* (K 477), and *Die Zauberflöte* (K 620).

The elegiac *Maurerische Trauermusik* (Masonic Funeral Music), written for the *Pompes Funèbres* or Lodge of Sorrows in Commemoration of Duke Georg August of Mecklenburg-Strelitz and Count Franz Eszterházy von Galantha in 1785, has a dark, mysterious atmosphere, the musical equivalent of some Neoclassical designs for subterranean tombs, like those by Desprez.[7] This short

work for orchestra is permeated with the figure three, not only in its tripartite form, but in its sixty-nine measures with the *Te decet* plainsong used by Michael Haydn in his *Requiem* of 1771 (which also influenced Mozart in his own *Requiem* of 1791). The use of bassett-horns and a contrabassoon anticipates the opening pages of Mozart's *Requiem* (K 626).

In 1785 Joseph II ordered a reduction in the number of Viennese Lodges: there was unease at the growing popularity of Freemasonry and at the influence of known Masons in all walks of life. The important Lodge *Zur wahren Eintracht* amalgamated with two other Lodges to become *Zur Wahrheit* (Truth), while *Zur gekrönten Hoffnung* (Crowned Hope), Mozart's Lodge *Zur Wohltätigkeit*, and *Drei Feuern* (Three Fires) joined to become *Zur neugekrönten Hoffnung* (New-Crowned Hope), an event Mozart immortalized by referring to Joseph's 'Benevolence' and the joy of the Brethren in having their 'Hope Newly Crowned' in his Masonic Song *Zerfliesset Heut', Geliebter Brüder* (K 483). The Emperor also required full lists of all members, information about activities, and so on, which were held on file by the Court. A list of Brethren of the Lodge *Zur gekrönten Hoffnung* (the 'neu' had been abandoned in or around 1789) for 1790 includes Mozart's name[8] as well as those of Count Johann Esterházy (Master of the Lodge and Imperial and Royal Chamberlain), Prince Nicolas Esterházy (Haydn's patron), various high-ranking personages in the Civil Service, legal world, publishing, the Church, Karl Ludwig Gieseke (who was to end up as Professor at Trinity College Dublin, and who claimed to have written at least part of the libretto of *Die Zauberflöte*), landowners, soldiers, musicians, artists, craftsmen, and a reigning prince (Anton von Hohenzollern-Sigmaringen).[9] An anonymous painting now in the Historisches Museum der Stadt Wien shows a Viennese Lodge of *c*.1790 arranged according to the St John's Lodge plan, with Mozart seated among the Brethren (who include at least two Churchmen [Colour Plate IV]).

Another picture of a Lodge interior featuring a man of genius also survives: this is the painting by Stewart Watson of the Inauguration of Robert Burns (1759–96) as Poet Laureate of the Lodge Canongate Kilwinning, Edinburgh, on 1 March 1787 [Colour Plate V]. It is indicative of the influence of Freemasonry in the eighteenth century that two almost exact contemporaries, both of whom became world-famous as creative artists, were dedicated Masons, appeared in paintings of Lodges, and were revered by their Masonic Brethren.

On the death of Joseph II in 1790 Austrian Masons awaited with considerable trepidation the next blow from the new Emperor, Leopold II. It must be remembered that repercussions from France were already

starting to worry European monarchs, and the link between progressive ideas, the growing power of the Third Estate, and French Freemasons could not be ignored. Professor H. C. Robbins Landon has suggested that in the uncertainty following the death of Joseph II, Mozart and Schikaneder took the risk of producing *Die Zauberflöte*, an allegorical opera in German that was part-*Singspiel*, which was intended to save the Craft by showing it in the best possible light. It was in 1790, too, that Queen Marie Antoinette warned her brother, the new Emperor Leopold, to take care over any associations of Freemasons, for it was by means of Freemasonry that the 'monsters' in France counted on succeeding elsewhere.[10]

Freemasonry, in 1791, was facing a real threat of being banned (its light extinguished), and in 1794 it closed the Lodges voluntarily *before* the new Emperor (Francis II), prohibited all secret societies in his realms. By that time, of course, the former Archduchess Maria-Antonia, as Queen (Marie Antoinette) of France, had been guillo-

94 *Title-page of Mozart's Masonic Cantata* Die Maurerfreude *(K 471), in the Viennese first Artaria edition of 1785, engraved by Sebastian Mansfeld after Ignaz Unterberger. The text was by Franz Petran, and the piece was written in honour of Ignaz von Born, Grand Master of the* Zur wahren Eintracht *Lodge. Emblems of Truth, Harmony, and Crowned Hope can be seen, all referring to Viennese Lodges* (BL. Music Library, Hirsch IV, 84).

tined, and the horrors of Jacobinism and the Terror had been unleashed. That there were sympathisers of revolutionary excess in the Holy Roman Empire with Masonic connections is now clear. Masonic revolutionary leaders elsewhere included Washington, Franklin, and probably most of those involved in 1789 in France, although the Terror and Regicide were not on the agenda then. The problem was that they happened, and

95 *Engraving by Ignaz Alberti, Vienna, of an imaginary scene from* Die Zauberflöte *from the first edition of the libretto of 1791. Note the rocky grotto, the fragments of masonry, the Masonic tools, the steeply pitched pyramid (or is it a fat obelisk?) with bogus 'Egyptian' symbols (although the* Ankh *is genuine enough). The vase with crouching figures and serpents, five-pointed star, and other elements should be noted* (BL. Music Library, Hirsch IV, 1385).

were not stopped by all the claims to brotherhood, fraternity, and benevolence.

In this respect Dr Guillotin's machine for severing heads from bodies in an efficient and supposedly humane manner is an interesting object, not only because it became an instrument of the Terror and of injustice (a corruption of its original intent), but because of the elements of its design. The square plate with the circle for the head and the triangular blade certainly suggest Masonic allegories: in the climate of the 1780s, when Masonic motifs would have been familiar to many, the connection might not have been as tenuous as we might think today.

Die Zauberflöte: Masonic Opera

Die Zauberflöte is based on *Séthos*, and it is clear that the author (or authors) of the libretto were familiar not only with Terrasson's work, but with the writings of Apuleius, Diodorus Siculus, and Lucian. Like Séthos, Tamino in *Die Zauberflöte* is a prince, and a travelling prince at that, who seeks education by journeying in foreign parts and by initiation into certain mysteries. But the *Flute* is not just derived from *Séthos*: like many concoctions of the period it owes debts to other works. These include *Thamos, König in Ägypten* by Gebler, the Opera *Oberon* by Paul Wranitzky which had been staged by Schikaneder in 1789 in a version by Giesecke, C. M. Wieland's collection *Dschinnistan* of 1786[11] which contains a fairy-story called *Lulu, oder die Zauberflöte*, and sundry works of Rococo *Exotica* popular at the time. In Wieland's *Stein der Weisen* there is a descent into a pyramid in Memphis for initiation rites involving Trials by Fire and Water. Indeed, Tamino, the Séthos-figure of *Die Zauberflöte*, is given an extra-exotic aura by being credited with a Japanese background, although his name, and that of Pamina, seem to be of vaguely Egyptian origin.

The illustrations for the printed libretto of *Die Zauberflöte* were engraved by Ignaz Alberti, a Freemason and Brother of Mozart's Lodge: one of these decorations contain much bogus 'Egyptian' allusion in the tall pyramid (or is it a fat obelisk?) with *Ankh* and other ill-observed details, as well as Masonic references in the mattock, pick, hourglass, and fragments of carved masonry. The overall gloom of the dark, cavernous scene, however, recalls images from Piranesi, and indeed the grotesque figures and urn recall the flavour of Piranesi's *Diverse Maniere d'Adornare i Cammini* of 1769. The Neoclassical Egyptian flavour was set [95].

At the very beginning of the opera the overture (in the

Masonic key of E flat major [i.e. with three flats]) starts with one chord followed by two more, the latter with anacruses, making five in all in the rhythm o–oo–oo. Now five combines the Duad and the Triad, and represents the flaming star of the female Order, or light itself. The following Adagio is a conventional representation of the Kingdom of the Night, or Darkness and Chaos. The opening of the fugue is *Ordo ab Chao*, the Kingdom of Light, with a rhythm suggesting the blows or tapping of mallets, that is, Masonic work. The fugue breaks off for the thrice-three chords of its Master's Degree with dotted rhythms (used in French Lodges under the Grand Orient which were about to be closed) before a darker section of self-examination in the minor key with many chromaticisms (suggesting a journey in sound) leads to the major closing bars, representing the victory of the sun. Was Mozart showing Austrian solidarity with his French Brethren, or was he referring to a Lodge in Prague which used the French Masonic ritual rather than that of the St John's Lodges? Throughout *Die Zauberflöte* Masonic allusions abound: the figure three runs through the opera, from the Three Knocks of the Overture and later, the key of E flat major with its three flats, the Three Ladies, the Three Boys, and certain rhythms of three in the scoring. Tamino is the initiate, taking vows of silence and symbolically making a journey, fasting, going through trials by fire, water, air, and earth, then finally passing from darkness to light. Sarastro, the High Priest of the Temple, is, of course, Zoroaster, and may be a portrait of Ignaz von Born, Master of the Lodge *Zur wahren Eintracht* which had Brethren drawn from the arts, sciences, Churches (both Roman Catholic and Protestant), civil servants, musicians, and aristocrats. Born died in July 1791, and it is possible that Sarastro was a kind of memorial to him as Master of an élite Lodge. Born, himself an Illuminatist, said that monks were ignorant, and that Jesuitry and fanaticism could be equated with roguery, ignorance, superstition, and stupidity.

There are many parallels with Isiac religion in *Die Zauberflöte*. Isis transformed herself into an old hag and then into a beautiful girl, just as happens to Papagena. Papageno the bird-catcher might have stepped from the banks of the Nile, with his reed-pipes. The magic bells may be a reference to the sacred *sistrum* and timbrels used in Isiac ceremonies, and indeed *sistra* replaced the bell in Ethiopian Christian liturgies, while the *crotalus* was used instead of the bell in Western European churches on Maundy Thursday. So the bells, roses, transformations, and even the bird-catcher with his pipes can be seen to have Isiac-Egyptian connotations. Furthermore, Monostatos, whose black visage and singular name pick him out as anti-social (his heart is as black as his face),

represents the obscure, the dark, hateful, and villainous. He may be an emblem of the black-robed clerics who serve the Church, and indeed that interpretation explains his devotion to the Queen and his servile and treacherous attitude to Sarastro and the Freemasons. One explanation of Monostatos is that he was a renegade Mason, but that does not quite fit the bill. The black-clothed cleric, black of heart and obscurantist of mind is better, but his hatred of the temple and of Sarastro (and therefore of Osiris-Isis) probably loosely identifies him with Seth of the South Wind, the murderer and dismemberer of Osiris,[12] as well as with bigoted anti-Masonic clergy. He is certainly given to lechery, to earthiness, and he is isolated: should the Night triumph then so will his carnality, and Pamina will be subjected. His chains and irons represent repression that can only be lifted when his intended victims are initiated to Enlightenment.

Die Zauberflöte is not just a re-hash of *Séthos*: it also contains elements of the St John ceremonial of Freemasonry as well as the 'Scottish Rites' and the Sovereign Rose-Croix Degree (No. 18 in the Ancient and Accepted Scottish Rite 33°). That memorable and very curious twenty-seventh scene in Act 2 which shows the Fire and Water through which Tamino must pass begins with *Zwei schwarzgeharnischte Männer* (Two men in black armour—not 'Two Armed Men' as has often been given in opera programmes)—who sing of the path of trials and of those trials through Fire, Water, Air and Earth (*Feuer, Wasser, Luft, und Erden*), of conquering the fear of death, of rising from earth to the sphere of heaven, of illumination, of consecration, and of the mysteries of Isis. In this scene Mozart used a *Lutheran* chorale, *Ach Gott, vom Himmel sieh' darein* to emphasize the solemn, even Biblical, nature of this extraordinary Trial scene. The Antique element is reinforced by the Two Men, who might be the two *telamoni* from the Villa Adriana at Tivoli, or even Jachin and Boaz themselves. The *telamoni*, of course, were Roman work in the Egyptian taste, and were similar to the Antinoüs figure, also from Tivoli. The Old Testament also promises that one who passes through waters will not be overflown, and that one who walks through fire will not be burned, nor will flame kindle upon the walker.[13]

H. C. Robbins Landon[14] points out that the solemnity, with the Protestant chorale, was very different from the liturgical experience of the average Roman–Catholic Austrian. He also tells us[15] that the orchestral introduction to this scene consists of eighteen groups of notes, that there are eighteen groups of priests, that part one of the chorus *O Isis und Osiris* is eighteen bars long, and that Papagena is eighteen, although when she says it she appears as an old hag. Eighteen is the degree of the Rose-

Croix, the number of priests who watched over Hiram's grave, and it is also six times three, and six is two times three.

Another point that completely eludes modern designers of this opera is the fact that roses played an important part in early productions: the flying machine of the Three Boys is covered with roses, and there was presumably scope for roses in the gardens, bowers, and other sets. Roses were used in Isiac rites; Lucius, in Apuleius, eats roses during his initiation, and the flower of Isis was the unfading rose. The Mystic Rose is an attribute of the Virgin Mary as it was of Isis herself.

The use of a Protestant chorale in *Die Zauberflöte* has a curious parallel at Maupertuis, where Alexandre-Théodore Brongniart designed the pyramid mentioned earlier which dominated an *Élysée*, or English garden: there the Marquis de Montesquiou held Masonic meetings. Antiquity was represented by the 'ruined' pyramid, while the segmental pediment, associated with Isis, was Masonic in its allusion. It is significant that Brongniart and Montesquiou also dignified their *Élysée* with a monumental mausoleum to the Protestant hero Admiral Gaspart de Coligny, in defiance of Papal persecution (Coligny was murdered on St. Bartholomew's Day in 1572) [see 91]. There appears to have been some form of ritual route through the *Élysée*: even the entrance was through a grotto beneath the pyramid representing a Terrasson-like descent to a subterranean vault, and many buildings were planned for the grounds, including an Arts Tower, a Temple with a spring representing Eternity, and several buildings by Ledoux, including his spherical Lodge and Ideal Village, all with Masonic connotations.[16] That the gardens at Maupertuis and the designs for Chaux were Masonic is beyond doubt.

Protestantism is alluded to in Mozart's *Requiem* as well, for the 'learned' fugal manner derived from Mozart's study of the works of Bach and Händel: the great *Kyrie* fugue has a first subject that is a direct quotation from Händel's *Messiah* (which Mozart had edited for performance). Thus even the *Requiem* embraces Antique and Protestant themes, and looks back to an ancient Jewish culture through the Old Testament. The parallels with the Temple and the Lodge will be obvious. With its dark colouring, its quotation of Plainsong, and its use of Händelian themes and fugues, the *Requiem*, too, has associations with Masonic designs that alluded to Protestantism, and cannot be seen only as a setting of the Mass for the Dead by an eighteenth-century composer of genius.

The last scenes of *Die Zauberflöte* include an attack by the Queen of the Night and her accomplices on the Temple (the Revenge Degree), and the dissipation of darkness by light:

> *Die Strahlen der Sonne vertreiben die Nacht,*
> *Zernichten der Heuchler erschlichene Macht*
> (The rays of the sun scatter the night
> Breaking asunder the might of the false dissembler).

Pamina and Tamino are welcomed by a chorus of priests with the words:

> *Es siegte die* Stärke *und krönet zum Lohn*
> *Die* Schönheit *und* Weisheit *mit ewiger Kron*
> (*Strength* is victorious and we a reward,
> *Beauty* and *Wisdom* are granted the eternal crown)

Strength, Wisdom, and *Beauty* are, of course, words with powerful Masonic connotations, associated with the St John and with the Scottish Rite: Strength is represented in Masonic symbolism by the Doric Order, Wisdom by the Ionic, and Beauty by the Corinthian. Strength, Wisdom and Beauty are the Three Principal Supports of Masonry, and are expressed in many ways, but usually by the Orders.

Finally, there has been much argument as to why the plot of *Die Zauberflöte* changed, altering the Queen of the Night and her retinue from forces of good into evil. The '*sternflammende Königin*' (star-flaming Queen) derives from the Queen of Heaven, and is therefore a figure from Antiquity, related to Isis/Astarte and the Moon. When Monostatos attempts to pounce on the sleeping Pamina he requests the Moon to be hidden, yet his request brings the Queen at once to protect Pamina, which was the opposite of his intentions.

The point about the beginning and the end of the *Flute* is that it teaches us two important truths: first, that things are not always what they seem, and, second, that the man who is 'more than a prince' by being a man, learns to cast aside the darkness by venturing through the gates of hell into the Underworld, metaphorically dies, and is resurrected after initiation and undergoing trials, overcoming the very terror of death itself. He also, when playing the flute, standing with the instrument in its transverse position, becomes an enigmatical representation of a word or a name by suggesting the Masonic Square.

The 'star-Flaming Queen', or Queen of the Night, is an image that would have been very familiar to Austrians: she is suggestive of the Virgin Mary,[17] and the image on her cresent-moon surrounded by stars suggests the Church. There is, however, a further subtlety that seems to have escaped most commentators on *Die Zauberflöte*: the Queen of the Night is the star-flaming Queen, and so she is a pseudo-Isis, the lady of light and flames, the fire of Hades. It is likely that the Queen, referred to in terms of deceit, superstition, and trickery, represents the Church's Virgin Mary as a usurper of Isis the benevolent, the good, the Mistress of the Word, the Beginning, Source of Grace and Truth, the Resurrection and the Life, the Mother of God, Supreme Deity as Maker of Monarchs, Shelter of the Living and of the Dead. Sarastro and the Priests pray to Isis and Osiris, but it is obvious from the opera that the star-flaming Queen of the Night is *not* Isis, although she has stolen her attributes in the moon and stars. The Queen and her black-clad ladies are not all bad, for they give Tamino the flute, making him into an Orpheus by that act, whereby he can then charm the fiercest animals; nevertheless, they obscure the truth with their darkness, misrepresentations, and deceit. At the very beginning of the opera the Three Veiled Ladies (veiled because Enlightenment cannot reach them) kill the serpent, symbol of Freemasonry, and Tamino is terrified of the serpent: the point is that his terror is due to ignorance, and the ladies show their true colours right at the start by attacking the Craft and trying to annex the young man for their cause.

In respect of *Die Zauberflöte* the Orpheus connection is also interesting, for that legend is one of the earliest and most obscure in Greek mythology, Orpheus was the type of poet and musician who ventured into the Underworld, suffered a great loss, originated mysteries to which men only were initiated, was murdered, and was dismembered by the Thracian women. The parallels with Osiris, the missionary going on a journey, who preaches goodness, culture, and music, are clear, even in his dismemberment. Tamino, by not speaking to Pamina, is undergoing a trial that recalls Orpheus and Euridice.

We learn also that Pamina leads Tamino through the Trials by Fire and Water, the way strewn with roses, while he plays the flute her father carved in a 'magic hour' from a thousand-year-old oak-tree during lightning, thunder, storm, and uproar. So her father, too, was a supernatural being like her mother (who disowns her because she will not kill Sarastro—i.e. the Grand Master); or is the 'mother' who disowns Pamina Mother Church, and therefore not her real mother at all? This seems very likely, because Pamina is not deeply disturbed by being disowned (as she would be were the Queen really her mother), and implores Sarastro not to punish the star-flaming Queen because the Queen's grief over losing Pamina was punishment enough. Pamina, by leading Tamino through the Trials by Fire and Water, guided herself by love, may be showing him the mysteries of life and death in a symbolic way.[18]

Now Hermes invented the lyre (the instrument of Orpheus) and was the guide to the dead in Hades, and if the flute is substituted for the lyre (Hermes also invented the shepherd's pipe), that gives Pamina an Hermetic-

Egyptian connection too. However, the priestly race of the Kerykes (of the Eleusinian Mysteries) claimed Hermes as head of their family, that is father, and, of course, those mysteries were festivals of Demeter (identified as Isis), and her daughter Persephone. The Egyptianization of *Die Zauberflöte* was complete.[19]

A reasonable interpretation of *Die Zauberflöte*, therefore, is that the Church and its agents put it about that Freemasonry is wicked and that its Brethren are up to no good (as, of course, happened, not only in Bulls but in many hysterical and paranoid publications). The truth, however, is different, for Wisdom, Strength, and Beauty are the rewards in the Enlightened precincts of the Temple (i.e. Freemasonry) and lead to a heaven on earth created by enlightened Mankind. The Three Boys refer to a secret that is not theirs to tell, and counsel Tamino to

Sei standhaft, duldsam und verschwiegen
(be resolutely staunch, patient, and silent)

before the temples of *Weisheit* (Wisdom), *Vernunft* (Reason), and *Natur* (Nature), the *Pforten* (portals) and *Säulen* (columns, pillars, or jambs) of which are inscribed with the words *Klugheit* (prudence), *Arbeit* (work), and *Künste* (Arts), all of which are Masonic [Colour Plate VII].

Mozart, it is known, took great comfort from Masonic views on death, as is clear from his letters to his dying father in 1787: he regarded death as the real purpose of life, as a best friend, as a comforter, with no terrifying image.[20] In other words Freemasonry gave Mozart a solace that the Church, with its terrible doctrine of Purgatory and Hellfire, could not give. The serenity of mind is that of a true son of the *Aufklärung* (Enlightenment), and of a dedicated Freemason who has symbolically passed from death to life in the Masonic ceremonies leading to the Master-Mason Degree, and who was wholly conversant with Masonic philosophies of death. It is clear from the Lodge of Sorrows for which Mozart composed the *Maurerische Trauermusik* that the Masons gave their departed Brethren a dignified memorial; Mozart himself was commemorated by a Lodge of Sorrows after his death which must have been a solemn and moving contrast to the perfunctory offices of St Stephen's Cathedral given by the priests of the Church. One final point ought to be made here: Mozart was given a third-class funeral (not a pauper's funeral), and the fact that the mourners dispersed after the church service was not unusual in the eighteenth century. Once a dead body was committed to the care of the Church, that was that: journeys to the communal ditches of the overspill burial-grounds were not usually undertaken, for city graveyards (or even suburban ones) were not pleasant places. This point, and the Masonic programme of reform that led to the establishment of landscape garden-cemeteries, will be elaborated upon below.

There are other intriguing aspects to *Die Zauberflöte* and Mozart. The *Palmenwalde* scenes remind us, not only of the Nilotic setting, but of many Continental Lodges named after palm-trees (palms, like acacias, chestnuts, limes, myrtles, and bays, had powerful Masonic connotations in Continental Europe). Mozart's use of secret codes and riddles is well known, and he often used code when writing to people he trusted, while his skill with mathematical puzzles and number-games was clear from an early age, so it is not surprising that the *Flute* is full of symbolic numbers and all sorts of coded musical messages, many of which escape the ear but become more obvious on paper. Mozart himself had plans to establish a secret esoteric society with Illuminatist–Masonic aims to be called *The Grotto*. He knew of several built rock-work grottoes, but he and his family were familiar with the grotto at Aigen near Salzburg, known as the Cave of the Illuminati; it is possible he had this site in mind for the scene with the Two Men in Armour, for a great waterfall roared down on one side.

Early in his life he had written a *Singspiel* for performance in Dr Anton Mesmer's garden in 1768: it was called *Bastien und Bastienne* (K 50), and had words by Friedrich Wilhelm Weiskern, after Favart, based on Rousseau's *Le Devin du Village*. Thus Wolfgang Amadeus Mozart, aged 12, had set a work that originated with one of the great figures of the Enlightenment for performance in the Vienna garden of a man who was to be involved with Cagliostro and with French Freemasonry.

It is submitted that *Die Zauberflöte*, like the Karlskirche, is unquestionably a Sublime work of Masonic Art, and, like the church, has many layers of meaning, and much deeply-felt symbolism, in both words and music, that can be understood only by deep study. The fact is that it, in turn, brought out the best in a whole generation of stage-designers, and these are rewarding to study for the sheer variety of invention they display. The architectural and Egyptian effects were remarkable, for accurate source-material relating to Ancient Egyptian design was available, not only from Quatremère de Quincy's works, but also from Denon's *Voyage . . .* of 1802 and the monumental *Description de L'Égypte . . .* of the Commission des Monuments d'Égypte published from 1809.[21]

The Stage-Sets and Egyptian Architecture

Only two years after the death of Mozart, the Quaglios produced designs for a new production of *Die Zauberflöte* at the Nationaltheater, Mannheim, in 1794. The Quag-

lios were involved in stage design in Vienna, Munich, Dresden, Zweibrücken, Mannheim, Schwetzingen, and other centres. Giulio III Quaglio (1764–1801), son of Domenico Quaglio, became official painter to the Court Theatre in Mannheim from 1785, and was a master of realistic architectural and landscape scenery. Most of his drawings appear to have survived as inventory sketches of the scenery archives of the Mannheim National Theatre in the 1790s, and some of the subjects were based on designs by Giulio, by his brother Giuseppe, or by his uncle Lorenzo. A design for *Ein Seltsames Gewölbe* ('a strange vault') in Act II, Scene 20, shows a fondness for Antique Roman motifs [96], although an Egyptian suggestion occurs in the presence of obelisks and sphinxes. *Gewölbe* also means a 'family vault', so the funereal character, indicated by the urns, *loculi*, and memorial plaques is further emphasized. This extraordinary design, with a torso hanging out of a *loculus* on the right, and the figures of Papageno and Papagena, is probably by Giuseppe (Joseph) Quaglio, and is signed by him.

The Esterházy family was deeply involved in Freemasonry, for, as has been indicated, Prince Nicolas Esterházy was Master of Ceremonies in the *Zur gekrönten Hoffnung* Lodge, while Count Johann Esterházy was Master in 1781 and 1791. *Die Zauberflöte* was given at Kismarton in 1804 under the baton of Johann Nepomuk Hummel (a pupil of Mozart and a Freemason), with designs by Carl Maurer, who was engaged by Prince Miklós III Esterházy in 1802 as his '*Hofkammermaler*' or official court painter. Maurer's weird designs are preserved in a sketch-book entitled 'Handzeichnungen Zum Theater Gebrauch von Carl Maurer Fürstlich Esterhazyscher Hof Theater Decorateur', dated Eisenstadt,

96 *Design, probably by Giuseppe Quaglio (1747–1828), for the Nationaltheater, Mannheim, production of* Die Zauberflöte, *in 1794. The subject is a 'vault inside a pyramid', for Act II, Scene 20, and shows Papageno and the crone Papagena (aged 18). The obelisks, sphinxes, torso hanging out of the* loculus *on the right, and funerary character should be noted, as should the curious use of ogee arches and the primitivist form of the opening on the left* (DT. No.S.Qu.44/II, neg. no. 2246).

97 *Carl Maurer's design for* Die Zauberflöte, *showing temple with segmental pediment, winged sphinxes, two columns before the temple (indicative of Jachin and Boaz), steep banded pyramid, and bogus hieroglyphs from the* Handzeichnungen, *p10* (Slovenská).

96

97

98

99

1812, and now in the Čaplovič library in Czechoslovakia[22] [97–99]. In spite of the availability of Quatremère de Quincy's work, Denon's *Voyage ...*, and other sources, Maurer's designs are inauthentic and ill-observed, although traces of Renaissance and Antique themes, such as the 'many-breasted' Diana, obelisks, segmental-pedimented temples based on Roman Isiac temples, Piranesian *carceri* interiors and Bernini-Poliphilus elephant with obelisk on its back, influenced these somewhat rustic and provincial offerings. Nonetheless, the strong Masonic connections of the Esterházy family must be borne in mind: the Egyptianizing sets were regarded as indicative of Freemasonry, and the allusions would not have escaped educated Austrian Masons.

Much more interesting, architecturally and archaeologically more scholarly, and in terms of imagery and flair quite outstanding, were the sets produced by Karl Friedrich Schinkel (1781–1841) in 1815 when Schinkel was appointed to design stage décor for the royal theatres in Berlin under the general management of Count Brühl. From 1815 to 1832 Schinkel designed more than thirty productions, but his work for *Die Zauberflöte*, given at the Berlin Königliche Schauspiele-Opernhaus in 1816 to celebrate the centenary of the coronation of the first Prussian King and the victory festival on 18 January after the Wars of Liberation, set a new standard of excellence. Schinkel selected the Egyptian style for historical correctness as well as for the grandeur and solemnity of the occasion and produced a masterpiece of Neoclassical theatre decoration in which architectural and historical accuracy were achieved without being slavish to pedantic correctness of every detail. These stunning designs were much admired at the time: E. T. A. Hoffmann in the *Dramaturgischen Wochenblatt* of 2

98 *Carl Maurer's design for* Die Zauberflöte, *showing a moonlit garden with Nilotic flora, an obelisk of five stages [cf. 7–12, 167, 170], a six-breasted bust representing Diana of Ephesus and Isis, and the fountain, an Isiac feature. From the* Handzeichnungen, *p15* (Slovenská).

99 *Carl Maurer's design for the entrance to the Trials by Fire and Water in Act II of* Die Zauberflöte. *The stepped corbels and angular openings derived from Piranesi's designs should be noted. Such forms were revived in Art-Déco work in the 1920s and '30s, and the angled 'arch' recurred in bridges over the M1 motorway designed in the 1930s. From the* Handzeichnungen, *p16* (Slovenská).

March 1816 waxed lyrical about them, praising the starry skies, dark vaults full of Sublime Terror, supernatural atmosphere, noble sphinxes, colossal scale of the Temple of the Sun, and the contrast between light and dark.[23]

The Fantastic Egyptian Temple in a rocky grotto (Act I, Scene 1) in which Tamino is pursued by the serpent and 'rescued' by the Three Ladies, gains additional menace by the inclusion of crouching, sinister, winged figures [100]. The Hall of Stars of the Queen of the Night (Act I, Scene 6) is an image of remarkable simplicity and directness: the dark vault of Prussian blue is suggested by the structural 'ribs' of stars, while the Queen seems to float on her crescent-moon [Colour Plate VI]. The allusions to the Immaculata are clear, for Marian symbolism was derived from that of Isis. For those who wish to pursue the interminable lists of objects, emblems, and ideas associated with the Virgin Mary, Antonio Cuomó's *Saggio apologetico della bellezza celeste e divina di Maria SS. Madre di Dio*,[24] Hippolytus Marraccius's *Bibliotheca Mariana alphabetico ordine digesta. . .*,[25] the same author's *Polyanthea Mariana, in qua libris octodecim . . .*,[26] Serafino Montorio's *Zodiaco di Maria* of 1715 (which treats of the varieties of Madonna to be found in Southern Italy alone), and St Alfonso Maria de'Liguori's *Glories of Mary*,[27] cover the subject in amazing detail. The Madonna is represented by the sun, the moon, the stars, the moon under her feet, the Stella Maris, the Rose of Sharon, the Lily among Thorns, the Tower of David, the Mountain of Myrrh, the Hill of Frankincense, the Garden enclosed, the Spring, the Spring shut up, the Fountain (working or sealed), the Palm Tree, the Queen of Mercy, Queen of Heaven and Hell, Ladder of Paradise, Gate of Heaven, Augusta, Aurora, a young heifer, and Medicina Mundi, among much else. She was protean, could multiply with bacteriological ease, and could be identified with virtually anything. As an antidote, Theodor Trede's *Das Heidentum in der römischen Kirche. Bilder aus dem religiösen und sittlichen Leben Süditaliens*, published in Gotha in 1889–91, provides a sober Lutheran's scholarly observations in a relentless account of improbable and syncretic happenings. A study of *Séthos*, of Isiac rites, and of the imagery used by Schinkel should clarify any doubts as to the identity of the Queen of the Night.

Schinkel's vault as a metaphor of the heavens had its parallel in a number of representations of the Temple of Solomon as a Pantheon-like structure; Martin van Heemskerck showed such a form in his version of the Temple [see 61]. The title page of a Prussian Masonic Song-Book of 1798 indicates how these ideas were merging [101]. The Pantheon also appears as an illustration to *Le Régulateur du Maçon* of 1801 [see 77].

For Act I, Scene 15 Schinkel set three Egyptian portals

100 *Schinkel's design for Act I, Scene 1 of* Die Zauberflöte *in the 1816 production of the opera at the Königliche Schauspiele-Opernhaus, Berlin, showing a fantastic Egyptian temple in a rocky grotto, treated quite freely, but with enormous verve. This, the domain of the Queen of the Night, has a suitably sinister flavour, appropriate for the palace of the 'Sternflammende Königin', who is also known as Astrifiammante in certain nineteenth-century versions of the opera. The crouching figures are suggestive of futuristic science-fiction fantasies mixed with more overt Egyptianizing architecture. From Thiele* (DT. A1627).

101 *Title-page of* Auswahl von Maurer Gesängen mit Melodien der vorzüglichsten getheilt; gesammlet und herausgegeben, von F. W. Böheim, *published in Berlin in 1798. This Masonic song-book had a vignette of a Pantheon-like structure with an Antique Doric portico flanked by sphinxes and obelisks* (UGLE).

102 *Schinkel's design for Act II, Scene 7 of* Die Zauberflöte *in the 1816 Berlin production at the Königliche Schauspiele-Opernhaus, showing a mausoleum consisting of a sphinx on a battered base set on an island with palm-trees. This 'Mondscheinlandschaft' is one of the most evocative of the entire set of outstanding designs. Carl Friedrich Thiele's version of Schinkel's original project (Schinkel Museum SM XXII c/102), from Thiele* (DT. A 1397).

AUSWAHL

von

Maurer Gesängen

mit Melodien der vorzüglichsten Componisten

in zwey Abtheilungen getheilt;

gesammlet und herausgegeben,
von
F. W. Böheim

Berlin, 1798.

in a unified composition within a lushly tropical land-scape [Colour Plate VII] to signify the sanctuary of Wisdom, Reason, and Nature. A distant view of the temple complex at Philae (or at least a group of buildings on an island that recall the Isiac temples at Philae) appears as a vignette in a *Palmenwalde* for Act II, Scene 1 of Schinkel's sets [Colour Plate VIII]; the luxuriant Nilotic plants and distant vignette may derive from Humboldt's travels and from Denon's *Voyage....*

The set for Act II, Scene 7 of *Die Zauberflöte* by Schinkel shows a landscape bathed in moonlight, with, as a central motif, an island on which is a mausoleum in the form of a sphinx on a battered base [102]. Hoffmann, in the *Dramaturgischen Wochenblatt*, felt the design was serious and solemn, with a mysterious colossus looking down on the silence of nature. The two kneeling figures with vases in the foreground, the palm trees, and the reflections in the waters add to the effect of serenity, of magic, and of mystery. Also dramatic, dark, mysterious, and reminiscent of catacombs, of the funereal designs of Desprez, and of Piranesi's *esquisses* for Egyptianizing fireplaces is the strange vault of Act II, Scene 20, with its massive piers, primitive forms, and brooding atmosphere [Colour Plate IX].

Two other Schinkel sets should be referred to here:

103 *Schinkel's design for* Act II, Scene 28 *in the 1816 Berlin production of* Die Zauberflöte *at the Königliche Schauspiele-Opernhaus, showing the exit from the Trials by Fire and Water on the right, and the entrance to the Temple of the Sun, with much Egyptian architectural treatment. The Architecture is derived from Denon's* Voyage . . . *(portico from Dendera), and from the title-page of F. Norden's* Travels in Egypt and Nubia *of 1757. Other elements are from Schinkel's own Diorama project* Das Labyrinth von Creta *of 1807, and from Mauro Tesi's* Racoltà di Disegni Originali *published in Bologna in 1787. From Thiele: this version of Schinkel's original project (Schinkel Museum SM XXII/119 and SM XVb/50–52) is by Carl Friedrich Thiele (DT. A 1398).*

104 *Schinkel's design for the Closing Scene of Act* II *and of the whole opera in the 1816 Berlin production of* Die Zauberflöte *at the Königliche Schauspiele-Opernhaus, showing the interior of the colossal temple of the Sun. In the background Osiris sits enthroned, flanked by Apis bulls. On either side are colossal statues of priests in attitudes of adoration. In the distance is a huge pyramid rising from the light of the sun behind the head of Osiris, with obelisks on each side. The colonnades* in antis *are based on Denon's* Voyage . . . *of 1802, while other elements derive from Piranesiesque designs, and from Schinkel's own Diorama project* Das Labyrinth von Creta *of 1807 (especially the* Tempelanlage von Edfu-*SM XXII e/62). The Osiris figure mixes the Hadrianic figure of Antinoüs, elements in Denon, and Piranesian flavours as the centrepiece of a spectacular final scene in which*

Die Strahlen der Sonne vertreiben die Nacht,
Zernichten der Heuchler erschlichene Macht

*(The rays of the sun scatter the night
Breaking asunder the might of the false dissembler.)*

Here Strength, Beauty, and Wisdom are lauded in the final chorus: words with powerful Masonic connotations. So Sarastro and his priests, presiding over the Egyptian Mysteries, represent the triumph of Benevolence and Freemasonry over the forces of superstition, lies, and darkness. From Thiele: this version of Schinkel's original project (Schinkel Museum SM Th/3) was made by Carl Friedrich Thiele (DT. A 1399).

105 *Simon Quaglio's pen-and-watercolour design for Act I, Scene 9 of* Die Zauberflöte *for the 27 November 1818 production at the Nationaltheater, Munich. This 'Egyptian interior' combines Greek and Egyptian features (note the palm-capitals and frieze, the Egyptian figures, the coffering, and the extraordinary Neoclassical glazing-bars to the window)* (DT. No.S.Qu.525, neg. no. 2252).

that for the penultimate scene (Act II, Scene 28) in which Tamino and Pamina, having passed the Trials, arrive at the Temple of the Sun [103], and that for the last scene, the Temple of the Sun [104]. In this context two further and less familiar or celebrated designs by Schinkel for opera sets may be mentioned. The opera was Spontini's *Olimpia*, and Schinkel's fine Neoclassical sets were prepared for the 1821 Berlin production. In both the *Olimpia* and *Die Zauberflöte* designs Schinkel explored many Graeco-Egyptian themes found in Masonic de-

signs. In *Olimpia*, for example, the Asiatic Artemis statue (*multimammiam*) is correctly shown with the curious rings of 'breasts' that are now through to represent testicles from sacrificed beasts, while the casing of the body, wrapped like an Egyptian mummy, is embellished with the heads of horned animals. The crescent moon of the more Grecian Artemis outside also identifies the goddess with Isis, who recurs as the Madonna-Isis in *Die Zauberflöte*. These Graeco-Egyptian motifs reappear in many Masonic designs of the Enlightenment and Romantic Neoclassical periods, and have parallels in the works of several designers.

Die Zauberflöte was well served by designers in the early part of the last century (which is more than can be said of the state of play today in which the Egyptian and Masonic elements tend to be ignored, thus making nonsense of the opera, which makes sense only when treated with Freemasonry and Egypt well to the fore). Simon Quaglio (1795–1878) was the son of Giuseppe Quaglio (1747–1828), and from 1814 painted architectural scenes for the Court Theatre in Munich; in 1824 he succeeded his father as chief scene-director there, a post

he occupied for the next half century, retiring in 1877. His style was influenced by those of his brother Angelo (1784–1815) and his father Giuseppe, but by 1818, when he produced sets for *Die Zauberflöte* to grace the opening of the Nationaltheater in Munich, he was treating his themes with a mixture of Romanticism and Classicism. Quaglio's Egyptian interior for Act I, Scene 9 combines Greek and Egyptian elements [105], but his spectacular forecourt of the Temple [106] combines convincing attention to Egyptian stylistic devices with an interesting slightly off-axis approach that contrasts with Schinkel's treatment. The obelisks, of course, suggest Jachin and Boaz. His vault inside a pyramid for Act II, Scene 20 is a powerful composition, with a strong whiff of mystery [107]. Dr Manfred Boetzkes opines that

> Quaglio's stage sets are fully equal in authority to those of Schinkel. . . . Quaglio, like Schinkel, seeks inspiration from Egyptian architecture, and his success in doing so may be seen from impressive studies like the Temple Forecourt and imaginative works like the Egyptian Interior.[28]

106 *Simon Quaglio's pen-and-watercolour design for Act II, Scene 2 of* Die Zauberflöte *for the 1818 production at the Nationaltheater, Munich. The forecourt to the Temple is shown, with massive pylons, obelisks, colonnades, and colossal seated Egyptian figures. Quaglio's slightly off-axis approach should be compared with Schinkel's deliberately balanced symmetry. The two massive obelisks are allusions to Jachin and Boaz, while looking suitably Egyptian in their context* (DT. No.S.Qu.532, neg. no. A. 1539).

Die Zauberflöte inspired many more designers, but few rose to the Quaglio/Schinkel heights. Norbert Bittner (1786–1851), the architectural painter and etcher, who was born in Vienna and remained there until his death, produced a series of etchings of stage-designs after Josef Platzer and Antonio de Pian from 1816 to 1818. Bittner's 'Egyptian interior' based on de Pian's 1818 designs for *Die Zauberflöte* at the Kärntnertortheater, Vienna, shows

107 *Simon Quaglio's pen-and-watercolour design for Act II, Scene 20 of* Die Zauberflöte *for the 1818 production at the Nationaltheater, Munich. This 'strange vault' combines built forms with natural rocks, and incorporates funerary* loculi, *Egyptian doorcases, two pillars that are like circular obelisks with coffers set around their sides, stepped Piranesian forms, caryatides with Egyptian head-dresses, hieroglyphs, and a seated colossal figure* (DT. No.S.Qu.530, neg. no. 2253).

an odd space owing more to the fairground than to scholarly research. Bittner's work was published in *Theaterdekorationen nach den original Skizzen des K. K. Hoftheater Mahlers Anton de Pian. Radiert und verlegt von Norbert Bittner*.[29] More convincing, yet tentatively drawn, is the vault between pyramids, also for the same 1818 production, which shows pylon fronts, canted openings, corbels, and obelisks [108].

Friedrich Christian Beuther (1777–1856), from Alsace, worked in Darmstadt, Wiesbaden, Bamberg, and Würzburg before moving to the Hoftheater, Weimar, in 1815, where Goethe was involved in management. When Goethe withdrew in 1818 Beuther moved to Brunswick, then to Kassel in 1823, where he remained until his death. His designs for *Die Zauberflöte* [109] show that he studied history and geography and the physical characteristics of land forms. Like Goethe, Beuther recognized the importance of aesthetic beauty and poetic truth, and he saw the significance of stage-design as a medium by which all the visual arts combined in a totality. His *Bemerkungen und Ansichten über Theatermalerei* of 1822 remains an interesting volume for the insight it gives us of notions current through the influence of Goethe.

Die Zauberflöte, then, and the great series of Egyptianizing stage-sets it inspired, are among the finest examples of the Art of Freemasonry, incorporating music, Isiac allusions, Eleusinian mysteries, Hermetic ideas, Egyptian themes, and much else besides. Mozart,

the man and artist who made the eighteenth century sing for ever in our ears, was not only one of the greatest creative personalities the world has ever known, but he was the quintessential artist of Freemasonry and of the *Aufklärung*.

Studies have been written on *Die Zauberflöte* alone, but there is scope for further research on Mozart as a Masonic artist, taking into account the layers of meaning in words as well as music. So it is with Masonic ideas expressed in Architecture and landscape: in the eighteenth century much of European cultural life was permeated by Freemasonry, and earlier, Freemasonry played various rôles we are only beginning to understand.

Mozart, composer of Elysian harmonies, left another Masonic masterpiece in his last three symphonies of 1788, which can be seen as a whole design, and herald *Die Zauberflöte*. Three symphonies, the first of which begins in the Masonic key of E flat major, suggest a journey, a Masonic initiation. The E flat symphony[30] has an

108 *Norbert Bittner's etching of a 'vault between pyramids' based on de Pian's design for* Act II, Scene 20 of Die Zauberflöte *in the 1818 production at the Kärntnertortheater, Vienna. No Egyptian pylons ever had columns set* in antis *within them (although the* in antis *distyle arrangement was seen as specifically Masonic), while the canted vault (echoed in the openings in the podium supporting the fat obelisks) derives from Piranesi's designs in* Diverse Maniere d'Adornare i Cammini, *as does the stepped form of the podium and of the doorway on the right (TMK. No.G.16939b).*

109 *Beuther's tempera-and-watercolour design for a garden with sphinx at night in Act II, Scene 7 of* Die Zauberflöte *in a production at the Kurfürstliches Hoftheater, Kassel, in 1821. Although the image is not as powerful as that devised by Schinkel, a strong Nilotic flavour is imparted.* (TMK. No.G.16928a).

electrifying opening with the use of a knocking rhythm, then a massive dissonance before the faster section, where the basic rhythm is three beats to a bar. (This dissonance is probably a representation of chaos, like the opening of the overture to *Die Zauberflöte*, the introduction to Haydn's *Die Schöpfung*, and the adagio opening of Mozart's 'Dissonance' string quartet (K 465), the last an unquestionably Masonic allusion). The second movement of the Symphony, Andante, has the deceptively simple lyrical quality of much of *Die Zauberflöte*. If number 39 suggests a Masonic opening, then number 40[31] (in the dark key of G minor, with its unusual, restless, opening and extraordinary *Andante* in six-eight knock-like rhythm in E flat), suggests the fear and despair of the night and the blackness of part of Masonic ceremony. Finally, number 41[32], with its miraculously complex counterpoint resolved in the glorious sun-like key of C major, suggests the light after the darkness and reception into the Temple set in Elysian Fields. This programme was realized in a number of garden designs and it is to that theme that we turn in the next chapter.

One other possible Masonic masterpiece that deals with a journey, and ends on a suitably desolate note appropriate for the *Hochmittermacht* of Austrian Freemasonry is Schubert's *Die Winterreise*. Müller's verses include a lime-tree, fountains, waterfalls, rocky chasms, a *Letzte Hoffnung* (last hope), a cemetery, funerary wreaths, and three suns, all of which have Masonic connotations.

Jean-Jacques Lequeu

If some of the designs for *Die Zauberflöte* are startling in their imagery, the esquisses of Jean-Jacques Lequeu (1757–1825) are even stranger. He produced an extraordinary drawing of a Lodge, which he unaccountably calls a 'Gothic House', illustrating the route along an axis based on Ancient Egyptian temples, and which is obviously derived from *Séthos* in that it shows a three-stage place of initiation [Colour Plate X; 110–113] Lequeu showed an elaborate section, much ornamented with quotations from Terrasson, with a huge shaft in which is an iron cage. The three-headed Cerberus guards chambers with corbelled roofs (very Piranesian [110]), then the route leads to a huge chamber above which are metallic tools for torture; this huge chamber is a furnace for the Trial by Fire, and looks like a kiln [111]. Three more bays of Piranesian corbelled-vaulted chambers lead

110 *Detail from Lequeu's 'Gothic House' (see Colour plate X) (there is nothing 'Gothic' about it) showing the first stage of initiation derived from descriptions in Terrasson's* Séthos. *There is a deep shaft with the three-headed dog Cerberus guarding the entrance to the Trials, which Lequeu called the* 'Porte des Intrépides' (BN. CE. AC, plate 61, fig. 156).

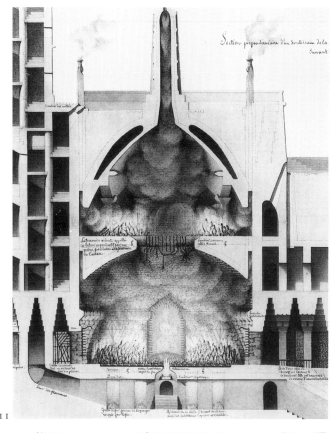

111

112

111 *The Trial by Fire by Lequeu, a detail from his 'Gothic House' shown in Colour Plate X. The form of the furnace recalls brick kilns and glass-making structures. Note the chains, pincers, and instruments of torture hanging. The Trial by Fire is the* 'Première Épreuve de l'aspirant' *(BN. CE. AC, plate 61, fig. 156).*

112 *The Trial by Water by Lequeu, a detail from his 'Gothic House' shown on Colour Plate X. This is the* 'Deuxième Épreuve' *in the tenebrous regions of the structure (BN. CE. AC, plate 61, fig. 156).*

113 *Lequeu's* Dernière Épreuve, *or Trial by Air, in which the aspirant is hoisted up to enter the sanctuary of Isis in which are the Cups of Memory and Forgetfulness. If the aspirant fails this last Trial he drops down into the tunnel and has to go back whence he came (BN. CE. AC, plate 61, fig. 156).*

113

to steps down into another chamber filled with water (the Trial by Water) [112]. Steps lead up to a space where the aspirant was hoisted through the air to reach the sanctuary dominated by Isis (who looks more like Britannia, and indeed represents Wisdom/Minerva), and containing the Cups of Memory and of Forgetfulness[33] [113]. These cups refer to mnemonic techniques developed from the sixteenth century, and we must remember that the Art of Memory was significant in Freemasonry.

The Trials by Fire, Water, and Air are illustrated in an extraordinary engraving in Alexandre Lenoir's *La Franche-Maçonnerie Rendue à sa véritable Origine, ou l'Antiquité de la Franche-Maçonnerie prouvée par l'explication des mystères anciens et modernes*, published in Paris in 1814 [114], and take place in a suitably Egyptianizing setting.

Lequeu is undoubtedly an odd case, as his curious Architecture and obscene drawings (*Figures Lascives*) show. He refers to the Great Architect of the Universe in the manuscript of his 'Architecture Civile', and draws on Gaspard Monge's descriptive geometry. Monge, professor at the École Polytéchnique, was entombed at the *Rond-Point des Peupliers* in the grand Egyptian tomb at Père-Lachaise [115]. Lequeu's work has recently come under scrutiny by a number of scholars,[34] and is perhaps even more baffling because we know so little about the man. Duboy says that Lequeu 'intended to impose on his public a masonic initiation which we can only describe as *frivolous*'.[35] All the plates in his 'Architecture Civile' are covered with obfuscatory notes in his neat bureaucratic hand, but these notes (and the mass of newspaper-cuttings and other documents) obscure rather than clarify. It does seem that in the meticulous drawings of imaginary buildings, details, instruments, and lascivious

114 *The Trials by Fire, Water, and Air for the reception of initiates in Memphis. A plate from Alexandre Lenoir's La Franche-Maçonnerie Rendue à sa véritable Origine . . . (Paris, 1814), showing the ceremonies of initiation described in* Séthos, *and purporting to apply to contemporary Masonic initiation. The setting is subterranean, mysterious, and unrelentingly Egyptian. On the right an initiate passes through fire, then water, and on the left is being hoisted through the air by an apparatus similar to that shown in 113.* (SJSM).

figures, Lequeu, if he was not actually mad, was making some kind of protest at the way in which craftsmen were being robbed of their trade secrets, having their skills paraded in the *Encyclopédie*, and reduced to the status of slaves by newfangled machinery. Lequeu himself was from an artisan background, and never tired of saying so. His drawings certainly have many allusions to Freemasonry, and it may be that his apparently frivolous Masonic images were a veiled protest against the popularization, vulgarization, and even corruption of Masonic ideas, as he saw it.

'Architecture Civile' seems disordered, for it consists of many ideas, themes, and images that do not seem to belong: it is disturbing in its incongruity. The productions of Boullée, Ledoux, and others were more reassuring because they were ordered, designed with flair and assurance, and pointed to a Utopian future. The problem, as Michael Foucault has pointed out, is that Heterotopias undermine syntax, order, reason, threaten

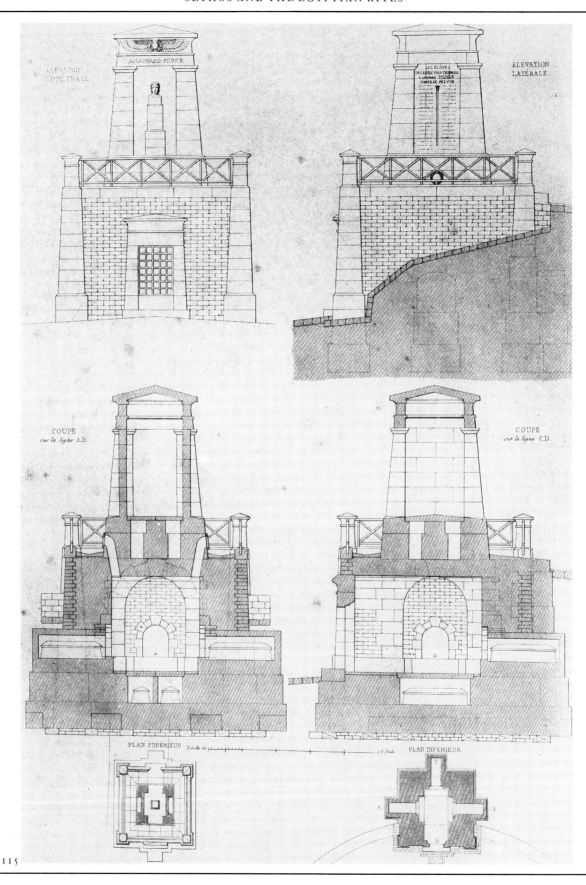

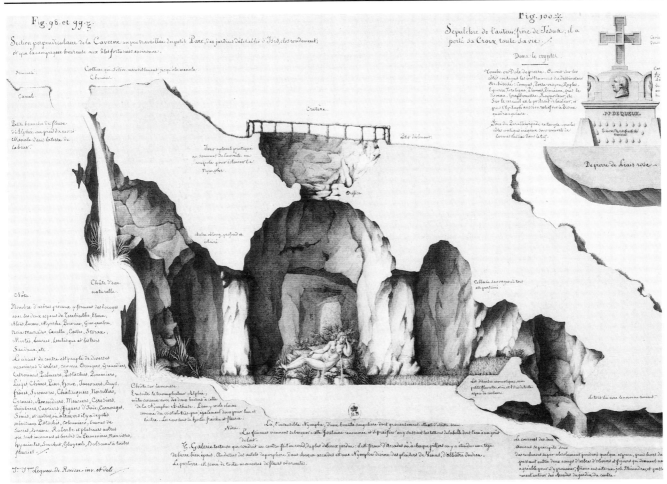

116 *Lequeu's perpendicular section of the (somewhat artificially adapted) Cavern in the little Park of the delectable Gardens of Isis, completely enclosed, and surrounded by the joyful landscape of the Fortunate Isles. The vignette on the right shows the sepulchre of the author, brother of Jesus, who has carried his Cross all his life. The Isiac idea of a healing spring is depicted, and the whole resembles to some extent the ideas behind the 'Gothic House' (BN. CE. AC, plate 33, figs. 98, 99 and 100).*

115 *Gaspard Monge's Egyptian mausoleum of 1820, in Père-Lachaise Cemetery, designed by Clochard. Monge was Professor at the École Polytechnique. From Normand's* Monumens Funéraires . . . (A).

grammar, tear apart mythology, and end in futility and chaos. Lequeu actually follows the definition of Architecture and its classification as set out in the *Encyclopédie*, and, by carrying his listings to absurd lengths, actually creates mayhem.[36] It is as though Lequeu were attacking the source of the artisan's alienation: the monument to rationality itself, the *Encyclopédie* of Diderot and his colleagues, was his target. Lequeu identified with Christ as Artisan and also with James the brother of Christ, who bore His Cross all his life [116]. But Duboy has described how the present cataloguing of Lequeu's works bears no relation to the inventory of the donation to what was the Royal Library in 1825; he states that, in his view, somebody has deliberately modified Lequeu's work 'to give it that air of a complex game that it now has'.[37] If this is so it raises interesting questions, but much further investigation is needed.

The Comte de Bouville, wealthy Freemason, and patron of Jean-Jacques Lequeu, built a Temple of Silence to Lequeu's designs in 1786 on his estate near 'Portenort' (*sic*). It was an amphi-prostyle octastyle temple with Tuscan columns and a Doric entablature, and in the pediment was a relief of Harpocrates/Horus,

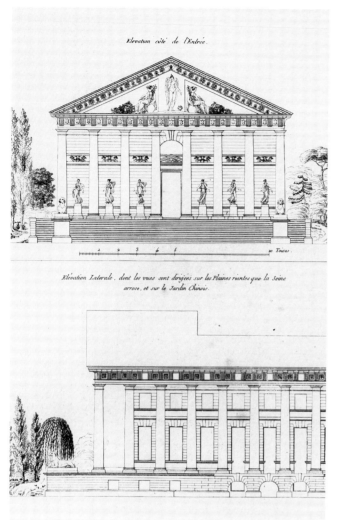

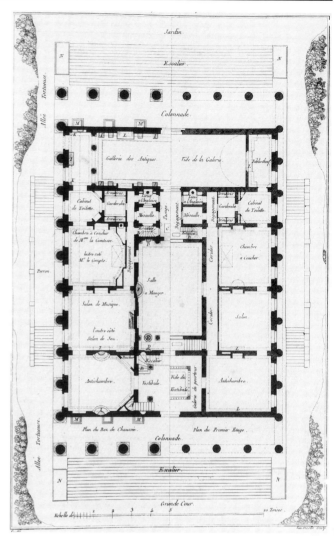

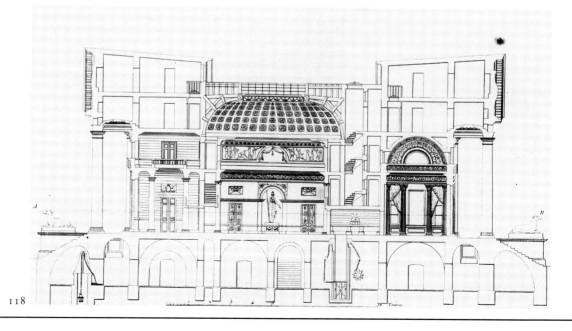

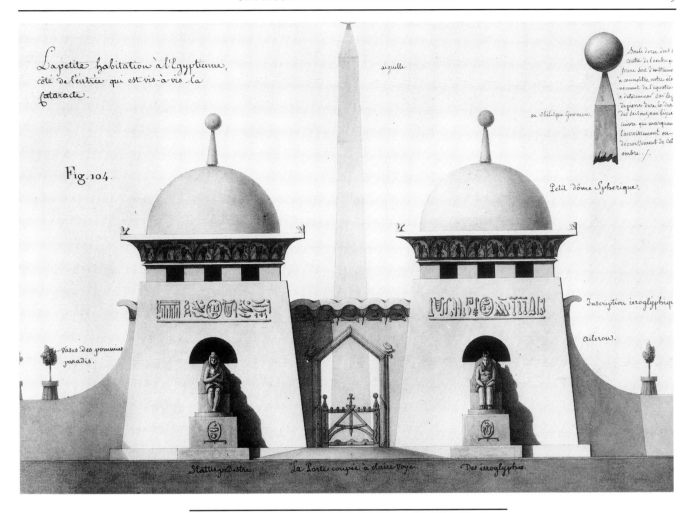

La petite habitation à l'Egyptienne,
côté de l'entrée qui est vis-à-vis la
fotaracte.

Fig. 104.

aiguille

ou obélisque Gnomon.

Petit dôme Syberique.

Inscription ieroglyphique

aileron.

Vases des pommes
paradis.

Statue d'Isatres.   La Porte coupée à claire-voye.   Des ieroglyphes.

120 *The small dwelling in Egyptian Style, showing the entrance that faces the waterfall, by Lequeu. This could almost be the set for the scene with Two Men in Armour in* Die Zauberflöte, *and so is associated with Masonic design (BN. CE. AC, plate 35, fig. 104).*

117 *Main and lateral elevations of Lequeu's country house known as the Temple of Silence, with Harpocrates, Commerce, and Abundance in the pediment, the dogs as symbols of household guardians, the goddesses of the twelve hours, turtles in the metopes, and an owl over the door. The lateral elevation had views over 'Meudon, Belvue, St Cloud, Madrid, Bagatelle, le Mont-Valérien, and the smiling plains watered by the Seine'. There was also a Chinese Garden. From Krafft (SJSM).*

118 *Section of Lequeu's Temple of Silence, showing the central dining room that could also double as a hall. Note the lifting devices, recalling the Trial by Air shown in 113 and 114. From Krafft (SJSM).*

119 *Plans of the House of Pleasure in the Antique style, called the Temple of Silence, by J. J. Lequeu, Architect. From Krafft (SJSM).*

121

121 *Temple of Verdure of Ceres by Lequeu. Note the identification with Artemis of Ephesus, and therefore with Isis, the spiral form of the columns (identified with Freemasonry), and the fountains (BN. CE. AC, plate 57, fig. 149).*

122 *Temple of Divination, by Lequeu. The building suggests Trials by Fire, and was intended to form the northern extremity of an Elysium (BN. CE. AC, plate 63, fig. 158).*

123 *(Top) Porch or vestibule which leads to the underground chambers and Pluto's dwelling, facing the right-hand side wall of the Temple of Wisdom, and* (bottom) *main entrance of the Temple of Wisdom. Both these Lequeu drawings show pronounced Egyptianesque leanings. Note the canted section of the vestibule, which is a favourite 'Egyptian' motif adopted by designers of the time. The Temple tympanum celebrates the statement that happiness, welfare, or prosperity lie in the angle, quoin, or corner where the wise are assembled: it is therefore unquestionably Masonic (BN. CE. AC, plate 67, figs 164 and 165).*

122

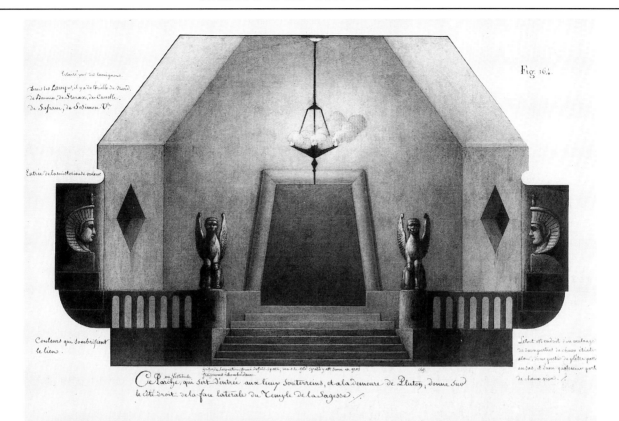

Fig. 164.

Ce Porche ou Vestibule, qui sert d'entrée aux lieux souterrains, et à la demeure de Pluton, donne sur le côté droit de la face latérale du Temple de la Sagesse.

Fig. 165.

LE BONHEUR EST DANS L'ANGLE
OÙ LES SAGES SONT ASSEMBLÉS.

Portail du Temple de la Sagesse, Côté de l'entrée principale.

123

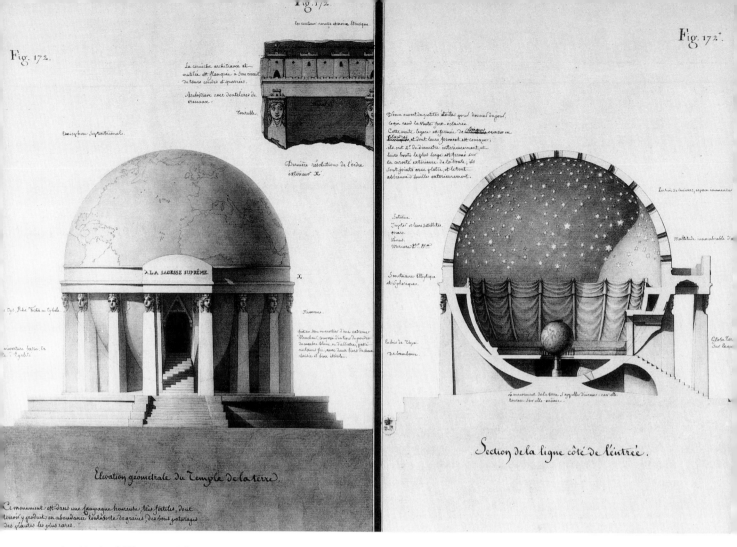

the God of Silence, with serpents; in the other (entrance) side was Harpocrates again flanked by 'Commerce' and 'Abundance'. Over the door was an owl, emblematic of night and death, and in the metopes were turtles; inside there was the sequence of rooms giving access to the gallery, and this sequence could also be approached from subterranean passages.

The building was illustrated by J. C. Krafft (who had studied at the same school of drawing in Rouen) in his *Recueil d'Architecture Civile*, published in Paris in 1812,[38] and appears to have been intended as dwelling-house and as a Masonic temple. Two dogs, symbolic of tutelary household gods, guarded the porticoes. Each portico had six pedestals bearing the goddesses of the Twelve Hours, the gatekeepers of Heaven, and the sides of the house had engaged columns, making the temple theme more obvious, yet the plan owes something to Palladio. Krafft could not see why Lequeu had given the name, design, and character of a temple to a house which according to its internal layout was intended as a residence. Lequeu responded by showing the Temple of Silence re-erected as such a temple at the gates of Paris. Krafft also illustrated Lequeu's house at Grawensel, the

124 *Elevation and section of a Temple of the Earth by Lequeu. Note the use of the sphere as an emblem of Wisdom and Nature, a theme also pursued by Boullée and Ledoux. The segmental-headed block over the entrance is inscribed to the 'Supreme Wisdom' (BN. CE. AC, plate 72, figs 172, 172°, 172°°.*

125 *Monument to a number of illustrious men of the city . . . for Victory Square, exhibited in Liberty Hall. The Time when human victims were being sacrificed to liberty, 1794. Design by Lequeu, showing his use of the garlanded column form, partly phallic, partly Masonic (BN. CE. AC, plate 72, fig. 176).*

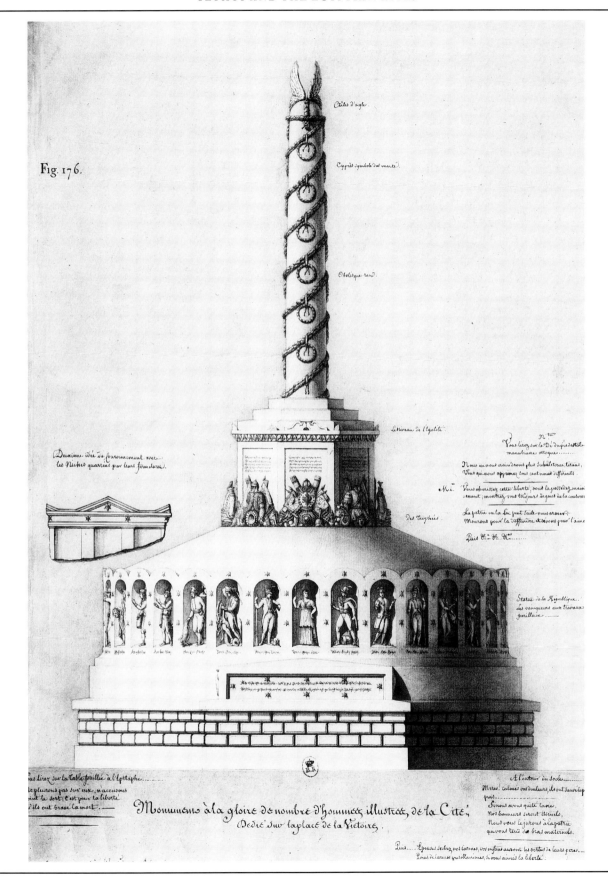

Fig. 176.

Monument à la gloire de nombre d'hommes illustres, de la Cité,
Dedié sur la place de la Victoire.

Casin de Terlinden, designed for the Dowager of Meulenaer in Belgium: an extraordinary house with a very ingenious plan.

Lequeu seems to have wallowed in the possibilities that designs for temples, monuments, and Lodges offered [120–126], for his use of motifs and Masonic allusions is highly inventive: he obviously knew his Terrasson, if not Mozart's *Die Zauberflöte*, for his design showing a 'Gothic' house could easily be used as a stage-set for that Sublime opera. With Lequeu we enter a deeply disturbing world. Even Ledoux's designs have a strangeness about them, but the case of Lequeu is very odd indeed.

126 *Interior of the cool room of a house in the Egyptian Taste by Lequeu. Various Masonic hints are suggested by the source of the living waters leaving the* Rocher. *Note the darkened room, the hieroglyphs, the canted fanlight, and the flowing waters on either side of the passage to the mysterious door* (BN. CE. AC, plate 58, fig. 150).

CHAPTER 7

ELYSIAN FIELDS

**Introduction; The Route and the Garden;
The Monument and the Tomb in the Garden; A National
Panthéon; Père-Lachaise; The Staglieno, Genoa;
The Kingdom of Death**

The cemetery is an open space among the ruins, covered in winter with violets and daisies.
It might make one in love with death, to think that one should be buried in so sweet a place.

Percy Bysshe Shelley
from the Preface to *Adonais*

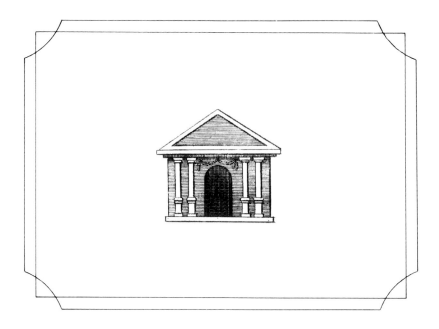

Introduction

Die Zauberflöte, the Masonic opera, is concerned with a journey, an initiation ritual, and much else, but its setting, emphasized by the many designs for sets described previously, is of great significance. The Orpheus legend, the Hermetic mysteries, *Séthos*, and other elements are combined in an Egyptian environment. The thunder, flashes of 'lightning', strange creatures, and dark cavernous vaults contrast with vistas, gardens, and temples. They occur in *Die Zauberflöte* and *Séthos*, and were seen as historical, going back to the beginnings of civilization. The idea of going down into the earth, or into caverns, vaults, or tombs, and passing through trials before acceptance as an initiate is very ancient, and is associated with death and rebirth or resurrection: it is therefore closely connected with the Isiac cults.

In *Séthos* the trials of fire, water, and air take place in vast underground caverns beneath the Great Pyramid itself [Colour Plate X; see 110–114]. The pyramid, of course, consists of four triangles set on a square, so would have pronounced Masonic significance, and the awakening interest in Egyptian Art and Architecture during the eighteenth century, spurred by Neoclassical experiments with stereometrically pure forms, and by

publications showing Egyptian buildings (such as F. L. Norden's *Travels in Egypt and Nubia* of 1757), together with the mysteriousness of Egypt (then part of the Ottoman Empire) and the still-uncracked meaning of hieroglyphs, brought Freemasonry and Egyptian motifs together.

Masonic artists and inventors of Masonic iconography sought devices in the Architecture and detail of Egypt, linking them with ideas of the Temple of Solomon, to produce some very curious stuff. Egyptian temples, false doors, pyramids, tombs, indecipherable hieroglyphs, strange creatures such as sphinxes and cynocephalic figures, obelisks, pylons, and the massiveness of Egyptian work appealed to the Enlightenment not only from the point of view of novelty, but because they were earlier, more primitive, and therefore nearer the beginnings than was the Classical Architecture of Greece and Rome. Richard Pococke's *Observations on Egypt* of 1743 and Norden's *Travels. . .* offered much in the way of description and image that provided Masonic designers with invaluable raw material [see 90].

The linear plans of Egyptian temples, involving courts, halls, pylons, avenues, and successions of spaces, were ideal for Masonic routes of initiation as symbols of journeys. Quatremère de Quincy's *De L'Architecture*

Égyptienne... of 1803, but written in 1785, analysed Egyptian Architecture, and dwelt on the massiveness and brooding grandeur that Boullée associated with monuments designed to withstand the ravages of time and which conjured up melancholy images of arid mountains and immutability. Quatremère de Quincy described and illustrated the temples at Karnak and Thebes, and some of the illustrations by Gaitte would have struck Masonic iconographers as peculiarly apt for the purposes of the Craft [see 88–90].

The Route and the Garden

The route became of considerable importance in Lodges during the last years before European Continental Freemasonry was all but crushed during the 1790s: it was the path along which initiates would journey from room to room, from space to space, and from volume to volume. Ancient Egyptian Architecture showed that a route could pass through portals into an open court, then into a hall, and so on, so gradually the idea of extending Masonic design *outside* buildings came to the fore. Such a movement would involve garden design embracing English landscape traditions.

127 *The temporary tomb of Jean-Jacques Rousseau on the* Île des Peupliers, *or* Elysée, *in the gardens of the Vicomte de Girardin at Ermenonville. View dated 1778 by J.-M. Moreau le Jeune* (BN).

Castle Howard acquired a mausoleum and a pyramid in its extensive grounds; Pope created a route through open and closed spaces at Twickenham that would terminate at an obelisk with a backdrop of evergreens erected in memory of his mother; William Shenstone made the walk at The Leasowes with its urn set among shrubs and inscribed *Et in Arcadia Ego*; and the Elysian Fields at Stowe, with the Temple of British Worthies set in a 'natural' landscape, created a new longing for the happiness of lost Antiquity and Arcadia, and, by associating commemoration with a garden, set a precedent for a new concept of cemetery design.

Jean-Jacques Rousseau, who was associated with a love of nature, an admiration for the primitive, and the nobility of savages, was entombed in 1778 at Ermenonville on the *Île des Peupliers* on the estate of René Louis Vicomte de Girardin (Gérardin), and his resting-place

128 *The* Île des Peupliers *at Ermenonville, showing the later permanent tomb of J.-J. Rousseau. An illustration by Mérigot fils of 1788. The tomb was designed by Hubert Robert, and the sculpture was by Le Sueur* (BN).

became a potent image to stir the Romantic imagination [127, 128]. The Arcadian landscape-garden, adorned with monuments, became an ideal possibility with considerable attractions compared with the unsavoury urban churchyards.[1] With the history of the development of cemeteries and of funerary Architecture, Freemasonry and its adherents are intimately connected.[2]

'Natural' landscapes were seen as contributing to the regeneration of Man and the improvement of the tone of society as a whole, and the fashionable ideas of the English garden were eagerly embraced on the Continent, especially by the owners of large estates. Such landowners, with pretensions to learning and fashion, could indulge fancy by creating gardens and temples away from prying eyes, could patronize intellectuals, and could even

establish places with esoteric symbolisms. The Marquis de Montesquiou and his architect Brongniart had created a route through a garden at Maupertuis inspired by English prototypes which Montesquiou called an *Élysée*; there, as has been noted, the garden was entered through the grotto under the famous masonry pyramid [see 91], and Ledoux planned other pavilions there of stereometrically pure type, much influenced by his Masonic affiliations.

Girardin is said to have designed his gardens at Ermenonville according to ideas in *La Nouvelle Héloïse*:[3] there he had his resident philosopher, an estate, and scope to develop temples and lodges in the gardens. Cagliostro built a pavilion on the estate of Sarasin near Basel in 1781 as a Lodge of Regeneration inspired by the Egyptian rites of his cult of Freemasonry. As with the Isiac cults of the Graeco-Roman world, an initiate would be confined for forty days in the pavilion, where tests and trials woul be undergone.[4] Here was a deliberate backward glance to Antiquity, to the mystery cults, to Christ's forty days of privation and temptation in the Wilderness, and to the initiations of the Graeco-Roman Isiac religions,[5] but it was also associated with an admiration for things English, for the poetic qualities of the English garden, and for the home of modern Freemasonry.

Ledoux had built a Lodge outside Paris in a large garden entered through a pyramid (a similar idea to that of Maupertuis).[6] Progress through the complex was through a great variety of rooms, all different, which alluded to the development of civilization from the primitive hut to a majestic hall (a similar idea to the Garden of Allusions). The Egyptianizing prototypes are clear, but the interesting departure is the inclusion of a garden in the overall scheme. William Beckford visited this Lodge during the 1780s, and was clearly aware of the significance, for he himself had given an 'Egyptian rout' at Fonthill in 1781 designed by Jacques de Loutherbourg, who knew Cagliostro and other Masons,[7] and who eventually claimed unlikely powers of prophecy and healing. (De Loutherbourg was buried at Chiswick, where a monument designed by the eminent Freemason and Architect Sir John Soane was erected in his memory.)[8]

The alleys of wood-piles in Ledoux's garden were lined with worked and unworked wood, and some of the

129 *The* Oïkéma*, or Temple of Sexual Instruction, at Chaux by Ledoux. The severe Neoclassical appearance belies the phallic plan-form at the upper level. From* L'Architecture (SJSM).

Coupe

Elevation

Echelle de   1   2   3   4   5   6   12   18 toises

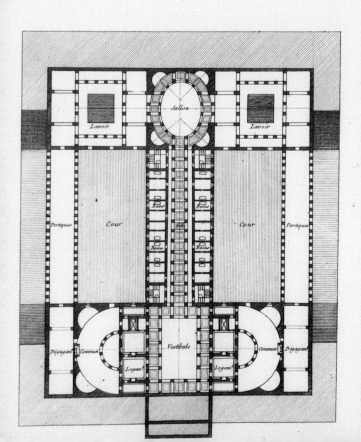

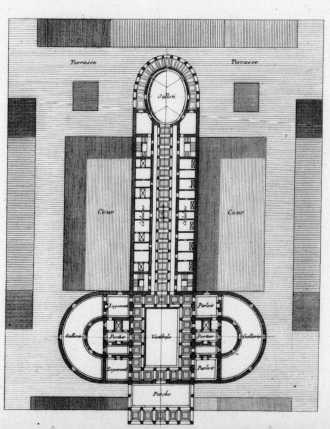

piles were in the form of primitive huts with thatched
roofs: Laugier, Freemasonry, Rousseau, and others were
influential in one way or another. It is clear that the
essence of such places was association, memory, allusion,
and, ultimately, mnemonic ideas, and that regeneration,
improvement through contact with nature, and notions
of a better society, a better world, were to the fore.

Even at his ideal town of Chaux, Ledoux allowed for
structures where various Lodges might meet.[9] At Chaux
('Lime') ideas of wholeness, peace, communality, harmony, union, memory (very significant), and advancement of crafts were to be promoted in ritual temples
(including one phallic-shaped whore-house, the *Oïkéma*,
in which young men would be initiated in the rites of
sexual congress) dedicated to them [129–132]. Masonic
emphasis on the importance of keeping vows could also
play its part in promoting marital fidelity in union and
harmony.

Ledoux and Chaux, therefore, are the forerunners of
people like Fourier and their *Phalanstères* (see below),
and, ultimately of those coercive notions that tried to
improve untidy humanity by means of institutionalized
totalitarianism. Out of Liberal Idealism comes regiment-
ation, just as out of Reason comes irrationality, as the
Terror demonstrated with awesome and irrefutable
effect. C. Fourier (1772–1837) noted that Freemasonry
had been like a precious stone, disdained, warped,
corrupted, and underestimated by society because its true
value was not even recognized.[10] Fourier, like Ledoux,
saw in Freemasonry scope for associations of people
which could be expanded infinitely to lead to major social
reforms (an idea central to Illuminism in Central Europe), so the 'revolutionary' nature of French Freemasonry was not mythological, but very real, and recognized as such by the Revolutionaries who closed it down.
Places where people could meet for social occasions
could play a civilizing rôle; by example, by association,
and by regeneration, society itself would be reformed on
rational, harmonious, optimistic, benevolent, humanist,
non-superstitious lines. Some of these ideas were to be
found in Fourier's exposition of his *Phalanstère*, published in *Le Nouveau Monde* in Paris in 1829. J. B. Godin,
in his *Familistère* at Guise, and in his *Solutions Sociales* of
1870, took Fourier's proposals further in terms of
practical association.

The idea of allusions as indicative of advanced ideas
was potent from the beginning of the eighteenth century
in Saxony. Designs by Lukas von Hildebrandt (who had
associations with Prince Eugen of Savoy) and Fischer
von Erlach (who also had Masonic connections) in
Vienna and elsewhere in the Empire employed an
unusually rich palette of motifs drawn from many
sources. Friedrich August II, nicknamed the Strong

130 *The Panarèthéeon, or Temple of Virtue and School of
Morals, from Ledoux's* L'Architecture (SJSM).

131 *The House in the Country, or Temple of Memory, from*
L'Architecture. *This extraordinary design recalls a fortress,
Trajanic columns, Palladian architecture, Greek, Roman, and
Moresque Islamic themes, and much else. It can therefore be
interpreted as a mnemonic of form, Architecture, and
civilization, for Ledoux himself referred to the desirability of
making the different characters of works of Architecture from
various civilizations known to all. The Temple of Memory was
intended to be free from the prejudices of Classically-trained
Architects, and suggested a wider culture, taking elements from
many centuries, languages of design, and civilizations (SJSM).*

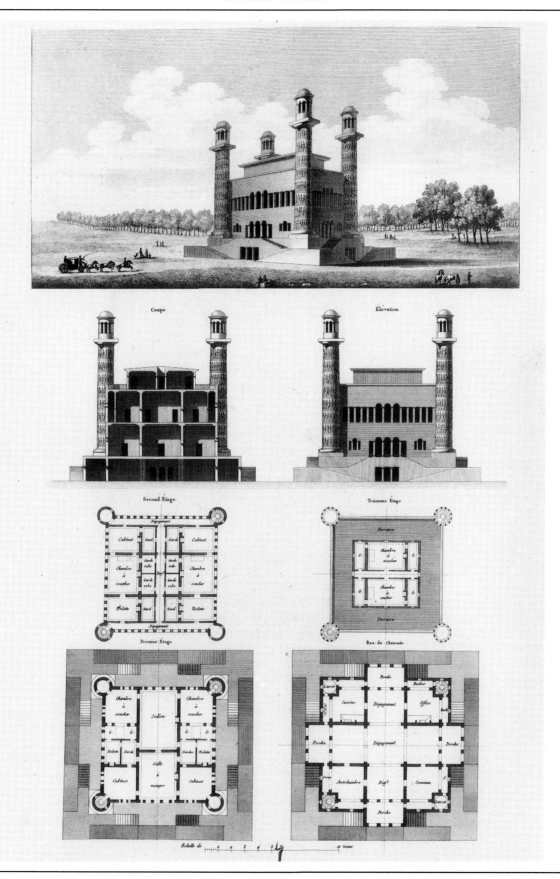

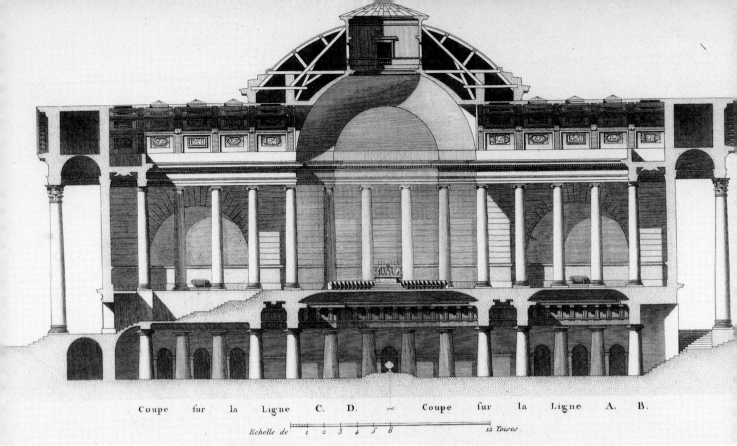

Coupe   fur   la   Ligne   C.   D.   ✕   Coupe   fur   la   Ligne   A.   B.

Echelle de   1   2   3   4   5   6   12 *Toises*.

132 *Section through the proposed church at Chaux (Lime)*
from Ledoux's L'Architecture considérée . . . *The crypt,*
with its primitive unfluted Doric columns, and the church
interior lit only by the oculus, are more suited, perhaps, to use as
Masonic Lodges than as Christian places of worship. Here the
Supreme Deity might be venerated, but the crypt is clearly
designed for use by a cult of some sort (SJSM).

(1670–1733), Elector of Saxony from 1694, created an
ideal climate in which eclecticism flourished, and which
produced extraordinary buildings such as the Zwinger
Palace in Dresden (part-Nymphaeum, part-Orangery,
part-formal garden, part-tournament-ground, part-
gallery) and Schloss Pillnitz (in the Chinese Taste by the
banks of the Elbe). The Elector's Court enamellers and
jewellers, Georg Friedrich Dinglinger and Johann Mel-
chior Dinglinger, produced some strange and beautiful
pieces for Augustus that alluded to Classical Antiquity,
to Ancient Egypt, and to Oriental cultures such as those
of China, Japan, and India.

The Court of Augustus was glittering and cosmopolitan, and when the Elector became King of Poland in
1697, converting to Roman Catholicism in the process,
the Protestant ethos of Saxony became confused and
weakened (his Queen-Electress Christine Eberhardine
remained a Protestant, and after his conversion, withdrew to Pretzsch, where she enjoyed the esteem of
Protestant Saxony, and especially of the city of Leipzig,
until her death in 1727), for Augustus was the hereditary
president of the *Corpus Evangelicorum* in the Imperial Diet
at Regensburg. The result was that Leipzig became one
of the most liberal and enlightened of centres for
publishing in all Central Europe as it was stultified by
neither strict Protestant primness nor excessive Papist
paranoia: Augustus and his successors smoothed over
almost every conflict between the Roman Catholic Court
and the Protestant culture of Saxony. Of course, the
conversion of the Elector to Catholicism was primarily a
political consideration in order to secure the Polish
Kingdom, and Augustus (athlete, glutton, and lecher
extraordinaire) seems to have carried out his religious
obligations with the minimum of conviction and the
maximum amount of splendour and theatrical show. His
lack of religious zeal was not unusual among princes of
the Enlightenment, and it is possible to discern in the
portraits of that remarkable monarch a superior intelli-
gence, an assured scepticism, and an air of being above all
superstition and theological debate. His encouragement
of eclectic tastes and his essential tolerance created an
ideal climate in which Freemasonry could flourish, and
indeed that was the case. Dresden acquired a National
Grand Lodge, and there were several other Lodges
there, while Leipzig had its celebrated Minerva of the
Three Palms Lodge, and Altenburg formed its Archi-
medes of the Three Tracing Boards Lodge later, in 1742.

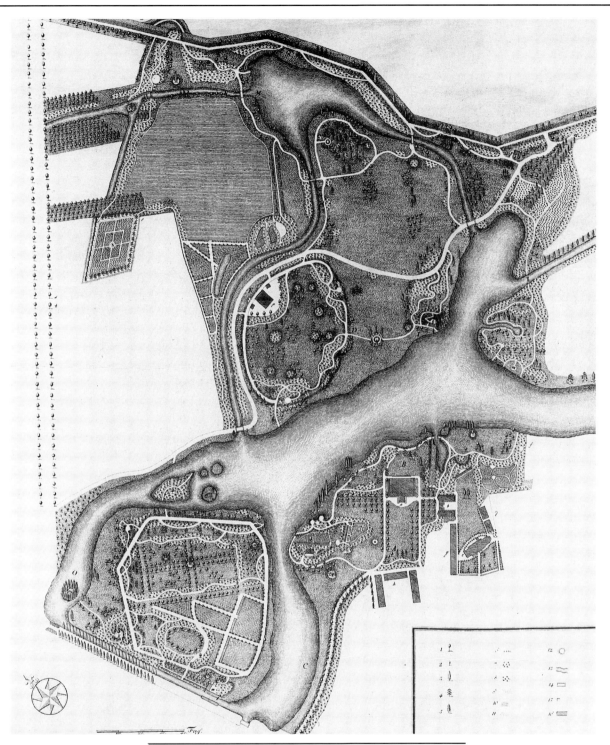

133 Erklärung des Grundriss des Gartens in Wörlitz
*(Explanation of the ground-plan of the gardens of Wörlitz) by
Israel Salomon Probst, the Jewish engraver of Dessau, 1784.
These remarkable 'English' gardens of allusion were created by
Prince Franz of Anhalt-Dessau and his friend, the Architect
Friedrich Wilhelm Freiherr von Erdmannsdorff* (Wörlitz,
Inv. No. IV, 354).

134 *The* Rousseau-Insel *at Wörlitz of 1782* (Dr Reinhard Alex, Wörlitz, 1989).

chinesisches Haus (before 1750) at Brühl and his infrequent diocesan visitations seated like some Mandarin on a Chinese palanquin are but two examples of this. Frederick the Great of Prussia (who corresponded with Voltaire on a number of matters connected with China) built (with advice from Johann Gottfried Büring) a Chinese Tea-Pavilion at Potsdam between 1754 and 1757 in the gardens near Sans Souci (where allusions may be found in plenty). The King, of course, was himself a Freemason, and interested in the wider aspects of wholeness and harmony promoted in the Enlightenment: intellectual curiosity could be said to be the order of the day.

One of the most perfect examples of a garden of allusions can be seen at Wörlitz in Saxony (now part of the German Democratic Republic) [133]. In the grounds of the Schloss, an impeccably Palladian essay, contemporary with and similar to Claremont (1771–74) (the latter by Henry Holland and Capability Brown) can be found a *Rousseau-Insel* [134] complete with poplars (modelled on Ermenonville); an extraordinary 'Gothic' House (with here and there a touch of Chinoiserie); a Temple of Venus; a Villa Hamilton (in celebration of Sir William Hamilton and his great collection of Classical antiquities), beside which is a rock-work 'Vesuvius' (to make the Neapolitan connections clear) [135, 136]; a labyrinth [137]; a *Limesturm* (or boundary-marker, based on a conjectural reconstruction of a watchtower or gatetower on Hadrian's wall in Northumberland); a pantheon (circular building with tetrastyle portico), and much else. There is nothing more startling in the dour Saxon context than a mini-Ironbridge (based on the

Such a climate, in which the various princes of Saxony were free to involve themselves fully in the *Aufklärung*, was ideal for the realization of architectural and landscaping schemes that would reflect the concerns of the time, and it is no accident that Freemasonry played a considerable part. Many interesting texts of the proto-Enlightenment, including much material germane to Freemasonry, was published in Leipzig during the eighteenth century, and that city was most significant in the history of the dissemination of Masonic ideas not only throughout Saxony, but Europe as well. Two of the smaller Courts, those of the Princes of Anhalt-Dessau and of the Dukes of Saxe-Weimar, were distinguished for their Masonic connections and their patronage of men of genius.

A wide-ranging eclecticism, then, was associated with a broadening of the mind and a liberalization of ideas: it indicated universality and freedom from bigotry. The Elector Max Emanuel of Bavaria created a Pagodenburg at Nymphenburg, while his son, Clemens August, Prince-Bishop of Cologne, was a devoted sinophil; his

135 *Villa Hamilton (1791–94) by F. W. von Erdmannsdorff, and rock-work 'Vesuvius' on the Stone Island (1788–96) at Wörlitz. Rock-work had a Masonic significance as a symbol of soundness and as the foundation of wisdom. The Villa celebrated the collection of Sir William Hamilton (1730–1803), diplomat and archaeologist, who witnessed and described the eruptions of Vesuvius, and who was an expert on volcanoes and volcanic rocks. He was a kinsman of William Beckford, and made several major collections of Greek and Roman antiquities, notably vases* (Wörlitz).

136 *The Stone Island* (Insel Stein) *at Wörlitz, with 'Vesuvius' erupting with fireworks. Aquatint by W. F. Schlotterbeck after Karl Kuntz, 1797* (Staatliche Galerie Dessau, Inv. No. G. 416).

137 *Inscription on the rock-work entrance to the Labyrinth at Wörlitz. It reads* Choose, Traveller, your Path with Reason (Waehle Wandrer deinen Weg mit Vernunft), *an inscription with clear Masonic overtones, for it could easily form part of the entrance to the Trials of Initiation to be read by a potential candidate* (Dr Reinhard Alex, Wörlitz, 1989).

138 Eiserne Brücke *at Wörlitz, with rock-work abutments, of 1791. This is based on the original Iron Bridge of 1778 at Coalbrookdale on the Severn in Shropshire. The Wörlitz version is scaled down (it is 7.75 [25 feet] metres in span), and is part of a vast scheme of eclectic references intended as mnemonics of the best of culture and knowledge, and as celebrations of achievements* (Wörlitz).

original in Shropshire) in the grounds of the Schloss.[11] The garden was thus commemorating not only the past, but current themes such as advanced technology and the rediscovery of Antiquity, and so was typical of the Enlightenment [138].

This marvellous ensemble was created by Prince Franz of Anhalt-Dessau (1740–1817) and his friend the Architect Friedrich Wilhelm von Erdmannsdorff (1736–1800). At Wörlitz the ideals of the Masonic Enlightenment found expression in a re-creation of an English landscaped park around the Anglo-Palladian Schloss (which is not a castle but a country house). It is important to realize that the English landscaped park was admired in Masonic and progressive circles on the Continent as an expression of modernity and enlightenment, while the Palladian style was closely associated with a Whig and Masonic Establishment, as has been mentioned above.

Schloss Wörlitz was built in 1769–73, and there were other English features in the grounds, including the informal and very beautiful landscape, the Gothic House, the Iron Bridge, and Pantheon, and various garden ornaments alluding to English precedents. Even the Rock Island (*Insel Stein*), representing Vesuvius, was intended to put the adjacent Villa Hamilton in context [see 135, 136]. Erdmannsdorff and his friend and patron developed ideas already begun in Saxony under Augustus the Strong, and created an extraordinary landscape, with routes, mnemonic ideas of allusion and eclecticism (to sum up, as it were, the best of cultural themes from Antiquity to the present), to give a total aesthetic and intellectual experience, triggering off further thoughts on the beholder. Even the labyrinth, the meaning of which has been outlined elsewhere in this study, has the inscription

> WAEHLE WANDRER
>
> DEINEN WEG
>
> MIT VERNUNFT

(Choose, Traveller, your path with Reason)

set in the rock-work [see 137]: a cautionary instruction with clear Enlightenment and Masonic overtones, and one that could have appeared in a setting of *Die Zauberflöte* itself. Rocks, of course, had Masonic significance in that they were symbols of soundness, good foundations, and wisdom, and it is not surprising that they recur in many gardens of the period.

Wörlitz (one of the great gardens of Europe) is indeed redolent with Masonic connotations, for it embodies Prince Franz's ideals of enlightened brotherhood, suggestions of other countries and the most progressive of ideas, and of a journey taking in a wide spectrum of stimuli. It also evokes admired England in its Palladianism, landscape, and Iron Bridge. Thus, Wörlitz is not

dissimilar to other gardens intended to evoke Elysium. Gardens such as those at Monceau, Maupertuis, Wörlitz, Franconville-la-Garenne and Ermenonville were intended as agents of elevating Mankind, and were the landscape equivalents of the Temple as indicative of creative perfection. Nature was good, Man in his natural state was good, and man-made 'natural' landscape evoked uncorrupted Elysium in which perfectability could be seen: so the garden, evoking Arcady and Elysium, embellished with eclectic Architecture and mnemonic devices, could help to bring about a new golden age of Enlightenment and ever-increasing perfection in society itself. This is a powerful Masonic ideal.

In 1789–90 the gardens of Wörlitz acquired a *Judentempel* designed by von Erdmannsdorff. It is a circular building divided into vertical panels by severe Tuscan pilasters, and is an allusion to those circular versions of the Temple in Jerusalem that were a feature of seventeenth- and eighteenth-century images of the Solomonic, Zerubabbel, and Herodian Temples [see 61]. Nevertheless, the inclusion of a Synagogue as part of an Enlightenment garden in Germany serves to emphasize that the *Aufklärung* actually meant something: Tolerance, Benevolence, and Wisdom were to rule with Reason and Nature.

There was another very important corollary, and that can be found in Terrasson too; the underground trials and ritual death in the built Hades led to initiation in the temple in a blaze of light, and that temple was set in a magical and evocative landscape through which ran routes, and in which priests also oversaw the initiates. Thus, certain 'English' gardens on the Continent had emblematic/allegorical meanings given to them by their Masonic creators far beyond what was the case in England. In fact the English model was seized upon for additional reasons over and above the poetic and picturesque aspects: gardens were agents of a fundamental change in sensibility.

That Masonic ideas were closely interwoven with the design of gardens may seem strange to English readers, but this would not be so far-fetched to Continentals. Take Goethe's novel *Die Wahlverwandtschaften*, for example; in that evocative work a garden with prospects is created, with a rustic moss-hut from which an unspoiled view may be enjoyed. In Chapter 9 a new garden building is being constructed, and the foundation-stone is laid with much ceremony. A mason dressed in his best suit and carrying a trowel in one hand and a mallet in the other delivers an address in which he says three things have to be taken into consideration when erecting a building. First of all, it has to be well sited, then have sound foundations, and be well made: the foundations are the mason's business, are the chief

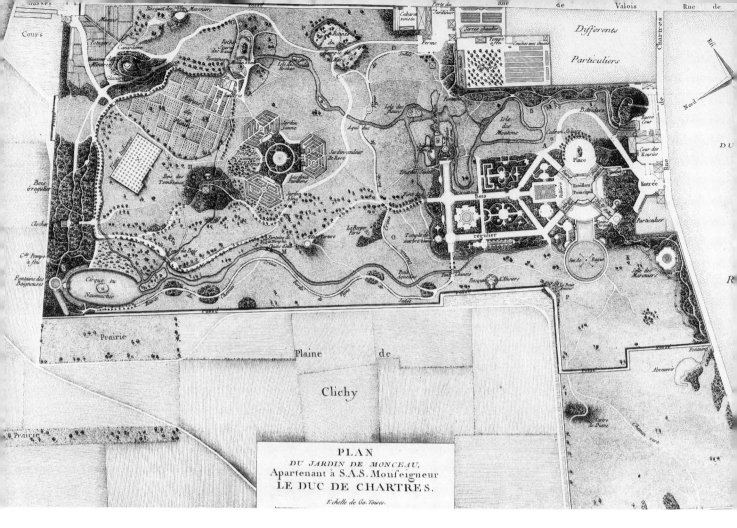

139 *Plan of the garden of Monceau, Paris, belonging to the Duc de Chartres, in 1779. Note the three mazes, or labyrinths, and the yellow, rose, and blue gardens to the north of which is the Bois des Tombeaux. Drawn by L. C. de Carmontelle and engraved by Bertrand* (BN).

business of the entire works, and are an earnest undertaking. The laying of the foundation in a narrow excavated space is secret labour, involving a well-hewn stone, the firm corner of which denotes the firm corner of the building. That square-cut stone is a symbol of the regularity of the edifice, of the perpendicular and horizontal denoting the trueness of the walls without and within, yet even that weighty stone must be bedded in a lime-mortar, for, as men who are inclined to association hold together in society better when they are cemented by the law, so stones whose shapes are well matched and truly cut are better united by this 'binding force' of lime. The stone is laid with a threefold blow of his mallet, indicating the union of the stone with the ground, or artifice with nature, and of Architecture with the landscape. Goethe, of course, was a prominent Weimar Freemason, and his Masonic references here and elsewhere are extraordinarily explicit. The mention of lime-mortar in this context is of singular interest, for it was an important Masonic symbol in Central Europe, although it seems to have declined in significance in Britain, the reasons for which are obscure.

Another marvellously allusive garden, complete with pyramid (the base and entrance to which are embellished with Egyptian symbols) designed by Langhans in 1792, obelisk, statue of Diana of Ephesus (called, significantly, Isis, in local usage), orangery (in a Ledoux-like stripped Neoclassical style with sphinx *couchant* on top of the *in antis* entablature), and much else, partially survives at the Neue Garten by the Heiliger See, Cecilienhof, Potsdam. The Hohenzollerns were closely involved with Freemasonry, and familiar garden themes of the Enlightenment occur throughout their former estates in Potsdam. Antiquity, the Exotic, and Nature combine.

Between 1773 and 1778 Carmontelle laid out the landscape of allusions at Monceau in Paris for the Duc de Chartres (a Freemason, as previously described), and this Parc (one of the first of the 'naturalistic' French landscaped gardens) was confiscated for 'public use' during

the Revolution. In 1801 Nicolas-Thérèse-Benoist Frochot proposed that the park should be converted into a
cemetery because real tombs could be integrated with the
cenotaphs in Carmontelle's 'Bois des Tombeaux', where
pyramids and other forms decorated the gardens [see 92;
139, 140]. The proposal did not come to fruition, and the
Parc Monceau, with Ledoux's *Barrière* at the entrance,
survives as a park, although some of the allusions are
missing. In due course Frochot purchased Mont-Louis
to the east of Paris, of which more anon. During the
1790s, Montmartre cemetery was laid out in the disused
quarry there, but it was messily done, and only acquired
its present character from a remodelling exercise of the
1820s and 1830s.

Several of the strands alluded to above started to come
together in an extraordinary way in the last quarter of the
eighteenth century, and the story deserves close investigation, though only the barest outline is possible here.

140 *View of the* Bois des Tombeaux *in the Parc Monceau,
Paris, in 1779, by Carmontelle, engraved by Bertrand* (BN).

The Monument and the Tomb in the Garden

Garden-cemeteries derive from several ideas and models
found in literature, poetry, landscapes, and gardens.
Rousseau's tomb on the Isle of Poplars at Ermenonville
[see 127, 128, 134] captured the imagination of a whole
generation for its beauty, its associations with Arcady
and Elysium, and, of course, the back-to-nature primitive
world so admired during the Enlightenment.

Another important prototype of the garden-cemetery,
and one with close Masonic associations, was the
extraordinary and imaginative garden of the Comte
d'Albon, partly inspired by his friend Court de Gébelin,
at Franconville-la-Garenne, laid out in the early 1780s.
Several views of this garden were drawn by the Comtesse
d'Albon, and these, with other illustrations by de Lussy
and Lepagelet, were published in *Tableau Pittoresque de la
Vallée de Montmorency, un des séjours le plus agréable des*

141

14

143

1.

141 Bosquet de l'Amitié *at Franconville-la-Garenne, from Lepagelet* (BL. 282. d. 17).

142 Rocher, *or artificial rock, at Franconville-la-Garenne, from Lepagelet* (BL. 282. d. 17).

143 *The pyramid (a memorial to the Comte d'Albon's ancestors) at Franconville-la-Garenne, from Lepagelet* (BL. 282. d. 17).

144 Caverne d'Young *at Franconville-la-Garenne, from Lepagelet. Edward Young (1683–1765) was the poet and author of* Night Thoughts, *a work influential in France and Germany* (BL. 282. d. 17).

145 *'Tomb' (actually cenotaph) of Haller at Franconville-la-Garenne, from Lepagelet* (BL. 282. d. 17).

145

Environs de Paris, published in 1790. The gardens contained a pantheon-like temple (a Masonic idea, as we have seen), an obelisk, a Temple of the Muses, a *Bosquet de l'Amitié* (very Masonic) [141], a *Cascade d'Ésope*, a *Palais de l'Aurore*, a Primitive Hut, a Priapus, an Isle, a Chinese Kiosk, rock-work [142], a fountain, a statue of Pan, the Devil's Bridge, an Asylum for Shepherds, a column, and a pyramid [143] which was a memorial to Albon's ancestors. The wide-ranging allusions to many styles and civilizations was, as we have seen, mnemonic and Masonic. More startling were the monument to William Tell and various other allusions to Switzerland (and therefore to freedom and nationalism), and the Caverne d'Young [144].

The latter was a memorial to Edward Young (1683–1765), the poet and author of *Night Thoughts*, a book influential in France and Germany. Young mentions the surreptitious burial of Protestants in Roman-Catholic territories in his works, and is said to have spent much time among the tombs. He also planted a celebrated avenue of limes at the Rectory in Welwyn, Hertfordshire. Young, Robert Blair, and James Hervey were three poets who dwelt on the macabre and the black side of death; their work, and the exemplars of Stowe and The Leasowes brought memorials and interment into the garden.

D'Albon erected a 'tomb' (actually a cenotaph) in memory of the Swiss botanist and physiologist, Albrecht de Haller [145], which consisted of a mound planted with four poplars, perhaps following the example of Ermenonville. Even more startling, though, d'Albon succeeded in obtaining the corpse of his friend, Court de Gébelin, the celebrated linguist and author of *Le Monde Primitif*, who had done so much to promote an understanding of early cultures. Now Court de Gébelin was a Freemason, who had written concerning the Eleusinian mysteries, and who was well-versed in Hermeticism and in Ancient Egyptian rites (he actually read his own version of the Eleusinian mysteries at Voltaire's initiation as a Freemason). He was convinced that symbol and allegory were keys to history and to the interpretation of history. He was also a Protestant, so his burial in the garden derives from Young, and has links with Maupertuis and with England. The tomb itself [146] has four ruined antique columns around a sarcophagus, suggesting markers, and has clear Masonic overtones. The four poplars on Haller's mound and the four ruined columns are, of course, connected as ideas.

D'Albon set up dispensaries, soup-kitchens, and other philanthropic establishments to ameliorate the condition of the poor on his estate, and his close connection with Freemasonry and with ideals of freedom and nationalism

were clear on every side. The Masonic aspects were
further reinforced when he erected a bust of Benjamin
Franklin (a prominent Freemason) in the garden.

Another interesting garden of the same period was
laid out at Méréville by the Duc Jean-Joseph de Laborde.
He erected a rostral column [147] on his estate to
commemorate his sons who were killed on the ill-fated
expedition of Lapeyrouse, and also built a cenotaph in
memory of Captain Cook that consisted of an urn on a
pedestal shaded by four severe Greek Doric columns
carrying a roof, a similar 'marked' plot to that of Court de
Gébelin. The Cook-Lapeyrouse connections were reminders that both expeditions came to sticky ends at the
hands of primitive societies so admired by the followers
of Rousseau and by those who cultivated ideas of
naturalness. Both monuments stood by the lake-shore,
evoking the sea-shores on which both the French and
British expeditions met disaster. A further mnemonic
idea was found in the island planted with exotic trees to
evoke the distant shores, while weeping willows and
poplars alluded to the elegiac nature of this strangely
beautiful memorial [148].[12]

Alexandre de Laborde, in his *Description des Nouveaux
Jardins de la France et de ses Anciens Châteaux*, published in
Paris in 1808, described a number of important French
gardens, including Ermenonville, Méréville, Morfontaine (with its pine of Lord Weymouth, black marble

146 *The tomb (actual) of Antoine Court de Gébelin at
Franconville-le-Garenne, from Lepagelet. Court de Gébelin, a
Protestant, was the distinguished author of* Le Monde
Primitif. *The form of the tomb, with the four markers,
appears to have Masonic significance for it recurs in several
eighteenth-century Masonic designs, and is associated with
marking out the territory* (BL. 282. d. 17).

147 *Rostral column at Méréville. Plate 54 of Laborde.
Designed by Constant Bourgeois and engraved by Gamble*
(Dumbarton Oaks Trustees for Harvard University).

149 *The pine of Lord Weymouth (an important eighteenth-century Freemason) and black marble tomb in the Little Park at Morfontaine. Plate 16 from Laborde* (SJSM).

148 (opposite) *'Tomb' (actually cenotaph) of Cook at Méréville. Plate 55 of Laborde* (Dumbarton Oaks Trustees for Harvard University).

tomb, bosquet at the entrance to the Little Park [149], and great rock complete with inscribed verse by Delille [150]), Plessis-Chamand (again with a tomb, this time of the wife of the owner [151]), and Maupertuis [see 91]. Both de Morfontaine and de Girardin were among the first French aristocratic landowners to promote a taste for 'irregular' gardens on the 'English' pattern. They favoured plantations of acacias and evergreens, significantly, and, of course, introduced tombs and memorials into their gardens, a precedent that was to have far-reaching effects.

Even earlier, Sir Edward Lovett Pearce (c.1699–1733) had designed an extraordinary obelisk set on a rock-work base, obviously influenced by Bernini's fountain in the Piazza Navona in Rome. It was sited in the grounds of Stillorgan[13] House, Co. Dublin, the estate of the Allen family, was erected in c.1732, and was intended as a mausoleum for the Allens [152]. Pearce was mentioned in the *Constitutions of the Free Masons*, published in Dublin in 1730, and both he and the Allens had Masonic connections: the Rt Hon. John Allen, third Viscount Allen of Stillorgan, was Grand Master of the Lodge of Free and Accepted Masons of Ireland in 1744. Lord Allen was the grandson of Sir John Allen, who seems to have inherited from John Allen (d.1641) a talent for design and building.[14]

The use of the gardens of Paris as settings in which to honour the dead grew in importance from 1790, when a bust of Linnaeus was placed on a truncated column[15] in the Jardin des Plantes. Linnaeus, who had advanced the progress of natural history, was thus granted one of the first of the Parisian real commemorations, as opposed to the purely symbolic tombs of the Parc Monceau. Both Delille's *Les Jardins* of 1782 and Bernardin de Saint-Pierre's *Études de la Nature* of 1784 celebrated the elegiac, moral, and improving possibilities of the landscaped garden, with its contrasting compositions and memorials to virtue, worthiness, and greatness.

It was Christian Cay L. Hirschfeld in his *Theorie der Gartenkunst I-IV*,[16] who praised great English gardens like Stowe and Hagley, but who also proposed incorporating real tombs into garden designs. He mused upon the fragility of life, and the melancholy of reflecting by such tombs, dwelling on the touching scenes where death is no longer frightening. Hirschfeld identified the Elysian Fields at Stowe as one of the very first modern examples of a garden devoted to commemorating the dead,[17] but Stowe, with its temple and monuments, did

150 *The great rock at Morfontaine with verse of Delille. Plate 20 of Laborde* (SJSM).

151 *Tomb of the wife of the owner in the gardens of Plessis-Chamand. Plate 68 of Laborde* (SJSM).

not go as far as the Garden of Danish Worthies at Jaegerspris near Roskilde of 1773–84. This remarkable garden contained over fifty monuments, arranged on a route, and all carefully sited in relation to planting, changes of level, and the like. The forms of many of the memorials expressed the characters or works of those commemorated.[18]

Quatremère de Quincy's entry on cemeteries in the *Encyclopédie Méthodique*[19] proposed mixing the Pisan *Campo-Santo* type of arcaded cloistered court with landscaped gardens, and leant heavily on Hirschfeld's work: the modern cemetery, from the Greek κοιμητήριον, meaning a dormitory or sleeping-place, would be infinitely more agreeable than the Church-managed dumps, and would have allusions to the noble cemeteries of Italy, with their Virgilian landscapes. At first, however, the designs for cemeteries were more like vast built structures [153, 154], and it was some time before the tendency to place monuments in gardens developed into

the first great garden cemeteries: formal compositions, with pantheons, pyramids, vast *exedrae*, enormous platforms, and apparently endless colonnades were produced in great numbers by ambitious Architects.

The Pantheon theme has been noted previously, and it entered into the Architecture of Death not only with the transformation of the Panthéon, but with the iconography of Pantheon-like structures as Masonic Temples, and the type of the church of the Holy Sepulchre in Jerusalem. The allusions were powerful, and these themes exercised designers for some time. Proposals such as Boullée's gigantic cenotaph for Newton combined the Pantheon motif with the Imperial Mausolea of Augustus and Hadrian, and expressed immensity, expanse, enlightenment, and the Sublime. Uniformity, vastness, unlimited vistas, and the elevation of the mind to enable celestial ideas to be encompassed were aspects of Boullée's design, where the visitor would be at the centre of a vast circle and be able to appreciate a huge spherical space. Newton's illumination of the mysteries of physics helped to explain nature, so the cenotaph was not only a Sublime monument to the genius of Newton, but a celebration of Nature itself [see 115, 117, 118].

It is at this point that the Age of Neoclassicism becomes so fascinating in respect of its response to the problems of designing for death. Pantheon-like forms combine with pyramids and obelisks, blank walls, and megalomaniac scale derived from Piranesi's visions of real buildings of Antiquity and of imaginary prisons. Often domes are coffered and placed inside pyramids: cones, hemi-domes, and other themes combine in compositions of severe grandeur and awesome scale. However, the search for simplicity, primitivism, and pure forms was almost a passion, from the publication of Laugier's *Essai*, and Laugier, as we have seen, was linked with Freemasonry, as were Ledoux and many others. Pyramids and Egyptian elements had strong Masonic associations.

It is to Germany, however, and especially to the Saxony of the *Aufklärung*, that we must return, for there, at Dessau in 1787, under the aegis of the enlightened Prince Friedrich Franz of Anhalt-Dessau[20] and of his friend the Architect Friedrich Wilhelm Freiherr von Erdmannsdorff (who was more than an Architect, being widely travelled and cultured, and interested in all sorts of progressive ideas), was created the first non-denominational and communal cemetery in all Germany—the *Stadtgottesacker*. This wonderful and little-known cemetery, one of the first of the garden-cemeteries in all Europe, has an entrance-portal that tells us

TOD IST NICHT TOD
IST NUR VEREDLUNG STERBLICHER NATUR

It contains the twin brothers Sleep and Death in its plain niches, and is surmounted by a figure of Hope with her Anchor [155]. The Dessau cemetery (of which the gates are unquestionably Masonic in inspiration) is therefore one of the first planned cemeteries of modern times, laid out with architectural pretensions, to be realized at a time when there was considerable debate about cemeteries in France, Germany, and elsewhere. In France, however, it seemed that the debate could easily go either way: towards the monumental built solution or towards the garden-cemetery as an Elysian ideal.

152 *The obelisk and rock-work base at Stillorgan, Co. Dublin, by Sir Edward Lovett Pearce, of c.1732, intended as a mausoleum for the Allen family* (A).

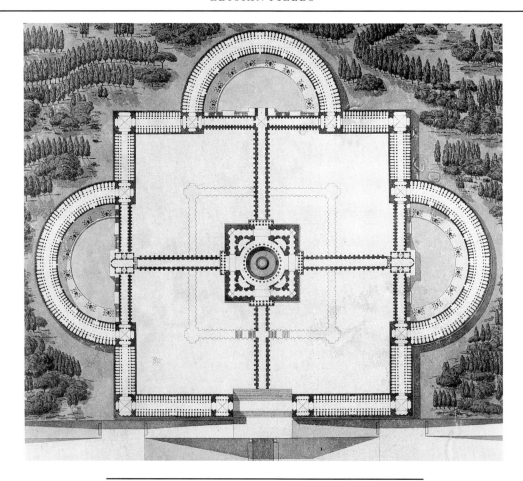

153 Élysée ou Cimetière Public. *A plan by Gasse for a gigantic Neoclassical built cemetery, the subject of a competition of 1799. The influence of Boullée and of other formalists is clear. In the centre is a communal monument with four octastyle porticos to receive the tombs of the illustrious. Underneath the vaults would serve as a depôt for the actual corpses* (A).

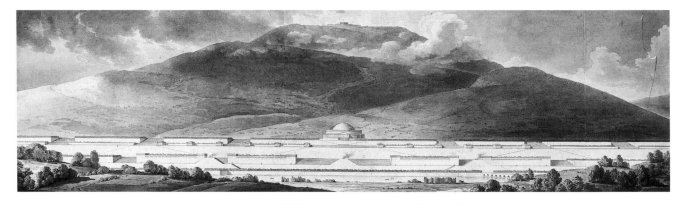

154 Boullée's Monument to the Supreme Being, *or cemetery in an Arcadian landscape. Charniers were to be set into the walls, and in the centre was an enormous domed Pantheon-like structure* (BN. CE. HA55, No. 25).

155 *Portal of the new cemetery in Dessau, the first public non-denominational communal cemetery unattached to a church in Germany, of 1787. Etching by Christian Friedrich Wiegand (1752–1832). The inscription reads* Tod is nicht Tod, ist nur Veredlung sterblicher Natur *(Death is not Death, only an ennobling of mortal Nature). The figures in the niches represent the twin brothers Sleep and Death, while Hope with her Anchor crowns the composition* (Staatliche Galerie Dessau, Schloss Georgium, Inv. No. G. 660).

A National Panthéon

In 1791, the French National Assembly decreed that the church of Ste Geneviève, Soufflot's Neoclassical domed masterpiece with its mighty portico in the Antique manner, should become the *Panthéon*, in which the greatest of French dead should be entombed, not only as part of an anti-clerical movement then gaining momentum, but to reinterpret Antiquity and to grant national figures (starting with Mirabeau) a suitable setting in death to give substance to the régime. The domed form of the Roman Pantheon and its identification with the Temple have been remarked upon previously, and these considerations seem to have weighed with the originators of the scheme.

A further proposal was made by Antoine-Laurent-Thomas Vaudoyer, who, like Brongniart (who worked at Maupertuis), was a Freemason:[21] Vaudoyer suggested making the *Champs-Élysées* into a modern Neoclassical Via Appia, and *Voie d'Honneur*, or *Voie Sacrée*, lined with mausolea, cenotaphs, and monuments of the distinguished dead of France. The name given to the great axial route and its tree-lined appearance suggested an Elysium in the Masonic sense of gardens like Maupertuis as well as a place of repose for the dead that would be instructive and educational as well as allusive and moving. Certainly the proposal would enable approved historical figures to be remembered, and the idea would assist in the regeneration of society to an approved pattern. Tombs and monuments would offer the passer-by not only fine Architecture and the best sculpture on the Antique model, but the inscriptions and eulogies would set a new tone, while the planting could also be arranged for mnemonic purposes. So the proposals for various types of cemeteries were not only concerned with hygiene and with breaking the monopoly of the Church when it came to Death: they were exemplary, were intended to teach, and were part of an ambitious scheme of social engineering.

There was much debate in Paris about the establishment of cemeteries, for it was not just the great who required graves, but the less august, who should be given a dignified last resting-place rather than an unsavoury communal ditch in an established burial-ground or churchyard.[22] Such notions savour of the new dignity accorded to the Third Estate (in theory at least), and of egalitarian principles promoted in the eighteenth century, not least by Freemasonry.

Quatremère de Quincy and others favoured the construction of massive, ideal, built cemeteries at first [see 153, 154], although at one stage it was proposed to demolish the fabric of Paris between what is now the *Odéon* and *Panthéon* to create a 'natural' setting for Soufflot's transformed building. This new *Élysée* would isolate the *Panthéon* from the squalor of the city, and the bosky nature of the new landscaped garden would contain sacred groves and 'philosophical' routes intended to promote feelings of veneration and improving thoughts.[23] This is unquestionably an idea derived from the Masonic concept of a symbolic journey or path with mnemonic features designed to evoke a specific response.

Today, we can have little conception of the horrific *fosses communales* in which hundreds of bodies were interred in churchyards and burial-grounds. It was little wonder so many people avoided seeing the committal, for conditions were repugnant, hideous, and inimical to feelings either of religious type or of reflective melancholy.

Many reformers sought to sunder burial of the dead from bones, skeletons, evil smells, and horrendous pits set in foul yards around which hundreds of thousands of bones were on view in the *charniers*. Death was to become a friend, the burial-ground a cemetery or sleeping-place, and the unmarked ditch a dignified place of rest marked by fine Architecture, suitable sculpture, and improving sentiments. Instead of the slime-covered ground, reeking of decomposition, urine, and faeces, gentle zephyrs would rustle the evergreens, and the dark foliage would set off the white stones of the sepulchres. There would be places of burial for poets, Architects, musicians, soldiers, philosophers, and routes through these areas would enable the reflective citizen to contemplate the richness of his nation's culture and be encouraged to emulate the nobility of mind once possessed by the dead.

Quatremère de Quincy proposed that the *Panthéon-Élysée* would contain the tombs of citizens less illustrious, perhaps, than those entombed in the *Panthéon* itself, but nonetheless important because they were human beings. Promenading Parisians would acquire soothing associations, and the Masonic ideas of an analogous theory by which Architecture and landscape could serve Utopian and improving ends would be implemented in the new Elysium. Quatremère had made the *Panthéon* into a tomb-like, forbidding, and mysterious pile by blocking up the windows, and this would be the grand focus, or centrepiece, of an Arcady in which Parisians would be buried and commemorated, would perambulate and reflect, and would be able to erect suitable memorials to their families, which would be together in death as in life. It was a more tender idea than anything the city graveyards of the eighteenth century could offer hitherto. Thus Quatremère's transformation of the *Panthéon* combined ideas of the *Panthéon*-like forms of Masonic images of the Temple and Lodge with the dark, severe, stripped style of Architecture adopted by Ledoux and others. The blocking of the windows was to give the building the character of a mausoleum: it was nothing to do with strengthening the structure.

The idea of a garden-cemetery itself became associated with that of a 'true pantheon' rather than the cold stone of Soufflot's building. In the garden-cemetery citizens would have ground for burial, and at the tomb contracts would be signed, promises sworn, and discord smoothed.[24] From 1793 the concept of egalitarianism gained ground, and the movement to found cemeteries as fields of rest was associated with secularization and equality, even in death. Cemeteries were to promote tender feelings in Elysian Fields which would be contrasted with the Church burial-grounds where skulls, bones, untidiness, and smells were all too obvious. Sweet, philanthropic ideals were to replace images of sadness and despair, hell-fire, and superstitition.[25] Rousseau's tomb at Ermenonville [see 127, 128, 134] was a visible statement of ideas about death that encapsulated notions from Antiquity: death was eternal rest, or sleep, and the ghoulish and macrabre images fostered in Baroque and Christian art were to be expunged. Thus the garden-cemetery, with its Masonic connotations, was also anti-Clerical, and offered gentler, more humane and beautiful images than those provided by the Church. Mozart's feelings about death as a true and best friend, whose image 'is not only no longer terrifying ..., but rather something very soothing and comforting'[26] were evolved after he became a Freemason, and are in marked contrast with the dark gloom and terror evoked by the Church, not only with Purgatory and Hell, but with unsavoury vaults, churchyards, and imagery such as the *Trois Morts et Trois Vifs*.

Père-Lachaise

Reference has been made above to Rousseau's tomb and to other examples of tombs, monuments, and cenotaphs in gardens. The acquisition of cadavers, over which monuments could be erected, to give added interest to a garden, will be a startling idea to many, yet, as has been demonstrated, it was taken up by several creators of gardens, and was a potent catalyst in the movement to form cemeteries.

A further model was the tomb of Jean-Paul Marat[27] in the garden of the former Cordelier's Monastery of 1793. This consisted of a rocky enclosure (very Masonic) planted with trees (including poplars to remind onlookers of Rousseau), in which stood a battered pedestal on which was an urn. The 'funerary bosquet' not only suggested a growing move away from buildings for entombment and towards a garden, but itself provided a powerful exemplar.

From the fifteenth century Mont-Louis had been noted for its charms as well as for its views of Paris and the surrounding countryside, and had been a Jesuit retreat until 1762, when the Order was expelled. The site had acquired formal gardens in the seventeenth century, when it had been the home of Francois d'Aix de la Chaise, Louis XIV's confessor, but little of this remained by the time Mont-Louis was purchased for the City of Paris in 1804.

Alexandre-Théodore Brongniart (who, it will be recalled, worked at Maupertuis, and seems to have found in Freemasonry not only a potential pool of patrons, but a completely new world in the social round of Masonic activities)[28] was commissioned to lay out the garden-cemetery of the east, known as Père-Lachaise cemetery. The Municipal Council responsible for acquiring and laying out the new cemeteries was dominated by the personalities of Frochot and Quatremère de Quincy, whose *De L'Architecture Égyptienne* . . . had come out in 1803, and who was clearly influenced by the Masonic beliefs in his interests involving ancient Egyptian Architecture and ideal typologies.

Brongniart originally proposed a large pyramid in the centre of the cemetery on the main axis leading from the Boulevard [156]. He mixed formal and naturalistic elements in his design, and created circuitous carriageways (as well as the straight axis) with *rond-points* [157], paths for pedestrians only, and some stunning architectural and landscape effects where levels changed. Brongniart was succeeded as Architect by Étienne-Hippolyte Godde, who was largely responsible for the appearance of the cemetery we see today. By 1825 Père-Lachaise Cemetery was being quoted by coemeterians on both sides of the Atlantic as the model for future developments, for it combined Neoclassical ideas about death and the Architecture of Death with the English landscaped-garden traditions.

This eighteenth-century style had introduced informal and 'natural' effects, as is well known, yet the important aspect of the English garden that gave a place to death and its commemoration within the 'natural' landscape setting has perhaps been underestimated until recently. The monument is as much an integral part of the 'picturesque' garden as the 'informal' path or the carefully contrived 'natural' clump of trees on a hill. Take the great English country-house mausolea at Cobham, Castle Howard, Brocklesby, Trentham, and elsewhere, for example, or the gentler, more allusive funerary urn at The Leasowes: here a literary note, struck again in Pope's garden at Twickenham, sets the elegiac tone.

Père-Lachaise is full of visual allusions to The Leasowes, Ermenonville, the gardens at Stowe, and other celebrated memorials set among landscapes. The new cemeteries, then, were to be based on images of Elysium and Arcady, where memorials to the dead would stand in pastoral landscapes and give solace to the bereaved. Monuments with 'drooping branches of a green tree falling over them' would gain in 'beauty and solemnity'.[29]

The cemetery of Père-Lachaise was the prototypical, grandest, and most magnificent of all the nineteenth-century funerary gardens that were to follow it. House-tombs of dignified Classical design lined the avenues which had distinctive planting [158, 159, 160]: the main axial approach up the hill was planted with limes, while the transverse path or *allée* had chestnuts. Poplars marked the *rond-point* [157] and also parts of the circuitous carriageway, while acacias were planted on this carriageway as it climbed the escarpment towards the chestnuts of the transverse *allée*. The escarpment itself had two lushly-planted *bosquets* as well as the clusters of magnificent tombs of Napoléonic soldiers.

The *Allée des Acacias*, of course, had Masonic connotations, for the acacia (*Mimosa Nilotica*) had not only Egyptian associations, but was a tree that grew in abundance around Jerusalem. Acacias, as markers where priests were not allowed to walk (as over a dead body), and, conversely, as identifications of routes that *could* be walked upon, have clear coemeterian allusions, while the tree is also emblematic of innocence and purity. A loose acacia was supposed to have been placed on the grave of Hiram, and the acacia was also said to be the Tree of Paradise, and the Tree of the Serpent. Claims for the acacia that it provided the wood for the Cross, for the Crown of Thorns, and even for the Burning Bush, demonstrate its importance as an emblem; it is also a symbol of immortality, of initiation and of resurrection. The true acacia (*Acacia Vera*) is also known as the Egyptian Thorn. Poplars (associated with Rousseau) are fast-growing, and their shape suggests the cypress and other lugubrious trees; and limes are suggestive of the *limonier*, or lemon-tree, of far-off southern lands.

In this respect Goethe's (noted by Gould as among 'writers of the Craft') evocative

> Kennst du das Land, wo die Zitronen blühn?
> (Do you know the land where the lemon-trees flower?)

is interesting, for it is suggestive of an Arcadian landscape where oranges glow in the dark foliage, and where a gentle wind blows, and where the myrtle stands quietly and the bay towers above. Goethe's house, with its roof on pillars, with gleaming halls and glittering

rooms, is also longed for, while the cloudy path and the dangers of fire and water (suggested in the dragons and streams) are indicative of a journey, dangers, and a house set in a sunlit landscape. The poem has three verses of six lines each:

> Kennst du ihn wohl? Dahin! Dahin
> Geht unser Weg! O Vater, lass uns ziehn!
> (Do you know it? There! There our way lies!
> Oh, father, let us go!)

The idea of longing, of a search for some ideal place, and the pleas to the Beloved, the Protector, and the Father, together with the house, pillars, fire, water, and so on, make this celebrated poem indubitably Masonic.

Chestnuts (*Marron d'Inde*) too can mean, as *marron*, a mark or a tally, but, significantly, it also means a curl tied with a ribbon, suggesting perhaps the knots of the cord with tassels. It is proposed that the scheme of planting at Père-Lachaise is not only allusive of Masonic routes and of certain ideas outlined above, but that the scheme of planting is also connected with Masonic emblems. Such a reasoned hypothesis is not as far-fetched at it might seem, for the number of tombs in the cemetery with Graeco-Egyptian or solely Egyptian flavours and overt Masonic emblems is apparent on any perambulation of it and other Parisian cemeteries. This should be no surprise

156 *Brongniart's first design for the cemetery of Père-Lachaise in Paris, showing the main entrance and the vast pyramid proposed for the centre (Musées de la Ville de Paris © by SPADEM 1987. Musée Carnavalet 86 Carn 250).*

158 *View of tombs of Napoléonic generals and admirals in Père-Lachaise Cemetery, Paris, drawn by T. T. Bury and engraved by Romney. On the left, the obelisk marks the tomb of L. André Masséna designed by Vincent Méry; then the Neoclassical sarcophagus-tomb of Marshal François-Joseph Lefebre, Duc de Dantzick, designed by Provost and David; and on the right is the sarcophagus-tomb on a high podium of R. Denis, Duc Decrès, Vice-Admiral, by Visconti. The large tomb in the background is that of Jean-Jacques-Régis Cambacérès, Duc de Parme, and Pro-Grand Master of the Grand Orient: it was designed by Marcel and sculpted by Plantar (A).*

157 The Rond-Point des Peupliers *in Père-Lachaise Cemetery, with Gaspard Monge's Egyptian mausoleum on the left, designed by Clochard. From Normand Fils* Monumens Funéraires choisis dans les Cimetières de Paris . . . *etc, Paris, 1832* (A).

given the affiliations of the designers and founders of those evocative garden-cities of the dead.

Père-Lachaise was regarded as a terrestrial paradise, a new Eden, an Elysium, an Arcady,[30] where earthly enchantment alleviated the gloom of the grave. The establishment of this great cemetery was part of a general movement that saw some startling realizations of ideas with strong Masonic connotations, although the Grand Orient of France closed its doors in 1791, and organized Freemasonry in France collapsed during the Terror. The Grand Orient was reconstituted in 1795 with membership much depleted: by 1796 there were only eighteen Lodges, three of which were in Paris.[31] By 1803 the Grand Orient reappointed *Grands Officiers Honoraires*, and in 1804 there were about 300 Lodges and the same number of Rose-Croix Chapters. French Freemasonry permeated the Napoléonic armies, and in 1804 Joseph Bonaparte became Grand Master, with Prince Cambacérès [see 86, 158] as Deputy Grand Master in charge of ensuring the good conduct of the Craft and its internal peace.[32] Cambacérès was entombed in one of the grandest of mausolea in Père-Lachaise.

159 *The tombs of Molière and La Fontaine in Père-Lachaise Cemetery, by Feuchère the elder. Molière and La Fontaine were buried at Père-Lachaise in order to give the cemetery status as a Pantheon, and to create a demand for fashionable burial there. To the left of the tomb enclosure is the grave of Louis Savart, bronze-caster and sculptor, and the urn on the pedestal commemorates N. Rambourg. The Corinthian column behind the poplars marks the tomb of Pierre Dufrenel, and the obelisk is the Gémon memorial. From Normand* (A).

160 *The tombs of Brongniart (left), by Lebas, and (right) of Jacques Delille, by Philippon, in Père-Lachaise Cemetery, from Normand's* Monumens Funéraires . . . *Brongniart's* Bourse *in Paris is shown in relief on his tomb. Brongniart was the architect of the cemetery, and the Abbé Jacques Delille was the author of* Les jardins, ou l'art d'embellir les paysages, *Paris, 1782, an influential work that helped to create the climate of opinion in which garden-cemeteries were first laid out* (A).

The Staglieno, Genoa

The grand urban cemetery, with its colonnades and necropolitan character, had been proposed by the French, but it was left to the Italians to realize it, just as they had realized the Campo Santo in Pisa (one of the most beautiful cemeteries in the world, which is essentially a large rectangular cloister round an open garth). The Cimitero di Staglieno in Genoa is a development of this characteristic enclosed and inward-looking cloister idea, carried to supreme heights, and is a celebration of death on a theatrical and monumental scale. While Père-Lachaise is possibly the most Arcadian, the Staglieno combines the qualities of urbanity, superb architectural effects, and a feeling for landscape in what is probably the grandest of all European cemeteries. It is the finest necropolis in Italy for the quality of its works of Art, sculptures, and Architecture.

The Staglieno was laid out in 1844–51, to designs by G. B. Resasco, on the north bank of the valley of the Bisagno, north-east of central Genoa, and consists of a walled and cloistered rectangular space on the floor of the valley, with flights of steps and broad ramps leading to the upper galleries that flank the Pantheon-like Rotunda. Above the galleries, and behind the Rotunda, the cemetery climbs the hill, in the manner of Père-Lachaise: that is, with individual tombs set among trees, so that the slope of the hill that rises above the town is covered with magnificent monuments, mostly Classical in inspiration, sitting among the dark-green foliage of myrtle and cypress. On axis, approached through the main gate, is a huge statue of Faith by Santo Varni that stands in the centre of the rectangular cloistered garth. Behind the statue, and dominating the main cloister, and indeed the whole composition, is the Pantheon or Rotunda, reached by a majestic flight of marble steps flanked by ramps. It was designed by Barbarino, and contains burial space inside for local worthies [161], an idea undoubtedly derived from the transformation of the *Panthéon* in Paris.

In the grounds of the Staglieno is a Cremation Temple. The Società Genovese di Cremazione was founded in the last century, and has long been associated with radical, progressive, and Masonic ideas. Indeed cremation in Italy and France has long been favoured by Freemasons, who tend in the Roman-Catholic countries to be associated with liberalism, anti-clericalism, and advanced opinions. (Cremation, as a mode of disposal of the dead, was a means of expressing aspirations not always in tune with orthodoxy in the Church.)[33]

Several family-tombs have pronounced Egyptian influences, and these, with the Pantheon, a severe Neoclassical flavour, and routes through the cemetery and the tree-covered slopes, have strong Masonic allusions. This cemetery does not glower: it reposes, with order and tranquillity. It seems assured and very grand, yet is silent and strong; it has found its place in the landscape.

161 *The Pantheon or Rotunda at the Staglieno Cemetery in Genoa, designed by Barbarino. The Pantheon-cemetery is a Masonic idea. In front of the steps is the statue of Faith by Santo Varni* (A).

162 *Design for an Egyptian tomb by Louis-Jean Desprez in pen and ink, with watercolour over black chalk. This is the Neoclassical Kingdom of Death, where a seated crowned skeletal figure with Egyptian head-dress presides. Note the* loculus *with cadaver feet on the right, the segmental form of the vault, and the segmental sarcophagus with bogus hieroglyphs. Desprez, clearly, was influenced by Piranesian images. The segmental forms were thought of as being peculiarly Egyptian from their use in the Graeco-Roman world in Isiac temples. The relationship to the crescent-moon and bow of Diana is obvious* (Courtesy of the Cooper-Hewitt Museum, the Smithsonian Institution's National Museum of Design. No. 1938-88-3951).

The Kingdom of Death

If the Staglieno judiciously mixed the mightier formal built-cemetery ideas of the French Neoclassicists with the landscaped garden, there was yet another type of necropolis. The underground cemetery had a long history in the Graeco-Roman world, and included hypogea (private underground groups of tombs) and catacombs (large public underground cemeteries). The Neoclassical catacombs of Paris have strong Masonic affiliations, and are theatrically effective: they could almost be setting for Trials in *Séthos* or *Die Zauberflöte*.

Louis-Jean Desprez (1743–1804) produced designs when he was in Rome from 1776 that have an intensely dramatic character. His imaginary tombs incorporating Egyptianizing ideas have a sombre funereal character enhanced by the semi-circular and segmental (as we have seen, a form associated with the crescent-moon and the bow of Diana, and therefore Isiac) arches of ashlar masonry beneath which the tombs are set. The gloomy, dungeonesque pictures suggest Piranesi's *Carceri* and other fantasies, but Desprez's images of skeletal Egyptianesque figures, corpses, and underground or cavernous structures conjure a Kingdom of Death where time has stood still [162]. Similar ideas occur in some of the sets for *Die Zauberflöte* discussed previously: indeed Desprez became interested in stage-design, and was employed as a theatrical designer by King Gustav III of Sweden from 1784, and lived in that country until his death.

The King's brother, Karl, was Grand Master of the Grand Lodge of Sweden from 1773, and Gustavus III is said to have promoted men of humble birth who had talent to positions of prominence and power. Gould stated that 'in no other country has the Craft been so intimately controlled and directed by the Royal

163 Vue Intérieur des Catacombes *showing the bones as arranged in a chamber by Héricart de Thury from 1810. From* Promenade aux Cimetières de Paris, etc, *by P. St-A . . . Paris, 1816* (A).

164 *View in the Crypte de Saint-Laurent in the Paris catacombs by Cloquet from Héricart de Thury's* Description des Catacombes de Paris, *published in Paris in 1815* (BN).

Family'.[34] Needless to say, Desprez had Masonic connections, and his designs display strong suggestions of Egyptianizing forms much favoured by the Craft at the time.

The closing of the famous cemetery of the Holy Innocents in Paris, which served several parishes, and the removal of the bones from the *Charniers* to the Montparnasse underground quarries from 1785 led to the renaming of the quarries as the 'catacombs', another allusion to Classical Antiquity. These catacombs were opened in 1786, and struck all those who saw them as completely severed from the land of the living: it was a world of darkness and of silence, except for the terrible noise caused when bones were thrown in. There Chaos reigned, with Destruction and Death. Later, in the 1790s and 1800s, the chaotic piles of bones were increased when remains were removed thither from newly-closed churchyards and crypts. The Sublime Terror of Death was clearly felt by observers, and a similar horrifying sensation may be experienced today beneath St Stephen's Cathedral in Vienna, where the chaotic piles of bones offer a ghastly sight to those who visit the catacombs there.

The catacombs of Rome and other cities had long attracted comment, and the reality of labyrinthine corridors crossing each other and entering large underground chambers in an apparently interminable network of various levels suggested not only Antiquity but the scenes of Trials in *Séthos*: here was the ideal setting for Masonic initiation, and the connection should be emphasized. Quatremère de Quincy (who lies in Montparnasse Cemetery) described the underground streets of those eerie cities of the dead in his *Encyclopédie Méthodique*;[35] other commentators saw the empty spaces as Architecture, and the dead as inhabitants, in a variety of inversion of a living city.

In due course, from 1810, Frochot and Héricart de Thury created Order (an architectural and Masonic skill) in this Kingdom of Chaos by arranging skulls and bones in carefully constructed walls lining corridors and spaces with all the severity of Neoclassical masonry [163]. Writers approved of the 'order and symmetry' which composed the ensemble of the catacombs. At the entry to the catacombs, on a stone lintel, is a line from Delille:

ARRÊTE! C'EST ICI L'EMPIRE DE LA MORT

The passages lead through various rooms: the *Crypte de Saint-Laurent* [164] containing the exhumed remains from that ancient churchyard; the *Grand Autel de l'Obelisque*; the *Sarcophage du Lacrymatoire* with the melancholy inscription:

SILENCE, ÊTRES MORTELS!
VAINES GRANDEURS, SILENCE!

the *Piédestal de la Lampe Sépulchrale* (with its question as to what is your destiny, presumptous Man, and the reminder that we are dust, and unto dust we will return), all have admonitory and mnemonic aspects. Many more rooms with inscriptions are linked by long corridors: Virgil and Delille are much in evidence (*inscriptions . . . d'un genre grave et sévère*), and grave and severe are words that describe much Neoclassical design.

The concern, even obsession, with Death, and the use of themes of mortality to create Sublime Architecture, is nowhere better seen than in the Parisian catacombs: here are Sublime Terror, the Journey, the passage from one room to another, the incorporation of a lamp, a fountain, an obelisk, a lachrymatory, a sarcophagus, and other familiar themes and artefacts. The catacombs, it is submitted, were intended not only as practical depositories for the millions of bones exhumed from Parisian churchyards, but as admonitory, educational places, where something of the nature of the Sublime could be imparted and where the Masonic/Egyptian/*Zauberflöte*/ *Séthos* subterranean journey in terrible vaults fraught with dangers and with reminders of mortality were given permanent form. The catacombs of Paris,[36] probably the most extraordinary of architectural experiences in a city peculiarly rich in architectonic delights, are related to the route at Ledoux's Lodge, to the gardens at Maupertuis, and to the Bois des Tombeaux at the Parc Monceau. They have unquestionable Masonic significance and ancestry, and epitomise *Ordo ab Chao*, one of the most important Masonic mottoes.

CHAPTER 8

CEMETERIES, MONUMENTS, AND MAUSOLEA

**Introduction; Early British Cemeteries;
Other Descendants of Père-Lachaise; The Monument
and the Tomb**

To subsist in lasting Monuments, to live in their productions, to exist in their names, and praedicament of *Chymera's*, was large satisfaction unto old expectations and made part of their *Elyziums*.

Sir Thomas Browne
Hydriotaphia
London, 1658

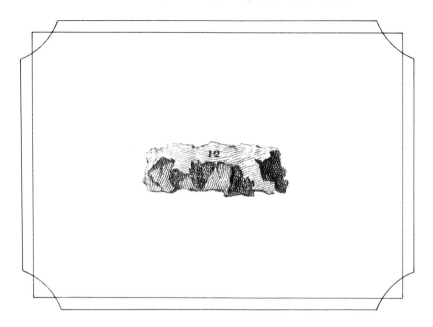

Introduction

The cemetery of Père-Lachaise quickly found its ad-mirers,[1] and in the 1820s the barrister George Frederick Carden began his campaign to get London to follow the example of Paris by forming new, hygienic garden-cemeteries to replace the unsavoury and overcrowded churchyards, crypts, and burial-grounds of London. The immediate proposal by Carden and his associates was for a new London cemetery on Primrose Hill (a site not unlike that of Père-Lachaise). This stimulated the Archi-tect Thomas Willson to exhibit a design for a General Metropolitan Cemetery in the shape of a pyramid to hold five million bodies.[2] This steeply-pitched pyramid based on the proportions of the tomb of Gaius Cestius in Rome also had an obelisk on the top, an image derived from the woodcuts in *Hypnerotomachia Poliphili* of 1499. However, Willson's ideas did not appeal to the promoters of the new cemeteries: it savoured too much of the vast Neoclassical proposals for built cemeteries by the Archi-tects of the French Academies in Paris and Rome, and these were tainted by the excesses of the Terror and of the French Revolution (which, arguably, set back the vari-ous progressive causes in Britain alone by at least a generation).

A scheme influenced by Père-Lachaise was favoured, and in February 1830 Carden convened a meeting to discuss his proposals, and this led to a public gathering in June in (appropriately) the Freemasons' Tavern, chaired by Lord Milton. A new Company was announced to be called The General Cemetery Company, and those present included Carden, Andrew Spottiswoode, MP, Sir John Dean Paul, the banker, and Lord Lansdowne.[3] Supporters of the new cemeteries came from persons of a pronouncedly 'progressive' side of the national spectrum of opinion, and Freemasons were well to the fore. At this meeting a splendid panorama of a proposed 'Grand National Cemetery'[4] designed by Francis Goodwin was shown, which consisted of a vast rectangular space, enclosed by colonnades, with chapels in the form of Greek temples, and Towers of the Winds at each corner of the colonnades.

Precedent to establish cemeteries unattached to churches had been set in Scotland, where the Reformed Church in the sixteenth century had provided burial-grounds that were physically removed from churches. This, of course, was in line with the abolition of chantries and the view that the doctrine of Purgatory was a vain opinion: the claims of the Church on corpses were weakened. The importance of Scotland in the development of speculative Freemasonry has already been emphasized (Chapter 3).

Early British Cemeteries

The movement to found cemeteries was thus first associated with the Reformed Religion (which, as we have seen, tolerated Freemasonry in Scotland and England to a remarkable degree), and then gradually became one of the concerns of persons of liberal and progressive ideas, many of whom were Freemasons. Norwich acquired its non-denominational Rosary Cemetery in 1821 (but mostly patronized by Dissenters), then Liverpool gained the Low Hill Necropolis of 1825 and, from 1825–29, the much larger Cemetery of St James, laid out in a disused stone quarry to designs by John Foster at a cost of £21,000 by a Joint Stock Company. St James's Cemetery was determinedly Neo-classical, with ramps leading down to the floor of the quarry, a perfect Greek-Revival temple as the mortuary chapel, routes carved through the solid rock (giving Sublimely Aweful effects), catacombs in the battered sides of the ramps, and a circular mausoleum of William Huskisson, MP. The planting was in clumps, and was by Shepherd, using the *bosquet* ideas prevalent in French elegiac gardens of the eighteenth century and later used at Père-Lachaise. By 1830 the Company was paying its shareholders a healthy dividend of 8 per cent, a figure considerably higher than could be expected from specu-lative housing or from railway stock. Liverpool, of course, had a strong Evangelical and dissenting element among its leading citizens, and Freemasonry was also powerful there.

The inter-denominational Glasgow Necropolis was formed by the Merchants' House in that city by promi-nent citizens, many of whom had Masonic affiliations. This severely Neoclassical cemetery is, in terms of Architecture, the most Sublime of all British cemeteries.[5] With the examples of Glasgow and Liverpool to emu-late, the General Cemetery Company in London deter-mined to press ahead with its proposals, and in July 1832 a Bill for establishing a cemetery in the neighbourhood of London received the Royal Assent. Passage of the Bill was no doubt smoothed by the fact that in October 1831 the first of a series of ferocious cholera epidemics struck, and, apart from the chaos caused in the already overcrowded churchyards, an added incentive to form cemeteries was provided by the belief that the epidemics were caused by the evil 'miasmas' that arose from the burial-grounds (not an illogical opinion given the appalling effluvium described so vividly by contempor-ary commentators.) The gratifyingly high dividend paid to shareholders by the joint-stock Company running St James's Cemetery in Liverpool doubtless encouraged the wheels to turn.

Francis Goodwin had his high hopes of becoming the Architect to the General Cemetery of All Souls at Kensal Green dashed when the Board decided to lay out the ground as a landscaped garden in which the public could erect any sort of monument it pleased. The Hon. Thomas Liddell, who prepared drawings under the eye of John Nash, appears to have been responsible for the original layout, with its great circle and winding paths (Père-Lachaise mixed with Regent's Park and the Eyre Estate designs), but, although a competition for the design of the building was won by H. E. Kendall, the buildings, all in a severe Greek-Revival style, together with the final layout of the grounds were designed by John Griffith of Finsbury (1796–1888), who much later became the Chairman of the Company.

By 1839 the General Cemetery Company was flourish-ing, and the original shares had doubled in value. The cemetery acquired many handsome monuments in the Neoclassical mode (including several, like that of Andrew Ducrow, in the Egyptian Taste), and was adorned with a wide variety of flowers and evergreens to augment the original landscape design. Like Père-Lachaise (where Abelard and Héloïse, Molière, Fontaine, and many other persons of distinction was translated in order to create a fashionable demand, replacing an earlier desire to be buried near the bones of Saints or votive statues), Kensal Green pulled off a coup when it acquired the bodies and handsome memorials of Princess Sophia (*d.*1848) and of her brother, the Duke of Sussex (*d.*1843) both children of King George III.

Augustus Frederick, Duke of Sussex (1773–1843), held robust and liberal opinions, and vowed he would never be buried at Windsor when he saw the state of the Royal Vaults there at the funeral of King William IV. The Duke became Grand Master of the Freemasons in 1813, and was President of the Society of Arts and of the Royal Society; he had a large collection of Hebrew and other ancient manuscripts, and seems to have been very interested in the problem of the design of the Temple. His genuine intellectual tastes and his deeply held Masonic beliefs (he only relinquished his leadership of Grand Lodge on his death) involved him with most of the issues of the day. His 'whole heart was bent on accomplishing that great *desideratum* of Masons, the Union of the Two Fraternities who had been mistermed *Ancient* and Modern'.[6] The Duke's interests were fully in accord with what one would expect of a reasonably educated Freemason in the period 1780–1840, and his burial at Kensal Green, like the interments of his fellow-Masons at Père-Lachaise, is wholly consistent with the man and his views.

In terms of allusion, the British cemeteries are less clearly Masonic than those in France or Italy, although Highgate (laid out by the London Cemetery Company to designs by Stephen Geary and James Bunstone Bunning from 1836 to 1842) has its spectacularly Sublime Egyptian Avenue and Cedar of Lebanon Catacombs, all in a powerful Kingdom-of-Death Egyptian Style that would be a marvellous setting for part of Act II of *Die Zauberflöte*. The West of London and Westminster Cemetery at Brompton, designed by Benjamin Baud, does contain a highly formalized avenue and circus, with a polygonal chapel on axis and circular galleries over the catacombs; it appears to be a reference to Bernini's colonnade at the west end of St Peter's in Rome mingled with a variant on the Pantheon types discussed above.

Entrance-gates and lodges in the Egyptian-Revival style at Abney Park Cemetery, Stoke Newington, designed by Professor William Hosking and Joseph Bonomi Junior, were more overtly Masonic, and the Architecture of the entrance was archaeologically correct and scholarly. In the case of Abney Park (the only London cemetery of the 1830s and early 1840s not to have any part of it consecrated for use by the Established Church) there was a complicated scheme of planting by George Loddiges, the nurseryman, and this highly ornamental cemetery 'as far as respects plants' had a complete arboretum, including all the hardy kinds of rhododendrons, azaleas, and roses in Loddiges's collection, as well as dahlias, geraniums, fuchsias, verbenas, petunias, and many others planted out in patches in the summer season[7]. Indeed, the 'complete arboretum', so admired by J. C. Loudon, had all its trees and shrubs fully named, which brings us to a consideration of one of the most startling notions the early nineteenth-century coemeterians entertained concerning their new cemeteries. 'Churchyards and cemeteries', wrote Loudon,[8] 'are scenes not only calculated to improve the morals and the taste, and by their botanical riches to cultivate the intellect, but they serve as *historical records*'. 'The country churchyard was formerly the country labourer's only library, and to it was limited his knowledge of history, chronology, and biography'.[9] Strang[10] had written in his *Necropolis Glasguensis* of 1831 that 'a garden cemetery and monumental decoration are not only beneficial to public morals, to the *improvement of manners*, but are likewise calculated to extend *virtuous and generous feelings*'.

Cemeteries, then, were educational and morally uplifting, and this exemplary concept is entirely Masonic in origin. Walking in the garden-cemetery the uninstructed could learn about varieties of trees and shrubs,[11] study the latest creations of the sculptor's art, acquire knowledge of Architecture and styles, and improve their sensibilities by becoming acquainted with the icono-graphy of death and its symbolism, as well as by reading affecting inscriptions and admonitory homilies. Thus would Benevolence and Wisdom be spread (again a powerful Masonic notion), and the idea of the cemetery as part of a scheme of social engineering found roots in Britain as well as in France. The Masonic connotations are clear. Ideas of suggestion were promoted by Loudon in his book on cemeteries in which he insisted that the planting of cemeteries should have a distinctive character quite unlike that of the public park or a pleasure-garden: he recommended evergreens, dark-leaved yews, and fastigiate trees found in Italian or Classical cemeteries because of their more Sublime forms, and because they were closely associated with plans of sepulture.[12]

Other Descendants of Père-Lachaise

The vast French literature on Death is an inexhaustible mine of material that puts the Anglo-Saxon world to shame. Philippe Ariès, in *The Hour of Our Death*[13] (an enormous and scholarly study), describes how, through Masonic ideas, the notion of granting the dead to be dealt with by a benevolent nature gained strength. He also points out that Roman Catholic writers in the 1870s were fulminating against cemeteries:

> the sophists . . . demanded . . . that the cemeteries be banished from the habitations of the living. Concern for public health was the mask behind which they hid . . . . The banishment of the cemeteries, demanded by the ungodly . . . was nothing but an empty excuse . . . . Concealed under the guise of public hygiene was an attack on the Catholic Church . . . . The banishment of the cemeteries was a good way promptly to extinguish the sense of filial piety toward the dead . . . . To separate the cemetery from the church was to disturb one of the finest and most salutary harmonies that religion ever created . . . . With two strokes of the pen, the pagan mind abolished the custom of centuries . . . . It is Freemasonry that demands the banishment of the cemetery to ten leagues from the capital and the establishment of a railroad for the dead . . . . And people persist in denying the disastrous influence of classical studies . . . . The nineteenth-century cemetery is the last arena of the desperate struggle between satanism and Christianity . . . . A nation that forgets its dead is a nation of ingrates . . . .[14]

Thus wrote Monsignor Gaume, in his *Le Cimetière au XIXe siècle* of 1875, quoted by Ariès in his magisterial volume. Gaume thus recognized the powerful Masonic victory in establishing cemeteries and weakening ties with the Church.

Certainly the more bigoted attacks on Freemasonry originated from Roman Catholic sources. The *Catholic Dictionary* of 1957 with *Nihil Obstat* and *Imprimatur* of 1950 suggests much that would be obnoxious if it were not such patent nonsense. Jews, of course, were admitted to Freemasonry, which prided itself on being tolerant, and tolerance is not something for which the Church has been noted, as Giordano Bruno knew full well, for it can lead to religious indifference. Freemasonry, according to the *Catholic Dictionary*, is anti-Christian, leads to religious indifference, is secretly manipulated by Jews, is politically subversive, has extensive power everywhere and spreads like *merulius lachrymans*, destroys legitimate authority, and brings all governments into contempt. In this view of Freemasonry, Communism is also an invention of Jews and Freemasons, an opinion shared by many: Nesta H. Webster, for example, in her *Secret Societies and Subversive Movements*,[15] talks of Jewish Perils, and other such familiar stuff.

The Rev. E. Cahill, SJ, in his *Freemasonry and the Anti-Christian Movement*, published in Dublin in 1929, describes Freemasonry as a 'child of the Protestant pseudo-Reformation', and goes on to attack it from several angles, but mostly because of its tolerance in matters of religion: he advocates a counter-movement inspired by supernatural and religious motives. How Mozart and Voltaire would have recognized the tones! Cahill also claimed that the British Army in Ireland was strongly permeated by Freemasonry, and that the Ulster rebellion of Carson and Craig was 'engineered largely through masonic intrigue'. While Freemasonry was strongly supported by the Anglo-Irish Ascendancy, and is still, to this day, powerful in Ulster, it must be remembered that the Protestant population of Ireland, especially in Ulster, includes a sizeable proportion of people of Huguenot and Moravian descent who had no reason to be either hopeful or happy about being governed by mentalities such as those of Cahill, who goes on to see Jewish machinations everywhere.

The Rev. Cahill was by no means alone: indeed he quotes chapter and verse from various Papal denunciations of Freemasonry, and refers in the most vitriolic terms to 'baneful Secret Sects who have come forth from the darkness for the ruin of Church and State'. And that 138 years after *Die Zauberflöte* was first given! The fact is that to Freemasons religious observance could be protean, and tolerance or even indifference were regarded as virtues unlikely to give birth to the zealous atmosphere that was to lead to a St Bartholemew's Day massacre or the repression of Protestants in Moravia and Bohemia in the seventeenth century. Furthermore, Freemasonry on the Continent all too often regarded Protestants (such as

Admiral Coligny and Court de Gébelin) as heroes and persons of substance, which would not go down too well with Cahill and his predecessors. Huguenots and their descendants were not likely to forget who had been their persecutors, and it is significant that there were plenty of Huguenot refugees in Prussia, Saxony, the Netherlands, England, and Ulster: it seems that through Huguenot Freemasons in the Netherlands the Craft was introduced to Vienna in the entourage of Prince Eugen of Savoy, an occurrence that explains much about Fischer von Erlach and Lukas von Hildebrandt.

For the purposes of the present study it is sufficient to point out that the coemeterian movement was originally inspired by many Masonic ideas, and that this fact was certainly recognized by Roman Catholic sources. Perhaps one of the problems was that the new cemeteries were very much more agreeable than the foul pits and slime-covered yards over which the Church presided. Indeed the Church, as Tenenti[16] has noted, has been somewhat vague when it comes to describing Heaven (and ecclesiastical opinion on the matter has been confusing, to put it mildly), although no such inhibitions occur where Hell and Purgatory are involved; yet to the rational mind of the Enlightenment, disagreeable Purgatory and a foul Hell were not attractive propositions, and, if the Church's running of the graveyards were anything to go by, a Catholic death should be avoided. The Masonic solution, as at Père-Lachaise, on the other hand, created an Elysium here on earth, and so accorded with the tenets of Freemasonry in that through the Brotherhood Benevolence, Friendship, Constancy, Enlightenment, Knowledge, Truth, Reason, and so on, Paradise on earth (or at least a great improvement) could be achieved rather than relying on some after-life from which no travellers returned to report on the facilities available. Père-Lachaise and its descendants offered a sense of repose, of beauty, and even of immortality through nature and finely crafted commemoration: Death and its horrors were conquered by Neoclassical grace and by the cemetery-garden in which stillness, scents, and charming vignettes could be enjoyed. Thus the undisturbed dead were ever-present, and near the survivors. Gone was the gloom of the grave, for over the cool serenity of the monument the honeysuckle and the rose would entwine in a terrestrial paradise that could be enjoyed and was indubitably real.

The Monument and the Tomb

Mention has been made of the designs of Boullée, Ledoux, and others that have Neoclassical concerns with stereometrical purity of form or Egyptian allusions. The

cemeteries of Paris contain many examples of monuments and mausolea with Egyptianizing and/or Masonic emblems. Sir John Soane's mausoleum in the burying-ground of St Giles-in-the-Fields attached to Old St Pancras churchyard is a 'monopteral temple' consisting of a block of stone under a canopy carried on four Ionic columns; a simple pediment surmounts each face [165]. This little canopy is sheltered by a bigger domed canopy with segmental pediments (very Isiac) carried on square piers. The whole is capped by a pineapple finial on a drum around which a serpent is coiled. (Herder's memorial in Weimar also featured a coiled serpent). Each segmental pediment has a wavy line incised on its flat surface, a very curious device. Soane, of course, was a Freemason, and from 1813 was superintendent of works to the Fraternity of Freemasons and designed the Council Chamber for Freemason's Hall. His extraordinary house in Lincoln's Inn Fields, with its collections of casts, pictures, and *objets d'art*, is itself a reminder to visitors of an enormous range of cultures in European civilization, while the mysterious tomb-like qualities of parts of the house, the routes, and the complex spatial inter-relationships, with folding walls, point to a mind steeped in theories of mnemonics, and a passion for exemplars. Soane's tomb has a number of Masonic allusions mixed with his stern, quirky variety of stripped Classicism, but the design had a long life, for it was the inspiration for Giles Gilbert Scott's cast-iron telephone boxes introduced between the two World Wars.

Even more startling is the monument to J. C. J. van Speyk of 1839 designed by J. D. Zocher. This is in the form of a lighthouse on the coast of Egmont, and consists of a massive Doric column set on a battered Neoclassical base of undoubted funereal character [166]. Freemasons are the 'sons of light', and the light of Freemasonry emanates from the source of all purity and perfection: Masons, coming from darkness into the light of inititation, are admonished to let the light in them shine out before all men, so that their good works can be seen, and the great fountainhead of that light be glorified.[17] In respect of lighthouses, the use of highly simplified Doric for the shaft, with Graeco-Egyptian doorcases and other Egyptian features was a characteristic of the series of buildings erected around the coasts of the British Isles during the first half of the nineteenth century.

Pyramids have powerful associations with death, with Egyptian rites, and with Freemasonry. A pyramid-monument in the churchyard of St Anne, Limehouse, has a close relationship to some of the sundials discussed in Chapter 3: it is very steeply pitched, and comes close to being either a thin pyramid or a fat obelisk, but it is divided vertically into five panels, and so is probably

166 *Monument to J. C. J. van Speyk, of 1839, by J. D. Zocher* (RIBA British Architectural Library Drawings Collection).

165 *Sir John Soane's mausoleum in the new burial-ground of St Giles-in-the-Fields adjacent to Old St Pancras churchyard in London. Note the Isiac segmental pediments, serpent twined round the drum at the top, and the incised wavy line* (A).

Masonic in the same sense as the Scottish sundials are indications of Masonic connections [167]. Soane designed an 'Egyptian Temple', published in 1778, which has an *in antis* arrangement of primitive Tuscan columns set against a pyramid with sphinxes at each corner, and used pyramids on the corners of a podium on which was a Pantheon-type of dome for the design for a mausoleum for James King. Pyramids with porticoes on all four faces were not uncommon designs by Neoclassical architects (Gilly produced such a proposal in 1791). A very elaborate pyramid-mausoleum with porticoes of banded Tuscan columns on all four sides which was designed in 1897 for the Counts of Henckel-Donnersmarck by Julius and Otto Raschdorff [168] is probably based on the Gilly design of over a century earlier. Count Henckel von Donnersmarck was elected Grand Master of the National Grand Lodge of All German Freemasons in 1838, retaining the position until his death in 1849.[18]

Obelisks, too, have clear Egyptian and Masonic associations. The Wellington Testimonial in Dublin, designed by Sir Robert Smirke in 1817–22, was erected in appreciation of one who had been initiated in Lodge No. 494, Trim, Co. Meath, and whose brother, the second Earl of Mornington, was Master of the Grand Lodge of Ireland.[19]

Another spectacular obelisk was erected at Rostrevor in Co. Down in 1826 to the memory of Major-General Robert Ross (1766–1814), the victor at Washington in the American War, who fell at Baltimore in 1814. The Ross family had close Masonic connections, and indeed Ross's uncle (also Robert) held high offices in the Grand Lodge of Free and Accepted Masons of Ireland in the 1780s. The massive obelisk on its Egyptianizing base hints at a Masonic reference, and indeed the gentry of Co. Down who contributed to the memorial were closely involved in Freemasonry [169].

It is in Ireland, too, that we find one of the most overt of Masonic memorials, and one in which are found not only many of the emblems described above, but also the five panels on the side of the shaft, previously noted in

167 *Pyramid in St Anne's churchyard, Limehouse, London. Note the panelled effect, and compare with the Scottish sundials described above* (A).

168 *Mausoleum of the Counts of Henckel-Donnersmarck, by Julius and Otto Raschdorff, 1897* (RIBA British Architectural Library Drawings Collection).

GRABSTÆTTE
DER GRAFEN
HENCKEL-DONNERSMARCK
A.DOM.MDCCCLXXXXVII

FINIS

169 *Massive granite obelisk with Egyptian pedestal incorporating a steeply battered die at Rostrevor, Co. Down. The massive cavetto cornice contains winged orbs with uraei on each side, and the relief on the die shows a sarcophagus draped with flags and military trophies and flanked by inverted torches. The monument was erected in memory of Major-General Robert Ross (1766–1814) in 1826, and was designed by William Vitruvius Morrison (1794–1838) (A).*

connection with sundials and pyramids. In the centre of the square of the little town of Comber, Co. Down, is a square shaft on a stepped base with a die, at the top of which is a statue: it is the monument of Major-General Sir Robert Rollo Gillespie (1766–1814), who came from an old Scots family which acquired lands in Down early in the eighteenth century. He had a life filled with incredible adventures, serving all over the world, until he was killed in India at Kalunga. Like the obelisk-sundials, the shaft of the column has five panels inscribed with the names of the places in which he saw action [170]. The dies of the pedestal contains a panel on each face: two have inscriptions, one has arms and trophies, and one has Masonic emblems. One of the inscriptions reads:

THIS TABLET

HAVING REMAINED BLANK SINCE THE ERECTION OF THE MONUMENT IN 1845,
IT SEEMS FITTING TO THE MASONIC BODY AND TOWNSMEN OF COMBER, TO RECORD
ON IT THAT THE BRILLANT [sic] REPUTATION OF SIR ROLLO, WAS MOST WORTHILY
MAINTAINED BY HIS GRANDSON
MAJOR-GENERAL ROBERT ROLLO GILLESPIE, C.B.
WHO FOR OVER 40 YEARS SERVED HIS COUNTRY
WITH THE SAME BRAVERY AND FIDELITY AS HIS ILLUSTRIOUS ANCESTOR
HE DIED ON THE 17TH NOV. 1890, IN COMMAND OF THE
MHOW DIVISION OF THE BOMBAY ARMY

JULY 5TH 1895   JOHN FRAZER COUNTY SURVEYOR ⎫
                                 WILLIAM WALKER ARCHITECT   ⎬ INSPECTORS
                                                             ⎭

The other inscription reads:

ROBERT ROLLO GILLESPIE
MAJOR GENERAL AND KNIGHT COMMANDER OF THE MOST
HONORABLE MILITARY ORDER OF THE BATH
BORN AT COMBER A.D. 1766:
AFTER A BRIEF BUT GLORIOUS CAREER,
FELL IN BATTLE BEFORE THE FORTRESS OF KALUNGA 24TH OCTOBER 1814.
HIS LAST WORDS WERE —
"ONE SHOT MORE FOR THE HONOR OF DOWN!"
A MONUMENT AT MEERUT IN THE EAST MARKS THE GRAVE WHERE HIS ASHES REST
A STATUE IN THE CATHEDRAL OF SAINT PAUL IN THE CITY OF LONDON
VOTED BY BOTH HOUSES OF PARLIAMENT ATTESTS THE GRATITUDE OF THE NATION.
HIS OWN COUNTRYMEN,
PROUD OF THE ACHIEVEMENTS WHICH HAVE SHED LUSTRE UPON HIS NATIVE LAND,
WITH A FEW OF HIS OLD COMPANIONS IN ARMS, HAVE RAISED THIS COLUMN
WITHIN THAT COUNTY WHICH CLAIMED HIS LATEST REMEMBRANCE
TO PERPETUATE HIS MEMORY AT THE PLACE OF HIS BIRTH.

170 *Monument of Major-General Sir Robert Rollo Gillespie in Comber, Co. Down. Note the five panels on the shaft* (A).

171 *Panel on the die of the pedestal of the Gillespie monument in Comber, Co. Down, showing Masonic emblems. The Two Pillars (Jachin and Boaz) with globes on top (an incorrect and unhistorical device which derives from sixteenth-century representations of Solomon's Temple), Masonic tools and instruments, the Square and Compasses (Both Legs Under), Euclid's forty-seventh proposition (the sum of the squares of two sides of a right-angled triangle equals the square of the* hypotenuse), *the Plumb-Line, the Hexalpha with the Triple Tau (T over H, meaning* Templum Hierosolymae *(Temple of Jerusalem)), the Pentalpha with G (meaning perhaps God or Geometry, but this is disputed), the Maul and Chisels, Levels and Rules, the Apron, the Sun, the Moon, the All-Seeing Eye, the Seven Stars, and the Motto* Audi, Vide, Tace *(Hear, See, Be Silent) (A).*

172 Fontaine de la Victoire *in the Place du Châtelet in Paris* (A).

A third panel contains the two Pillars, Jachin and Boaz, with globes on top, Masonic tools and instruments, the All-Seeing Eye, the Sun and the Moon, the Hexalpha (six-pointed star formed of two triangles), the Pentalpha (or five-pointed star), the proof of Euclid's forty-seventh proposition, and the motto *Audi, Vide, Tace* (Hear, See, Be Silent) [171].

It is not possible to be more specific than that, and Gillespie's Masonic affiliations are still there for all to see. In respect of the five panels on the shaft of the square pier, five, of course, is one of the sacred numbers of Freemasonry, and is formed of a combination of the Duad with the Triad, of the first even number with (excluding unity) the first odd number, two plus three. In the school of Pythagorean number systems five represents light, and so the Gillespie column is a mnemonic of a lighthouse. A five-pointed star is an emblem of health (triple triangle), and, of course, there are Five Orders of Architecture.

A similar subdivision into five sections can be seen on the palm-column [172] of the Fontaine de la Victoire in the Place du Châtelet in Paris, designed by J.-M.-N. Bralle in 1807. This fountain, and that in the Rue de Sèvres of 1809–44 (also by Bralle) in the form of an aedicule for the male Egyptianizing figure of Antinoüs by P.-N. Beauvallet, were reminders not only of the Napoléonic campaigns, but of the fact that the Napoléonic army was permeated with Freemasonry. Indeed Masonic zeal to improve the world, bring light where before there was darkness, and establish harmony throughout Europe and beyond was a powerful incen-

tive among the officer-corps of the Napoléonic armies. It is possible that the Châtelet column is not only a reminder of the campaigns, but a specifically mnemonic device to suggest the Nilotic adventures by reference to the Pharos at Alexandria.

A comparison of the lists of Freemasons and the names of the illustrious dead in the part of Père-Lachaise reserved for Napoléonic officers is sufficient to show the close connection. *L'égyptomanie* meant more than an enthusiasm for an architectural style: it was an emblem of a way of life, of a philosophy, of a system that almost swept through the world through the force of French arms, and it was a reminder of the power and potency of progressive forces. In the centre of the Place de la Concorde is a real Egyptian obelisk from Luxor that was given to Charles X of France in 1829, and set up under the direction of J. B. Lebas in the reign of Louis Philippe. On the main axis of the Champs Élysées it is not only an axial marker, but has meanings beyond mere architectural devices.

The Comber monument, however, is certainly one of the most interesting and less obscure of all Masonic commemorative edifices, and its iconography (in spite of mistreatment by slogan-writers and paint-sprayers) can be studied today with benefit. That it is related to obelisks, lighthouses, sundials, and Pythagorean theories adds to its intrinsic interest. While Scottish tombstones and sundials often have clear Masonic attributes, it is not very often that a public memorial actually advertises its Masonic connections, yet there is such a monument at Comber, and it is an amazing example.

CHAPTER 9

CONCLUSION

**Introduction; The Masonic Peace Memorial and
Other Masonic Buildings; Pictorial Cards; Is there a
Masonic Style?; Epilogue**

In the world today there exists a great organization with
a ritual and a code of conduct that entitle it to be called the direct descendant
of the mysteries of later antiquity.

R. E. Witt
Isis in the Graeco-Roman World
London, 1971, p157

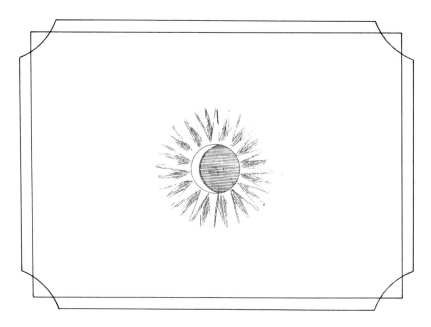

Introduction

There is not very much more to be said, for this book is essentially an *introduction* to the Art and Architecture of Freemasonry. Any of the aspects that have been touched upon could be expanded into a major book. The Masonic tombs in the cemeteries of Père-Lachaise, Montmartre, and Montparnasse alone, for which lack of space has prevented coverage, could fill a major volume, while the mnemonic side of things, the elegiac gardens, and the iconography would each account for a large tome. One is conscious of skimming the surface, of merely offering tantalizing glimpses, but it is hoped that the study, such as it is, proposes a few vignettes of a vast world that is unaccountably left unmentioned in most investigations. Several standard and scholarly reference books dealing with Architecture and with Architects very oddly do not mention Freemasonry at all, except obliquely if an Architect is known to have designed a Lodge or a Masonic Hall. One looks in vain for mention of Masonic affiliations in such works, although in some cases (as in Soane's) these are well known, and there is no case for concealment. One suspects that to a certain type of English academic mind Freemasonry, like Rosicrucianism or Alchemy, is so suspect that it is ignored. Yet to

ignore it distorts the picture, and there is no need to do so for there is an enormous amount of material available (although care must be exercised to concentrate on real publications, actual images, and scholarship rather than to make use of any of the peculiar ravings that have made investigations more difficult rather than enlightening over the years).

The Masonic Peace Memorial and Other Masonic Buildings

The entire complex of buildings that formed the Freemasons' Hall in London, and in which so many important meetings that shaped the nation in the nineteenth century were held, was superseded by the magnificent Masonic Peace Memorial in Great Queen Street, built to designs by Ashley and Winton Newman, after a two-stage architectural competition judged by Sir Edwin Lutyens, Walter Cave, and A. Burnett Brown in 1926. This Memorial consists of a meeting hall and Temple, with administrative, executive, and display rooms, including a large and impressive library and museum (to which this study is indebted). Ingeniously arranged on an awkward site, the massive pile-up of Neoclassical

motifs at the corner remains a familiar London landmark [173].

Purpose-built Masonic Halls became usual during the nineteenth century as Lodges found meeting in public-houses increasingly inconvenient, not least because pubs were no longer regarded in the same light as formerly. One of the most distinguished designs was that for the Freemasons' Hall at York Street in Bath by William Wilkins (1778–1839), erected in 1817–19. As the author of *The Antiquities of Magna Graecia*,[1] and the Architect of Downing College, Cambridge (1807–20) (the Grecian style of which was backed by Thomas Hope), Wilkins was suitably versed in Grecian architecture, and his Masonic Hall was considered at the time to be of 'strict Masonic appearance'. The distyle *in antis* arrangement of the façade suggests Solomon's Temple in its Renaissance variants, while the battered Graeco-Egyptian archi-traves, triangular knockers, and Egyptian chimney pots in the shape of Egyptian pylons also suggest the Antique origins of Freemasonry. This distyle *in antis* motif is a particularly Masonic element: it was found in Sandby's Hall and recurs in many places in the Masonic Peace Memorial building—the most important Masonic build-ing in Britain—and is common to a great number of Masonic Halls throughout the United Kingdom.

173 *Perspective of the Masonic Peace Memorial, headquarters of the United Grand Lodge of England in Great Queen Street, London. The building was designed by Ashley and Winton Newman in 1926. Note the* in antis *arrangement of the columns, and the mighty pile-up of masonry. The tower is an interesting composition, with its aedicules,* in antis *columns, and arched forms* (UGLE).

Buildings where ceremonies of the Craft are perform-ed are necessarily inward-looking, so that frequently Masonic Halls are top-lit (if illuminated by daylight at all). Any fenestration occurs where office, executive, or non-ceremonial uses are required. Soane used top light-ing for his museum at Lincoln's Inn Fields, and, of course, at the Bank of England, where the severe interiors and windowless exterior walls had a certain Masonic quality. Both the Greek and Egyptian styles of Architecture lent themselves admirably to the window-less façade, but Egyptian styles especially suggested the early history and legends of Freemasonry in which Abraham, Hermetic Wisdom, Egyptian Learning, Solomon, Hiram, Euclid, Enoch, Jabal, and many others

feature. Two of the most overtly Egyptian of all British Masonic Halls, both with fine architectural qualities, were erected in Boston, Lincolnshire, and in Edinburgh.

At Boston the Freemasons' Hall [174], again with the distyle *in antis* arrangement of columns (this time with palm capitals and tall *abaci*), is based on Ancient Egyptian prototypes, part-pylon, and part-temple façades (though much shortened and paraphrased) from Edfu, Dendera, and Philae, as illustrated in the seminal works of Denon,[2] of the Commission des Monuments,[3] and of artists such as David Roberts (1796–1864).[4] The interior was coloured chocolate, with ornaments of gilt-bronze, and the ceiling was dark blue, with gilt stars. Eschewing all modesty, the splendid, tough, assertive, pylon-like front, made of brick with stone dressings, proclaims in hieroglyphs that its foundation dates from 1860. In the covered cornice is the winged globe with *uraei*.

At No. 78 Queen Street, Edinburgh, the lavish Egyptian Chapter Room was built in 1900–01 to designs by Peter Henderson (1849–1912) for the Supreme Grand Royal Arch Chapter of Scottish Freemasons [Colour Plate XI]. Henderson's scheme using Egyptian elements included the carpets and furnishings, and the whole was brilliantly coloured.[5]

Masonic Halls of the twentieth century became very grand. The 'finest Masonic Temple in London', as the Abercorn Rooms in the Great Eastern Hotel in Liverpool Street were described in *The Freemason*,[6] was completed by Hampton & Sons to designs by Messrs Brown and Barrow, and was indeed lavish. While the old Temple in the basement was in the Egyptian style, the new Edwardian Temple was in the purest Greek, with features representing Wisdom, Strength, and Beauty. Its Grecian motifs included Doric and Ionic aedicules that incorporated the All-Seeing Eye and acted as canopies for the ceremonial chairs: these designs would not have been unworthy of Thomas Hope at his best a century earlier. The opulent interior was photographed by Bedford Lemere on completion [175].

Masonic allusions are not always overt in the Architecture of Freemasonry, especially that of Masonic Halls: it is as though the Lodge wished to carry its secrecy into architectural anonymity, although that is clearly not the case with the triumphal and noble pile of the Masonic Peace Memorial. Masonic Halls in certain areas, such as Ulster, are immediately identifiable: like the Gillespie monument in Comber they are adorned with Masonic symbols. Masonic bashfulness is not a concern in that part of the world, and many halls have Masonic emblems displayed in prominent positions to make the building identifiable. Many Masonic Halls in Ulster are similar in general form to that of Nonconformist churches, where a decent Classical simplicity predominated in the last century.[7] However, such examples rarely rise to architectonic heights of splendour, and as a building type, Masonic and other Halls, of, say, the Orange and Hibernian Orders, tend to be relatively unpretentious, and there is little to choose between them.

The interiors of some of the grander Lodges, however, are, in terms of Architecture, exceedingly ambitious. The Grand Royal Arch Chapter Room of Freemasons' Hall in Dublin, for example, was in a powerful Graeco–Roman–Egyptian style. In Barnstaple in Devon the 'Bath' furnishings of the Lodge Room of Loyal Lodge No. 251 [176] were justly celebrated for their magnificence: Jachin and Boaz, with their 'lily-work chapiters' and bowls, and other Masonic items, were of the finest quality. Some exteriors (such as Freemasons' Hall in London) were noble conceptions, even if the Masonic symbolism tended to be lavished on the interiors. Certain Continental Lodges were more overt in their advertisement, such as the Temple 'Le Droit Humain' in Paris [177].

Masonic jewellery, ornaments, details, and so on would fill several volumes if discussed in any thorough way. Clocks and watches with Masonic symbols occur in plenty, and Freemasons' Hall in London has a fine collection [178]. Dials are usually decorated with Masonic implements or attributes, while triangular forms are in evidence, for obvious reasons.

Pictorial Cards

In 1819 R. Ackermann published *Pictorial Cards, in Thirteen Plates, Each containing four subjects, Partly Designed from the Subjoined Tale of Beatrice; or The Fracas*. Ostensibly playing cards, these curious designs 'by an artist of Vienna' have a strongly Masonic flavour, and have certain affinities with the 1791 illustrations of *Die Zauberflöte*. 'The figures', Ackermann observes, 'are beautifully drawn, the architecture well imagined, and the *accessoires* of every description are introduced with a

174 *Freemasons' Hall, Mainridge, Boston, Lincolnshire, of 1860–3. Of stock brick with stone dressings, this pylon-like front with a distyle* in antis *arrangement (recalling Jachin and Boaz before the Temple) of palm-leaf capitals has an inscription in hieroglyphs which states when it was built. Note the winged disc with* uraei. *Although it is based on published sources such as Denon's* Voyage . . ., *with Dendera, Edfu, and Philae in evidence, the palm-capitals have extra non-Egyptian ornament which may be attempts to introduce architectural enrichment as allusions to Solomon's Temple as described in the Bible (A).*

176 *'Bath' furniture in the possession of Loyal Lodge No. 251, Barnstaple, Devon. Note Jachin and Boaz, complete with 'lily-work chapiters' and bowls, and the relationship with sixteenth-century images of the Temple (UGLE).*

175 *Masonic temple in the Abercorn Rooms, London, photographed by Bedford Lemere in 1912 (GLCL).*

177 *Temple* Le Droit Humain *in Paris, an Egyptianizing façade on which is an inscription extolling the rights of women. Over the door is the inscription 'Order out of Chaos' much favoured in French Masonic circles from 1802* (UGLE).

peculiarly tasteful feeling'.[8] Certainly the illustrations are oddly exotic, and only a few will be described here. The Nine of Diamonds, 'is made to form an Egyptian sepulchre; two obelisks form the entrance, leading to a massive pyramid, which composes the background of the picture, and the diamonds are converted into characteristic embellishments'. Bogus hieroglyphs and winged globes complete the picture. The Six of Hearts has two seated Egyptian female figures on either side of a portal leading to a darkly menacing route: the sources are derived from Piranesi, much modified, with bogus hieroglyphs. The Four of Spades features a canopy carried on four columns sheltering a pyramid and a

globe, and the Two of Diamonds features pyramids and a fountain (very Isiac). This very odd series of designs contains many allusions to funerary Architecture, to tombs and temples, to Egypt and to Neoclassical subterraneous vaults. Masonic stars, crescent-moon, tripod, square, Two Pillars, and other emblems can be found in these strange cards [179].

Is there a Masonic Style?

In the course of researching and writing this book an awareness of certain stylistic aspects has developed, but these are extremely hard to define, for they depend on nuance, on hints, on feeling, and on mood as much as anything. Overt displays of Compasses, Square, All-Seeing Eye, and other attributes do not constitute a style, while two columns or two pillars (with or without globes on top) may or may not be Masonic.

In music there seems to be a well-defined style, apart from the use of certain keys, notably the 'heroic yet humane' key of E flat major, that is associated with

Freemasonry. That style embraces the 'learned' manner of Baroque counterpoint and fugue, chorale-like tunes, and a certain *gravitas* of manner. Examples of a type of musical style that might be termed Masonic would include the opening of Haydn's Symphony No. 22 in E flat (*The Philosopher*), the scene in *Die Zauberflöte* with the Two Men in Armour, and the grave-digging scene in Beethoven's *Fidelio*. A similar mood prevails in the *Verwandlung* music in Act 1 of Wagner's *Parsifal* which, like the Two Men in Armour scene in *Die Zauberflöte*, is associated with a journey and a quest.

In landscape design an elegiac note is struck, and varied allusions are made, as at Monceau, Wörlitz, Maupertuis, and other gardens outlined above. Those gardens have a grave beauty and serenity, a balance, that is also found in Mozart's music: their eclectic, ecumenical, and stylistic vagaries testify to open minds, a rejection of bigotry and cant, and a celebration of various aspects of past and present. Walking by the lake at Wörlitz, a sense of ineffable loss is experienced: memory is jogged, places are recalled, ideas are floated in a

178 *Collection of watches and clocks with Masonic allusions. Note the triangular forms, Jachin and Boaz, and Masonic implements and signs. Time, through which we pass, is important, and the Mason, setting his alarm clock at night, would be reminded of the Craft before going to sleep and when rising in the morning* (UGLE).

gracious solitude. Somehow in those enchanted gardens sunlit mischiefs and the regrets of farewell are amalgamated. The Palladian house, the garden of allusions, and the temples of memory whisper of some radiant truths: there is a benevolent thread that draws us together, that suggests affection and calm in those luminous demesnes. An eighteenth-century garden of allusion, with all its gentle melancholy, seems to heal us of tendencies to introspection, and gently reminds us that what is here, what is felt, what is seen, what is beautiful, can be the basis for resignation and acceptance not only of life as it is, but of what it might be: it is wholesome, true, and

entirely rational, humane, and natural. It does not depend on Clergy, on obfuscation, on superstition, or on cant. The spirit of Mozart pervades such places, and helps us to feel kinship with the past, present, and future: futilities and dissonances are far away, and can be abandoned as unnecessary baggage.

And what of the descendants of such places, the early cemeteries? There, too, the style (humane, sound, of the earth, with allusions to the past and to the recent present) mingles formal buildings derived from Classical Antiquity with Elysian landscapes of allusion. In Père-Lachaise we find a land of austere simplicity on the surface, mixed with hints of the garden of memory, the memorial against the dark bank of foliage, the poplars of Rousseau's island, the acacias of ancient times.

In Architecture, laboured Egyptianisms and other exotica can be Masonic (as in the Edinburgh case), but a truer Masonic style is found in the simplified unshowy Neoclassicism of the vault in Weimar where Goethe and Schiller lie, in the Portal to the new cemetery at Dessau, in the Eben Mausoleum in Berlin-Kreuzberg, and in the ultra-stripped Classicism of Ledoux. Again, heroic yet humane might be the best way of describing it, and there is no question that the simple geometry and the absence of unnecessary frippery or show suggest a style appropriate to the Third Estate, to a gravity of mind, and to the virtues of thought, unassuming gentility, and sensibility without sentimentality.

Egyptian Architecture, with its stereometrically pure forms, blank walls, and massive simplicity, entered into the canon of Neoclassical design, and coincided with a high point of Masonic influence in France and Germany: it is not surprising, therefore, that a simplified stripped Classicism, much influenced by the Architecture of Ancient Egypt, found favour with the *avant-garde*, many of whom were Freemasons. A severe Neoclassical language of Architecture was felt appropriate to many institutional buildings after the Napoléonic Wars, for it became associated with classes that were neither clerical nor aristocratic, but that represented endeavours of the mind, of the Third Estate, and of a group that generally lacked political clout in previous centuries, but rose to

prominence in the second half of the eighteenth century. That group might be described as intellectual aristocrats, and would include such giants as Franklin, Mozart, Haydn, Washington, and many others. A Masonic Style, therefore, would have to include not only many later compositions of Mozart, but the Constitution of the United States of America, many of Goethe's works, and virtually all of the *oeuvres* of those French and Prussian Architects who reduced Classicism to its essentials, elevating Geometry and proportion above decoration and even the Orders, and who have been so mis-named 'Revolutionary'. In its essence, Masonic Style is summed up in the opening chorus of Mozart's *Requiem* in D Minor (K 626), which employs the darker colouring of such works as the *Maurerische Trauermusik* (K 477), the 'Learned' style, the elegiac funereal allusions, allusions to Antiquity (in the *Requiem's* case a fragment of Plainsong), and the severe character of stripped Neoclasicism. This *Requiem aeternam* suggests the green funereal garlands of Neoclassical coemeterian design, as at Père-Lachaise and as in gardens of allusion, and also the dark vaults of Desprez or Héricart de Thury.

So a Masonic Style is an amalgam of many things, but it has a distinctive flavour that is instantly recognizable once the subject has been studied and understood. It is a style that pervades the second half of the eighteenth century and the first two decades of the nineteenth; it is, in fact, the essence of Neoclassicism, the kernel of a movement that changed the world, and might have gone on changing it, had not reaction, retrogression, and bigotry replaced what seemed to be a genuine dawning of true Enlightenment.

Epilogue

Lurking somewhere under the conventional histories that deal with the Renaisssance, Baroque, and Neoclassical periods is a strange world that is only recently being gingerly uncovered in any systematic way. From the fifteenth century of our era the Hermetic-Egyptian traditions played an important rôle in cultural affairs, and from the sixteenth century they were associated with a radical reformation that envisaged a great change in society, in education, in religion, and in awareness, taking in every aspect of human activity. In the latter phase of the Enlightenment the symbolic and allegorical aspects of Antiquity began to be seen as presiding over much that was admired, and the ceremonies and systems of Freemasonry were explored as keys to the understanding of Antiquity itself.

What is starting to emerge is that during the Enlightenment many philosophers and others were thinking of Freemasonry and its organization as possible means of

179 *Four pictorial cards from R. Ackermann's* Pictorial Cards, in Thirteen Plates . . . *of 1819. These curious designs 'by an artist of Vienna' have a strong Masonic flavour similar to Alberti's decorations for the libretto of* Die Zauberflöte *of 1791. Top left is the Four of Spades, top right is the Six of Hearts, bottom left is the Two of Diamonds, and bottom right is the Nine of Diamonds* (GLCL and The Worshipful Company of Playing Card Manufacturers).

changing society itself. Fourier, for example, clearly envisaged his *Phalanstère* and its organization in Masonic terms: there would be a harmony between the interests of rich and poor based on association what would be reached after *seven* historic periods or phases (note the Masonic allusion) had been gone through.[9] Benevolence, equality, and individual interest in the *Phalanstère* as a whole would be encouraged, although enforced egalitarianism would be eschewed since variety would be possible through differing qualities and abilities of the people.

Freemasonry, then, was seen as an agency for improvement, for creating an ideal society in buildings and landscapes that themselves would reflect the aspirations of the Brotherhood. Sociability, groups, associations, and the good fellowship of the Lodge were to become the bases for a new society. The asylums of happiness and prosperity found in the Elysiums and Lodges were to become the very foundation of a new state, and through Architecture and its results (the strongly built and firm masonry structures) not only would the grandeur and lost Antiquity be rediscovered, but an ideal world based on that Antiquity grow again.

Yet the Enlightenment, like the clear meridian splendour of the south, held within it the terrible demon of mid-day: *non timebis a timore nocturno ... ab incursu et demonio meridiano*, and the noontide demon, bringing fright and a sudden chill, passed by, something half-seen in the corner of the eye, something primeval, and incredibly old, rustling behind the acacias and the bay-leaves, and seeming to darken the sun itself. It can be sensed in the work of Lequeu, in Viennese pictorial cards, and in the Kingdom of Death as depicted by several Neoclassical artists. Is it altogether fanciful to see aspects of darkness in the chilly schemes of Boullée, in some of the designs of Piranesi, or in the stark geometry of Ledoux? I think not, for all the marvellous advances of the *philosophes* in late eighteenth-century France seemed to herald a new world, but Rationalism and Enlightenment were obviously not enough. So it was in the 1790s, when the euphoria of liberty passed to the anguish of terror: gone was an ancient and longed-for equipoise. From the tenebrous realms of occultism and Hermetic

mysteries, from the longing for paradise on earth, from the removal of the supernatural in matters of religion, something grew, but it was not Rationalism.

For a brief period in the eighteenth century Freemasonry was at the heart of much that was enlightened, forward-looking, and promised a regeneration of society. The searches for wisdom, to rediscover Antiquity, to replace superstition by reasoned philosophy, to better mankind, and to find expressions for the new age in Architecture, music, and in all the arts, reached their zenith in the years before the end of the eighteenth century, but a promised land did not materialize, in spite of Napoléonic successes which promised the implementation of some Masonic ideas.

Freemasonry played an important rôle in the foundation of the United States of America, in the break-up of the Spanish Empire in South America, in nationalist aspirations in the German Lands, in the lead-up to the French Revolution and the Napoléonic reorganization of Europe, and in Italian Unification. In terms of Architecture, so closely connected with Freemasonry in historical terms, the impact during the Enlightenment of the Craft on design, both of buildings and gardens, was enormous, while, as has been discussed, many new ideas, such as those of the garden-cemetery, were largely Masonic in concept. That France and Scotland should have played such a significant part is not very surprising, because both countries were tied by systems of historical alliances, and relations between the two were close.

An association of Egyptian Architecture and Freemasonry is also clear, for the concern with Hermetic ideas and with ancient mysteries, together with the search for primitive, pure forms, led to Egypt. Eternal verities and ageless serenities are suggested in the immutability and clarity of Egyptian Architecture, but the iconographical, decorative, and architectural manifestations of ancient Egyptian culture are only a few aspects of an influence which has permeated Western European and American civilization, yet has not attracted the attention it deserves. It is hoped that this preliminary study will prompt further investigations into what is an enormous area for future work to be done. There is certainly no shortage of materials.

GLOSSARY OF TERMS

REFERENCES

SELECT BIBLIOGRAPHY

INDEX

GLOSSARY OF TERMS

Beyond the obvious facts that you are a bachelor,
a solicitor, a Freemason, and an asthmatic,
I know nothing whatever about you.

Sir Arthur Conan Doyle
The Memoirs of Sherlock Holmes:
The Norwood Builder

This brief list is by no means exhaustive, but may help readers to identify some of the more common motifs found in the iconography of Freemasonry. Those who wish to delve into every Masonic or quasi-Masonic term are referred to Kenneth Mackenzie's *The Royal Masonic Cyclopaedia* (Wellingborough, 1987), to Bernard E. Jones's *Freemasons' Guide and Compendium* (London, 1956), to the same author's *Freemasons' Book of the Royal Arch* (London, 1969), to Albert G. Mackey's *A Lexicon of Freemasonry* (London, 1919), to *The Oxford English Dictionary* (Oxford, 1933), to Joseph Gwilt's *An Encyclopaedia of Architecture, Historical, Theoretical, and Practical* (London, 1903), to Lenning's *Allgemeines Handbuch der Freimaurerei* (Leipzig, 1900), and to my own *English Architecture: an Illustrated Glossary* (Newton Abbot, 1987): a combination of these source is recommended.

Aaron
The Initiated. Aaron's Rod is associated with the Royal Arch and is one of the Three Holy Things kept in the Ark.

Abaciscus
A square compartment enclosing a part or the entire pattern or design of a Mosaic Pavement.

Abacus
The slab at the top of a capital, crowning the column. In the Tuscan, Doric, and Antique Ionic Orders it is flat and square, but in the richer Orders (Later–Roman, Ionic, Corinthian, and Composite) its four sides are concave.

Abbreviations
A Masonic abbreviation is distinguished by three points in a triangular form (∴) following a letter, and may refer to the Three Lesser Lights. The Three Points were often used by the Grand Orient of France. A few examples are given here. A∴C∴ Year of Destruction, associated with the Knights Templar; A∴Dep∴ Year of Deposit; A∴E∴ In the Egyptian Year, used in the Hermetic Fraternity. It is obtained by adding 5044 to the ordinary or vulgar date; A∴H∴ In the Hebrew Year, obtained by adding 3760 to the ordinary date; A∴Inv∴ Year of the Discovery; A∴L∴ Year of Light (+4000); A∴L∴G∴D∴G∴A∴D∴L∴U∴ *À La Gloire du Grand Architecte de L'Univers*; A∴L'O∴ To the East; A∴M∴ Year of the World; A∴O∴ Year of the Order, associated with the Templars; B∴A∴ Burning Bush (*Buisson Ardente*); B∴B∴ Burning Bush; C∴C∴ Celestial Canopy; E∴A∴ Entered Apprentice; F∴ Brother; F∴C∴ Fellow Craft; FF∴ Brethren; G∴ Grand; G∴L∴ Grand Lodge; G∴M∴ Grand Master; I∴T∴N∴O∴T∴G∴A∴O∴T∴U∴ In the Name of the Great Architect of the Universe; J∴W∴ Junior Warden; M∴M∴ Masonic Month (March in France); M∴·∴ Master-Mason; M∴W∴ Most Worshipful; R∴A∴ Royal Arch; R∴+∴ Rose Croix; R∴W∴M∴ Right Worshipful Master; S∴S∴S Three Greetings, or *Salut* × 3; S∴W∴ Senior Warden.

A rectangle is a Lodge; two overlapping rectangles are Lodges. A triangle (delta) is the emblem of the Chapter in Royal Arch Masonry, and represents a Trinity. The Latin Cross is the Cross of the Passion (and is distinguished from the Greek Cross by having one leg longer than the other three). The Templar Cross is like a Maltese Cross, but with straight ends to the arms rather than V-shaped. The Swastika is associated with the Hermetic Mysteries. A Templar Cross over a Delta is a sign of the Rose-Croix and signifies the Lodge of St John.

Abditorium
A secret place for hiding records, associated with the columns of Solomon's Temple, which were supposed to be hollow.

Abracadabra
An amulet in the form of a triangle.

```
A B R A C A D A B R A
  A B R A C A D A B R
    A B R A C A D A B
      A B R A C A D A
        A B R A C A D
          A B R A C A
            A B R A C
              A B R A
                A B R
                  A B
                    A
```

Abraxas
The Supreme Deity using the Pythagorean system of numbers: $\alpha = 1$, $\beta = 2$, $\rho = 100$, $\alpha = 1$, $\xi = 60$, $\alpha = 1$, $\zeta = 200$, totalling 365, i.e. the Ancient Length of Days in a Year.

Acacia
Mimosa Nilotica or *Acacia Vera*, associated with grave markings, with immortality, and with innocence. Jewish priests were not permitted to pass over graves, so it was necessary to mark the places of burials with acacias. Routes where it *was* possible to walk might therefore be lined by acacias, which is the reason for avenues of acacias at Père-Lachaise cemetery.

Acanthus
A plant (*Acanthus Spinosus*) with leaves that are the model for those in the Corinthian Order.

Accepted
Initiated, meaning the acceptance by the Operative Masons of others adopted into the Order, or who have received the Freedom, as of a Guild or a Livery Company.

Acclamation
Words used in connection with the 'battery' or 'firing', or breaking of glasses after a toast, or banging of glasses or beakers after such a toast.

Acknowledged
Candidates invested with the Masters' Degree.

Adoptive Masonry
Organization established for the initiation of females.

Adytum
A secret, impenetrable chamber; the Holy of Holies; the place where oracles were delivered.

Affiliated
A Mason who joins a Lodge other than that he first joined. A Profane (i.e. non-Mason) is initiated, while a Mason is affiliated.

African Architects
Eighteenth-century Masonic research society in Prussia, founded under Frederick the Great, a celebrated Freemason.

Age
Apprentice three years, Fellow Craft five years, Master-Mason seven years.

All-Seeing Eye
Superintending Providence, knowing and seeing all. It is an emblem in the Degree of Master-Mason, for God is All Eyes, and represents T∴G∴A∴O∴T∴U∴.

Almond
The tree which budded was Aaron's Rod and an almond.

Alpha and Omega
The beginning and the end, the first and last.

Alphabet
Hebrew and Greek alphabets have numerical equivalents. As this matter would fill a book in itself, readers are referred to Mackey and Mackenzie for further enlightenment.

Altar
A cube or double cube with four horns with Bible, Square, and Compasses (the Three Great Lights), surrounded by Three Lesser Lights, from which the grateful incense of Brotherly Love, Relief, and Truth rise. It is sometimes synonymous with pedestal, but this is corrupt.

Ancient Craft Masonry
Degrees of Entered Apprentice, Fellow Craft, and Master-Mason.

Androgynous Masonry
Masonry for initiation of both sexes.

Ankh
A cross surmounted by a circle ( ), used in Ancient Egyptian hieroglyphs, and sometimes identified with the nimbus and Cross of the Crucifixion. It is also known as the *Crux Ansata* and is associated with Eternal Life.

Anniversaries
Festivals of SS John the Baptist and Evangelist.

Anno Lucis
In the Year of Light

Antis, In
An *Anta* is a species of pilaster used in Classical Architecture to terminate the side walls of temples. When the pronaos or porch in front of the cell is formed by the projection of the pteromata (side walls) terminating in *antae*, with columns between, it is described as being *in antis*. The base and capital of *antae* differ from those on adjacent columns. *In antis* two-column arrangements are common in the Architecture of Freemasonry because of the suggestion of the porch of the Solomonic Temple.

Aphanism
Part of the legend of the Craft in which the body was concealed.

Apis
The sacred Egyptian Bull, associated with Osiris/Serapis.

Apprentice
Entered Apprentice is the First Degree.

Apron
The first gift bestowed on a newly initiated Apprentice. It is an

emblem of purity in life and conduct.

Arch of Heaven
An arch carried on two columns, signifying the Higher Degree or Royal Arch. The columns signify Wisdom of the Supreme Architect and the Strength of the Universe's stability.

Architecture
The art or science of building or designing edifices of any kind that gives them intellectual and poetic qualities over those of mere buildings. An Architect is a skilled professor of the art of building who designs and frames any complex structure. An Architect is also the Creator.

Arithmetic
The science concerned in measurement, and therefore in building. Freemasons are required to add to their knowledge, never to subtract, always to multiply benevolence, and to divide assets with poor brethren. Many numbers have emblematic significance.

Ark
The chest containing the Commandments: it is used in Freemasonry to mean the Lodge, or even a chest containing Masonic warrants, jewels, and emblems. It is also associated with Noah and safety.

Ark and Anchor
Hope and a Good Life.

Arts, Liberal
Grammar, Rhetoric, Logic, Arithmetic, Geometry, Music, and Astronomy.

Ashlar
Stone in its rough state is ignorant, unpolished Man. The fully dressed ashlar, smoothed and squared, represents expanded intellect, controlled passions, and purified life: it is symbolic of the initiated Mason taking his place in the Lodge. *See* **Jewels.**

Ass
Stupidity and ignorance.

Astrology
A system of divination by studying the planets in their relations to each other and to the earth, much used by alchemists, occultists, and Hermetic philosophers.

Astronomy
Images of the Sun and Moon suggest the regularity and precision of Wisdom and Prudence; the blazing star in the east is the Divine Being, but also suggests the inundation of the lands by the Nile (and therefore Resurrection), and the Seven Stars are the seven planets which completed the astronomical system.

Atelier
A Lodge.

Audi, Vide, Tace
Hear, See, Be Silent.

Aufklärung
Enlightenment: the spirit and aims of eighteenth-century intellectuals in imparting or receiving mental or spiritual light through reason, the acquisition of wisdom, and the study of and respect for nature. Light in this sense is identified with Freemasonry.

Austria
A great many intellectuals and artists were Freemasons in eighteenth-century Austria, notably in Vienna, where Mozart and Haydn attended Lodges.

Babel
Confusion, where language was confounded and the science of Masonry lost.

Baldachin
Canopy over the Oriental Chair in the Lodge: it signifies the covering of the Lodge.

Beauty
One of the three principal supports of Freemasonry, represented by the Corinthian Order. It is also represented by the Junior Warden, the meridian sun, and the third in rank of the Masters of the Temple.

Beehive
Industry and regeneration: an emblem of the Ark.

Bible
A Greater Light of Freemasonry.

Black
Grief and Mourning.

Blazing Star
Divine Providence bringing blessings and giving life and light; Prudence; associated with Hermeticism.

Blue
The colour of the first three Degrees, signifying friendship and benevolence and the Heavens.

Blue Lodges
Degrees of Entered Apprentice, Fellow Craft, and Master-Mason are called Blue Masonry; Lodges in which the degrees are conferred are called Blue Lodges.

Boaz
The column on the right-hand of the Temple as one approached the portal (left as one left the Temple). It signifies strength. It is also associated with the First Degree of Apprentice, and with the Senior Warden in its meaning of Strength.

Bone
This is supposed to refer to the Builder, Hiram. The word also signifies a core or inmost part. A bone consists of animal matter and the salts of carbonate and phosphate of lime, so is related to mortar and to chalk.

Book of Constitutions
The Book of Constitutions of the Freemasons edited by James Anderson, published in 1723. Also known as the Old Charges, and containing the rules, regulations, and legends of the Craft.

Book of the Law
The Bible

Brazen Serpent
Redemption, Mediation, but mostly associated with the Royal Arch.

Broken Column
The fall of a supporter of the Craft. Life ended or cut off. Death.

Brother
The term given by Freemasons to each other.

Brotherly Love, Relief, and Truth
The three great principles of the Craft, involving Benevolence, helping those in need, and uprightness.

Burning Bush
The source of Masonic Light, or Truth.

Cabbala
Mystical interpretation of the Scriptures, and metaphysical speculations. The oral tradition handed down from Moses to the Rabbis of the Mishnah and the Talmud. An unwritten tradition, a secret and esoteric doctrine. In the Cabbala words and letters have numerical values in the Gematria system.

Cabiri
Inventors of shipbuilding and navigation, who founded mysteries. One of them was murdered by the other three (shades of Hiram), and this murder was commemorated in the ancient secret rites, involving the wearing of an apron and an olive branch. The Mysteries of the Cabiri were still being enacted in the Graeco-Roman world in the first century of our era, and seem to have become identified with Isiac and other mysteries.

Cable Tow
A cord with four tassels enclosing a tracing-board referring to the Four Cardinal Virtues and the bonds of affection uniting the Brethren. It is associated with the Entered Apprentice Degree.

Caduceus
The wand of Hermes in the form of an olive staff entwined with serpents: it signifies the messenger, immortality, and peace.

Cagliostro
Founder of an esoteric Egyptian rite in eighteenth-century Paris in which Alchemy and Mesmerism mixed. His Seal was an S-shaped serpent pierced by an arrow.

Calendar
The Masonic Calendar varies according to the different rites. Usually 4000 is added to the actual date, so 1990 would be A∴L∴ 5990; Ancient Craft +4000; Scottish Rite +3760; Royal Arch +530; Knights Templar −1118.

Capitular Degrees
1. 4° = Scottish Rite, Secret Master; 5° = Perfect Master; 6° Intimate Secretary; 7° Provost and Judge; 8° Intendant of the Building; 2. 9° Scottish Rite, Master Elect of Nine; 10° Grand Elect of Fifteen; 11° Sublime Knight Elect; 3. 12° Scottish Rite, Grand Master Architect; 13° Knight of the Royal Circle; 14° Scotch Elect; 4. 15° Scottish Rite, Knight of the East; 16° Prince of Jerusalem; 17° Knight of the East and West; 18° Knight of the Rose Croix. This system is French.

Carbonari
An Order of Charcoal Burners organized on similar lines to Freemasonry that was closely involved in the ideals of a United Italy, and had close connections with Scotland and with France.

Cardinal Virtues
Prudence, Fortitude, Temperance, Justice.

Carpet
Emblems of a Degree. A flooring- or tracing-board.

Cassia
Acacia (corruption of).

Catafalque
A wooden bier decorated with funereal emblems, used in a Lodge of Sorrows. It is also associated with the Third Degree in French Rites.

Centre, Opening on
A Lodge in the Third Degree is opened at the centre, for all stand upon the same level, and every point on the circumference of a circle is the same distance from the centre.

Cephas
A cube of stone.

Chain
A circle of Brethren holding hands with arms crossed, known as *chaine d'union*.

Chalk, Charcoal, Clay
The three qualifications for the servitude of an Entered Apprentice used to mark the Lodge, emblematic of freedom, fervency, and zeal. Chalk is also associated with lime, as used in mortar. Chalk, Charcoal, and Clay (*Kreide, Holzkohle, und Erde*) are old Masonic symbols.

Chamber of Reflection
A room furnished in sombre fashion where the Candidate is placed for meditation.

Chapiter
A capital to a column.

Charges
The Laws of the Craft as set out in the *Book of Constitutions*.

Charity
One of the Ecclesiastical Virtues, usually shown with children.

Chisel
A Masonic tool, an emblem of the effects of education on the mind, for the Mason transforms the rude block of stone to the finely squared ashlar.

Circumambulation
Procession around the altar.

Circumspection
A duty in Freemasons to be cautious in words and carriage.

Cock
Courage and Resurrection.

Coffin
The Pastos or Bed, signifying symbolic death: deliverance is termed rising from the dead.

Colours
Each Grade has a colour. Green = immortality, hope; Blue = First three Degrees, signifying universality of the Heavens; Red = Royal Arch Masonry, fire, ardour, zeal, regeneration, purity, and the reconstruction of the Temple; Purple = Mark, Past, and Most Excellent Masters, compounded of Blue (=Craft Masonry) and Red (=Royal Arch Masonry); White = purity; Black = suffering, grief, mourning, and death; Crimson = fervency and zeal, associated with Royal Arch Masonry.

Column
That part of the Order of Architecture that is upright, and supports the entablature. It has a base, shaft, and capital, except for Greek Doric, which has no base.

Compasses
A symbol of the sun, (like the pyramid), and an architectural and Masonic implement. Virtue, the measure of life and conduct, the additional light to instruct in duty and keep passions within bounds.

Composite Order
One of the Five Orders, mixing Ionic and Corinthian, combining Wisdom and Beauty.

Consecration Elements
Corn, Wine, and Oil (health, plenty, peace).

Copestone
The last stone laid. To celebrate the copestone is to mark the completion of the edifice.

Corinthian Order
One of the Five Orders of Architecture, with a distinctive capital of acanthus leaves, stalks, and small scrolls at the corners. It signifies Beauty, and is associated with the south.

Cornerstone
First stone in the foundation, laid in the north-east.

Cornucopia
The Horn of Plenty, a symbol of abundance and fecundity; it is associated with the Nile, and with the tears of Isis.

Covering of the Lodge
The canopy of Heaven with innumerable stars.

Cowan
One of the Profane, i.e. unitiated. It seems to mean a roughmason, dry-stone waller, or one not permitted to work with lime.

Craft
The whole body of Freemasonry.

Crata Repoa
An Egyptian Rite of Seven Degrees.

Cross charged with a Rose
Rose-Croix Masonry emblem, usually with an eagle and a pelican at its foot.

Crow
A bar to raise weighty stones.

Crux Ansata
A cross surmounted by a circle, known as the *Ankh*.

Cube
An important Masonic emblem, the Perfect Ashlar. The Perfect Lodge should be a double cube.

Cubit
A measure of length based on the distance from the elbow to the middle fingertip, and sometimes associated with the amount by which the Nile rose in flood.

Cynocephalus
Man with a dog's head.

D
Door.

Dagger
Vengeance.

Darkness
Ignorance, a state of preparation, an emblem of chaos, the state of Man before birth, the state of the uninitiated. The Kingdom of Night, or Chaos.

Degrees
Ancient Craft Masonry, or the St John's Masonry, has Three Degrees of Entered Apprentice, Fellow Craft, and Master-Mason. There are other Degrees in other rites, but they need not concern us here. *See* **Capitular Degrees**.

Delta
A Triangle; it is also the luminous Triangle enclosing the Ineffable Name.

Design
The search for Truth.

Doric Order
The oldest of the Orders, prized for its sturdiness and simplicity. It is associated with Strength.

Drop Cloth
Raising-sheet used in the Third Degree.

Duad
Two, or a line between two points.

Eagle, Double-Headed, Crowned
With a wavy sword in the claws. An emblem of Scottish Rite Masonry. A single-headed Eagle is the emblem of St John.

Ear of Corn
Plenty.

East
Where the sun rises, dispensing light (Wisdom).

Egg
An emblem of the creation of the world and of wholeness. It is associated with the *Ankh*, with the *Vesica Piscis*, with the Kneph, and with immortality.

Egyptian Mysteries
Ancient rites described in Graeco-Roman texts, involving the mysteries of Isis and the final mysteries of Osiris. They were probably the models for Masonic ceremonies, and are described by Terrasson in the eighteenth century.

Eleusinian Mysteries
The most sacred and august of the mysteries of the Graeco-Roman world, like Isiac mysteries much concerned with wanderings, trials, death, and light.

Emblem
An occult representation of something by a sign.

Enlightenment
See **Aufklärung**

Enoch
The builder of Two Pillars to record the principles of knowledge, identified with Hermes Trismegistus, builder of cities.

Entered
One who has received the First Degree.

Epopt
One who has passed through the great mysteries and has seen the light.

Euresis
The discovery of the Body, perpetuated in the Third Degree.

Faith
The lowest round in the theological ladder, frequently suggested by a female figure with a Cross.

Fellow Craft
Second Degree of Craft Masonry.

Five
A sacred number, combining the Duad and Triad (the first even with the first odd, excluding unity). It represents light, and is symbolized by the five-pointed star of the triple triangle. There are Five Orders of Architecture, Five Points of Fellowship, and Five Senses. Five was also the number of knocks of the Lodges of Adoption, was associated with female Orders, with the Virgin Mary, and the flaming star. Five chords commence the overture to *Die Zauberflöte*.

Fixed Lights
Three windows in the east, south, and west.

Flaming Sword
A sword with a spiral, wavy, or twisted form, used by the Tyler or Tiler when guarding the Lodge.

Flooring
A board or canvas on which the emblems of a Degree are depicted, also called Carpet or Tracing-Board. The floor of a Lodge should properly be covered with alternate squares of white and black, symbolizing the Mosaic Pavement of King Solomon's Temple. The chequerboard pattern refers to the vicissitudes of life, or the chequered existence, and also to the Trials of a candidate.

Form
An oblong square (rectangle), with the greatest length lying east-west. A double cube. It represents the Lodge, the Temple, and the World.

Fortitude
One of the Four Cardinal Virtues.

Forty-Seventh Proposition
In any right-angled triangle the square described on the side opposite the right angle is equal to the sum of the squares described on the sides containing the right angle. This discovery is credited to Euclid (who is identified with Hermes Trismegistus) and to Pythagoras. The 3-4-5 Triangle was called the Egyptian Triangle by Plutarch. The base represented Osiris, the perpendicular Isis, and the hypotenuse Horus. The principle is fundamental to surveying and to Architecture because by setting out a triangle with sites proportional to 3, 4, and 5, a right angle can be accurately arrived at. It is called Euclid's Forty-Seventh Proposition.

Forty-Two
The number of judges before whom a dead Egyptian had to appear. The Chorus *O Isis und Osiris* sung by the priests of the Temple in Act II of *Die Zauberflöte* is forty-two bars long.

Fountain
An Isiac and Marian emblem associated with purity and with healing.

Four Crowned Martyrs
Four Christian Masons who were martyred in the reign of Diocletian. Pope Melchiades (or Miltiades) ordered them to be commemorated as the *Quatuor Coronati*.

Fourteen
An important number, including the Fourteen Saints, the fourteen days of burial in the Master's Degree, the fourteen pieces into which Osiris was cut by Seth or Typhon, and the fourteen days between the full moon and the new. The moon (Isis) at the end of fourteen days after the full moon, enters Taurus and becomes united with the Sun from which she collects fire on her disc during the fourteen days which follow.

France
Of immense importance in the history of Freemasonry and its influence on the developments of architectural theories and a variety of primitive Neoclassicism, a short entry on France cannot do it justice. The huge contribution of France and of

French Masonic Architects in the development of stereometrically pure forms, Graeco-Roman-Egyptian syntheses, the *Élysée*, and the cemetery is discussed in the text. The size of that contribution will be evident in the Bibliography. France also produced three of the most influential works associated with the Egyptian Revival and with the spread of an Architecture associated with Freemasonry: Quatremère de Quincy's *De l'Architecture Égyptienne* ... of 1803, Denon's *Voyage dans la Basse et la Haute Egypte* ... of 1802, and the Commission des Monuments d'Égypte's *Description de L'Égypte* ... of 1809–28.

Freemason
A member of a class of skilled workers in stone; a member of the Fraternity of Free and Accepted Masons; one Free of a Company, Guild, Incorporation, or Fraternity.

Freemasonry
A system of morality, veiled in allegory, and illustrated by symbols; a secret or tacit Brotherhood. An organization based on a Lodge, with unique and elaborate rituals and secrets, with members drawn to it by the rituals and by the significance of the Craft.

G
Equals 400 or, with a line over it 40,000. G is associated with one of the sacred names of God, and with Geometry.

Gavel
A tool for breaking off corners of rough stone, with a cutting edge: a stonemason's hammer.

Geometry
The science which teaches the properties of what can be measured, and which enables figures to be set up in precise relation to each other. Geometry is of fundamental importance in surveying and in Architecture.

Germany
A most important country in Masonic terms, which produced some of the most distinguished Masonic writers, including Lessing, Herder, Kloss, Bode, Findel, Schneider, Begemann, Krause, Lenning, Moritz, and many others. Germany, in the wider eighteenth-century sense, also produced Mozart and his Masonic masterpieces. It also produced Johann Wolfgang von Goethe (1749–1832) who became a Freemason in 1780. His writings are full of Masonic allusions, and are imbued with the spirit of the Fraternity. His influence on the creation of the Elysian *Weimarer Friedhof* (Cemetery) in 1818 was considerable, and he lies with Schiller in the stern Neoclassical Graeco-Egyptian mausoleum in the form of an Antique temple designed by Clemens Wenzeslaus Coudray (whose tombstone has the Square and Compasses as he, too, was a Freemason). Also in Weimar are buried the eminent Freemasons Johann Joachim Bode (1730–93) (his gravestone features a cornucopia and an obelisk), and Johann Gottfried von Herder (1744–1803), who was one of the first writers of the eighteenth century to see the relevance of Egyptian Architecture to the striving for primitivism. His tombstone features a serpent eating its tail, a blazing sun, Alpha and Omega, and the words 'Light, Love, Life'. Weimar, in fact, was one of the chief centres of Freemasonry in Saxony, as a visit to the churchyards and the cemetery will make clear, for Masonic symbols on the memorials abound. The intellectual, artistic and progressive liberal views of the princely family ruling Saxe-Weimar created a climate in which the *Aufklärung* flourished.

Girdle
A symbol of chastity and purity, analogous to the Masonic apron, and associated with the strength and power. Graeco-Roman cult statues of Isis show the goddess with a girdle tied with the Isiac or mystic knot at the front, just under the breasts.

Globe
The Supreme Being. In Freemasonry the celestial and terrestrial globes are indicators of the universal claims of the Craft, and of the widespread need for charity. A globe is an emblem of power and enlightenment, is associated with the winged disc with *uraei* of Egypt, and represents the earth and the heavens.

Golden Ass of Apuleius
The *Metamorphoses* contain an important story in which many allusions to ancient mysteries are made, with trials, initiation, and so on. The connection with Isiac rituals, with Graeco-Roman initiation rites, with *Séthos*, with *Die Zauberflöte*, and with Freemasonry is interesting and clear.

Grammar
One of the Seven Liberal Arts and Sciences which, with Logic and Rhetoric, form a Triad, the support of Language.

Grand, or Great Architect of the Universe
The Deity, the Grand Geometrician, Kneph the Maker, Demiurgos of the Platonic system, and a double form of divinity and humanity.

Grand Lodge
Every Lodge was once independent. Grand Lodges were established to regularize practice. The matter is complex, and the histories of Grand Lodges and the Grand Orient may be studied in several standard works. A Grand Lodge is really a supervising central authority, and is the Court of Appeal in case of dispute.

Grand Master
The presiding officer of the Craft with extensive powers.

Ground Floor of Lodge
The plan of the Lodge based on the Temple of Solomon. It has an altar (a remembrance of Abraham's sacrifice, of David's altar, and of Solomon's altar—known as the Three Grand Offerings).

Hand
A symbol of a builder. The left hand is the symbol of equity.

Harpocrates
God of silence and secrecy, identified with Horus the Enlightener, son of Isis. Isis, as the fount, and as Navigatrix, is also an enlightener.

Hermes

The messenger, identified with Hermes and Thoth, and by Diodorus Siculus as the Secretary of Osiris. The second Hermes was Hermes Trismegistus, the Thrice Great (note the Masonic and Isiac Three), who invented hieroglyphics, who is identified with Euclid (and hence with Pythagoras), and after whom Hermetic (or Egyptian) wisdom is named.

Hermetic Rite

A system for teaching alchemy and the rites of Hermes Trismegistus.

Hexagon

A figure formed with six triangles described using the points of seven stars.

Hieroglyphics

When they were unreadable they were given a status of awesome importance, and were the subject of innumerable studies of a speculative nature. Hieroglyphs were figures standing for a word, or, in some cases, syllables or sounds, forming elements in a type of writing found in Ancient Egyptian monuments. A hierogrammatist was someone entrusted with the keeping of records, and with the superintendence of monumental inscriptions.

High Twelve

Noontide, when the Craft was called from labour to refreshment. It is referred to in Wagner's *Parsifal*.

Hiram

The gavel of the Worshipful Master. Hiramites are Freemasons. Hiram, King of Tyre, sent Solomon men and materials to build the Temple. Hiram the Builder was supposed to be the Architect and builder of the Temple, and was murdered by the Three with Three Blows during attempts to extract secrets from him.

Hochmitternacht

High midnight, when the Craft was proscribed in Austria, and Freemasonry fell on hard times.

Hope

The second round (or rung) in the ladder. She, as a figure, is depicted with an Anchor.

Hour-glass

The transitory nature of life.

Illuminati

A Bavarian society founded by Weishaupt in the 1770s that was supposed to be anti-Clerical, and was denounced as anti-Christian. It infiltrated Freemasonry on the Continent, and saw Ingolstadt (where Weishaupt had the Chair in Canon Law) as Eleusis, Austria as Egypt, Munich as Athens, and Vienna as Rome. It played an important rôle in promulgating Enlightenment ideas throughout the Holy Roman Empire.

Illustrious Elected of Fifteen

A Degree that commemorates the Fifteen Conspirators, the Twelve who recanted, and the Three killers of Hiram.

Implements

Those tools used in Operative Masonry that are used in Speculative Masonry for instruction. They include the gauge, the gavel, the mallet, the chisel (Apprentice), square, level, plumb (Fellow Craft), and the trowel (Master-Mason), symbolizing the skills and Degrees. The trowel, of course, was used to lay mortar for jointing, and implies a skill not possessed by a Cowan.

Indented Tassel

The rope around the pavement, frequently knotted and tasselled.

Ionic Order

One of the Five Orders of Architecture, distinguished by its volutes. It represents Wisdom, and is placed in the east.

Isis

Egyptian Goddess who was sister and bride of Osiris. She resurrected Osiris when he was killed and dismembered by Seth, and she gave birth to Horus by parthenogenesis. Her tears caused the Nile to flood, she could blind with a stroke of her *sistrum*, and her fountains could restore sight. Her attributes are the moon, the cow's horns, the rose, the fountain, the lotus, and much else, and she is clearly the forerunner of the Marian *cultus* of the Christian Church. Her mysteries have interesting parallels with Masonic rituals, and she is discussed by a number of writers in Antiquity, including Diodorus Siculus and Plutarch.

Italy

Freemasonry was closely associated with liberal-progressive ideas from the eighteenth century, when a Lodge was established in Florence. Garibaldi established a Grand Orient based on the Scottish Rite, and the Craft was closely associated with Italian Unification, and with French Freemasonry.

Jachin

The name of the left-hand column when viewed from front (right-hand when leaving) of the Solomonic Temple. It is associated with establishment and legality, with the Junior Warden, and with the Fellow Craft.

Jacob's Ladder

A Masonic symbol, usually of seven rounds, but sometimes a ladder of five is depicted, although this does not appear to be the Jacob's variety.

Jehovah

The *Nomen Tetragrammaton*, or ineffable name of God.

Jerusalem

The Ideal City, the City of God, Paradise, seat of the Temple, something that is longed-for, was lost and destroyed, but exists as a symbol of the Ideal.

Jewels

All Lodges have six Jewels, three fixed, and three movable: in American usage the movable Jewels are the Rough Ashlar, the Perfect Ashlar, and the Trestle-Board, while in England they are the Square, Level, and Plumb-Line; the fixed Jewels in

America are the Square, Level, and Plumb, while in England they are the Rough and Perfect Ashlars, and the Tracing-Board. Why they are reversed is unclear. Jewels are also the names of the emblems worn by officers of the Fraternity as badges of office.

Jumper
A long chisel or lever.

Justice
One of the Four Cardinal Virtues, shown with scales and bandaged eyes, but in Freemasonry it can be suggested by other means associated with uprightness and by the left hand.

Key
Silence. Also a symbol of the disclosing of the conscience before the judges. It means the tongue, and is often made of ivory. A keystone is the wedge-shaped stone at the top of an arch which completes the arcuated system.

Knee
Knee to knee is one of the Five Points of Fellowship, and is associated with support.

Kneph
A winged egg or globe enclosing Masonic emblems, and surrounded by a serpent; it was the emblem of the Antient and Primitive Rite, and signifies the creative Principle, or the Grand Architect of the Universe, the Maker, Divinity, Humanity, and the Divine in Man.

Labyrinth
A symbol of a journey or a pilgrimage or even of life itself with all its wrong turnings and false starts. Found in gardens and in the floors of cathedrals such as Chartres.

Landmarks
It was the custom to mark the boundaries of lands by means of stone markers. Columns carrying a canopy, as over a shrine or a tomb, do the same. Landmarks are upright stones but they are also principles. Masonic landmarks are modes of recognition, the Degrees of Freemasonry, the government of the Fraternity, prerogatives of the Grand Master, and much else described by Mackey, Mackenzie, *et al*. They are also associated with funerary and commemorative designs.

Level
An emblem of equality and probity, and a Masonic implement that ensures accurate working.

Lewis
A metal wedge-shaped cramp inserted in a cavity in stone whereby a heavy piece of masonry can be lifted into place. It also means the son of a Freemason. A *Louveteau* means a young wolf: in the Isiac mysteries initiates wore a wolf's mask, so a wolf was a candidate, therefore a *louveteau* also means, like Lewis, a Mason's son. The cynocephalus figures of Ancient Egypt may be connected with allusions to initiation.

Light
The object of all ancient mysteries, in the sense of illumination. A lighthouse is a symbol that Freemasons have passed from darkness into light, for the light shines before all men that in good works may be seen. Light issuing from a triangle within a dark circle is an emblem of the Knights of the Sun. Lesser lights are the lights placed east, west, and south, and are often in the form of columns of the three Orders. Fixed Lights are dormer-windows to the east, west, and south. The Three Great Lights are the volume of the Sacred Law, the Square, and the Compasses.

Lily
An emblem of purity, and part of the ornaments of the Temple. It was similar to the lotus in Egyptian art, and had profound symbolic meaning, associated with the Isiac religion and with the Virgin Mary.

Lime
A tree (*see* **Trees**), but also the mortar or cement used in building. When limestone (carbonate of lime) is submitted to a red heat the carbonic acid is driven off, leaving quicklime, a powerful alkaline substance which, if mixed with water, gives off heat and forms hydrated or slaked lime, the most important part of mortar used in masonry. A Cowan was a builder of dry-stone walls (that is, without using mortar), and was without the Word, unitiated in the secrets of Freemasonry, outside the Craft, or profane. His status was not as high as that of a Mason, and the key to his status was his lack of possession of the Word and his familiarity with dry-stone work rather than with masonry bound with lime mortar. Needless to say, mortar (and lime) implies connections by binding (like the rope or indented tuft), and the attributes of the Craft. Lime in French is *Chaux*, hence Ledoux's ideal town. If mnemonic techniques are accepted as part of Freemasonry, the lime-tree can be associated with mortar, as can the lemon-tree, and the acacia (especially the locust-tree or false acacia with its lemon flowers). Significantly, a trowel is a tool of the Master's Degree. Well-tempered and slaked lime for mortar was significant in Continental Masonry during the Enlightenment. Lime is also associated with chalk, an old Masonic symbol.

Line
Any means of describing a straight line by stretching a cord between two points, or establishing a vertical by fixing a weight to a cord. It represents moral rectitude.

Lodge
A room in which Freemasons assemble. The Masons assembled. It represents the world and the Temple. It is also the Ark in which the warrants and other precious objects are kept. A Lodge room ought to be orientated east-west, should be isolated from other buildings, and should preferably be on an upper floor. Decorations should be Masonic emblems, Triangles, Triple Tau, Square, Compasses, Death's Head, and so on, and the floor should be carpeted, made of mosaic pattern. Ceilings should represent the 'clouded canopy'.

Logic
One of the Seven Liberal Arts and Sciences.

Mahabyn
A secret word, the origins of which are obscure. It is also

described as Maughbin, Magboe and Boe, Mahhabone, Marrow in this Bone, Mac Benac, and Mackbenah. Marrow may refer to a secret within the bone, and it may, like Maugh, refer to a colleague or a partner. One interpretation is that the word refers to the rotten flesh coming from the bone during the Raising of Hiram, or to decay extending even to and within the bone, but Mahabyn or its variants do not seem to have a Hebrew origin, although it has been associated with building, the builder, and the body of Hiram. A bone itself has a meaning related to the inmost part or the core, and bones consist partly of salts or carbonate and phosphate of lime, which might suggest a relationship with lime-mortar and the trowel of the Master's Degree. Maught means strength, and Maugrabin apparently refers to a man of the west, or even to an African Moor. It also may signify universality, in the sense of from the highest to the lowest.

If there is any derivation from *mahal*, meaning private lodgings (*halla* means to lodge in Arabic), or a palace, and *bin* or *byn* derives from *ben*, meaning an inner or best room, the strange word *mahabyn* may indicate the accessibility of innermost rooms or innermost secrets to those who were initiated to the Degree of Master-Mason. Boaz seems to be the word relating to the Apprentice Grade, and Jachin that of the Fellow Craft. According to the Sloane Catechism the third word is Mahabyn, and is associated with the Third, or Master's Degree. However, a further intriguing possibility is suggested by the techniques of mnemonics, and the associations of the trowel, mortar, and Degree of Master. The word *Mahoe* is the name of several trees, and is applied with qualifications to similar plants of various genera: it can also mean a malvaceous tree, *paritium tiliaceum*, and tileaceous means belonging to the Natural Order *Tiliaceae*, typified by the genus *Tilia*, the lime or linden-tree. If Mahabyn means something like the inner meaning among trees, then it could refer to lime-mortar, as the great binding agency holding all Masons together, and not used by Cowans or the profane. In other words, *mahabyn* may be a mnemonic for lime, and especially lime-mortar, but this is only a hypothesis which I offer as a possible explanation for a word that appears to be nonsensical, on the surface. My explanation is as reasonable as any other, and it is not insignificant that a trowel is a tool associated with the Degree of Master-Mason, and that a trowel is used when jointing stones with lime mortar. The explanation may be even simpler, however, in that the 'marrow-in-the-bone' aspect of the Hiramic legend may be an Art-of-Memory technique for remembering the word itself.

Mallet
A tool emblematic of correcting irregularities, depressing malignity, and moderation. It is often confused with the gavel, but is quite different, as it has a large round head, while the gavel has a small one with a triangular pointed edge.

Mark
A device given to a particular Mason. It enabled work by any Mason to be identified, and helped in the administration of building contracts.

Masons, Worshipful Company of
A London Livery Company, thirtieth in Order of Precedence, founded in the Middle Ages.

Memory, Art of
A system of mnemonics evolved in Classical times, using large and complex buildings and routes through them as triggering mechanism for memory.

Monde Primitif
Antoine Court de Gébelin, himself a Freemason, produced this remarkable evocation of a Primitive World, with accounts of the ancient mysteries.

Moon
An Isiac symbol, indicative in Freemasonry of the light shed in the night, for the Lodge has a universal meaning.

Mopses
A variety of German Freemasonry (androgynous from 1776), found in Roman Catholic states. From *Mops*, meaning a pug-dog or mastiff, indicative of fidelity.

Mortar
Lime mortar is an important symbol in Continental Freemasonry as a binding agent. The trowel is a symbol of the Master-Mason, and the Cowan cannot work with lime. Mortar, tempered and slaked, is a significant symbol, and indicates that passions and fiery temperaments are under control, transformed by the process. Untempered mortar indicates that the lessons of the Craft have not been fully assimilated.

Mosaic Pavement
A floor of small differently coloured stones. The term seems to have been applied to the chequerboard pattern of black and white squares on floors, but this usage must have started with a misunderstanding, for chequerboards have large slabs rather than small *tesserae*.

Nine
A significant Masonic number, involving the important 3, consecrated to the spheres ($360° = 3$ and 6 and $0 = 9$).

Noah
Involved in rescuing with the Ark, and keeper of a secret, who was 'raised' by his sons.

North
Darkness and Night. Ignorance.

Numbers
Pythagorean number systems are far too complex to be discussed here. Only a few numbers will be mentioned. Equal numbers are female and odd ones are male because even ones can be divided, so suggest generation. One equals God, the point within the circle, love, concord, piety, fidelity, because it is indivisable. It is associated with harmony and preserving light, and friendship. Two, on the other hand, was evil and dark. Three was again harmony, friendship, concord, peace, and temperance, and is regarded as perfect. Four was sacred to the name of God (the *tetragrammaton*). Five was light, nature,

marriage (female = two plus male = three), and is associated with the triple triangle (it is a significant beginning of the overture to *Die Zauberflöte*). Six was health and justice, and was perfect because it could be divided by both two and three and because one, two and three added equal six (aliquot parts). Seven was associated with creation. Eight was a cube (two × two × two), and meant friendship, prudence, justice, counsel; it was associated with nature and equality. Nine was perfection, and was three + three + three or three × three as well as the gestation period for humans. Ten, as the union of one, two, three, and four was perfect and represented Heaven.

The first three numbers (one, two, three) are called Monad, Duad, Triad. The Monad is male and creative. The Duad is female, ever-changing, and is matter capable of form. Monad plus Duad equals Triad, which is the world formed by the creative principle out of matter, and is the basis for the Pythagorean right-angled triangle and the squaring of the sides. The Isiac connections are clear.

Obelisk

A monolith, square on plan, tapering slightly towards the top, which terminates in a pyramid. Hieroglyphs were carved on all four faces. Obelisks were associated with the sun, were both phallic and gnomons, and were symbols of continuity, power, regeneration, and stability. As markers of axial routes they appear in Masonic iconography, usually in association with Continental Masters' Degrees.

Oblong Square

A parallelogram or four-sided figure, all of which angles are equal, with two sides longer than the others. A symbol of the Lodge, the Ark, the Temple.

Octagon

Some representations of the Temple showed circular or polygonal buildings, clearly derived from the Dome of the Rock, the Holy Sepulchre in Jerusalem, and the Pantheon. Octagons were used in this respect, and also suggest the Crosses of the Knights of St John and of the Templars, as well as the Eight Beatitudes.

Ogee

An arched form composed of two convex and two concave curves, rising to a sharp point, like two cyma reversa sections meeting at a point. It occurs in various eighteenth- and nineteenth-century designs with Masonic connections (often in association with Egyptian or Classical elements, which is odd, for the ogee arch is Gothic), but its precise meaning remains obscure. It *may* refer to the Outside Guardian (O∴G∴).

Operative Mason

A stonemason who practises his craft by working with stone, as opposed to a speculative Mason.

Orders of Architecture

There are Five Orders (Tuscan, Doric, Ionic, Corinthian, and Composite), and they consist of bases (except for Greek Doric which has no base), shafts, capitals, and entablature. Columns include the bases, shafts, and capitals, and entablatures consist of architraves, friezes, and cornices.

Ordo ab Chao

Order from Chaos, an important Masonic motto, suggesting the Art of Architecture itself.

Orient

The East. The supreme Masonic bodies on the Continent are called Grand Orients.

Oriflamme

The Royal Standard of France based on the banner of the Basilica of St Denis, of red silk, it was a banderole of two or three points, sometimes powdered with golden flakes of fire. Various Masonic bodies possess banners on poles or lances which are called Oriflammes, and have tassels of silk as well.

Ornaments

Mosaic pavement, indented tassel, and blazing star.

Orphic Mysteries

Further mysteries of the Graeco-Roman world, again involving remembrance of a murder (this time of Bacchus). Interesting from our point of view was the crowning of initiates with poplar and the carrying of serpents in the rituals.

Osiris

Husband/brother of Isis, he was infinitely wise, went on journeys, was murdered and dismembered by Seth (Typhon), put together again, and resurrected by Isis. Osiris is the lost sun, monarch of the infernal regions, supreme judge, and the embodiment of wisdom. His emblem was the sun, and goodness was his manifestation. Like Isis, he is of great importance in Freemasonry, notably in Continental rites, while the Egyptian Rites of the eighteenth century accord him great significance. One of his symbols is the Apis Bull. In the Graeco-Roman world he became Serapis, and his temples often had a Lady Chapel attached which was dedicated to Isis.

Parallel Lines

SS John the Baptist and Evangelist, the patrons of Masonry.

Pastos

A chamber or a couch, the Ark, a coffin, emblems of mortality. Aspirants in Antiquity were sometimes placed in a cell called a Pastos which commemorated the death of a god.

Pedal

Feet (*pes* = foot) planted firmly on the principles of right cause a man to be upright and just. It symbolizes justice.

Pedestals

When the columns of Wisdom (east), Strength (west), and Beauty (south), are not erected in the Lodge, the pedestals represent them, and at these the three superior officers sit.

Pediment

The triangular gable set over columns or pilasters. The form makes it Masonically significant. Segmental pediments were associated particularly during the Roman Empire with Isiac cults (the crescent-moon, bow of Diana, horned form, etc.), and recur in Masonic Architecture and Art.

Pelican
The Redeemer, or Charity.

Pentalpha
A geometrical figure with five points formed of three triangles.

Perpendicular
Upright and erect, Justice, Fortitude, Prudence, Temperance, associated with the Plumb, Level, Triangle, and Square.

Phallus
The erect male member, associated with the gnomon, the obelisk, the pillar, the column, and point within a circle.

Pickaxe
Working tool to lift stones and break them. An emblem in Royal Arch Freemasonry.

Piece of Architecture
Any literary work dealing with Freemasonry.

Pillar
Obelisks. Free-standing vertical elements, not to be confused with columns.

Pillars of the Porch
The two of brass erected at the Solomonic Temple by Hiram, with capitals of lily-work (lotus), one called Jachin (God-established) and the other Boaz (in strength). These did *not* have globes on top. Between these Pillars the Fellow Craft is encouraged to seek and acquire knowledge.

Plumb
An instrument for erecting perpendicular lines consisting of a cord and a weight. It symbolizes upright codes of conduct.

Points of Fellowship
The pentalpha or triple triangle.

Point within a Circle
The individual Brother within the boundaries of his duty. The phallus, or fecundity. The Universe.

Pomegranate
Used on the capitals of the Solomonic Temple 'pillars' (Jachin and Boaz), it appears to have been associated with fruitfulness.

Pommel
A sphere on a column.

Prudence
One of the Four Cardinal Virtues.

Prussia
An important country in the history of Freemasonry, not least because of the membership of the Fraternity of Kings Frederick II and Frederick William IV, and, in the case of the latter, because of the patronage given to building (the masterpieces of Schinkel), to painters and sculptors, and to the famous expedition of Dr Karl Richard Lepsius to Egypt of 1842–5 which produced the beautiful and magisterial *Denkmäler aus Aegypten und Aethiopien*, published in Berlin in 1849–59, one of the greatest works ever devoted to a detailed study of Antique remains.

Pythagoras
Students of Pythagoras and his system of numbers (as Sage of Croton) had to go through various tests and trials that sound something like the Isiac and other mysteries. Indeed the various Institutions established by Pythagoras resembled Masonic themes in many ways. There were secret signs, much symbolism, and admonitory injunctions to keep silent. Right angles were moral and just; equilateral triangles were God, Light, and Truth; the Square was divine; the Cube was the mind of man, purified by piety; the Point within the Circle was the universe; the triple triangle was health; and much else. Pythagoras evolved an eclectic system in which there was much that was Egyptian, and much that seemed to stem from more Eastern notions. His chief importance is his development of Geometry.

Rainbow
A sign of hope, often used in Central European Freemasonry during the *Aufklärung*. It also seems to have been associated with the stair and with arcuated construction.

Raised
The reception into the Third Degree, or resurrection. Hence Raising Sheet.

Red
The colour of Mark Masonry and Royal Arch Masonry.

Rhetoric
One of the Liberal Arts, associated with the development of Language.

Right Angle
Two lines meeting at ninety degrees embrace a right angle, or quarter of a circle. It represents virtue and uprightness.

Right Hand
Fidelity and inviolability.

Rising Sun
Worshipful Master.

Rock, Rocks
Symbols of soundness. Foundations for Wisdom. Rock-work is frequently associated with grottoes, labyrinths, and gardens of allusion.

Rose
Associated with Isis and Horus/Harpocrates, the rose is the flower of silence and secrecy, hence *sub rosa*. It is the emblem of the Virgin Mary and of Isis.

Rosicrucians
Some claim that the Rosicrucians, or Fraternity of the Order of the Rosy Cross, influenced Freemasonry. The subject is discussed at length by Frances A. Yates in her *The Rosicrucian Enlightenment*. Rosicrucians seem to have been involved in Hermetic Wisdom, Alchemy, and other activities, and their organization was not unlike that of the Jesuits. Rosicrucianism seems to have heralded a proto-Enlightenment, and, despite indignant claims by Masonic writers that Rosicrucians had no connection with the Masonic Fraternity, careful reading

of the evidence of sixteenth-century intellectual movements before the Newtonian revolution seems to point to several cross-influences that indicate Renaissance-Hermetic-Cabbalist-Alchemical ideas permeated a number of groups. It does seem unlikely that Freemasonry escaped unscathed.

Royal Arch

Royal Arch Masonry has been described as the 'root, heart, and marrow of Masonry'. It appears to satisfy Master-Masons because it repairs a loss. It is the quintessence of Masonic philosophy, and it contains symbolism of the most elaborate variety. It is concerned with discourses of Light and Truth, and is associated with the keystone of an arch without which the whole edifice collapses. See Jones, Bernard E., *Freemasons' Book of the Royal Arch*. London, 1969.

Rule

The instrument that enables straight lines to be drawn, proportion to be ascertained, and measurements made. The Master observes his duty, and veers neither to left nor to right.

St John's Masonry

A term like 'Ancient Craft', which means the three basic Degrees.

St John the Almoner

Otherwise known as St John of Jerusalem, he has been claimed as a Patron Saint of Freemasonry.

St John the Baptist and St John the Evangelist

Usually regarded as the Patron Saints of Masonry, but the claims of St John of Jerusalem are also interesting in this respect.

Scallop

With staff and sandals, is part of the emblems of a Masonic Knight Templar.

Schaw Manuscripts

A code drawn up at the end of the sixteenth century by William Schaw for the conduct of Operative Masons in Scotland.

Scotland

A country of immense importance in the history of Freemasonry, for it was in Scotland that much of what became modern Freemasonry developed. The Scottish Rite is called the Ancient and Accepted Rite.

Scythe.

Death.

Seal of Solomon

The pentangle or a double triangle.

Seeing

The Mason sees with special sight, for the unitiated are in darkness, and are blind.

Serpent

Wisdom. With tail in mouth it is Eternity. Winged globe and *uraei* symbolize the trinity of the deities. A serpent is also a symbol of healing.

Setting Maul

Instrument of the Third Degree: it is a wooden hammer to set the stones, and was associated with the murder of Hiram. It should not be confused with the gavel.

Seven

A sacred number, much so in Freemasonry. The Creation, the Deluge, the companions of Noah, and the seven years for the building of the Temple are but a few examples. The Seven Stars represent the Pleiades, the mystical seven Churches, and the Apocalypse.

Shibboleth

A test-word to distinguish the Ephraimites (who could not pronounce *sh*) from the Gileadites; therefore a word used to detect the profane or the uninitiated, associated with the Fellow Craft and with Jachin, plenty, ears of corn, and a waterfall.

Shovel

Tools of Royal Arch Masonry. A shovel removes spoil, so in speculative Freemasonry it symbolizes the casting off of dross.

Skeleton

Reminder of Mortality: the skeleton at the feast.

Skirret

An instrument which acts on a centre pin, from which a line is drawn to mark out the extremities of the new building.

Skull

The seat of the soul, symbol of mortality, an emblem of death and the grave.

Solomonic Column

A twisted, spiral, or barley-sugar column, associated with the Temple. The form is found in columns or piers near particularly sacred sites, such as altars or shrines in cathedrals, e.g. the *Baldacchino* in St Peter's in Rome. This sacred imagery makes the form important in Masonic iconography.

Sorrow Lodge

A commemorative Lodge held for departed Brethren.

South

The sun is at its meridian so refreshment can be taken. Beauty, Junior Warden, and the Corinthian Order.

Speculative Masonry

Using the tools and implements of operative Masonry, speculative Masonry instils a moral system by referring to the symbolic meaning of those tools and implements. The speculative Mason is taught to build a spiritual work of Architecture, pure, strong, beautiful, and a fit Temple. It is a progressive process, and not to be attained in any Degree of perfection except by time, patience, and considerable application and industry. No candidate can be admitted to the profoundest secrets or the highest honours of Freemasonry until he has imbibed the lessons of secrecy and morality.

Sphinx

An enigma in the form of an Egyptian statue of a woman's

head on a lion's body. It is a symbol of mystery, and as such is adopted by Freemasons.

Spiral or Twisted Column
Columns of the barley-sugar type or that are garlanded or covered with spirals, are associated with the Temple and with the Winding Stair. Also called Solomonic.

Square
An angle of ninety degrees which enables great exactness in building to be achieved. It is also a symbol of moral probity, and is one of the Three Great Lights. Masons meet 'on the Square', with a moral meaning (to act honourably) enhanced by the chequerboard patterns of floors.

Square and Compasses
Emblems of Ancient Craft Masonry.

Star
Five points of fellowship. The Blazing Star is an emblem of Divinity, and of resurrection. The Seven Stars are the Pleiades.

Steps
Three Degrees; Youth, Manhood, Old Age; Life, Death, Immortality.

Strength
A principal support. The Doric Order. The Senior Warden. Hiram King of Tyre. Boaz.

Sun and Moon
With the Master, are associated with the Three Lesser Lights. The Sun and Moon represent Wisdom, power, and goodness, and emphasize the omnipresent rule by night and by day.

Supports
Wisdom, Strength, and Beauty support the Lodge in the forms of the Ionic, Doric, and Corinthian columns.

Tassels
The Four Cardinal Virtues attached to the cord forming the border of a Tracing-Board. Also the four Principal Points: the Guttural, Pectoral, Manual, and Pedal.

Tau
A Greek T, symbolizing eternal life. It is associated, with the halo over it, with the *Ankh*. A Triple Tau is three crosses meeting at a point, and therefore looks like a T over an H, the emblem of the Deity, and Jewel of the Royal Arch. It also stands for *Templum Hierosolymae*, as a monogram of Hiram of Tyre, and as a corruption of *Shin*, the sacred abbreviation of God's name.

Tears (*Guttes*)
In Continental Lodges, and in most of the Higher Degrees, tears are strewn on the hangings of the Lodge.

Telamoni
Male figures used to support an entablature: the male equivalent of caryatides. Two celebrated telamoni from the Villa Adriana now in the Vatican have Egyptian head-dresses and appearance.

Temperance
One of the Four Cardinal Virtues.

Temple of Solomon
The model for Lodges, the perfect building which was lost, and that was built under divine guidance through Hiram. It was destroyed by the Babylonians. It was built by the Wisdom of Solomon, the Strength of King Hiram's wealth and power, and adorned by the Beauty of Hiram the Builder's workmanship.

Temple of Zerubbabel
When the Jews were liberated they built a second temple under Zerubbabel. Descriptions of this have played a part in the iconography of the Temple and the Lodge. According to some authorities, this temple was a restoration of the Solomonic Temple, which was not completely destroyed.

Tesselated Border
Laid with various small stones, properly, but it also has come to mean the *houpe dentelée* or cord of strong thread intertwined with knots, at each end of which is a tassel, signifying the fraternal bonds and the Cardinal Virtues.

Tetragrammaton
A word of four letters, the ineffable name of God.

T∴G∴A∴O∴T∴U∴
The Great or Grand Architect of the Universe.

Theological Virtues
Faith (with book and Cross), Hope (with Anchor), and Charity (with children), the principal rounds of the Masonic Ladder.

Third Degree
That of Master.

Three
A sacred number, the fork, Cerberus, Fates, and Furies, the Trinity, and Isis, Horus, Osiris. In Freemasonry the Three Lights, Three Tenets, Three Jewels, Three Rounds, Three Working Tools, Three Degrees, Three Principal Orders of Architecture, Three Knocks, Three Fellow Crafts, and many others testify to the importance of three.

Three Globes
The Lodge that became the Prussian Grand Lodge in 1765.

Three Steps
Three stages of life and the Three Degrees.

Tiler
Officer with drawn sword guarding the door of the Lodge.

Tracing-Board
Each Degree has its tracing-board, which shows the emblem for that Degree.

Trees
Certain trees have Masonic connotations, including the palm (with its Nilotic and Biblical overtones) and the acacia, or Egyptian thorn (*Acacia Vera*), associated with funeral wreaths, graves, immortality, and the Tree of Paradise (with

serpent). The acacia has also been identified with *Mimosa Nilotica* (i.e. with clear Egyptian Associations), and is an emblem of innocence. This false acacia has lemon-coloured flowers. Acacias were planted in gardens and cemeteries (e.g. Père-Lachaise) to remind us of the ancient custom of marking graves with acacias so that nobody would walk over them, of initiation, of the journey, and of immortality. The palm is coincident with the acacia, and is associated with the Egyptian Mysteries of certain Continental rites. The myrtle seems to have had similar associations for the Greeks, and so also has Masonic connotations. The German *Myrte* seems also to be a mnemonic for *Mörtel*, meaning mortar made from lime.

The lime-tree is also Masonic (at least in eighteenth-century Continental terms), and, like the palm, was used as the name of Lodges, notably in German-speaking countries. The German *Linde, Linden* is associated with the lime-tree (as in the Berlin Unter den Linden), but the French *Limonier* is also found in Masonic contexts, such as Père-Lachaise Cemetery. The German *Zitronen*, as in Goethe's *Mignon*, is usually translated as 'lemon-trees', but, if we consider the lines

> *Kennst du das Land, wo die Zitronen blühn,*
> *Im dunkeln Laub die Gold-Orangen glühn,*
> *Ein sanfter Wind vom blauen Himmel weht,*
> *Die Myrte still und hoch der Lorbeer steht?*

(Do you know the country where the lemon-trees flower, where golden oranges glow among the dark leaves, where a gentle wind blows from the blue heavens, where the still myrtle and the high bay stand?)

we find allusions to limes, myrtles, and bay-trees (the latter associated with triumph and with the higher Degrees of the Scottish Rite). Goethe's poem has other Masonic allusions, including a blue sky, the glowing golden elements (the stars, perhaps?), the roof or canopy resting on pillars, the marble statues, and a reference to dragons and streams (fire and water). Beloved, Protector, and Father are not without significance either. *See* **Lime** *and* **Mahabyn**.

Trestle-board
The board on which the master lays designs. Symbolic of the erection of temples in the heart and mind.

Triangle
Double triangles are symbols of the Deity, while triple triangles (Pentalpha) are symbols of health and of fellowship. Equilateral triangles are symbols of the Deity and of perfection.

Triple Tau within Triangle
Emblem of Royal Arch Masonry.

Trowel
Tool of the Master's Degree, symbolic of the binding together of the parts of a building, and therefore of Freemasonic fellowship. Significantly, a trowel is used to apply lime mortar. A trowel in a triangle is an emblem of cryptic Masonry.

Tubal Cain
Supposedly the inventor of brass and/or bronze, and a password.

Turtle
Conjugal affection and constancy, perhaps confused with the turtle-dove and only significant in esoteric French use.

Tuscan Order
The simplest and most primitive of the Orders, it is like Roman Doric, but is unfluted, and there are no triglyphs and metopes.

Two Knights on One Horse
Poverty, associated with the Knights Templar.

Waterfall
Plenty, the Fellow Craft, and Jachin. A fountain, an Isiac attribute.

Widow's Son
Hiram the builder.

Winding Stair
A way up to the middle chamber of the Temple, suggested by spiral columns or by garlanded columns, which therefore have Masonic significance.

Year of Light
The era of Creation.

Zerubbabel
Building of the sacred Temple. Called after the founder of the Second Temple.

REFERENCES

In the course of time the scope of masonic
history has undergone great changes.

Douglas Knoop and G. P. Jones
The Genesis of Freemasonry
Manchester, 1949, p1

Abbreviations

AQC
Ars Quatuor Coronatorum. Transactions of the Quatuor Coronati Lodge. No. 2076. London.

BN
Bibliothèque Nationale.

Curl, *Celebration*
Curl, James Stevens, *A Celebration of Death. An introduction to some of the buildings, monuments, and settings of funerary architecture in the Western European tradition.* London and New York, 1980.

Curl, 'Cemeteries'
Curl, James Stevens, 'The Design of Early British Cemeteries' *Journal of Garden History*, Vol. 4, No. 3, July–September, 1984.

Curl, *ER*
Curl, James Stevens, *The Egyptian Revival. An Introductory Study of a Recurring Theme in the History of Taste.* London, 1982.

Curl, 'Gardens'
Curl, James Stevens, 'The Design of Historical Gardens: Cultural, Magical, Medical and Scientific Gardens in Europe' *Interdisciplinary Science Reviews*, Vol. 13, No. 3, 1988, pp.264–81.

DNB
The *Dictionary of National Biography*. Oxford, from 1917.

Etlin
Etlin, Richard, *The Architecture of Death. The Transformation of the Cemetery in Eighteenth-Century Paris.* Cambridge, Mass., and London, 1984.

Gould
Gould, R. F., *The History of Freemasonry.* Edinburgh, 1884–87.

J
Jones, Bernard E., *Freemasons' Guide and Compendium.* London, 1956.

KJ
Knoop, Douglas and Jones, G. P., *The Genesis of Freemasonry. An Account of the Rise and Development of Freemasonry in its Operative, Accepted, and Early Speculative Phases.* Manchester, 1949.

KJH
Knoop, Douglas, Jones, G. P., and Hamer, D. (Eds), *Early Masonic Pamphlets.* London, 1963

KJ(*M*)
Knoop, Douglas and Jones, G. P., *The Mediaeval Mason. An Economic History of English Stone Building in the Later Middle Ages and Early Modern Times.* Manchester, 1967.

Landon
Landon, H. C. Robbins, *Mozart's Last Year.* London, 1988.

LC
Lepper, John Heron, and Crossle, Philip, *History of the Grand Lodge . . . of Ireland.* Dublin, 1925.

M
Mackey, Albert G., *A Lexicon of Freemasonry.* London, 1919.

M & R
MacGibbon, David and Ross, Thomas, *The Castellated and Domestic Architecture of Scotland from the Twelfth to the Eighteenth Century.* Edinburgh, 1887–92.

OED
The Oxford English Dictionary. Oxford, 1933

R
Rosenau, Helen, *Vision of the Temple: the Image of the Temple of Jerusalem in Judaism and Christianity.* London, 1979.

S
Stevenson, David, *The Origins of Freemasonry. Scotland's Century 1590–1710.* Cambridge, 1988.

S-L
Saint-Léon, E. Martin, *Le Compagnonnage.* Paris, 1901.

Sv
Svanberg, Jan, *Master Masons.* Stockholm, 1983.

Vidler
Vidler, Anthony, *The Writing of the Walls. Architectural Theory in the Late Enlightenment.* Princeton, 1987.

Witt
Witt, R. E. *Isis in the Graeco-Roman World.* London, 1971

Wittkower
Essays in the History of Architecture Presented to Rudolph Wittkower. London and New York, 1969.

Yates, *Bruno*
Yates, Frances A., *Giordano Bruno and the Hermetic Tradition.* London, 1964.

Yates, *Memory*
Yates, Frances A., *The Art of Memory.* London, 1966.

Yates, *Occult*
Yates, Frances A., *The Occult Philosophy in the Elizabethan Age.* London, 1979.

Yates, *Rosicrucian*
Yates, Frances A., *The Rosicrucian Enlightenment.* London, 1972.

Chapter 1   An Outline of Some of the History of the Craft

1 *OED.*
2 KJ, p1, and *passim.* KJ is an indispensable book, and this chapter owes much to it.
3 Ibid., p62.
4 Ibid., p65
5 Ibid., p65.
6 Ibid.
7 Ibid., p66.
8 Curl, *ER, passim.* See also Witt, *passim.*
9 Curl, *ER,* Chapter 1 and *passim,* and KJ, p66.
10 KJ, p66
11 Ibid. See also Curl, *ER, passim.,* and Witt, *passim.*
12 The *Regius MS* is BM Bibl. Reg. 17 A1 and the *Cooke MS* is BM Add. MS. 23198. See also Knoop, Jones, and Hamer, *The Two Earliest Masonic MSS.* Manchester, 1938.
13 Gwilt, Joseph, *An Encyclopaedia of Architecture,* revised by Wyatt Papworth. London, 1903, p1312. See also Findel, J.G., *Geschichte der Freimaurerei . . .* Leipzig, 1861–62, also translated into English as *History of Freemasonry,* and published in 1865. See p51.
14 Begemann, Wilhelm, *Die Tempelherrn und die Freimaurer.* Berlin, 1906.
15 KJ(*M*), *passim.*
16 Knoop and Jones, *The Scottish Mason and the Mason Word.* Manchester, 1939. See also S, p11.
17 S, p11.
18 KJ(*M*), p82. See also City of London *Cal. Letter-Books.* B, 9, and other sources mentioned in KJ.
19 *AQC,* LI, 1938.
20 AQC, XLVIII, 1935.
21 KJ, pp12–13.
22 Williams, W. J., *AQC,* XLV, 1932. See also KJ, *passim.*
23 KJ, p15.
24 KJ(*M*), p108. See also KJ, p15.
25 OED, Vol IV, p527.
26 Ibid.
27 Act 23, *Henry VI,* c 12.
28 Act 11, *Henry VII,* c 22 §1 of 1495 and Act 2 and 3 *Edward VI,* c 15 §3, among others.
29 KJH, pp40–41, and KJ, p15.
30 KJH, pp108 and 200–202.
31 *Memorandums.* 18 May 1691. See also Conder, E., *The Hole Craft and Fellowship of Masons.* London, 1894.
32 KJ, *passim.*
33 Curl, James Stevens, 'Legends of the Craft. The Architecture of Masonic Halls' *Country Life,* 21 August 1986, pp581–3. See also KJ, *passim,* and S, *passim.*
34 Sv p53.
35 S goes into this in detail, and is essential as a study of early Renaissance Scotland.
36 KJ, p56.
37 S-L. See also Sv, *passim,* and KJ, p56 and *passim.*
38 See Curl, James Stevens, *The Londonderry Plantation 1609–1914. The History, Architecture, and Planning of the Estates of the City of London and its Livery Companies in Ulster.* Chichester, 1986, *passim* for a discussion of the Companies.
39 KJ, p57.
40 S-L, *passim.*
41 Ibid. See also KJ, p58.
42 S-L, p24, and KJ, p59.
43 S, p123.
44 Ibid.

45 Ibid.
46 Ibid., p124. I am grateful to Doctor Stevenson for permission to quote from his work.
47 Ibid.

Chapter 2   The Important Legends

1 KJ, p67.
2 Ibid.
3 Ibid. and *passim*.
4 Ibid., p67.
5 Ibid., p68
6 Ibid.
7 Ibid.
8 Ibid., p69.
9 Cooke MS. BM Add. MS. 23198.
10 Ibid.
11 KJ, p69.
12 An Egyptian Cubit was based on the sixteen measures by which the Nile flooded when Isis wept for Osiris. There is a celebrated statue of the Nile, Cornucopia, and sixteen Cubits as *putti* in the Vatican (Plate 12 of Curl, *ER*). It was also based on the length of the human forearm, and varied. The Egyptian Cubit was about 52.42cm, while the Roman *cubitus* was about 44.19cm.
13 *I Kings* 7, 13–20.
14 *II Chronicles* 3, 15.
15 J, p357. Flavius Josephus (37–*c*.98) was a Jewish soldier who became a Roman citizen, was presented by Titus with many rare books after the sack of Jerusalem, and who wrote several important works including a book on Jewish Antiquities.
16 Ibid., p358.
17 See also Böcher, O., 'Die Alte Synagogue zu Worms'. *Der Wormsgau*. Supp 18, 1960.
18 KJ, p88.
19 The *Graham MS* of 1726.
20 KJ, p89.
21 *II Kings* 4, 33–36.
22 KJ, p91.
23 Ibid., p92.
24 This point is discussed in S, pp135–69. Stevenson is excellent on the ramifications of Freemasonry in Scotland.
25 *II Kings* 23, 13.
26 Illustrated in R, p109.
27 Merkelbach, R., *Roman und Mysterium in der Antike*. Berlin, 1962, p187 and *passim*.
28 Witt, R, E., 'The Egyptian Cults in Macedonia between Alexander and Galerius'. *Balkan Studies*. Thessalonica, 1970.
29 Erman, A., *The Literature of the Ancient Egyptians*. London, 1927.
30 Witt, p157.
31 Ibid., 157f.
32 Seyffert, Oskar, *A Dictionary of Classical Antiquities*. London and New York, 1899.
33 Curl, 'Gardens'.
34 Ibid.
35 Sv, pp144f.
36 Ibid., p146.

Chapter 3   The Renaissance Period and Freemasonry

1 See Yates, *Rosicrucian, passim*, for discussions on these matters. See also Yates, *Occult, passim*.
2 Ibid.
3 Evans, R. J. W., *Rudolf II and his World. A Study in Intellectual History*. Oxford, 1973, *passim*. Evans and Yates are essential reading for an understanding of European Renaissance thought.
4 Ibid. See also the works of Frances A. Yates cited in the Bibliography.
5 Curl, *ER, passim*.
6 Rome, 1643.
7 Rome, 1666.
8 Rome, 1650.
9 Rome, 1652–4.
10 Rome, 1636.
11 n.p., 1647.
12 Amsterdam, 1676.
13 Amsterdam, 1679.
14 Yates, *Bruno, passim*.
15 Godwin, Joscelyn. *Robert Fludd: Hermetic Philosopher and Surveyor of Two Worlds*. London, 1979.
16 See *Utriusque Cosmi Historia, Tomus Primus, De Microcosmi Historia*.
17 Yates, *Rosicrucian, passim*.
18 See Yates, *Rosicrucian, passim* and Evans, R. J. W., *Rudolf II . . . passim*.
19 The Council of Europe Exhibition in Florence in 1980 featured works of an occult and magical nature in which designs that included Egyptianizing motifs were much in evidence.
20 Yates, *Rosicrucian*, p85. See also Patterson, Richard, '"The Hortus Palatinus" at Heidelberg and the Reformation of the World' in *The Journal of Garden History*, 1(1), pp67–104, and 1(2), pp179–202, 1981.
21 Yates, *Rosicrucian*, pp9–12. See also Yates, *Bruno, passim*. See also Curl, 'Gardens'.
22 Illustrated in Yates, *Rosicrucian*, plate 6(a).
23 John Rylands University Library of Manchester Rylands Latin MS 32, folio 79r.
24 These matters are discussed and illustrated in Curl, *ER, passim*.
25 Yates, *Bruno*, pp273–4 and *passim*.
26 Pp273–4.
27 S, p7. Doctor Stevenson's study of the sixteenth-century evidence is essential to any understanding of this tortuous and labyrinthine period.
28 Ibid., p85. I am grateful to Doctor Stevenson for permission to quote from his work.

29 Doctor Stevenson also notes this point.
30 My italics.
31 J, p529.
32 Ibid., pp338–9.
33 Ibid., p129.
34 See Yates, *Memory*. What follows is derived from her book.
35 Ibid. See also S, p87.
36 S, pp87–96.
37 Ibid.
38 Ibid. Doctor Stevenson on memory and the late Doctor Frances Yates on the same subject are invaluable.
39 M, p420.
40 Yates, *Memory*, pp128–170.
41 S, pp87–96. Doctor Stevenson expounds on Dickson at some length.
42 Ibid., p95
43 Yates, *Memory*, pp286–7 and *passim*.
44 Ibid.
45 S, p49 and *passim*.
46 Ibid.
47 Baigent, Michael and Leigh, Richard, *The Temple and The Lodge*. London, 1989.
48 M & R, pp357–512. S, pp113–8. See also Somerville, Andrew R., 'The Ancient Sundials of Scotland' in *Proc. Soc. Antiq. Scot.*, 117 (1987), pp233–64.
49 See Jacob, Margaret C., *The Radical Enlightenment: Pantheists, Freemasons, and Republicans*. London, 1981, p111.
50 See Yates, Frances A., *Astraea. The Imperial Theme in the Sixteenth Century*. London, 1975, *passim*. See also S, p148.
51 S, p148.
52 Ibid., pp150–1.
53 Ibid., p151.
54 See Carr, Harry, *The Minutes of the Lodge of Edinburgh, Mary's Chapel, No. 1, 1598–1738*, London, 1962, and the same author's work on the Word and Catechisms in *AQC*, 1970, 1971, and 1972. See also S, p151.
55 J, pp355–6.
56 Ibid., p348.
57 Ibid., p349.
58 Ibid., p353.
59 *Dampier's Voyage*, 356, of 1697.
60 Fielding, *Amelia*, I, X. See also Sir Walter Scott's *Family Letters*, 24 February 1824.
61 *OED*.
62 J, p399.
63 Ibid.
64 Ibid., p400.
65 Ibid., p395.
66 Ibid., pp398–403.

Chapter 4   The Great Prototype

1 For a discussion of the Temple and its iconography see R.
2 Ibid. See especially Doctor Rosenau on the Synagogue of Dura-Europos and others.
3 See Yale Judaica Series, Vol XII, *The Code of Maimonides, Book Eight. The Book of Temple Service*. New Haven and London, 1957.
4 See Curl, *Celebration*, pp28–30.
5 BN, MS Latin 358 and 461.
6 R, *passim*.
7 Ibid., p39.
8 See Epstein, I (Ed), *The Babylonian Talmud*. London, 1948.
9 See Hermann, Wolfgang, 'Unknown Designs for the "Temple of Jerusalem" by Claude Perrault'. *Wittkower*.
10 Taylor, René, 'Architecture and Magic: Considerations on the *Idea* of the Escorial'. *Wittkower*.
11 Baring-Gould, Rev. S., *The Lives of the Saints*. Edinburgh, 1914.
12 Yates, *Occult*, pp9–15.
13 See footnote 10.
14 Quoted in Taylor, op. cit. p90.
15 See Yates, Frances A., in the Bibliography, Rosenau on the *Temple*, and on *Ideal Cities*. See also S and J.
16 See Curl, *ER*, *passim* and Ch.4.
17 Aurenhammer, Hans, *J. B. Fischer von Erlach*. London, 1973, p132.
18 Ibid., p135.
19 Ibid., p136.
20 *Tractate of the Mishnah*, *Middoth* Cap 4, *Mishnah* 7. Quoted in R, p187.
21 Wittkower, R., *Art and Architecture in Italy, 1600–1750*. Harmondsworth, 1958, pp115 and 347.
22 See Ward-Perkins, J. B., 'The shrine of St Peter and its twelve spiral columns', *Journal of Roman Studies*, XLII (1952) pp21–33. See also Fernie, Eric, in *Architectural History*, 32 (1989) pp18–29.

Chapter 5   Masonic Design and Architecture

1 Material for the early part of this chapter derives from J and K J.
2 And often (alas!) infinitely tedious.
3 K J, p169.
4 Ibid.
5 See Yates, *Rosicrucian* (see Bibliography) for details too broad in scope for discussion here. See also Webster, Nesta H., *Secret Societies and Subversive Movements*. n.p., 1924.
6 Jacob, Margaret C., *The Radical Enlightenment: Pantheists, Freemasons, and Republicans*. London, 1981, pp111, 127, and 242.
7 Ibid., p147.
8 Ibid., p110.
9 Ibid., p256.
10 Chevallier, Pierre, *Les Ducs sous l'Acacia, ou Les Premiers Pas de la Franc-Maçonnerie Française, 1725–1743*. Paris, 1964, *passim*.
11 Ibid.
12 Chevallier, Pierre, *La Première Profanation du Temple Maçonnique, ou Louis XV et la Fraternité*. Paris, 1968, *passim*, for reports and inventories.

13 Larudan, the Abbé, *Les Francs-Maçons Écrasés*, Amsterdam, 1747, described this in great detail.

14 Béyerlé, Jean-Pierre Louis de, *Essai de la Franc-Maçonnerie*. 'Latomopolis', 1784. An exhaustively detailed volume.

15 Paris, 1804–46.

16 Braham, Allan, *The Architecture of the French Enlightenment*. London, 1980, p160.

17 Ibid., pp193–4.

18 Vidler, p93.

19 Ibid., footnote 29, p208. See also Grandidier, Abbé, *Essais Historiques et Topographiques sur l'Église Cathédrale de Strasbourg*. Strasbourg, 1782. The footnotes of Professor Vidler's book contain much interesting and relevant material which can be studied with profit.

20 Ibid., p93. I am grateful to Professor Vidler for permission to quote from his work.

21 See Wilton-Ely, John, *Piranesi*. London, 1978.

22 Curl, *ER*, *passim*. See also Gould, III, p285.

23 Alméras, Henri d', *Cagliostro*. Paris, 1904 and Köppen, Karl Friedrich, *Crata Repoa, oder Einweihung der ägyptischen Priester*. Berlin, 1778.

24 *État du G∴O∴ de France*. Paris, 1777, 1,4, *passim*.

25 I, 1, p67.

26 Vidler, p95.

27 J, p448.

28 Ed. Mackenzie, Wellingborough, 1987, pp82–3.

Chapter 6 Séthos and the Egyptian rites

1 *The Life of* SÉTHOS, *Taken from Private Memoirs of the Ancient* EGYPTIANS. *Translated from a* Greek *MANUSCRIPT into FRENCH. And now faithfully done into* English *from the* Paris *EDITION*; By Mr Lediard. In Two Volumes, London, 1732.

2 Ibid., I, p34.

3 Ibid., I, p187.

4 Quoted in Dent, Edward J., *Mozart's Operas. A Critical Study*. London, 1960.

5 Landon, pp55–56.

6 Grand Lodge of Austria.

7 Curl, *ER*, p92.

8 Published by H. C. Robbins Landon in 1982.

9 Landon, pp59–60.

10 Ibid., p60. See Thomson, K., *The Masonic Thread in Mozart*. London, 1977, p133.

11 *Lulu oder die Zauberflöte* was by A. J. Liebeskind, and was included in the collection by Wieland and other.

12 See Witt, *passim*, and Curl, *ER*, for discussion of Egyptian deities and syncretism.

13 *Isaiah*, 43, 2.

14 Landon, p130.

15 Ibid.

16 Laborde, A. de, *Description des Nouveaux Jardins de France*. Paris, 1808, and Rivière, C., *Un Village de Brie au XVIIIe Siècle: Maupertuis*. Paris, 1939.

17 Curl, *ER*, pp6, 32–4, 61–2, 73–4.

18 Brophy, Brigid, *Mozart the Dramatist*. London, 1988, p189.

19 For details of deities and personalities see Seyffert, Oskar, *A Dictionary of Classical Antiquities*. London and New York, 1899.

20 Mozart to his father, 4 April 1787.

21 Curl, *ER*, discusses this at length.

22 Ibid., p134 and *passim*. See also Horányi, Mátyas, *The Magnificence of Eszterháza*. London and Budapest, 1962.

23 See *Karl Friedrich Schinkel. Architektur, Malerei, Kunstgewerbe*. Catalogue of Exhibition in Berlin, 1981. Items 210a–h.

24 Castellamare, 1863.

25 Rome, 1648.

26 Cologne, 1710.

27 London, 1852.

28 *The Age of Neo-Classicism*. Catalogue of the Fourteenth Exhibition of the Council of Europe. London, 1972, item 755 Addenda.

29 Vienna, 1818.

30 K. 543.

31 K. 550.

32 K. 551.

33 Vertical Section of Cellars of Gothic House in Lequeu's Architecture Civile, plate 156, Cabinet des Estampes, BN.

34 See Philippe Duboy's *Lequeu. An Architectural Enigma*. London, 1986.

35 Ibid., p15.

36 This is discussed at length by Duboy.

37 Duboy, op. cit. p35.

38 Plates 37–39.

Chapter 7 Elysian Fields

1 Curl, 'Cemeteries', p223, and *passim*.

2 Curl, *Celebration*, mentions names connected with the cemetery movement, many of whom were Freemasons.

3 Girardin, René de, *De la Composition des Paysages*. Paris, 1777.

4 Vidler, p99, and *passim*. See also notes 68 and 79 in Vidler's book, p210. I am grateful to Professor Vidler for permission to quote from his work.

5 See Witt, *passim*.

6 Oliver, J. W., *The Life of William Beckford*. London, 1932, pp172–81. See also Vidler, p101, and notes 75 and 76 on p211 of his book.

7 Vidler, p211, n73, and *passim*.

8 *DNB*.

9 Ledoux, C.-N., *L'Architecture Considérée . . . passim*., but see p118. See also Vidler, p211, n73 and *passim*.

10 See Curl, James Stevens, *European Cities and Society*. London, 1970, pp143–4. See also Fourier, C., *Théorie des Quatre Mouvements*. Lyons, 1808, p195 and *passim*. See also Vidler, p102, which also quotes this source (p211 n82). For further developments see Curl, James Stevens, *The Life and Work of Henry Roberts (1803–76), Architect*. Chichester, 1983, on Fourier and Godin.

11 Alex, Reinhard and Kühn, Peter, *Schlösser und Gärten um Wörlitz*. Leipzig, 1988, *passim*. See also the catalogue *Friedrich Wilhelm von Erdmannsdorff 1736–1800*. Wörlitz, 1986, *passim*.

12 Etlin, p224, and *passim*.

13 Curl, *Celebration*, p181, and Craig, Maurice, *The Architecture of Ireland from the Earliest Times to 1880*. London, 1982, pp167 and 169.

14 LC, p176.

15 Illustrated in Etlin, p231.

16 Dresden, 1778–85.

17 Kryger, Karin, *Studier i det nyklassicistiske gravmaele i Danmark 1760–1820*, Copenhagen, 1985, pp163–70.

18 Hirschfeld's work was also published in the French edition as Hirschfeld, Christian Cay L., *Théorie de l'Art des Jardins*. Leipzig, 1779–85. See pp226–74.

19 Paris, 1788–1825.

20 Alex and Kühn, op. cit.

21 The remarkable connection between Architects and Freemasonary is made clear by Brengues and Mosser in Ligou, D., *Histoire des Francs-Maçons*, Toulouse, 1981. Alain Le Bihan's *Francs-Maçons Parisiens du Grand Orient de France*, published in Paris in 1966, contains lists of Architects with Masonic connections. See also Vaudoyer, A.-L.-T., *Idées d'un citoyen français sur le lieu destiné à la sépulture des hommes illustres de France*. Paris, 1791.

22 Curl, 'Cemeteries', Etlin, *passim.*, and Curl, *Celebration*, *passim*.

23 Etlin, p233.

24 Laveaux, J.-C., 'Sur les Sépultures des Grands Hommes, et Celles des Autres Citoyens' in *Journal de la Montagne*. 19 July 1793. Etlin discusses these matters further.

25 Etlin, *passim*. Etlin's book is the most detailed work to be published so far on the genesis of the French garden-cemetery: his work is indispensable.

26 *Briefe und Aufzeichnungen*. Kassel, 1962–3, IV, p41.

27 Illustrated in Etlin, p170.

28 See footnote 21 of the present work in this chapter.

29 Miller, Thomas, *Picturesque Sketches of London Past and Present*. London, 1852.

30 See Etlin for a very full discussion of this.

31 Gould, Vol. III, p162.

32 Ibid., p165.

33 Curl, James Stevens, 'Europe's Grandest Cemetery?' *Country Life*. 15 September 1977.

34 Gould, Vol. III, p198.

35 Vol. I, p545 and *passim*.

36 See St-A, M.P., *Promenade aux Cimetières de Paris, aux Sépultures Royales de Saint-Denis, et aux Catacombes*. Paris, 1816.

Chapter 8   Cemeteries, Monuments, and Mausolea

1 Discussed at length in Etlin and in Curl, *Celebration*.

2 See Willson, Thomas, *The Pyramid. A General Metropolitan Cemetery to be Erected in the Vicinity of Primrose Hill*. London, 1842, also illustrated in Curl, *Celebration*, pp212–15.

3 See *The Literary Gazette and Journal of the Belles Lettres*. 12 June 1830, and *The Morning Chronicle*, 10 June 1830.

4 'Intended for the prevention of the Danger and Inconvenience of burying the Dead within the Metropolis . . .'.

5 See Curl, *Celebration*, pp209–11.

6 Gould, Vol. II, p491.

7 Loudon, John Claudius, *On the laying out, planting, and managing of Cemeteries . . .* London, 1843, p22.

8 Ibid., p13.

9 Ibid.

10 Quoted in Loudon, p11.

11 Curl, 'Cemeteries', pp223–54.

12 Loudon, op. cit. pp20–1.

13 London, 1981.

14 Ariès, Philippe, *The Hour of Our Death*. London, 1981, pp546–7.

15 Christian Book Club of America, but originally published in 1924. See also *A Catholic Dictionary* by William E. Addis and Thomas Arnold, London, 1957, p362.

16 Tenenti, Alberto, *La Vie et La Mort à travers l'Art du XVe Siècle*. Paris, 1952, p72.

17 M, p195.

18 Gould, Vol. III, p258.

19 LC, p216.

Chapter 9   Conclusion

1 Cambridge, 1807.

2 Denon, Dominique Vivant, *Voyage dans la Basse et la Haute Egypte pendant les campagnes du Général Bonaparte*. Paris, 1802.

3 *Description de l'Egypte, ou Recueil des observations et des recherches qui ont été faites en Egypte pendant l'expédition de l'armée française, publié par les ordres de Sa Majesté l'empereur Napoléon le Grand*. Paris, 1809–28.

8 Roberts, David, *The Holy Land, Syria, Idumea, Arabia, Egypt and Nubia*. London 1842–9.

5 See Conner, Patrick (Ed), *The Inspiration of Egypt: Its Influence on British Artists, Travellers and Designers, 1700–1900*. Brighton, 1983, p96.

6 Of 9 November 1912.

7 See Curl, James Stevens, *Classical Churches in Ulster*. Belfast, 1980.

8 I am grateful to Mr Ralph Hyde for drawing these to my attention.

9 Curl, James Stevens, *European Cities and Society*. London, 1970, p143.

SELECT BIBLIOGRAPHY

It requires more courage to face the unknown
than the known. A straight stair, a ladder, hides neither
secret nor mystery at its top. But the stairs
which wind hide each step from the climber; what is
just around the corner is unknown.

Carl H. Claudy
Introduction to Freemasonry
New York, 1932

ACERELLOS, R. S., *Die Freimaurerei in ihren Zusammenhang mit den Religionen der alten Aegypter, der Juden und der Christen.* Leipzig, 1836.

ACQUIER, HIPPOLYTE and NOEL, ALBERT, *Les Cimetières de Paris, ouvrage historique, biographique et pittoresque.* Paris, 1852.

AGULHON, MAURICE, *Pénitents et Francs-Maçons de l'ancienne Provence.* Paris, 1968.

ALBON, COMTESSE D', *See* LUSSI and LEPAGELET.

ALBRECHT, THEODOR, *Freimaurers Weltreise.* Leipzig, 1914.

ALEMBERT, JEAN LE ROND D', Entries in Diderot's *Encyclopédie.*

ALEX, REINHARD and KÜHN, PETER, *Schlösser und Gärten um Worlitz,* Lèipzig, 1988.

ALLAIS, L.-J., DÉTOURNELLE, A., and VAUDOYER, A.-L.-T., *Grands Prix d'Architecture: projets couronnés par l'Académie d'Architecture et l'Institut de France.* Paris, 1806.

Allgemeine Musikalische Zeitung. Leipzig, from 1798.

ALMÉRAS, HENRI D', *Cagliostro.* Paris, 1904.

ALMÉRAS, HENRI D', *La Vie Parisienne sous la Révolution et le Directoire.* Paris, n.d.

AMAURY-DUVAL, L., *Des Sépultures.* Paris, 1801.

AMBELAIN, ROBERT, *Cérémonies et Rituels de la Maçonnerie Symbolique,* Paris, 1966.

ANDERSON, E. (Ed.), *The Letters of Mozart and His Family.* London, 1966

ANDERSON, JAMES (Ed.), *The Constitutions of the Free-Masons.* London, 1723.

ANDERSON, JAMES (Ed.), *The New Book of the Constitutions of the Antient and Honourable Fraternity of Free and Accepted Masons.* London, 1738. This important source-book is known as *Anderson's Constitutions.* See also W. J. Hughan's *Introduction* to the facsimile edition of Anderson's work in *Quatuor Coronatorum Antigrapha,* Vol. VII. London, 1890.

ANONYMOUS, *O∴ ou Histoire de la fondation du Grand Orient de France.* Paris, 1812.

ARIÈS, PHILIPPE, *The Hour of Our Death.* London, 1981.

ARNAUD, C.-P., *Recueil de tombeaux des quatres cimetières de Paris.* Paris, 1813.

Ars Quatuor Coronatorum. Transactions of the Quatuor Coronati Lodge, No. 2076. London, various dates.

AULARD, F.-A., *Le Culte de la Raison et le culte de l'Être suprême 1793–94.* Paris, 1892.

AVRIL, J.-B., *Rapport de l'Administration des Travaux Publics sur les cimetières . . . etc.* n.p., 1794.

AURENHAMMER, H., *J. B. Fischer von Erlach.* London, 1973.

BALLIN, E. M., *Der Dichter von Mozarts Freimaurerlied 'O Heiliges Band'.* Tutzing, 1960.

BALTARD, L.-P., *Athenaeum, ou Galerie française des productions de tous les arts . . .* Paris, 1807.

BALTARD, L.-P. and VAUDOYER, A.-L.-T., *Grands Prix d'Architecture, Projects couronnés par l'Académie Royale des Beaux Arts de France.* Paris, 1818.

BALTRUŠAITIS, JURGIS, 'Eighteenth-Century Gardens and Fanciful Landscapes'. *Magazine of Art.* April, 1952, pp172–81.

BALTRUŠAITIS, JURGIS, *Le Moyen-âge fantastique*. Paris, 1955.

BALTRUŠAITIS, JURGIS, *La Quête d'Isis. Introduction à l'Égyptomanie. Essai sur la légende d'un mythe*. Paris, 1967.

BÄR, CARL, *Mozart: Krankheit, Tod, Begräbnis*. Salzburg and Kassel, 1966.

BARBER, W. H., et al., *The Age of the Enlightenment. Studies Presented to Theodore Besterman*. London, 1967.

BARTHES, ROLAND, *Sade, Fourier, Loyola*. Paris, 1971.

BATTEAUX, C., *Les Beaux-arts réduits à un même principe*. Paris, 1776.

BAUER, WILHELM A. and DEUTSCH, OTTO ERICH, *Mozart: Briefe und Aufzeichnungen*. Kassel, 1962–75.

BAYLOT, JEAN, *Dossier français de la Franc-Maçonnerie régulière*. Paris, 1965.

BEALES, D., *Joseph II*. Cambridge, 1987.

BEGEMANN, GEORG E. WILHELM, *Die Tempelherrn und die Freimaurer*. Berlin, 1906.

BEGEMANN, GEORG E. WILHELM, *Vorgeschichte und Anfange der Freimaurerei in Schottland. Die alten schottischen Werklogen*. Berlin, 1914.

BERGMAN, J., *Ich bin Isis. Historia Religionum 3*. Uppsala, 1968.

BERLIOZ, HECTOR, 'La Flûte Enchantée et les Mystères d'Isis' in *Les Musiciens et la Musique*, edited by Hallays. Paris, 1903.

BERNIGEROTH, JOHANN MARTIN, *Les Coutumes des Francs-Maçons dans leurs assemblées, principalement pour la réception des apprentifs et des maîtres, tout nouvellement et sincerement découvertes*. Leipzig, 1745.

Betbuch für Freymaurer in hochwürdigste Provinzialloge von Böhmen und allen Freimäurern dieses Sprengels. Prague, 1784.

BEUREN, OTTO, *Die innere Urwahrheit der Freimaurerei*. Mainz, 1884.

BEUTHER, *See* JUNG.

BIHAN, ALAIN LE, *Francs-Maçons Parisiens du Grand Orient de France*. Paris, 1966.

BITTNER, NORBERT, *Theaterdekorationen nach den Original Skizzen des K. K. Hoftheater Mahlers Anton de Pian. Radiert und verlegt von Norbert Bittner*. Vienna, 1818.

BLACK, A., *Guilds and Civil Society in European Political Thought from the Twelfth Century to the Present*. London, 1984.

BLONDEL, JACQUES-FRANÇOIS, *Discours sur la nécessité de l'étude de l'architecture*. Paris, 1754.

BOAS, *See* LOVEJOY.

BÖHEIM, F. W. VON, *Auswahl von Maurer Gesängen mit Melodien der vorzüglichsten Componisten in zweij Abtheilungen getheilt*. Berlin, 1798.

BORD, GUSTAVE, *La Franc-Maçonnerie en France des Origines à 1815*. Paris, 1908.

BORDELON, LAURENT, *La Coterie des Anti-Façonniers*. Paris, 1716.

BORN, IGNAZ VON, *Physikalische Arbeiten der einträchtigen Freunde in Wien*. Vienna, 1783–88.

BORN, IGNAZ VON, 'Über die Mysterien der Ägypter' in *Journal für Freymaurer*. Vienna, 5784 (1784). See pp15–132.

BOULLÉE, ÉTIENNE-LOUIS, *Architecture, Essai sur l'Art*. Paris, 1968.

BRAHAM, ALLAN, *The Architecture of the French Enlightenment*. London, 1980.

BRANSCOMBE, P., '*Die Zauberflöte*: Some Textual and Interpretative Problems'. *Proceedings of the Royal Musical Association*. 1965–6, 92, pp45–63.

BRENGUES, J., *La Franc-Maçonnerie du bois*. Paris, 1973.

BRONGNIART, A., *Plans . . . du Cimetière Mont-Louis . . . etc*. Paris, 1814.

BUCK, J. D., *Symbolism of Freemasonry or Mystic Masonry and the Greater Mysteries of Antiquity*. Chicago, 1946.

BUSINK, T. A., *Der Tempel von Jerusalem von Salomo bis Herodes*. Leiden, 1970.

CABRIÈRE, J., *Court de Gébelin*. Paris, 1899.

CAHILL, REV. E., *Freemasonry and the Anti-Christian Movement*. Dublin, 1929.

CALCOTT, WELLINS, *A Candid Disquisition of the Principles and Practices of the Most Ancient and Honourable Society of Free and Accepted Masons. . . .* London, 1769.

CARMONTELLE, LOUIS CARROGIS, *Jardin de Monceau, près de Paris, appartenant à . . . M. le duc de Chartres*. Paris, 1779.

CARR, H., *The Mason and the Burgh. An Examination of the Edinburgh Register of Apprentices and the Burgess Rolls*. London, 1954.

CARR, H., *The Lodge Mother Kilwinning, No. 0. A Study of the Earliest Minute Books, 1642 to 1842*. London, 1961.

CARR, H., *The Minutes of the Lodge of Edinburgh, Mary's Chapel, No. 1, 1598–1738*. London, 1962.

CARR, H., *The Early French Exposures*. London, 1971.

CAYLUS, ANNE-CLAUDE-PHILIPPE DE THUBIÈRES, COMTE DE, *Recueil d'Antiquités Égyptiennes, Étrusques, Grecques et Romaines*. Paris, 1752–67.

CHAILLEY, JACQUES, *The Magic Flute: Masonic Opera*. tr. H. Weinstock. London, 1972.

CHAMOUST, RIBART DE, *L'Ordre François Trouvé dans la Nature*. Paris, 1783.

CHAPMAN, GUY, *Beckford*. London, 1937.

CHAUSSARD, PIERRE, *Monuments de L'heroïsme français: nécessité de ramener à un plan unique . . . etc*. Paris, 1800.

CHETWODE CRAWLEY, W. J., *Caemeteria Hibernica*. Dublin, 1895–1900.

CHEVALLIER, PIERRE, *Les Ducs sous l'Acacia, ou Les Premiers Pas de la Franc-Maçonnerie française, 1725–1743*. Paris, 1964.

CHEVALLIER, PIERRE, *La Première Profanation du Temple Maçonnique, ou Louis XV et la Fraternité, 1737–1755*. Paris, 1968.

CHEVALLIER, PIERRE, *Histoire de la Franc-Maçonnerie française. La Maçonnerie: école de l'égalité, 1725–1799*. Paris, 1974.

CLARK, H. F., 'Eighteenth-Century Elysiums: the Rôle of "Association" in the Landscape Movement'. *Journal of the Warburg Institute*. 1943, Vol. 6.

CLAUSEN, ERNST, *Die Freimaurer. Einführung in das Wesen ihres Bundes*. Berlin, 1922.

CLERE, MARCEL LE, *Cimetières et Sépultures de Paris*. Paris, 1978.

COHEN, REV. A., *Lessing's Masonic Dialogues*. London, 1927.

COMAY, JOAN, *The Temple of Jerusalem*. New York, 1975.

COMMISSION DES MONUMENTS D'ÉGYPTE, *Description de l'Égypte, ou Recueil des observations et des recherches qui ont été faites en Égypte pendant l'expédition de l'armée française, publié par les ordres de Sa Majesté l'empereur Napoléon le Grand*. Paris,

1809–28. Another edition was published 1821–9 in 24 volumes, with atlas.

COMPIÈGNE DE VEIL, LOUIS, *Mishnah Torah*. Illustrated by Claude Perrault. Paris, 1678. The full title is *De Cultu divino, ex Mosis Majemonidae secunda Lege seu Manu Forti liber VIII etc . . . Hunc librum ex Hebraeo Latinum fecit . . . Ludovicus de Compiègne de Veil. . . .* Paris, 1678.

COUPÉ, JACQUES-MICHEL, *Des Sépultures en politique et en morale.* Paris, 1795.

COURET, *See* VILLENEUVE.

COURT DE GÉBELIN, ANTOINE, *Monde primitif, analysé et comparé avec le monde moderne.* Paris, 1787.

CROSSLE, PHILIP, *See* LEPPER, JOHN HERON.

CURL, JAMES STEVENS, 'Mozart Considered as a Jacobin'. *The Music Review.* 1974, Vol. 35, pp131–41.

CURL, JAMES STEVENS, *A Celebration of Death. An introduction to some of the buildings, monuments and settings of funerary architecture in the Western European tradition.* London and New York, 1980.

CURL, JAMES STEVENS, *The Egyptian Revival. An Introductory Study of a Recurring Theme in the History of Taste.* London, Boston, and Sydney, 1982.

CURL, JAMES STEVENS, 'The Design of the Early British Cemeteries'. *Journal of Garden History.* Vol. 4, No. 3, July–September 1984, pp223–54.

CURL, JAMES STEVENS, 'Entstehung und Architektur der frühen britischen Friedhöfe' *O Ewich is so Lanck. Die Historischen Friedhöfe in Berlin-Kreuzberg. Eine Ausstellung im Landesarchiv. Berlin, 22 April 1987 bis 26 Juni 1987.* Berlin, 1987, pp267–82.

DARNTON, ROBERT, *Mesmerism and the End of the Enlightenment in France.* New York, 1970.

DAUBERMESNIL, FRANÇOIS-ANTOINE, *Rapport fait au nom d'une Commission spéciale, sur les inhumations.* Paris, 1796.

DAVID, JACQUES-LOUIS, *Rapport sur la fête héroïque pour les honneurs du Panthéon.* Paris, n.d., but probably 1794.

DELESPINE, PIERRE-JULES, *Marché des Blancs-Manteaux . . . suivi du Tombeau de Newton.* Paris, 1827.

DELILLE, ABBÉ JACQUES, *Les jardins, ou l'art d'embellir les paysages.* Paris, 1782.

DENON, BARON DOMINIQUE VIVANT, *Voyage dans la Basse et la Haute Egypte pendant les campagnes du Général Bonaparte.* Paris, 1802.

DENT, EDWARD J. *Mozart's Operas. A Critical Study.* London, 1960.

DESCHAMPS, REV. N., *Les Sociétés Secrètes et la Société.* Paris and Avignon, 1881.

DESMONCEAUX, ABBÉ, *De la bienfaisance nationale.* Paris, 1789.

DESPREZ, LOUIS-JEAN, *Ouvrage d'architecture. . . .* Paris, 1781.

DÉTOURNELLE, *See* ALLAIS.

DEUTSCH, OTTO ERICH, *Mozart und die Wiener Logen.* Vienna, 1932.

DEUTSCH, OTTO ERICH, *Das Freihaustheater auf der Wieden.* Vienna, 1937.

DEUTSCH, OTTO ERICH, *Mozart: die Dokumente seines Lebens.* Kassel, 1961.

DEUTSCH, OTTO ERICH, *See* BAUER, WILHELM A.

DIDEROT, DENIS, *Encyclopédie ou dictionnaire raisonné des sciences, des arts, et des métiers, par une société de gens de lettres.* Paris, 1751–80.

DINAUX, ARTHUR, *Les Sociétés badines, bachiques, littéraires et chantantes.* Paris, 1867.

DRING, E. H., 'The Evolution and Development of the Tracing or Lodge Board'. *Ars Quatuor Coronatorum.* 29, 1914.

DUBOY, PHILIPPE, *Lequeu. An Architectural Enigma.* London, 1986.

DÜLMEN, R. VAN, *Der Geheimbund der Illuminaten.* Stuttgart, 1975.

DUPUIS, CHARLES-FRANÇOIS, 'Initiation, initié' *Encyclopédie Méthodique: Antiquités, Mythologie.* Paris, 1790.

DURAND, J.-N.-L., *Recueil et Parallèle des Édifices en tous Genres.* Paris, 1799–1801.

DURAND, J.-N.-L., *Précis des leçons d'architecture données a l'école polytechnique.* Paris, 1802, 1805. Also the *Nouveau Précis* of 1813.

EARNSHAW, BRIAN, *See* MOWL, TIM.

EBERS, KARL FRIEDRICH, *Sarsena, oder der vollkommene Baumeister, enthaltend die Geschichte und Entstehung des Freimaurerordens und die verschiedenen Meinungen darüber . . . etc.* Bamberg, 1817.

ECKERT, M., *La Franc-Maçonnerie en Elle-même et dans sa rapport avec les autres Soc. Sec. de l'Europe.* Liège, 1855.

EINSTEIN, ALFRED, *Mozart. His Character. His Work.* tr. A. Mendel and N. Broder. London, 1956.

EMPEREUR, CONSTANTIN L', *Talmudis Babylonici Codex Middoth sive de Mensuris Templi.* Leyden, 1630.

ENGEL, L., *Gesichte des Illuminaten-Ordens.* Berlin, 1906.

EROUART, G., *Jean-Laurent Legeay, un Piranésien français dans l'Europe des lumières.* Paris, 1982.

ETLIN, RICHARD A., 'Landscapes of Eternity: Funerary Architecture and the Cemetery, 1793–1881' *Oppositions.* 1977, Vol. 8, pp14–31.

ETLIN, RICHARD A., 'The Geometry of Death'. *Progressive Architecture.* May 1982, pp134–7.

ETLIN, RICHARD A., *The Architecture of Death. The Transformation of the Cemetery in Eighteenth-Century Paris.* Cambridge, Mass., and London, 1984.

EVANS, R. J. W., *Rudolf II and His World. A Study in Intellectual History.* Oxford, 1973.

FAY, BERNARD, *La Franc-Maçonnerie et la révolution intellectuelle du XVIIIe Siècle.* Paris, 1961.

FESCH, PAUL, *Bibliographie de la franc-maçonnerie et des sociétés secrètes.* Brussels, 1976.

FICHET, FRANÇOISE, *La théorie de l'architecture à l'âge classique. Essai d'anthologie critique.* Brussels, 1979.

FINDEL, J. G., *Geschichte der Freimaurerei von der Zeit ihres Entstehens bis auf die Gegenwart.* Leipzig, 1861–62.

FISCHER VON ERLACH, JOHANN BERNHARD, *Entwurff einer Historischen Architektur, in Abbildung unterschiedener verühmter Gebäude, des Alterthums und fremder Völker.* Leipzig, 1725.

FORESTIER, RENÉ LE, *Les Illuminés de Bavière.* Paris, 1913.

FORESTIER, RENÉ LE, *La Franc-Maçonnerie Templière et Occultiste aux XVIIIe et XIXe Siècles.* Paris, 1970.

FOURIER, CHARLES, *Théorie des Quatre Mouvements*. Lyons, 1808.

FRANKL, P. and PANOFSKY, E., 'The Secret of of the Medieval Masons', *Art Bulletin*. March 1945.

FRASER, D., HIBBARD, H. and LEWINE, M. J. (Eds), *Essays Presented to Rudolf Witthower*. London, 1967.

Free-Masons' Melody, The, Brief and General Collection of Masonic Songs. Bury, 1818.

Freimaurerei und Joseph II: Die Loge Zur Wahren Eintracht. Catalogue of Exhibition at Schloss Rosenau. Zwettl, 1980.

FRERE, A. S., *The Grand Lodge, 1717–1967*. Oxford, 1967.

FRICK, KARL, *Die Erleuchteten. Gnostischtheosophische und alchemistischrosenkreuzerische Geheimgesellschaften bis zum Ende des 18. Jahrhunderts*. Graz, 1973.

FRIEDEL, J. G., *Geschichte der Freimaurerei*. Leipzig, 1861.

G......, J..., *Mahhabone: or, The Grand Lodge Open'd. Wherein is Discovered The Whole Secrets of Free-Masonry, Both Ancient and Modern . . . etc.* London, 1776.

G., G., *Promenade sérieuse au Cimetière du Père La Chaise . . .* Paris, 1826.

GABANON, L. (pseudonym of LOUIS TRAVENOL), *Nouveau Catéchisme des Francs-Maçons*. 'Jérusalem' (i.e. Amsterdam), 1740.

GALLET, M., *Claude-Nicholas Ledoux, 1736–1806*. Paris, 1980.

GANAY, ERNEST, COMTE DE, *Les Jardins de France et Leur Décor*. Paris, 1949.

GANNAL, FÉLIX, *Les Cimetières depuis la fondation de la monarchie française . . . etc.* Paris, 1884.

GATTY, H. K. F. and LLOYD, ELEANOR, *A Book of Sundials*. London, 1900.

GAUME, MGR., *Le Cimetière au XIXᵉ Siècle*. Paris, n.d.

GAUTIER-LA CHAPELLE, A., *Des Sépultures*. Paris, 1801.

GAY, PETER, *The Enlightenment: An Interpretation. The Rise of Modern Paganism*. London, 1967.

GENLIS, STÉPHANIE-FÉLICITÉ, COMTESSE DE, *La Botanique historique et littéraire*. Paris, 1810.

GIRARD, J., *Des Tombeaux, ou de l'influence des institutions funèbres sur les moeurs*. Paris, 1801.

GIRARDIN (GÉRARDIN), RENÉ-LOUIS DE, VICOMTE D'ERMENONVILLE, *De la Composition des Paysages, ou des moyens d'embellir la Nature autour des Habitations, en joignant l'agréable à l'utile*. Geneva and Paris, 1777.

GIRARDIN (GÉRARDIN), RÉNE-LOUIS DE, VICOMTE D'ERMENONVILLE, *An Essay on Landscape*. London, 1783.

GIRARDIN, STANISLAS-XAVIER, Comte de, *Promenade ou Itinéraire des Jardins d'Ermenonville*. Paris, 1788.

GIRAUD, PIERRE, *Les Tombeaux, ou essai sur les sépultures . . . etc.* Paris, 1801.

GOETHE, JOHANN WOLFGANG VON, *Die Wahlverwandtschaften*. Tübingen, 1809.

GOULD, ROBERT FREKE, *History of Freemasonry: its Antiquities, Symbols, Constitution, Customs, etc.* Edinburgh, 1884–87.

GOULD, ROBERT FREKE, *History of Freemasonry Embracing an Investigation of the Records of the Organizations of the Fraternity in England, Scotland, Ireland, British Colonies, France, Germany, The United States of America, and Other Countries*. Revised, edited, and brought up to date by Dudley Wright, London,

1931. Another edition of the above, from which mention of France, Germany, and Other Countries has been dropped from the title, was revised, edited, and brought up to date by Rev. Herbert Poole. London, 1951. Gould, in all his editions, must be used with extreme caution.

GRANDIDIER, ABBÉ, *Essais Historiques et Topographiques sur l'Église Cathédrale de Strasbourg*. Strasbourg, 1782.

HAFENREFFER, MATTHIAS, *Templum Ezechielis*. Tübingen, 1613.

HALL, MANLY PALMER, *The Secret Teachings of All Ages: An Encyclopedic Outline of Masonic, Hermetic, Qabbalistic and Rosicrucian Philosophy*. Los Angeles, 1928–75.

HAMILL, J., *The Craft. A History of English Freemasonry*. London, 1986.

HARCOURT, FRANÇOIS-HENRI, DUC D', *Traité de la Décoration des dehors, des jardins, et des parcs*. n.p., n.d.

HAUTECOEUR, LOUIS, *L'art sous la Révolution et l'Empire en France*. Paris, 1958.

HAVEN, M., *Le maître inconnu. Cagliostro*. Lyons, 1964.

HENKEL, A. and SCHÖNE, A., *Emblemata: Handbuch zur Symbolkunst des XVI und XVII Jahrhunderts*. Stuttgart, 1967.

HENNE AM RHYN, OTTO, *Die Freimaurer, deren Ursprung, Geschichte, Verfassung, Religion, und Politik*. Leipzig, 1909.

HERDER, JOHANN GOTTFRIED VON, *Älteste Urkunde des Menschengeschlechts*. n.p., 1774.

HÉROLD, FERDINAND, *Rapport présenté par M. Hérold, . . . sur le projet de création d'un cimetière parisien a Méry-sur-Oise*. Paris, 1874.

HIRSCHFELD, CHRISTIAN CAY L., *Théorie de l'art des jardins, traduit de l'allemand*. Leipzig, 1779–85.

HORNE, A., *King Solomon's Temple in the Masonic Tradition*. Whitstable, 1972.

HORÁNYI, MÁTYÁS, *The Magnificence of Eszterháza*. London and Budapest, 1962.

ISTEL, EDGAR, *Die Freimaurerei in Mozarts Zauberflöte*. Berlin, 1928.

IVERSEN, ERIK, *The Myth of Egypt and its Hieroglyphs in European Tradition*. Copenhagen, 1961.

IXNARD, PIERRE MICHEL D', *Recueil d'Architecture*. Strasbourg, 1791.

JACOB, MARGARET C., *The Radical Englightenment: Pantheists, Freemasons, and Republicans*. London, 1981.

JAHN, OTTO, *Life of Mozart*. London, 1882.

JONES, BERNARD E., *Freemasons' Guide and Compendium*. With a Foreword by J. Heron Lepper. London, 1956.

JONES, BERNARD E., *Freemasons' Book of the Royal Arch*. London, 1957.

JONES, G. P., *See* KNOOP.

JONES, G. P., 'Building in Stone in Medieval Western Europe', *Cambridge Economic History of Europe*. Cambridge, 1952.

Journal of Garden History. July–September 1984, Vol. 4, No. 3. A special issue entitled *Cemetery and Garden* with contributions by Richard A. Etlin, James Stevens Curl, Barbara Rotundo, Keith N. Morgan, David Schyler, Martine Paul, and Frances Clegg.

JUNG, O., NIESSEN, C., and BEUTHER, R., *Der Theatermaler Christian Friedrich Beuther und seine Welt*. Emsdetten, 1963.

JUNK, VIKTOR, *Goethes Forsetzung der Mozartschen Zauberflöte*. Berlin, 1900.

KAT, W., *Een Grootmeestersverkiezing in 1756*. The Hague, 1974.

KELLER, LUDWIG, *Die Freimaurerei. Eine Einführung in ihre Anschauungswelt und ihre Geschichte*. Leipzig, 1914.

KING, ALEC HYATT, *A Mozart Legacy. Aspects of the British Library collections*. London, 1984.

KINNANDER, MAGNUS, *Svenska frimureriets historia*. Stockholm, 1943.

KLAPP, LUDWIG, *Maurerische Reden*. Hamburg, 1905.

KLOSS, GEORG, *Bibliographie der Freimaurerei und der mit ihr in Verbindung gesetzten geheimen Gesellschaften*. Frankfurt-a-M., 1844.

KLOSS, GEORG, *Die Freimaurerei in ihrer wahren Bedeutung aus den alten und ächten Urkunden der Steinmetzen, Masonen, und Freimaurer*. Leipzig, 1846.

KLOSS, GEORG, *Geschichte der Freimaurerei in England ... etc*. Leipzig, 1848.

KLOSS, GEORG, *Geschichte der Freimaurerei in Frankreich ... etc*. Darmstadt, 1852–53.

KNEISNER, F., *Geschichte der deutschen Freimaurerei*. Berlin, 1912.

KNOOP, DOUGLAS and JONES, G. P., 'Castle Building at Beaumaris and Caernarvon in the early fourteenth century' *Ars Quatuor Coronatorum*, XLV. 1932.

KNOOP, DOUGLAS and JONES, G. P., 'The Building of Eton College, 1442–1460' *Ars Quatuor Coronatorum*, XLVI. 1933.

KNOOP, DOUGLAS and JONES, G. P., 'London Bridge and its Builders' *Ars Quatuor Coronatorum*, XLVII. 1934.

KNOOP, DOUGLAS and JONES, G. P., *The London Mason in the Seventeenth Century*. London, 1935.

KNOOP, DOUGLAS and JONES, G.P., 'The Bolsover Castle Building Account 1613' *Ars Quatuor Coronatorum*, XLIX. 1936.

KNOOP, DOUGLAS and JONES, G. P., 'The Rise of the Mason Contractor' *RIBA Journal*. October, 1936.

KNOOP, DOUGLAS and JONES, G. P., *The Scottish Mason and the Mason Word*. Manchester, 1939.

KNOOP, DOUGLAS and JONES, G. P., *Begemann's History of Freemasonry*. n.p., 1941.

KNOOP, DOUGLAS and JONES, G. P., *A Handlist of Masonic Documents*. Manchester, 1942.

KNOOP, DOUGLAS and JONES, G. P., *The Scope and Method of Masonic History*. Oldham, 1944.

KNOOP, DOUGLAS and JONES, G. P., *The Genesis of Freemasonry. An Account of the Rise and Development of Freemasonry in its Operative, Accepted, and Early Speculative Phases*. Manchester, 1949.

KNOOP, DOUGLAS and JONES, G. P., *The Mediaeval Mason. An Economic History of English Stone Building in the Later Middle Ages and Early Modern Times*. Manchester, 1967.

KNOOP, DOUGLAS and JONES, G. P., *An Introduction to Freemasonry*. Manchester, n.d.

KNOOP, D., JONES, G. P., and HAMER, D. (Eds), *The Two Earliest Masonic MSS*. Manchester, 1938.

KNOOP, D., JONES, G. P., and HAMER, D. (Eds), *Early Masonic Pamphlets*. Manchester, 1945.

KNOOP, D., JONES, G. P., and HAMER, D. (Eds), *Early Masonic Catechisms*. Revised by H. Carr. London, 1963.

KOCH, RICHARD, Br∴ *Mozart, Freimaurer und Illuminaten, nebst einigen freimaurerischen kulturhistorischen Skizzen*. Bad Reichenhall, c.1911.

KÖCHEL, LUDWIG RITTER VON, *Chronologisch-thematisches Verzeichnis sämtlicher Tonwerke Wolfgang Amadé Mozarts*. Wiesbaden, 1983.

KOMORZYNSKI, EGON, *Emanuel Schikaneder, Ein Beitrag zur Geschichte des deutschen Theaters*. Vienna, 1951.

KÖPPEN, KARL FRIEDRICH, *Les Plus Secrets Mystères des Hauts Grades de la Maçonnerie Dévoilés*. 'Jérusalem' (i.e. Amsterdam), 1766.

KÖPPEN, KARL FRIEDRICH, *Crata Repoa, oder Einweihung der ägyptischen Priester*. Berlin, 1778.

KRAFFT, J. C., *Recueil d'Architecture Civile*, Paris, 1812.

KUÉSS-SCHEICHELBAUER, —, *200 Jahre Freimaurerei in Österreich*. Vienna, 1959.

KÜHN, SEE ALEX.

LABORDE, ALEXANDRE DE, *Description des Nouveaux Jardins de France et de ses Anciens Châteaux*, Paris, 1808.

LALANDE, JÉROME DE, *État du G∴O∴ de France*. Paris, 1777.

LALANDE, JÉROME DE, 'Francs-maçons' *Encyclopédie Supplement*. Paris, 1777.

LAMY, BERNARD, *De Tabernaculo Foederis, de Sancta Civitate Jerusalem, et de Templo EJUS*. Paris, 1720.

LANDON, H. C. ROBBINS, *Mozart and the Masons. New Light on the Lodge 'Crowned Hope'*, London and New York, 1982.

LANDON, H. C. ROBBINS, *Mozart's Last Year*. London and New York, 1988.

LANKHEIT, KLAUS, *Der Tempel der Vernunft: Unveröffentlichte Zeichnungen von Boullée*. Basle and Stuttgart, 1968.

LARUDAN, ABBÉ, *Les Francs-Maçons écrasés. Suite du livre intitulé, L'Ordre des Francs-Maçons Trahi*. Amsterdam, 1747. See also *Die Zerschmetterten Freymaurer*. Frankfurt and Leipzig, 1746, which also contains a plate by Bernigeroth.

LAUGIER, ABBÉ MARC-ANTOINE, *Observations sur l'architecture*. The Hague and Paris, 1765.

LAUGIER, ABBÉ MARC-ANTOINE, 'Prédicateur du Roi' in *Essais Historiques et Topographiques sur l'Église Cathédrale de Strasbourg*. Strasbourg, 1782.

LAWRENCE, JOHN T., *The Perfect Ashlar and other Masonic Symbols*. London, 1912.

LEDIARD, THOMAS, *The Life of Séthos, Taken from Private Memoirs of the Ancient Egyptians. Translated from a Greek Manuscript into French. And now faithfully done into English from the Paris Edition. By Mr Lediard*. London, 1732.

LEDOUX, C.-N., *L'Architecture considérée sous le rapport de l'Art des Moeurs et de la Législation*. Paris, 1804.

LEDOUX, C.-N., *L'Architecture de Claude-Nicolas Ledoux*. Paris, 1847.

LEE, DUNCAN CAMPBELL, *Desaguliers of No 4 and His Services to Freemasonry*. London, 1932.

LEICESTER REPRINTS, *Masonic Reprints*. Lodge of Research, No. 2429, Leicester.

LENNING, C., *Allgemeines Handbuch der Freimaurerei*. Leipzig, 1900.

LENOIR, ALEXANDRE, *La Franche-Maçonnerie rendue à sa véritable Origine, ou l'Antiquité de la Franche-Maçonnerie prouvée par l'explication des mystères anciens et modernes*. Paris, 1814.

LEPAGELET, M. and LUSSI (LUSSY), DE, *Tableau Pittoresque de la Vallée de Montmorency, un des séjours le plus agréable des Environs de Paris*. Paris, 1790.

LEPPER, JOHN HERON and CROSSLE, PHILIP, *History of the Grand Lodge of Free and Accepted Masons of Ireland*. Vol. 1. Dublin, 1925.

LEPSIUS, KARL RICHARD, *Denkmäler aus Aegypten und Aethiopien*. Berlin, 1849–59.

LESSING, G. E., *Ernst und Falk. Dialogues Maçonniques* . . . Paris, 1946.

LESUEUR, ÉMILE, *La Franc-Maçonnerie Artésienne au XVIIIᵉ Siècle*. Paris, 1914.

LETI, GIUSEPPE and LACHAT, LOUIS, *L'Ésotérisme à la scène: La Flûte Enchantée, Parsifal, Faust*. Annecy, 1935.

LIGOU, D., 'La Franc-maçonnerie française au XVIIIᵉ Siècle'. *L'Information Historique*. 3, 1964.

LIGOU, D. and others, *Histoire des Francs-Maçons en France*. Toulouse, 1981.

LINDNER, ERICH J., *Die königliche Kunst im Bild. Beiträge zur Ikonographie der Freimaurerei*. Graz, 1926.

LLOYD, ELEANOR, *See* GATTY, H. K. F.

LOVEJOY and BOAS, *A Documentary History of Primitivism and Related Ideas*. Baltimore, 1935.

LUSSI, M. DE, *Vues des monumens construits dans les jardins de Franconville-la-Garenne, appartenans à Madame la Comtesse d'Albon, gravés d'après ses dessins et ceux de M. de Lussi*. Paris, 1784.

LYON, DAVID MURRAY, *History of the Lodge of Edinburgh. (Mary's Chapel), No. 1, Embracing an Account of the Rise and Progress of Freemasonry in Scotland*. London, 1900.

LYRA, *See* NICOLAUS DE LYRA.

MACGIBBON, DAVID and ROSS, THOMAS, *The Castellated and Domestic Architecture of Scotland from the Twelfth to the Eighteenth Century*. Edinburgh, 1887–92.

MACKENZIE, KENNETH R. H., *Fundamental Constitutions of the Primitive and Original Rite of Freemasonry*. London, 1877.

MACKENZIE, KENNETH R. H., *The Mark Work*. London, 1884.

MACKENZIE, KENNETH R. H., *The Royal Masonic Cyclopaedia*. Wellingborough, 1887.

MACKEY, ALBERT G., *A Lexicon of Freemasonry; containing a Definition of all its Communicable Terms, Notices of its History, Traditions, and Antiquities*. London, 1919.

MAIMONIDES (MOSES BEN MAIMON), *De Cultu divino, ex R. Mosis Majemonidae secundae Legis seu Manus Fortis libro VIII*, translated into Latin by Louis Compiègne de Veil. Paris, 1678; later reprinted in *Fasciculus sextus Opisculorum quae ad historiam ac Philologiam sacram spectant*. Rotterdam, 1696.

MAIMONIDES (MOSES BEN MAIMON), *The Code of Maimonides, Book Eight. The Book of Temple Service. Yale Judaica Series, Vol. XII. New Haven and London, 1957*.

MARCHANT DE BEAUMONT, FRANÇOIS-MARIE, *Vues pittoresques,*

historiques, et morales du Cimetière du P. La Chaise . . . Paris, 1821.

MARCHANT DE BEAUMONT, FRANÇOIS-MARIE, *Itinéraire du curieux dans le Cimetière du P. La Chaise* . . . Paris, 1825.

MARET, H., Article on Cemeteries in *Supplément à l'Encyclopédie* . . . Amsterdam, 1776.

MARRACCIUS, HIPPOLYTUS, *Bibliotheca Mariana alphabetico ordine digesta* . . . Rome, 1648.

MARRACCIUS, HIPPOLYTUS, *Polyanthea mariana, in qua libris octodecim* . . . Cologne, 1710.

MARTY (author) and LASSALLE (lithographer) with ROUSSEAU (Architect), *Les Principaux Monuments Funéraires Du Père-Lachaise, de Montmartre, du Mont-Parnasse et autres Cimetières de Paris* . . . Paris, n.d.

MASSIN, JEAN and BRIGITTE, *W. A. Mozart*. Paris, 1959.

MICHEL, A. G., *La Dictature de la Franc-Maçonnerie sur la France*. Paris, 1924.

Mishnah. Amsterdam, 1698 ff. See the celebrated edition of G. Surenhusius published in Amsterdam. Part 5 of 1702 contains illustrations of the Temple by Constantin L'Empereur and C. Huyberts.

MORITZ, CARL PHILLIPP, *Die Symbolische Weisheit der Aegypter*. Berlin, 1793.

MOSSER, *See* RABREAU.

MOSSER, M. and others, *Alexandre-Théodore Brongniart, 1739–1813*. Paris, 1986.

MOWL, TIM and EARNSHAW, BRIAN, *John Wood: Architect of Obsession*. Bath, 1988.

MOZART, W. A., *Die Zauberflöte*. Vocal Score.

Mozart und das Theater. Catalogue of the Exhibition. Düsseldorf, 1970.

MÜLLER, D., *Aegypten und die griechischen Isis-Aretalogien*. Berlin, 1961.

München Theatermuseum, *Das Bühnenbild im 19. Jahrhundert*. Munich, 1959.

Music Review, The

MYLNE, R. S., *The Master Masons to the Crown of Scotland*. Edinburgh, 1893.

MYLONAS, G. E., *Eleusis and the Eleusinian Mysteries*. Princeton, 1961.

N . . ., M., *Apologie Pour L'Ordre des Francs-Maçons*. The Hague, 1742.

NAUDON, PAUL, *La Franc-Maçonnerie*. Paris, 1967.

NAUDOT, JEAN-J., *Chansons notées de la très vénérable confrérie des maçons libres*. Berlin, 1746.

NAUMANN, J. G., *Vierzig Freymaurer-Lieder*. Berlin, 1784.

NETTL, PAUL, *Mozart and Masonry*. New York, 1970.

Neugekrönten Hoffnung, Zur, *Verzeichnis der Brüder und Mitglieder der St Joh. zur Neugekrönten Hoffnung im Orient zu Wien*. Vienna, 1986.

NEWTON, SIR ISAAC, *Chronology of Ancient Kingdoms Amended*. London, 1728.

NICOLAUS DE LYRA, *Prologus Primus . . . fratris Nicolai de Lira in testamentum vetus, et . . . Explicit postilla* . . . Nürnberg, 1481.

NIESSEN, *See* JUNG.

NORDEN, F. L., *Travels in Egypt and Nubia*. London, 1757.

NORMAND FILS, *Monumens Funéraires choisis dans les Cimetières de Paris . . .* Paris, 1832.

NOWINSKI, JUDITH, *Baron Dominique Vivant Denon.* Rutherford, Madison, Teaneck, 1970.

OLIVER, J. W., *The Life of William Beckford.* London, 1832.

OSTI, GIUSEPPE, *Istituzione Riti e Ceremonie dell'Ordine de' Francs-Maçons.* Venice, 1785. (Contains Laradan's illustrations of Lodges.)

PALOU, JEAN, *La Franc-Maçonnerie.* Paris, 1966.

PARREAUX, ANDRÉ, *William Beckford.* Paris, 1960.

PASS'D MASTER, A, *Shibboleth: or, Every Man a Free-Mason, etc.* Dublin, 1765.

PAUL, ALBERT-N., *Histoire du Cimetière du Père La Chaise.* Paris, 1937.

PÉRAU, ABBÉ GABRIEL-LOUIS, *Le Secret de la Société des Mopses, dévoité & mis au jour par* Monsieur P***. Amsterdam, 1745.

PÉRAU, ABBÉ GABRIEL-LOUIS, 'Le Secret des Francs-Maçons'. Originally written in 1742 or thereabouts, appeared in *L'Ordre des Francs-Maçons Trahi.* Amsterdam, 1742.

PÉRAU, ABBÉ GABRIEL-LOUIS, *Les Secrets de l'Ordre des Francs-Maçons.* Amsterdam, 1745.

PÉROUSE DE MONTCLOS, J. M., *Étienne-Louis Boullée, 1728–1799.* Paris, 1969.

PERRAULT, C., *See* COMPIÈGNE DE VEIL, LOUIS.

PEVSNER, NIKOLAUS (Ed.), *The Picturesque Garden and its Influence outside the British Isles.* Washington, 1974.

Pictorial Cards in Thirteen Plates each containing four subjects, etc. London, 1819.

POSNER, OSKAR, *Bilder zur Geschichte der Freimaurerei.* Reichenberg, 1927.

PRADO, JERÓNIMO, *See* VILLALPANDO.

QUATREMÈRE DE QUINCY, ANTOINE-CHRYSOSTÔME, *Encyclopédie Méthodique.* Paris, 1788–1825.

QUATREMÈRE DE QUINCY, ANTOINE-CHRYSOSTÔME, *Rapport sur l'édifice dit de Sainte-Geneviève . . .* Paris, 1791

QUATREMÈRE DE QUINCY, ANTOINE-CHRYSOSTÔME, *Rapport fait au Directoire du Département de Paris, sur les travaux entrepris, continués ou achevés au Panthéon français. . . .* Paris, 1793

QUATREMÈRE DE QUINCY, ANTOINE-CHRYSOSTÔME, *De L'Architecture Égyptienne, considérée Dans son Origine Ses principes et son goût, et comparée Sous les mêmes rapports à l'Architecture Grecque.* Paris, 1803.

QUATREMÈRE DE QUINCY, ANTOINE-CHRYSOSTÔME, *Histoire de la vie et des ouvrages des plus célèbres architectes du XIᵉ Siècle jusqu'à la fin du XVIIIᵉ.* Paris, 1830.

QUATREMÈRE DE QUINCY, ANTOINE-CHRYSOSTÔME, *Dictionnaire d'histoire d'architecture comprenant dans son plan les notions historiques, descriptives archéologiques . . .* etc. Paris, 1832.

QUATREMÈRE DE QUINCY, ANTOINE-CHRYSOSTÔME, *Rapport fait au Conseil-Général . . . sur l'instruction publique . . . l'érection de cimetières . . .* et. Paris, n.d.

RABREAU, D., MOSSER, MONIQUE, AND OTHERS, *Charles De Wailly, peintre architecte dans l'Europe des lumières.* Paris, 1979.

RANFT, GERTRUD, *Historische Grabstätten aus Weimars klassischer Zeit.* Weimar, 1985.

REINALTER, HELMUT (Ed.), *Freimaurer und Geheimbünde im 18. Jahrhundert in Mitteleuropa.* Frankfurt-am-Main, 1983.

RIGAUD, JEAN, *Stowe Gardens in Buckinghamshire.* London, 1746.

RITZ, SÁNDOR, *Le Città Celesti dei primi Cristiani: quella dell'Apocalisse Secondo Eusebio, e quelle sul Monte Celio in Roma.* Rome, n.d.

RITZ, SÁNDOR, *La Nuova Gerusalemme dell'Apocalisse e Santo Stefano Rotondo.* Rome, 1967.

RIVIÈRE, C., *Un Village de Brie au XVIIIᵉ Siècle: Maupertuis.* Paris, 1939.

ROBERTS, DAVID, *The Holy Land, Syria, Idumea, Arabia, Egypt and Nubia.* London, 1842–9.

ROBISON, JOHN, *Proofs of a Conspiracy against all the Religions and Governments of Europe, carried on in the secret meeting of Free Masons, Illuminati, and Reading Societies.* Dublin, 1798.

ROCHEFORT, ELÉONORE-MARIE DESBOIS DE, Article on Cemeteries in *Encyclopédie méthodique, Économie politique et diplomatique, partie dédié et présentée à Monseigneur le baron de Breteuil.* Paris, 1784.

ROGER, *Le Champ du repos, ou le Cimetière Mont-Louis . . .* Paris, 1816.

ROHR, R. R. J., *Les Cadrans Solaires Anciens d'Alsace.* Colmar, 1971.

ROHR, R. R. J., *Les Cadrans Solaires.* Strasbourg, 1986.

ROSENAU, HELEN, *The Ideal City in its Architectural Evolution.* London, 1974.

ROSENAU, HELEN, *Vision of the Temple. The Image of the Temple of Jerusalem in Judaism and Christianity.* London, 1979.

ROSENBERG, ALFONS, *Die Zauberflöte, Geschichte und Deutung von Mozarts Oper.* Munich, 1964.

ROSENSTRAUCH-KÖNIGSBERG, EDITH, *Freimaurer im Josephinischen Wien.* Vienna and Stuttgart, 1975.

ROSS, T., 'The Ancient Sundials of Scotland', *Proc. Soc. Antiq. Scot.,* 24 (1890), pp161–273.

S . . . M∴, R∴ DE, *Le F∴ La Maçonnerie, considérée comme le résultat des religions égyptienne, juive, et chrétienne.* Paris, 1833.

SADLER, HENRY, *Masonic Facts and Fictions Comprising A New Theory of the Origin of the 'Antient' Grand Lodge.* With an Introduction by John Hamill. Wellingborough, 1985.

ST-A, M. P., *Promenade aux Cimetières de Paris, aux sépultures royales de Saint-Denis, et aux catacombes.* Paris, 1816. Also an expanded edition of 1825.

Sarastro Club Bulletin, Official Publication of the Sarastro Masonic Club. Vienna, 1962 f.

SCHEIBE, J. A., *Vollständiges Liederbuch für Freymaurer.* Copenhagen and Leipzig, 1776.

SCHEIDER, RENÉ, *Quatremère de Quincy et son intervention dans les arts, 1788–1830.* Paris, 1910.

SCHIFFMAN, G. A., *Die Freimaurerei in Frankreich in der ersten Hälfte des XVIII Jahrhunderts.* Leipzig, 1881.

SCHINKEL, KARL FRIEDRICH, *Decorationen auf den beiden Königlichen Theatern in Berlin unter der General-Intendantur des Herrn Grafen von Brühl.* Carl Friedrich Thiele's versions of the Schinkel designs for *Die Zauberflöte.* Berlin, 1823.

SCHMIDT, PAUL, *Court de Gébelin à Paris, 1763–1784.* Paris, 1908.

SCHÜTZ, F. W. VON, *Versuch einer vollstaendigen Sammlung Freimaurer . . .* Hamburg, 1790.

SEELEY, BENTON, *Stowe: A Description of the . . . House and Gardens. . . .* London, 1797.

SERBANESCO, G., *Histoire de la Franc-Maçonnerie Universelle.* Paris, 1963–66.

SÉROUX D'AGINCOURT, J.-B.-L.-G., *Histoire de l'art par les monuments depuis sa décadence au IVe siècle jusqu'à son renouvellement au XVIe.* Paris, 1811–23.

SKALICKI, W., 'Das Bühnenbild der Zauberflöte'. *Maske und Kothurn,* 2. 1956.

SOMERVILLE, ANDREW R., 'The Ancient Sundials of Scotland' in *Proc. Soc. Antiq. Scot.,* 117 (1987), pp233–64.

SONGHURST, W. J. (Ed.), *Quatuor Coronatorum Antigrapha. Masonic Reprints of the Quatuor Coronati Lodge, No. 2076,* Vol. 10. London, 1913.

STARCK, JOH. AUG. VON, *Über die alten und neuen Mysterien.* Berlin, 1782.

STAROBINSKI, JEAN, *1789, les emblèmes de la raison.* Paris, 1973.

STEVENSON, DAVID, 'Masonry, Symbolism, and Ethics in the life of Sir Robert Moray, FRS', *Proc. Soc. Antiq. Scot.,* 114 (1984), pp405–31.

STEVENSON, DAVID, *The First Freemasons. Scotland's Early Lodges and their Members.* Aberdeen, 1988.

STEVENSON, DAVID, *The Origins of Freemasonry. Scotland's Century 1590–1710.* Cambridge, 1988.

STEVENSON, W. B., 'Sundials of Six Scottish Counties, near Glasgow', *Trans. Glasgow Archaeol. Soc.,* 9 (1940), pp227–86.

SURENHUSIUS, GUGLIELMUS, *Mishnah, sive Legum Mischnicarum liber qui inscribitur Ordo Sacrorum,* etc. Amsterdam, 1702.

TAUTE, REINHOLD, *Maurerische Bücherkunde. Ein Wegweiser durch die Literatur der Freimaurerei . . .* Leipzig, 1886.

TENETI, ALBERTO, *La Vie et La Mort à travers l'Art du XVe Siècle.* Paris 1952.

TENENTI, ALBERTO, *Il senso della morte e l'amore della vita nel Rinascimento,* Turin, 1957.

TERRASSON, JEAN, *Séthos, histoire ou vie tirée des monumens anecdotes de l'ancienne Égypte . . .* Paris, 1731. Also the 1732 translation by Lediard.

THIÉBAUT, ARSENNE, *Réflexions sur les pompes funèbres,* Paris, 1797.

THIÉBAUT, ARSENNE, *Voyage à l'isle des peupliers.* Paris, 1798.

THIELE, *See* SCHINKEL.

THOMSON, KATHARINE, *The Masonic Thread in Mozart.* London, 1977.

THREE DISTINCT KNOCKS, THE, *Or the Door of the most ANTIENT FREE-MASONRY, Opening to all Men, Neither Naked nor Cloath'd . . .* etc. London, 1763.

THURY, LOUIS HÉRICART DE, *Descriptions des Catacombs de Paris.* Paris, 1815.

TRAHARD, PIERRE, *La Sensibilité Révolutionnaire (1789–1794).* Paris, 1936.

Transactions of the Manchester Association for Masonic Research.

TRAVENOL, LOUIS, *Catéchisme des Francs-Maçons.* 'Jérusalem' and Limoges, 1744.

TRAVENOL, LOUIS, *La Désolation des Entrepreneurs Modernes du Temple de Jérusalem, ou Nouveau Catéchisme des Francs-Maçons.* Paris, 1747.

TRAVENOL, LOUIS, *Nouveau Catéchisme des Francs-Maçons.* 'Jérusalem' (Amsterdam), 1749.

TREDE, THEODOR, *Das Heidenthum in der römischen Kirche. Bilder aus dem religiösen und sittlichen Leben Süditaliens.* Gotha, 1889–91.

TSCHUDY, THÉODORE HENRI DE, *L'Étoile Flamboyante, ou La Société des Francs-Maçons Considérée sous tous les aspects.* Frankfurt and Paris, 1766.

UNITED GRAND LODGE OF ENGLAND, *Constitutions of the Antient Fraternity of Free and Accepted Masons, Under the United Grand Lodge of England, Containing the General Charges, Laws and Regulations, etc., etc.* London, 1926.

VACQUIER, ANDRÉ, 'Les Jardins du Comte d'Albon à Franconville-la-Garenne'. *Paris et Île-de-France. Mémoires publiés par la Fédération des Sociétés Historiques* Vol. 8. Paris, 1957.

VACQUIER, J., *Les Anciens Châteaux de France.* Paris, 1913.

VARTANIAN, ARAM, *Diderot and Descartes. A Study of Scientific Naturalism in the Enlightenment.* Princeton, 1953.

VAUDOYER. *See* ALLAIS and BALTARD.

VIDLER, ANTHONY, 'The Architecture of the Lodges: Ritual Form and Associational Life in the Eighteenth Century'. *Oppositions.* 1976, Vol 5, pp75–97.

VIDLER, ANTHONY, *The Writing of the Walls. Architectural Theory in the Late Enlightenment.* Princeton, 1987.

VILLALPANDUS, JUAN BAPTISTA (WITH JÉRONIMO PRADO), *In Ezechielem Explanationes et Apparatus urbis ac Templi Hierosolymitani, commentariis et imaginibus illustratus.* Rome, 1596 and ff. See especially *De Postrema Ezechielis Prophetae Visione.* Rome, 1631.

VILLENEUVE, MARTIN COURET DE, *L'École des Francs-Maçons.* 'Jérusalem' (Amsterdam), 1748.

VILLENEUVE, MARTIN COURET DE, *Projet de Catacombes,* pour la ville de Paris, en adaptant à cet usage les carrières qui se trouvent tant dans son enceinte que dans ses environs. Paris, 1782.

VILLENEUVE, MARTIN COURET DE, *Vues pittoresques, plans, etc. des principaux jardins anglais qui sont en France: Ermenonville.* Paris, 1788.

VOLTAIRE, FRANÇOIS MARIE AROUET DE, *Essai sur les Moeurs.* In *Oeuvres Complètes.* Paris, 1878.

W.-O. V-N, *The Three Distinct Knocks, Or the Door of the most Antient Free-Masonry.* London, 1763.

W., T., *Solomon in all his Glory: or, the Master-Mason* etc. London, 1766. (Actually Thomas Wilson).

WADE, IRA, *The Clandestine Organisation and Diffusion of Philosophic Ideas in France from 1700 to 1750.* Princeton, 1938.

WAHREN EINTRACHT, ZUR, *Die übungslogen der Gerechten und Volkommene Loge zur Wahren Eintracht im Orient zu Wien.* Vienna, 1984.

WAILLY, C. DE, *Projets de Reconstruction*. Paris, 1819.

WAILLY, C. DE, *Vues sur le Panthéon*. Paris, 1796.

WAITE, A. E., *A New Encyclopaedia of Freemasonry*. London, 1921. New revised edition, 1970. Must be used with extreme caution.

WANGERMANN, E., *From Joseph II to the Jacobin Trials*. Oxford, 1969.

WARREN, CHARLES, *The Free Mason stripped Naked: or, the whole Art and Mystery of Free-Masonry, Made Plain and Easy to All Capacities . . . etc.* Dublin and London, n.d.

WATELET, CLAUDE-HENRI, *Essai sur les jardins*. Paris, 1774.

WEBSTER, NESTA, *Secret Societies and Subversive Movements*. London, 1924.

WHATELY, THOMAS, *Observations on Modern Gardening*. London, 1770.

WHATELY, THOMAS, *L'Art de former les jardins modernes, ou l'art des jardins anglais. . . .* Paris, 1771.

WHITROW, M. (Ed.), *Isis. Cumulative Bibliography*. London, 1971.

WIEBENSON, DORA, 'Le Parc Monceau et ses "Fabriques"' *Les Monuments Historiques de la France*. 1976.

WILSON, THOMAS, *Le Maçon Démasqué, ou Le Vrai Secret des Francs Maçons*. London, 1751.

WILSON, THOMAS, *Solomon in All His Glory: or, the Master-Mason*. Belfast, 1772.

WISCHNITZER, R., *The Architecture of the European Synagogue*. Philadelphia, 1964.

WITT, R. E., *Isis in the Graeco-Roman World*. London, 1971.

WOLLIN, NILS GUSTAV, *Desprez en Suède*. Stockholm, 1939.

WOOD, JOHN, *The Origin of Building: or, the Plagiarism of the Heathens Detected*. Bath, 1741.

WYZEWA, T. VON and SAINT-FOIX, G. DE, *Wolfgang Amadée Mozart*. Paris, 1912–46.

YATES, FRANCES A., *The French Academies of the Sixteenth Century*. London, 1947.

YATES, FRANCES A., *Giordano Bruno and the Hermetic Tradition*. London, 1964.

YATES, FRANCES A., *The Art of Memory*. London, 1966.

YATES, FRANCES A., *The Rosicrucian Enlightenment*. London, 1972.

YATES, FRANCES A., *Astraea. The Imperial Theme in the Sixteenth Century*. London, 1975.

YATES, FRANCES A., *The Occult Philosophy in the Elizabethan Age*. London, 1979.

ZENKERT, A., *Katalog der ortsfesten Sonnenuhren in der DDR*. Berlin-Treptow, 1984.

ZINNER, E., *Alte Sonnenuhren an Europäischen Gebäuden*. Wiesbaden, 1964.

ZUCKER, P., *Die Theaterdekoration des Klassizismus*. Berlin, 1925.

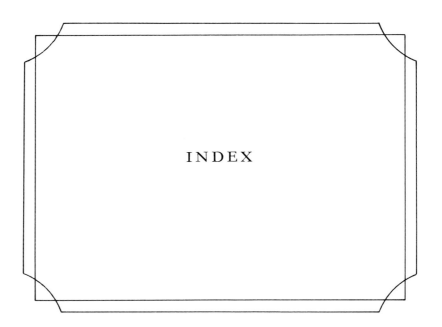

INDEX